Charles Evans Hughes and
the Dawning of Modern America

Charles Evans Hughes and the Dawning of Modern America

Joanne Reitano

University Press of Kansas

Published by the University Press of Kansas (Lawrence, Kansas 66045), which was organized by the Kansas Board of Regents and is operated and funded by Emporia State University, Fort Hays State University, Kansas State University, Pittsburg State University, the University of Kansas, and Wichita State University.

Library of Congress Cataloging-in-Publication Data

Names: Reitano, Joanne R., author.
Title: Charles Evans Hughes and the dawning of modern America : how US amphibious units in Europe helped win World War II / Joanne Reitano.
Description: Lawrence : University Press of Kansas, 2025. | Includes index.
Identifiers: LCCN 2024042510 (print) | LCCN 2024042511 (ebook) | ISBN 9780700638864 (cloth)
ISBN 9780700638871 (ebook)
Subjects: LCSH: Hughes, Charles Evans, 1862–1948 | Judges—United States—Biography. | Governors—United States—Biography. | Statesmen—United States—Biography. | United States. Supreme Court—Officials and employees—Biography. | United States. Supreme Court—History—20th century.
Classification: LCC KF8745.H8 R45 2025 (print) | LCC KF8745.H8 (ebook) |
DDC 347.73/2634 [B]—dc23/eng/20240911
LC record available at https://lccn.loc.gov/2024042510.
LC ebook record available at https://lccn.loc.gov/2024042511.

British Library Cataloguing-in-Publication Data is available.

Authorised Representative Details: Easy Access System Europe
Mustamäe tee 50, 10621 Tallinn, Estonia | gpsr.requests@easproject.com

For
Adam, Bobbi Jo, and Elliot.
Paul, Karlie, Anabelle, and Charles.

Contents

Illustrations

Acknowledgments

My greatest debt is to Lewis L. Gould, Eugene C. Barker Centennial Professor Emeritus in American History at the University of Texas at Austin. I have benefitted from his kindness and support ever since he reviewed my 1994 study of the 1888 tariff debate. He not only suggested this book on Hughes but also gave me all his research material for the 1916 election. Along with articles, brochures, and speeches were important materials from manuscript collections otherwise inaccessible to me. They included Chester I. Long (Kansas Historical Society), Theodore Roosevelt (the Library of Congress), Elihu Root (the Library of Congress), and William H. Taft (the Library of Congress). Most importantly, he provided much needed encouragement and wise counsel over time. My gratitude runs deep.

Researching this book has been an extended affair. It was pursued in fits and starts during and between terms until I retired in 2016. But even then, I adjuncted until finally (and reluctantly) being driven out of the classroom by COVID-19 and "remote learning." Then I faced a daunting "remote research" landscape that prevented further microfilm work, required buying books, and necessitated new Internet skills. I became even more dependent on librarians, especially those at the New York Public Library. Pre- and post-pandemic, I received valuable assistance from librarians at the Columbia University Oral History Project, the Folklife Center at Crandall Public Library (Glens Falls, New York), the Hennepin County Library (Minneapolis, Minnesota), LaGuardia Community College, the Library of Congress, and New York University. Gracious staff at the LaGuardia-Wagner Archives of LaGuardia Community College enabled me to read the Hughes manuscripts on microfilm.

It was an honor to be reviewed by law professor Richard A. Epstein, diplomatic historian Edward Rhodes, and law professor William G. Ross. Although they had different perspectives, they were equally constructive in solidifying the final product. I cannot properly acknowledge one anonymous scholar who provided an extensive, provocative, and important critique. All four reviewers strengthened the scholarly context of the book. In addition, I was delighted to receive valuable input from Hughes's great-granddaughter Sandra Hughes Wadell, president of the now defunct Charles Evans Hughes Memorial Foundation. Of course, remaining errors and inadequacies are my own.

At the University Press of Kansas, I was privileged to work with David Congdon, senior editor for history. His high standards, limitless patience, and practical guidance definitely enhanced the book. Andrea Laws helped with permissions and marketing. The final stages of publication depended on the expertise of art director Karl Janssen, copyeditor Jenn Bennett-Genthner, typesetter Larisa Martin, and the ever-gracious production editor Erica Nicholson.

Age has taken a toll but has not significantly muted my compulsive work habits. Personal shortcomings notwithstanding, family and friends have been consistently supportive. They deserve more appreciation and gratitude than I can ever convey.

Introduction

From 1905 to 1941, Charles Evans Hughes had a remarkable career as a lawyer, law professor, public investigator, governor of New York State, associate justice of the US Supreme Court, presidential candidate, secretary of state, judge at the Permanent Court of International Justice, and chief justice of the US Supreme Court. The scope and accomplishments of his public service were exceptional. How could one person fulfill so many different roles and earn widespread respect at each juncture? Hardly mentioned today, Hughes was, according to Associate Justice Felix Frankfurter, "among the very few really sizeable figures of my lifetime. He is three-dimensional and has impact."[1]

Everyone agreed that Hughes was brilliant, impressive, influential, nationally prominent, and world renowned, but he had plenty of critics. As Frankfurter observed, "A dominant figure is bound to be controversial." That makes Hughes all the more interesting, especially since the debate over his significance raises important questions about leadership in a democracy. Was he a moralistic, impractical idealist or a thoughtful, responsive pragmatist? Was he liberal or conservative, a statesman or an obstructionist? Could he have simultaneously been behind, in tune with, and ahead of his time? Historian Lewis L. Gould called Hughes "one of the most enigmatic figures in American politics."[2]

Hughes was never boring. During the first forty years of the twentieth century, he played critical roles concerning the nation's most complex challenges in politics, foreign policy, and the law. As a structural reformer, his central goal in each career was to improve the existing system so that its practice better reflected its promise. Considered one of America's most successful progressive governors, he confronted bossism, big business, labor issues, upstate-downstate and urban-rural tensions. He addressed criminal justice, urban congestion, public health, and conservation. Hughes almost became president but narrowly lost the 1916 election to Woodrow Wilson. It was his only major failure. As secretary of state after World War I, he helped the nation redefine its role as a major force in a vastly changed, traumatized world despite

Figure 0.1. "Charles Evans Hughes," artist unknown, Harris and Ewing. *The Brooklyn Daily Eagle*, February 12, 1922.

virulent isolationism. Consequently, Hughes has been judged the best secretary of state after John Quincy Adams and William H. Seward.

On the US Supreme Court during two separate terms, Hughes was important in adapting the Constitution to modern realities and expanding civil liberties. Most famously, he maintained the integrity and independence of the Court when threatened by court packing during the New Deal. Hughes was often compared to Chief Justice John Marshall. Through it all, he was America's most prominent lawyer as well as the president of numerous legal and civic organizations. A sketch of Hughes at age forty captured his thoughtful intensity (see figure 0.1). His lifetime of public service provided a window into the nation's challenges as it moved from the nineteenth to the twentieth century. Precisely because Hughes's decisions reverberated beyond one man, it is important to understand that man.

For such an exceptional life, books about Hughes are surprisingly few and his reputation is surprisingly mixed. A brief look at the scholarly record introduces the controversy. There are two overview biographies from the 1950s, a 1966 study of his tenure as secretary of state, and a 1967 book about his two terms as governor. In addition, a brief overview essay was published in 1973. Hughes's service on the Supreme Court received detailed analysis in 1916 and 1951. Several later works focused on his role during the New Deal and two covered him as chief justice. In addition, countless scholarly books and articles touched upon his various public services. They all contributed to the lasting debate about Hughes as a person and as a public figure. Of course, critiques of his motivation, successes, failures, and significance should be assessed in the light of Hughes's own priorities as revealed by his own words.

This biography focuses on the dilemmas of democracy that Hughes confronted, all of which remain compelling today. They included federal versus state power, reform versus the status quo, integrity versus corruption, opportunity versus oppression, equality versus inequality, private versus public interests, isolationism versus internationalism. To be sure, no single human being could possibly resolve all of these conflicts. Few even try. Consequently, a life dedicated to constructively addressing such complexity can offer insights into our past and lessons for our future.

Hughes never advocated panaceas or proposed revolutionary, transformative solutions. But he had strong ideals and clear objectives that propelled him to leadership in a transitional era replete with domestic and foreign challenges. Hughes did not seek any of the positions he held but was repeatedly summoned to serve by presidents and the people. His determination to be principled but reasonable enhanced his reputation as a practical idealist. At the same time, it allowed critics to dismiss him as too moderate, reactionary, or hypocritical. Examining different interpretations reveals how Hughes's fundamental commitment to justice, democracy, and world peace simultaneously limited, broadened, and integrated the different aspects of his life. The term *practical idealist* is not an oxymoron. As one biographer suggested about his own subject, it is possible for "the idealist to inform the pragmatist."[3]

Across three careers, Hughes embraced Progressivism, which historian James T. Kloppenberg described as a transatlantic commitment to equality in the interest of democracy. Being reason-based, fact-oriented, pluralistic, and pragmatic, Progressivism endorsed experimentation to address contemporary problems. The goal was to replace conflict with harmony by emphasizing public over private interests. However, being nonideological, multifaceted, and flexible precluded clear, consistent (and reassuring) solutions. Instead of the rigid formalism of classical liberalism and Victorianism, Progressive ethics embraced a broad commitment to justice, a crucial concept for Hughes. Because he held such influential positions, Hughes's pursuit of and struggles with progressivism in politics, foreign policy, and the law illuminated the challenges of change in the twentieth century.[4]

The original studies identified the major controversies surrounding Hughes. Other studies will be discussed as appropriate, but these provide essential starting points. The most positive account of Hughes was published in 1951 by *The Washington Post* associate editor Merlo J. Pusey. An authorized biography simply titled *Charles Evans Hughes,* it was based on extensive interviews with Hughes, his family, his associates; public and private documents; plus the draft of Hughes's autobiographical notes. While covering Hughes's public roles, Pusey highlighted his private life in order to humanize a man who was often depicted as cold and aloof. Pusey's two-volume study was awarded the Pulitzer and Bancroft Prizes. It remains the most exhaustive, most sympathetic account of Hughes. However, it has been faulted for being too celebratory and for relying too heavily on Hughes's own version of events. In that context, legal historian Laura Kalman pointed out that Hughes chose Pusey as his biographer only after reading Pusey's editorials and popular pamphlet criticizing court packing.[5]

The 1916 and 1951 examinations of Hughes on the Supreme Court were complimentary and complementary. Judge William Lynn Ransom's *Charles Evans Hughes, The Statesman* assessed his time as associate justice. Lawyer and professor of government, Samuel Hendel's *Charles Evans Hughes and the Supreme Court* covered Hughes as associate justice and as chief justice. Both authors emphasized Hughes's common sense "application of fundamental concepts to new conditions." They praised him as a strong defender of the Court's independence and separation of powers within the federal government, between national and state governments, as well as between governmental power and individual rights. These and later scholars suggested that Hughes's efforts to promote a seamless economy in the public interest, his reassessment of judicial review, and his commitment to civil liberties were his most lasting legacies. Although, his resistance to overturning precedent and occasional inconsistencies remain perplexing, even an ardent critic concluded that Hughes was "one of the most important public figures of this century. He may also be one of our greatest Chief Justices."[6]

In 1956, diplomatic historian Dexter Perkins published a concise biography, *Charles Evans Hughes and American Democratic Statesmanship.* Perkins highlighted Hughes's efforts to strike "a just balance between conservativism and liberalism." Viewing Hughes as "flexible" and "practical" within the context of his times, Perkins considered Hughes an outstanding secretary of state and "one of the great figures of American history." Historian William E. Leuchtenburg disagreed. To him, "adaptability" was less "a virtue" than "a vice" because it limited Hughes's vision and impact. In the final analysis, wrote Leuchtenburg, Hughes "was a valuable civil servant, but he was not a great political leader." Compared to Theodore Roosevelt, Woodrow Wilson, Franklin Delano Roosevelt, William Jennings Bryan, Robert M. LaFollette, and Eugene Debs, Hughes was second-rate.[7]

The most negative book about Hughes was political scientist Betty Glad's *Charles Evans Hughes and the Illusions of Innocence* published in 1966. It was previewed by a brief but strikingly similar critique written in 1952 by law professor Alphaeus T. Mason, "Charles Evans Hughes: An Appeal to the Bar of History." Both scholars claimed that Hughes's puritanical parents determined his development into a rigidly perfectionist moralist. Combining psychological theory with the realist school of power politics, Glad considered Hughes emotionally encumbered and intellectually ill-equipped for leadership in the twentieth century. Glad's study was nominated for a Pulitzer Prize and is widely cited along with Mason's article, which she did not acknowledge. To be sure, psychobiography explored important aspects of human motivation. However, political scientist James MacGregor Burns pointed out that it could obfuscate human complexity by downplaying influences and experiences after childhood. Indeed, historian Richard Leopold suggested that Glad's book revealed the limits of trying to "force her subject into a preconceived interpretative mold."[8]

In 1967, historian Robert F. Wesser published *Charles Evans Hughes: Politics and Reform in New York, 1905–1910,* which examined Hughes as governor. Wesser depicted Hughes as a principled Progressive confronting a boss-dominated political system complicated by upstate-downstate, rural-urban conflicts. Hughes emerged as a tough crusader, a "fighting governor," who achieved popular (and national) acclaim. Against great odds, he secured concrete reforms in corporate regulation, labor conditions, public health, criminal justice, and conservation, as well as administrative accountability and efficiency. The political reforms he could not get passed were adopted later. For all his efforts, Hughes weakened bossism but did not vanquish it. Wesser's account was sometimes considered too positive but was generally upheld by subsequent scholars.[9]

A brief but important assessment of Hughes's life was written in 1973 by political scientist Daniel J. Danelski and historian Joseph S. Tulchin as the introduction to *The Autobiographical Notes of Charles Evans Hughes*, which they edited. Footnotes throughout the text drew upon memoranda compiled by Henry C. Beerits, a Princeton graduate working under Hughes's supervision. Like other authors, Danelski and Tulchin tried to resolve the contradiction between Hughes's positive attributes and negative image. To them, Hughes's "unusual intelligence, strong sense of duty, and self-sufficiency" defined his life story.[10]

Although Hughes claimed that his *Autobiographical Notes* were not "an apologia," he hoped they would correct "inaccuracies" in the record. At seventy-one, Hughes organized his papers for posterity and at seventy-nine, began working on the *Autobiographical Notes* "not as a memoir, but to provide a body of facts for reference." Thus, the *Autobiographical Notes* captured his major concerns and provided context for secondary sources. Danelski and Tulchin saw the *Notes* as the rejoinder to oversimplified versions of a multifaceted human being.[11]

Having been embroiled in so many controversies during his lifetime, Hughes wanted to get his perspective on the record. Most public figures do. Hughes understood the delicate role historians play in assessing prominent people's contributions. As a lawyer and an Enlightenment man, Hughes always hallowed the power of reason and the importance of facts. Yet, he feared that there was simply too much information for any one person to absorb and that "the truth would seem to await a strange fate in being overwhelmed and buried by facts." Therefore, he suspected that "the historian may be compelled to take refuge in his intuitions, his appreciation of tendencies, and his assumptions as to personalities and motives." The result would resemble "impressionism." But, he quipped, "no one cares to think how he would look in an impressionist picture." Hughes was right. Historians do their best to comprehend the past but are always limited by their own perspectives, the material they use, and the time frame in which they function. Their conclusions are necessarily conditional. The most they can do is interrogate, and hopefully enrich, the ongoing dialogue about the past.[12]

This biography begins with Hughes's childhood, personal development, and dramatic rise to national prominence. It then examines his efforts to balance change with continuity in politics, foreign policy, and on the Supreme Court. In assessing his leadership and impact, any portrait of Hughes must apply several different brushes to a large canvas. Biography, wrote historian John A. Garraty, should show the "subject's point of view" while avoiding "the twin perils of the whitewash and the tar barrel."[13]

Hughes's life is a barometer for the first four decades of the twentieth century. Ultimately, the reader will have to decide whether he was significant or insignificant, an inspiration or a disappointment. Certainly, the complexity of his personality and the challenges he faced as governor, presidential candidate, secretary of state, and Supreme Court justice are inherently interesting and ever-relevant. Through his lifelong pursuit of democracy, peace, and justice in domestic politics, international relations, and constitutional development, Charles Evans Hughes directly influenced America's transition to modernity. He deserves a fresh look.

1 | Becoming Hughes, 1862–1906

A man . . . should exhibit that spirit of self-reliance, that sense of individual responsibility in forming and stating opinion, which proclaims that he is a man, not a marionette.

—Charles Evans Hughes, 1910

Growing Up

Outstanding from the start, Charles Evans Hughes was born on April 11, 1862, in Glens Falls, New York. At the tender age of six, little Charlie already demonstrated "that spirit of self-reliance, that sense of individual responsibility" that dominated his life. It was evident when he petitioned his parents to let him study at home instead of attending school. After all, Charlie had been reading since age three-and-a-half. His mother, a former teacher, tutored him in the three *R*s: French, German, and mathematics. She gave him a large-print New Testament at age five. His father, a Baptist minister and former classics teacher, added a children's history of England and Wales. For his sixth birthday, Charlie received a children's *Wonders of Science* and, two years later, a New Testament in Greek. At age nine, he astonished the Baptist church elders with his mastery of religious lore and concepts. No wonder school was boring.[1]

For a child, Charlie had an unusual ability to memorize coupled with a striking amount of self-discipline. The six-year old's "Plan of Study" included not only the topics he would pursue but also a schedule for studying them. He pledged to start early in the morning before his parents woke up. After finishing his planned work, he would read interesting books from his father's library. Its existence constituted an important parental influence because books were a costly luxury on a preacher's salary. Charlie particularly enjoyed *Gulliver's Travels, Pilgrim's Progress,* and *Robinson Crusoe.* He even seems to have understood the stories, if not the subtlety, of Shakespeare. Charlie eagerly absorbed everything and, when his parents considered adopting another child for company, Charlie insisted that they should just focus on educating him.

From an early age, he was self-assured, aware of his advantages, and determined to maximize them.[2]

Two other factors shaped Charlie's childhood. One was poor health. He was small, prone to illness, and preferred crackers and pancakes to meat and vegetables. Like his future associate, Theodore Roosevelt (TR), Charlie worked hard to become stronger by using a horizontal bar and two flying rings that his father installed in the yard. He enjoyed playing with other children, especially sledding, baseball, and, perhaps prophetically, cops and robbers. The second factor was his parents' love of learning and devout religiosity. His father, David Hughes, followed his own father's profession as a printer, which provided access to material for self-education. David was so inspired by Benjamin Franklin's *Autobiography* that he migrated to the land of freedom and equality. Because he had trained as a Methodist preacher, he envisioned having a pulpit in the New World, even though he knew no one there.

Defying family objections, David Hughes arrived in 1855. Welsh heritage may have contributed to a warm, outgoing personality that brought him success as a preacher in upstate New York. But he craved more schooling and taught in order to earn enough money for one year at Wesleyan University. Then he returned to the pulpit and mastered Latin, Greek, and Hebrew. At about this time, love motivated him to become a Baptist because of a charming young lady who shared his dedication to learning and religion. Her parents were not pleased. Old stock Americans of Irish and Dutch lineage, they scorned foreigners, including "this upstart, this dark-hued Welshman."[3]

However, once she had made up her mind, Mary Catherine Connolly would not be deterred. She was serious, strong-willed, and independent, attributes that also defined her son. Eager for an education, she attended two institutes for young women, which was exceptional at the time. After teaching at a small village school, she opened her own school in Kingston, New York. In contrast to David's "black hair, snapping black eyes, and olive complexion," Mary Catherine was "very fair, with golden hair and light blue eyes." While he was "emotional, impulsive," she was "reserved, reflective, and cautious." With complementary differences bridged by shared intellectual interests and religious devotion, they were a perfect match.[4]

Because the Reverend Hughes served in Oswego, New York; Newark, New Jersey; New York City; and Greenpoint, Brooklyn, the family moved often and lived modestly. As loving but strict disciplinarians, they instilled in their only child a deep sense of duty and morality. David Hughes was an ardent abolitionist who greatly admired Abraham Lincoln, as would his son. Hughes later hallowed his father as "an evangelical preacher of persuasive power" known for "his unvarying kindliness, his tender interest in the afflicted and unfortunate, his unflagging industry and unselfishness [that] inspired respect and won him many lasting friendships." The Reverend Hughes retired in 1901 but continued preaching at various pulpits around New York. After he suffered a stroke while preaching in 1909, both parents moved into the governor's executive mansion in Albany where David died later that year. Hughes inherited his father's library, most of which he "distributed to colored ministers in Washington" when he left the capital in 1916. This simple act revealed that his father also bequeathed him a social conscience.[5]

Despite his parents' hope that he would become a preacher, Charlie decided to pursue their values in secular ways. Outwardly obedient, he was inwardly restless and chafed under parental domination. He was, he said, "eager for new experiences [and] greater freedom." Riding a hobby horse in the attic, his imagination carried him to times and places he read about. His fondest memories of childhood were visiting his grandfather upstate where he learned to ride a real horse, pick berries, and appreciate the Hudson River. He was thrilled by a trip to Europe in 1873, meeting Welsh relatives and helping plan excursions to London and Paris.[6]

Charlie attended formal school irregularly, mainly studying at home and, he said, developing "an insatiable appetite" for English novels. He attended school in Oswego and Newark, where he formed a boys' club and acquired his first taste of leadership. When his parents moved to New York City in 1874, he was admitted to the top tier of the graduating class at New York City's best Public School, #35. Class salutatorian at age thirteen, he later reported that "my spirit had begun to flutter in its cage." However, being too young for college, he spent a year exploring the city and preparing for the college entrance examination. With great persistence, Charlie convinced his parents to let him attend Madison College (now Colgate University) in upstate New York. They conceded only because it was a Baptist institution that prepared young men for the ministry and lowered its fees for ministers' sons. Nonetheless, his mother lamented that "her little boy left home and never came back."[7]

Living conditions at Madison were harsh. The unfurnished rooms lacked central heating, lighting, and running water. Each student got

Figure 1.1. *Mr. Hughes at the Age of Sixteen.* The Miriam and Ira D. Wallach Division of Art, Prints and Photographs, the New York Public Library.

water from a pump outside, used an outhouse, and had a small stove fired by coal, which was stored in the closet. They brought kerosene lamps and minimal furniture from home. There were no servants. The Reverend and Mrs. Hughes worried about the effect of college on their precocious son. (Hughes always denied being a child prodigy.) Their letters urged him to guard his health, study hard, and pray often. Throughout his life, he would follow his mother's admonition to "*be thorough, be thorough. BE THOROUGH* in all you undertake."[8]

At the same time, he was slowly wandering from the fold by playing cards (especially whist) and smoking. College pranks, he wrote, "gave me a happy sense of freedom from the discipline to which I had been subjected at home." Yet, he was grateful that being small "saves me from all rough handling." Charlie joined Delta Upsilon, founded in 1834 as the world's oldest non-secret, non-hazing fraternity, a significant choice on his part. There he formed life-long friendships, developed as a leader, and discovered a talent for public speaking. He embraced Delta Upsilon's emphasis on upright character, liberal culture, service, and the advancement of justice. At age sixteen, he was increasingly self-confident (see figure 1.1).[9]

After two years, Hughes said, "I began to wish for a more liberal atmosphere and for wider opportunities." He prevailed upon his parents to let him transfer to Brown University, another Baptist institution where he received an annual scholarship and free board as a minister's son. Brown had more students, a broader curriculum, fewer restrictions, and the city of Providence nearby. Living conditions were similarly stark, but there were toilets in one college building and servants kept the rooms clean. Charlie enjoyed himself. He smoked often, drank beer occasionally, learned to play poker (for matches not money), and attended the theater. He participated in college politics and pranks, wrote for the student newspaper, joined Phi Beta Kappa, and was active in Delta Upsilon. Although pleased by the compliments he received whenever he spoke at fraternity events, he resolved not to become "egotistical" or "conceited."[10]

Being poorer than most students, Charlie tutored other boys but constantly had to ask his parents for money in order to be properly attired for college events, previewing a lifelong concern with his appearance. A telling episode occurred when he agreed to ghostwrite another student's paper for a fee in order to buy a second-hand pair of skates. At first, he justified the affair as a "laudable" way to help a friend and earn money. But his father's disapproval stung and he soon repented, even though he enjoyed using the skates. The youngest member of his class, Charlie excelled as a student and graduated with the third highest grades. He earned an award for "ability, character, and attainment," key elements of his adult life.[11]

According to political scientist Betty Glad, the Brown professors who most influenced Hughes reinforced his parents' puritanical emphasis on discipline and duty but couched those qualities in secular concepts of reason, the harmony of interests, justice, and serving the common good. Without denying religious precepts, they opened the door to slow, orderly social change without really threatening the status quo. For Hughes, college had created "a different youth with a broadened outlook." However, for Glad, the combined effect of his parental and collegiate conditioning made Hughes a conservative, inflexible adult. From her perspective, Hughes was imbued with a self-righteous faith in reason and justice that blinded him to the inequities of his day and the realities of power politics. Referencing psychologist Karen Horney, Glad saw in

Hughes a neurotic need for approval that made him moderate and cautious rather than bold and creative. It was a damning assessment.[12]

Another possibility is that Hughes's past was a springboard, not a prison. To be sure, Hughes was profoundly influenced by his parents' emphasis on discipline, duty, and decency. So, too, he consistently adhered to his professors' faith in reason, harmony of interests, public service, and, above all, justice. Under their tutelage, however, he began to see government and law as the agents of progress, beyond relying on God. Law professor Richard D. Friedman even suggested that "the law replaced the religion he had learned from his minister father." This important shift prepared Hughes to become progressive in politics and on the bench. As "a tool for social betterment," enlightened government could complement religion's emphasis on individual betterment. Omitting any discussion of Horney's concept that people could control their neuroses and shape their futures to achieve self-actualization, Glad underestimated Hughes's ability to build on his past and grow.[13]

For example, in his *Autobiographical Notes,* Hughes reported that the college professor whom Glad cited "fully persuaded" him to be a free trader. However, when no longer "under the spell of his expositions," Hughes became a lifelong protectionist. Reflecting on his college years, he observed "first, that there was so much that we did not learn, and, second, that we learned so many things that were not so." This is the attitude one would expect from an intellectually vibrant person. In fact, when discussing that Brown professor, Hughes extolled not his ideology but his pedagogy, particularly the emphasis on independent research and thinking. Hughes never wanted to be a marionette.[14]

By his senior year, Hughes had outgrown college. Only nineteen upon graduation, he put childhood behind him and started looking for a job. He wanted to teach but because of his age was rejected everywhere except by a small school for boys in Delhi, New York. The skeptical headmaster offered him a position at a meager salary. However, Hughes soon won over the headmaster and the students with his charm, humor, and enthusiasm, not to mention his ability to clearly convey Latin, Greek, algebra, and plane geometry. For extra money, he tutored two town girls in French. Hughes was so successful that he was offered a permanent position with a significant raise. Gratitude notwithstanding, he declined.[15]

The reason was that Hughes had developed a love for the law. After teaching, he read law books in the office of a local retired judge. As the county seat, Delhi enabled him to observe trials in the New York State Supreme Court. His mind was made up, but first he had to convince his parents to support him through the required two-year law program. With their regretful blessings, he applied to Columbia Law School, passed the entrance examination, and was accepted. His path was set and he admitted to his parents, "Now don't you think I am ambitious, but I would like to be something in this world."[16]

Getting Established

During the intervening summer of 1882, Hughes took a clerical job with a New York City railroad company agent. His employer was charming and the pay was excellent. When Hughes was asked to make a modest investment in the company as a condition for the job, he reluctantly asked his father for the sum, expecting to reimburse him quickly from the generous salary. However, while working with the company's records, Hughes noticed irregularities. Some letters and telegrams were written by the agent but signed by others, including himself. Exhibiting the penchant for facts that would make him famous, Hughes researched his employer in old newspapers and discovered a pattern of financial corruption, arrest, conviction, escape abroad, extradition, and yet more deception while awaiting retrial. After some unpleasant exchanges when Hughes, his father, and the company president confronted the agent, Hughes got his father's refund, two weeks salary, and, he said, "a new insight into the ways of men."[17]

This experience made studying law at Columbia even more compelling and consumed Hughes entirely. But he still wanted to work. As luck would have it, after being rejected at a prominent law office, he literally bumped into the firm's senior partner, Walter S. Carter. Kindly engaging the embarrassed young man in conversation, Carter was impressed enough to offer Hughes an unpaid summer clerical position. The result was exposure to an outstanding group of lawyers and a job upon graduation in 1883. He passed the New York State Bar examination in 1884 at age twenty-two. But he did not know that he had scored an unprecedented 99.5 until 1944 when the record was discovered among the papers of one of the questioners. He was none other than the grandfather of Benjamin Cardozo, Hughes's future friend and US Supreme Court colleague.[18]

Graduating at the top of his class earned Hughes a coveted two-year fellowship (1885 to 1886) that provided a stipend and a job as "quiz master" for two hundred students for two hours on two nights a week. When two dozen seniors asked for a special tutorial, he added two more hours on two more evenings. Then, he faced a long trip home to Jersey City Heights, where his parents had relocated. In appreciation, the students gave him a gold watch that he used throughout his life, including as chief justice. In the second year of the fellowship, he taught a course on common law pleading at the law school.

Meanwhile, Hughes was building a reputation in the Carter firm and won his first case only a year out of law school. It involved a man whose wife absconded with their children while he was hospitalized recovering from injuries sustained by rescuing the children from a fire. Already demonstrating his prosecutorial skills, Hughes demolished the lies of the wife and her brother. The father won custody and Hughes's lifetime patterns were set. As both teacher and lawyer, he was characteristically well prepared, in control of the facts, methodical, and clear. He always enjoyed and exceled at learning, teaching, and litigating. He also tended to overwork because, as one of his secretaries later commented, Hughes "goes to a new piece of work like a hungry man at a meal." In each career, his "spirit and energy: inspired others."[19]

In 1887, at twenty-five years old, Hughes was promoted to partner. At last, he considered it proper to court Carter's daughter Antoinette. A Mayflower descendant and graduate of Wellesley College, she was smart, sweet, and beautiful but had a difficult youth. Merely an infant when her mother died, she was raised by an aunt while her father—lawyer, art collector, and patron of the arts—moved from place to place and married three more times. Antoinette must have welcomed the stability that Hughes offered. In turn, Hughes forever cherished her charm, intelligence, and loyalty. She remained the light of his life for fifty-seven years. They were married in 1888 and had a son, Charles Jr., in 1889.[20]

By now, Hughes was an imposing figure, "nearly six feet tall, of large and powerful frame." While vacationing on Nantucket, far from his barber at New York City's Hotel Astor, he grew a thick mustache and beard. Thus, he acquired the distinctive appearance that delighted cartoonists and inspired the nickname "Whiskers." It was not always meant fondly. A wit later remarked that Hughes was "a cross between Jehovah and Bernard Shaw . . . a cousin to Mark Twain and a brother of Santa Claus." The joy at becoming a father was multiplied by the birth of daughter Helen in 1892. At that time, the young family was in Ithaca, New York, where, at age twenty-nine, Hughes became the youngest full professor at Cornell Law School. He loved practicing law but had worked so hard that his health suffered and he was depressed. An emaciated 127 pounds, he could not even get life insurance. Nonetheless, his father-in-law was indignant that Hughes would voluntarily relinquish a promising, prosperous legal career for poorly compensated academic obscurity.[21]

Cornell was paradise. Teaching nurtured Hughes's insatiable craving for intellectual development enhanced by a peaceful, beautiful campus. He learned new approaches to teaching case law and new subjects like international law, which proved useful later. He also formed an enduring friendship with Cornell's future president Jacob Gould Schurman, who wrote the introduction for a collection of Hughes's speeches and served as minister to China when Hughes was secretary of state. Schurman's brother became one of Hughes's law partners. According to a former student (by then a judge himself), Hughes always "bore himself with dignity but without aloofness." He was "not only capable but kindly, a man truly desirous of assisting us to develop ourselves, not a bogey man looking to 'bust' someone." Hughes relished every moment at Cornell. As proof, he gained weight and got life insurance. Despite several offers, Hughes never resumed teaching full time. However, he gave guest lectures at law schools, delivered many speeches, wrote numerous court decisions, and published five books. Later, he reflected that of all his careers, "I think that I enjoyed teaching most of all."[22]

Unfortunately, it was hard to survive financially on a professor's salary, which was a quarter of his lawyer's salary. In 1893 his father-in-law formed a new law firm and asked him to return to New York City as full partner. Carter promised that that Hughes would have help from junior lawyers, interesting cases to handle, and a substantial salary. Moreover, he suggested that his daughter and her two children would do well to get out of "a one-horse town like Ithaca." Hughes was torn by protests from his Cornell colleagues, especially Schurman. Nonetheless, he decided to do what was "best for the little family." His father-in-law rejoiced at the prodigal's return.[23]

Hughes immediately "plunged" into his work and excelled at deciphering, mastering, and winning difficult cases. His signature strategy was investigating every aspect of even the most arcane subjects. For example, he learned German and studied beet manufacturing in order to interrogate German engineers in a factory malfeasance case. Once, he had a mechanical piano player brought home so that he could fully examine its workings. Overwhelming the experts, he easily won his cases and thoroughly impressed the opposing lawyers, including Henry W. Taft, the future president's brother. As in the classroom, Hughes was adept at demystifying complicated topics in court. After copious research, but using only sketchy outlines, he rapidly dictated briefs and speeches to stenographers. Then, he delivered everything perfectly from memory. Truly "formidable," wrote one reporter, Hughes was "a lawyer's lawyer."[24]

Character

Hughes was not just a lawyer. Whenever he worked himself into a state of nervous exhaustion and depression, he took a break, thereby demonstrating an ability to address his own mental and physical health. Time and again, the lovely scenery, the fresh air, the bracing walks renewed his strength and his spirit. His only regret was travelling to Europe alone after Antoinette bore Catherine in 1898 and Elizabeth in 1907. Back in New York City, they enjoyed the theater and bicycle riding. During summers, they vacationed upstate or in Europe. Hughes took canoe trips with his wife or son, fished, hiked, climbed mountains, and later learned to play golf. The family was a constant source of joy. He delighted the children by reading stories or inventing new ones, by imitating a monkey or playing the only song he knew on the piano. He also read Uncle Remus and Mr. Dooley in dialect. In one photograph a family cat perched on Hughes's shoulder; in another a cat sat on his hat. Muckraker Ida Tarbell appreciated Hughes's sense of humor and the characteristic "twinkle in his eye."[25]

When he was away, Hughes exchanged heartfelt letters with his wife and children. He even dabbled in verse, like a stanza penned for his daughter Catherine:

> My dearest Katrine
> As you are nineteen
> It's time that I write you a letter;
> Enclosed you will find
> Not a piece of my mind
> But a check which no doubt
> You'll like better

Later making fun of his reputation as a cold, stern, narrow-minded chief justice, he sent the following to Antoinette:

Intent upon "opinions" terse,
I have no time or skill for verse.
How can I hope to meet your pleasure
In vain attempt to write in measure!
Enough—that hard judicial lives
Are made serene by charming wives.

This was a side of his personality that few beyond his family ever saw.[26]

There were only three known occasions when Hughes cried openly. Two involved family—one when his cherished older daughter succumbed to tuberculosis at age twenty-eight. The second was when his beloved wife Antoinette died in 1945. The third came in 1932 after the painful duty of urging his good friend, Oliver Wendell Holmes Jr., to retire from the Supreme Court at age ninety-one. On Holmes's ninetieth birthday, Hughes gave a nationally broadcast speech affirming that, far from being old, Holmes was "the exemplar and prophet of the young," capable of "making the old serve the new. . . . We honor him, but what is more, we love him. We give him tonight the homage of our hearts." As Hughes left Holmes's house a year later, Holmes's secretary saw "tears streaming down" his face. The iceberg could melt.[27]

Starting with his "Plan of Study" at age six, Hughes followed a schedule throughout his life. The couple appeared for breakfast at precisely the same time every morning, fully dressed for the day. He was characteristically organized and disciplined. As Hughes himself admitted, he was driven to excellence from childhood and set the highest possible standards for himself and others. All sources agree that Hughes was a perfectionist and a "glutton for work." His biographer, Merlo J. Pusey, called him "a bundle of nerves." Suggesting that Hughes "inherited a mercurial temperament from his Welsh-Irish-Scotch forebears," one colleague compared him to a ship that usually was "plowing along steadily" but sometimes hit "stormy seas" and was "pitching heavily." If Hughes became too anxious or depressed, he knew to pause. Summers became crucial opportunities for rest and recuperation. Hughes was aware of his limitations. Through it all, wrote diplomatic historian Dexter Perkins, Hughes "knew what his scale of values was, . . . what he believed and what he did not believe." His core was strong.[28]

Glad interpreted Hughes differently. Using psychologist Karen Horney's concept of neurotic needs, she deduced that Hughes's perfectionism overcompensated for a fundamental sense of inadequacy. As proof of his insecurity and instability, Glad cited an 1893 letter to Antoinette in which Hughes confessed, "I lack nerve—wifey—confidence, cheek—I could [do] so much better if I had it. And the older I get the less I have." In an 1897 letter, he called himself "a neurotic, abnormal, cranky, crotchety, absurd husband." Such statements could reveal a healthy dose of self-criticism and humility, but Glad viewed them as unhealthy. On the one hand, she suggested that insecurity led Hughes to isolate himself from others, resist criticism, battle depression, and develop a duodenal ulcer. On the other hand, she claimed that insecurity made Hughes ambitious. His need for constant approval simultaneously drove and crippled his leadership. From this perspective, Hughes's professed sense of duty and moral purpose in public service masked insecurity and fortified a self-righteousness that promoted arrogance and precluded admitting error. The result was a "political innocence" devoid of "creative vision" or "new solutions to the problems he encountered." His core was weak.[29]

The personal letters and anecdotes that Pusey presented revealed that Hughes's marriage provided crucial emotional sustenance. Indeed, Hughes claimed that Antoinette "spoiled me for friendship" because "the quiet, restful companionship of love unfits me for the conventions of social intercourse." Many letters and poems to his beloved "wifey" revealed how much he counted on her support and devotion, neither of which he ever took for granted. A note to Antoinette in 1937 captured his appreciation: "To my Dearest—to whose care and love, unfailing watchfulness and encouragement, I owe everything—health, peace of mind, the most congenial companionship and the unbroken happiness of forty-nine years. How could the evening of life be more glorious! How can I express the love that feeds upon the years?" Nonetheless, when thoroughly exhausted from work and aware that "my psychology has suffered," Hughes went on recuperative trips alone. He had enough self-awareness to pursue coping strategies when necessary and valued her understanding. As he put it, "You loved me well enough to let me leave you. I love you too much to let me leave you again." The tough prosecutor, the determined politician, the deft diplomat, the reserved judge was a romantic.[30]

Hughes was frequently depicted as aloof, cold, sanctimonious, and supercilious. This image originated with his political enemies in New York and was reinforced by his formal professional persona over time. Hughes was always gracious but never one of the boys. His secretary, Robert Fuller, reported that "nobody ever slapped him on the back and called him Charlie." According to Lloyd C. Griscom, foreign diplomat and chairman of New York City's Republican Party, Hughes had a unique "ability to detach himself and concentrate" on an issue. Hughes admitted having "a positive genius for privacy" and being "always jealous of my independence." Although these attributes could convey "coldness," said Griscom, they really reflected "a devotion to his work and a single mindedness of purpose that was outstanding among men of his day." They defined "a mind of great power."[31]

Moreover, said Felix Frankfurter, Hughes's penchant for detachment kept him from personalizing differences of opinion. When the justices conferred, Hughes would argue his case without begrudging those who disagreed. Once the case was settled, rather than "crying over spilled milk," he would make jokes or engage his opponents in conversation and move on. Offering an interesting distinction, Frankfurter concluded that Hughes "was self-critical rather than self-righteous."[32]

Independence and integrity propelled Hughes to fame, but sometimes he carried them too far. For example, he once refused to give a job to a man who had worked on his gubernatorial campaign because, Hughes said, "I can't very well appoint you because you are a personal friend." Another time, he coldly responded to a warm greeting from Chief Justice William H. Taft prior to arguing a case before the Supreme Court. When asked about the incident, Hughes explained, "I did it intentionally as I intend to win my cases on their merits and not through friendship with the judges." Such attitudes hardly enhanced his reputation. According to one critic, "If Hughes were more of a human being, and a little less like a heathen god, he would be much stronger with the people."[33]

In contrast to this misanthropic image, Pusey described Hughes as engaging and dynamic. Frankfurter recalled "the power and charm of his personality." Apparently, Hughes easily dominated a room and quickly won over people who expected him to be austere. Apprehensive about joining Hughes for lunch at the office, Griscom "found him to be a most genial and amusing companion and host. . . . I could hardly believe that this was the individual who had a fixed public reputation of extreme frigidity and inaccessibility." A reporter who regularly covered Hughes considered him "inconceivably industrious, absolutely fearless . . . but humanly approachable and friendly, good natured, reasonable, jovial." A State Department employee noted that an "occasional caustic manner" was offset by "his booming laugh" and "fascinating" conversation. Others made similar remarks. Although he was a demanding supervisor with a short temper, his staff was thoroughly dedicated to him in each of his careers.[34]

A quote often used to bolster Hughes's cold, antisocial reputation was from Herbert Hoover, his colleague in President Warren G. Harding's cabinet. In 1951, Hoover called Hughes the "most self-contained man I ever knew . . . [who] simply had no instinct for personal friendship that I could ever discover." Yet, in his 1952 *Memoir*, Hoover incorporated "A Note on Secretary Hughes" where he reported that "we built up a warm friendship out of four years of constantly working together." Hoover noted that, "in his previous gubernatorial and Presidential campaigns, [Hughes] had been reputed to be cold and indifferent in personal relations." But, Hoover clarified, "In fact, he was a man of great reserve who did not reach out for friends; but when he gave his friendship, it was deep and lasting." Maybe, mused Hoover, a more outgoing Hughes would have been president. Nonetheless, Hoover, who could be reserved and formal himself, appreciated Hughes as "the soul of courtesy, fair dealing, and devotion to his family. His abilities in law [and] his sense of justice were transcendent. He had a mental and moral stature that commanded my unceasing admiration."[35]

Like Glad, H. Stuart Hughes couched an analysis of his grandfather in psychological terms, but with different insights. Agreeing that Hughes was insecure, he identified a sense of discomfort in high society. Although he "married up" and "could pass for a patrician," Hughes never forgot his modest origins and always considered himself "an outsider." In addition to his moral principles, this factor may have influenced his lifelong empathy with the underdog. Hughes's grandson connected it to his friendship with the three Jews on the Court—Louis D. Brandeis, Benjamin N. Cardozo, and Felix Frankfurter. As the last surviving member of the group, Frankfurter often visited Hughes in retirement. To be sure, Hughes had a close relationship with Oliver Wendell Holmes Jr. but his grandson attributed it to "awe" for the older man.[36]

William T. Gossett, Hughes's law clerk and later his son-in-law, also suggested that Hughes's background gave him perspective and kept him humble. His religious upbringing and moral principles led him to view law as a bond of human decency. Thus, said Gossett, Hughes was "sensitive in his relations with others without being sentimental, witty without being frivolous, purposeful without being stubborn." As a professional, Hughes "reasoned closely without being closed minded, was tolerant without being lax, and calm without being indifferent." Most notably, "he was of rock-ribbed integrity without monolithic righteousness." Perhaps too generous for any mortal soul, Gossett's description nonetheless captured Hughes's many sides and reflected the limitations of binary analyses. After all, human beings are inherently complicated and interact with different people in different ways. Hughes was a multifaceted person whose very complexity highlighted his humanity.[37]

Over time, Hughes experienced a religious metamorphosis. It began at Brown where he attended Congregational and Episcopalian churches instead of the Baptist one. Although admitting that "it is impossible to get outside of one's early training," he began questioning his father's "long established and stereotyped methods of thought." Hughes later explained that his parents' "constant and rigorous religious discipline" backfired "by creating in me a distaste for religious formalities." He later suggested that as a youth "what interested me most was the dialectic rather than the premises" of religious dogma.[38]

On reflection, Hughes concluded that religious ritual often "cheapened" religious conviction by substituting "formalism and vain repetition" for substance. Consequently, he started seeing religion in more ecumenical terms and remained only loosely tied to the Baptists, whom he "cherished" primarily for their contribution to "the struggle for religious liberty." At a 1922 commemoration of Roger Williams, the colonial champion of religious freedom, Hughes emphasized the connection between religious and civil liberty. "Men of all religious beliefs," he said, must "stand equal before the law" in order to prevent "bigotry" and tyranny. It was crucial not only to separate politics from religion but also to "look beyond form and ritual." Only then could a democracy protect "the liberty of the soul."[39]

In 1889, Hughes returned to his religious origins, if not his parents' evangelical form. At New York City's Fifth Avenue Baptist Church, he became acquainted with, but never worked for, John D. Rockefeller. The most he did was provide pro bono advice to a church worker upon Rockefeller's request. In addition, John D. Jr. attended Hughes's Sunday school classes and took over after Hughes resigned. Innocent as these associations were, they provided fuel for future attacks. The church was important for other reasons. After moving and rebranding several times, it ultimately became the interdenominational Riverside Church. While the Rockefellers provided the money, the Reverend Harry Emerson Fosdick provided the inspiration that made Riverside famously liberal and ecumenical.

During the 1920s and 1930s, Fosdick was the leader of the Protestant modernist movement that rejected fundamentalism in favor of a Protestantism that moved with the times and addressed social problems. It suited Hughes well. Coincidentally, Fosdick attended Colgate, belonged to Delta Upsilon, and was a Baptist. Later, when Hughes was president of the alumni association and a college trustee, he pressured Brown to stop requiring the president and most trustees to be Baptists. He did likewise as a trustee of the University of Chicago. The spirit of modernism infused Hughes's secular life. He believed that being truly Christian meant reaching beyond denomination and dogma to value "faith without credulity; conviction without bigotry; charity without condescension; courage without pugnacity; self-respect without vanity; humility without obsequiousness; love of humanity without sentimentality; and meekness with power. That is our ideal."[40]

In Hughes's opinion, the historical figure who best embodied that ideal was George Washington—not just for his accomplishments but for his character. To Hughes, Washington's life taught "the lesson of the supremacy of duty. It is the lesson of honor, of fidelity to trust." Uninterested in pure power or prestige, Washington never sought the positions he held but accepted them out of a sense of responsibility to the nascent nation. Moreover, he refused to profit personally from his status and insisted that reimbursing his expenses was sufficient compensation. Washington never embraced "self-seeking or base motive." If only those values permeated business, courts, the press, and politics today, said Hughes, "we should neither need nor seek governmental panacea." However, because morals ultimately rested with the individual and "there is no legislative road to character," he hoped that all Americans would take Washington's example "to heart."[41]

Hughes followed suit. He too did not seek the offices he held and insisted on being compensated only for expenses when campaigning. He often cut suggested fees in half, delivered all speeches pro bono, and gave much of his personal time to public causes. To be sure, Hughes was a financially successful lawyer and a forceful power holder, but he never relinquished the basic moral values that he acquired as a child and revitalized as an adult. He held onto them even when scorned as a moralist and outfoxed as a politician.[42]

From 1894 to 1904, Hughes focused on his practice and built his legal reputation mainly dealing with businesses. He argued or prepared briefs for over twenty-five cases before the New York Court of Appeals, numerous other cases before lower courts, plus cases tried in other states and in Europe. Because all of his work was done on a case-by-case basis, Hughes was never retained by or obligated to any specific company. He modeled himself after another lawyer who was a public servant, one whom his father admired, and who also was criticized for defending corporations, like railroads. To Hughes, Abraham Lincoln was the paragon of "scrupulous honesty." He admired in Lincoln the very attributes that he pursued throughout his professional life. He considered Lincoln "a man of caution. As a lawyer, he studied thoroughly his opponent's cause and knew it as well as his own. As a statesman, he patiently considered every possible objection to his policy and did not take the final attitude until he was sure of his ground. But when he had once determined upon his course, he did not flinch."

Hughes frequently repeated these points, which echoed his own values. In his eyes, Lincoln set the highest standard for dedication to public service and "patriotic duty." He was a perfect model for the life of public service that Hughes embraced. Accordingly, a bronze bust of Lincoln always occupied a prominent place in his home office.[43]

Lincoln may also have influenced Hughes on the subject of racial equality. This was one area where Hughes diverged from mainstream progressives, who, noted historian Michael McGerr, "readily accepted the inequitable arrangement of segregation" partly because of "condescension and indifference," partly because they feared "dangerous social conflict." In 1906, as president of New York City's Baptist Social Union, Hughes invited the prominent African American educator Booker T. Washington to be an honored guest at a formal dinner. Protests from church members only reinforced his contempt for hypocrisy and prejudice. The dinner proceeded as planned with Mr. and Mrs. Washington seated at the head table with Mr. and Mrs. Hughes.[44]

Speaking at a Tuskegee Institute fundraiser in 1908, Hughes declared that protecting civil liberties and economic opportunity for African Americans was in the interests of all Americans. He believed that "in this land, the door of opportunity must be wide open to our citizens." Most importantly, he said, "We want neither slaves nor serfs, nor any body of citizens permanently below the standards which must be maintained for the preservation of the Republic." The principle was simple: "We cannot maintain our democratic ideals as to one set of our people and ignore them as to others." Hughes upheld this commitment throughout his life, especially on the Supreme Court. In 1939, he and Mrs. Hughes were sponsors of Marion Anderson's concert held at the Lincoln Memorial after she was denied permission to sing before an integrated audience at the Daughters of the American Revolution (DAR) hall in Washington, DC. Antoinette belonged to the DAR.[45]

Hughes's 1909 commencement speech at Union College unveiled his priorities. Declaring that "the man who is rich only in information is poor indeed," he urged the graduates to broaden their horizons to include art, poetry, and the world "because we live in the Twentieth Century . . . not the Thirteenth or Fourteenth Centuries." In addition to honesty and efficiency, they should develop "social sympathy and intense love of democracy." Aware of his own modest origins, Hughes cautioned against "intellectual snobbishness" and scorn for boys "toiling in shops or working as clerks." After all, they were being educated in "the great school of life . . . and there may be a Lincoln hard at work making the best out of his meager advantages who will outshine all the products of our great universities." Instead of just focusing on personal security and prosperity, Hughes urged the graduates to render public service and never "go forth . . . bearing the sign: For Sale." Admitting that democracy was subject to "misuse" by special interests, he remained optimistic that open debate and open elections would ultimately enable reason to prevail.[46]

Toward that end, Hughes valued public education. Like Thomas Jefferson and Benjamin Franklin, he genuinely believed that "the safeguards of democracy are education and public discussion," core progressive concepts. Thus, Hughes declared: "Our country is safe as long as our schools are full." He condemned elementary education that focused on "the mere learning of dates of battles or the birth and succession of kings." Rather, children should be introduced to "the actual operations of our government" and its "vital relation" to their own lives so that they will become discerning citizens, immune to both corruption and "indifference." Similarly, when a fifteen-year-old wrote the chief justice asking how to prepare for a political career, Hughes advised him "that the best preparation of public office is to be a good citizen," to keep abreast of current events, and to value integrity in all aspects of life. Such qualities, he insisted, would lead to many opportunities for public service.[47]

So saying, Hughes identified his lifelong quest for practical ways to promote a democracy dedicated to the Enlightenment ideals of reason and fairness. He was singularly well-suited for the job. Hardly perfect, Hughes was a perfectionist ardently dedicated to honesty, duty, equal opportunity, and justice for all. Outstanding as he was, Hughes's awareness of his own shortcomings kept him humble. He learned to balance obsessive work with vacations. He compensated for his gravitas, independence, and insistence on integrity with a few deep friendships, a loving family life, and a twinkle in his eye. Significantly, he had a sense of humor, which is essential for acquiring perspective on yourself and on life in general.

Hughes repeatedly fought against people who took advantage of liberty and put self-interest above public interest. He knew that "trying to cheat the public is a game that is constantly being played." Yet, on both the domestic and world stages, he remained optimistically dedicated to the proposition that people could get along if they respected each other and treated each other fairly. These basic values defined his complex character and shaped his various careers. Hughes expressed them well in 1910 as he defined the *true American.* First and foremost, the term itself must "ever be a word of the spirit and not of the flesh." Consequently, there should be no discrimination on the basis of "custom or religion, . . . bigotry of creed or relation." Furthermore, he said, "neither birth nor station, neither circumstance nor vocation" should "win or prevent the esteem to which fidelity, honesty, and sincerity are alone entitled."[48]

Rather, a true American should "look neither up nor down" but assess each person with a "sympathetic relation" to others by upholding both "individual interests and . . . community interests." All people engaged in "honest work" should be respected. They should not be seen "merely as economic factors of work, but human beings of like passions and possessed of the unalienable rights" cherished by all. As he noted, "Almost every man is solicitous for individual rights when he is thinking of his own. The true concern is for the interests . . . of another as well as for my own." Democracy ultimately depended on people rising above self-interest to develop "a keen sense of their collective interest [and] co-operative vigilance" for the general good. Hughes's personal values informed his public values. These statements reflected a faith in democracy based on meritocracy, personal success based on character, and social solidarity based on mutual respect. Hughes's challenge was to harness his personal convictions and professional attributes to promote a better world by reforming state government, improving international relations, and modernizing the law.[49]

Going Public

Hughes's reputation as a lawyer spread quickly and earned him stature in the Bar Associations of New York City, New York State, and the United States. Arguing often in court, he learned from arrogant judges the importance of being even-handed and gracious on the bench. Previewing his career as a political and judicial reformer, Hughes called for simplifying the civil code and eliminating imprisonment for debt. Not only was it "unsound in principle" but it was "easily made a means of extortion and oppression in the case of the ignorant and friendless poor." As judges began referring their most difficult cases to him, he was mentioned as a potential judge himself. But Hughes insisted that he was not interested.[50]

Nor, at age forty-three, was Hughes anxious to lead the 1905 New York State legislative investigation of New York City's gas and electric lighting companies. He had little knowledge of the gas industry and less experience in politics. He wasn't even the committee's first choice. Nonetheless, he accepted reluctantly after recommendations from several top lawyers, including Henry Taft, and persistent appeals by State Senator Frederick C. Stevens, who chaired the investigating committee. Always concerned about integrity, Hughes obtained Stevens's promise that he would "be allowed to make a thorough inquiry without political interference" and publicized that agreement in the daily papers. The press was not convinced. They accused Hughes of being an ally of the Rockefellers and a former associate of a utility company lawyer. Furthermore, they branded him with the negative stereotypes that plagued him henceforth: "Coldness, solitude, aloofness, silence, frigidity, ice."[51]

Set against the background of municipal reforms already under way in European cities, late-nineteenth-century New York anti-corruption campaigns, and early-twentieth-century urban reforms across the United States, the investigation was not just a local matter. At first, the hearings seemed bland and boring. However, as the questioning intensified, the public cheered and the press reassessed. Using the records of six companies comprising the Gas Trust, Hughes exposed shocking irregularities. He interrogated witnesses with deceptively calm courtesy and total mastery of their companies' financial records. When it became clear that he knew more than they did about their own businesses, the company officials admitted charging household customers three times the actual cost of delivering electric current and overcharging the city even more.

In addition, the gas companies inflated their value to enhance their stock while deflating their value to reduce their taxes. The gas company presidents were mortified and the public was furious. Hughes's report and recommendations resulted in a state commission to regulate the gas and electric companies. More powerful than any previous commissions, it could investigate company finances, establish standards, and regulate rates. It was an important step toward promoting business accountability in the interests of public welfare, which became one of his lifelong goals.[52]

Hughes then joined his family in Europe thinking that his was work done. But it had just begun. While relaxing in the Alps, he received a telegram from New York State Senator William M. Armstrong asking him to lead an investigation of the life insurance industry. Unlike the gas industry, Hughes was familiar with the issues through a case concerning the Equitable Life Assurance Society. Internal fighting exposed scandalous financial dealings that were publicized by Joseph Pulitzer's *New York World* and spurred public demand for an investigation. Hughes immediately withdrew from that case in order to eliminate any conflict of interest and again secured promises that the new investigation would be free from political interference. Thus assured, he accepted the offer in the belief that it "would be the most tremendous job in the United States." It was an ironic twist of fate for someone who once failed to qualify for life insurance.[53]

The hearings proved explosive. True to form, Hughes mastered complicated data and posed penetrating questions. Journalist Mark Sullivan observed that although Hughes was "as undramatic himself as an adding-machine, he brought about such a series of dramatic revelations as had the effect, on the public, of a tumbling cascade of sensations." When the insurance company officers testified, Hughes allowed them to make opening statements and honored appropriate requests from

Figure 1.2. "The Gridiron," artist unknown. *New York World*, September 14, 1905.

their lawyers. Yet, they were unable to answer Hughes's questions or explain their own company's financial records. Hughes "made the books live," wrote journalist Ida Tarbell: "Made them reveal tales of human weakness and wrongdoing—of favoritism, grafting, extravagance, hypocrisy, law-breaking." These realities "sickened our hearts while they strengthened our hands. Nothing eluded him; nobody was spared." Hughes repeatedly exposed corrupt practices, including manipulating company procedures to increase executive salaries plus benefiting from using policyholder's payments to invest in stocks. A *New York World* cartoonist depicted him grilling the life insurance executives on a barbeque (see figure 1.2).[54]

Through what one observer called "steady, impassive, remorseless interrogation," Hughes uncovered evidence that New York Life, Mutual, and Equitable jointly influenced legislators and the public—not just in New York but across the country. For the past ten years, Mutual (often with Equitable) financed a "House of Mirth" in Albany where legislators were entertained and sometimes lived. The insurance companies also paid legislators as consultants and contributed to their election funds, including TR's 1904 presidential campaign. Key culpable politicians included former Democratic Governor David B. Hill, Republican US Senators Thomas C. Platt and Chauncey Depew, plus Republican State Senator William Barnes Sr., father of a future adversary.[55]

Hughes exposed an alliance between former Republican Governor Benjamin B. Odell Jr. and railroad tycoon Edward H. Harriman. When Hughes asked Harriman whether he had acquired "political influence" through Odell, Harriman replied that Odell "had political influence because of his relations with me." According to Oswald Garrison Villard, grandson of abolitionist William Lloyd Garrison and progressive editor of the *New York Evening Post,* Hughes was "keen, fearless, unapproachable." A cartoon in *The Brooklyn Daily Eagle* depicted him as a pied piper luring the rats out of the (New York) Life Insurance building and sending them off to oblivion. In the process, he destabilized New York State politics.[56]

Hughes was so impressive that people wanted him to run for mayor. Even William Randolph Hearst, controversial publisher of the *New York Journal* and future Hughes foe, applauded the hearings and supported the idea. Accordingly, the Republican Party offered Hughes the nomination. Some party men were undoubtedly sincere, but others wanted to divert Hughes from the investigations because, wrote one journalist, he had become "the personification of outraged America." Hughes's letter declining the nomination explained that running for public office would undermine his credibility and independence. It would look like he was putting self-interest over public interest. Rather, he was determined to complete the job he started with, "unremitting toil and undivided attention," because it raised "questions vital to the interests of millions of our fellow citizens throughout the land." Besides, he was uninterested in political office.[57]

After concluding an exhausting four months of hearings, Hughes spent six more weeks writing a 440-page report that summarized the testimony and proposed remedial legislation. It called for laws to protect the rights of insurance policyholders, prevent firms from abusing their policyholder's funds, forbid political contributions by corporations, require candidates to account for their campaign funds, and prohibit lobbying. Amazingly enough, these ambitious recommendations became state law. They inspired forty-two other states to explore the issue and twenty-nine states to pass similar bills. In essence, wrote historian Michael McGerr, Hughes had "presided over a revolution in policymaking." Ironically, the new restrictions helped the life insurance industry restore its reputation over time. However, they angered some wealthy Brown trustees who opposed Hughes as a commencement speaker and made sure that that the men who invited him were replaced.[58]

According to historian Richard McCormick, "The importance of the life insurance investigation . . . as a turning point in New York State politics cannot be overstated." By arousing public indignation, the exposures weakened nineteenth-century bossism and the party discipline on which political machines depended. As independents organized and ticket splitting spread, politicians rethought their strategies, especially in large cities. The public furor that had been building for decades finally forced legislators to address corporate abuses. The investigations, wrote McGerr, became "the catalyst in the political ascendancy of progressivism in New York State." Although big businesses still dominated the economy and influenced politics, they had to work with (and sometimes manipulate) the new standards and restrictions.[59]

To the liberal Boston lawyer Louis D. Brandeis, the New York State revelations were gratifying. They supplemented his own investigations in Massachusetts, stimulated his reassessment of political economy, and initiated a lifelong friendship with Hughes. Both men helped rewrite the relationship between politics and private enterprise for the twentieth century. Indeed, said Hughes, "the supreme issue of the day" was governmental supervision of corporations that handled what Adam Smith, and later Brandeis, called "other people's money." In the process, wrote historian Michael E. Parrish, Hughes and Brandeis became pioneers in helping the legal profession transition from an exclusive focus on private litigation to a broader concern with public policy. The result was a new integration of private, academic, and public law. Few people had the ability to function in all three domains; Hughes did.[60]

The gas and insurance investigations changed Hughes's life. Considering the critical importance of the investigations and his initial reluctance to assume a public role, it was fortunate, wrote *The Brooklyn Daily Eagle,* that "the event and the man met." As the hearings were covered all over the country, Hearst's *New York American* proclaimed Hughes "counsel for the people." Nonetheless, the hearings left him divided. On the one hand, they justified returning to his law firm by reinforcing his belief that "of all vanities there is no vanity like that of politics." On the other hand, the hearings gave Hughes a sense of accomplishment that fed his idealism as well as his ambition.[61]

Hughes's compulsive work habits, photographic memory, and lawyerly skills, combined with his courteous but firm and formal demeanor, proved unexpectedly useful and effective in the public arena. He earned respect by doing a difficult job well while maintaining his integrity and promoting reform. As one commentator put it, "Mr. Hughes began this work as a skilled attorney. When he finished it, he was a statesman, if to be a statesman is to awaken the national consciousness upon the gravest questions affecting the national life." Charles Evans Hughes had become a political star.[62]

Yet, Hughes's controversial persona and equally controversial positions reinforced negative stereotypes that pursued him relentlessly and still pepper historical literature. Frankfurter thought that the image of Hughes as a "cold, unfeeling mental machine" was a "caricature" that missed the essence of the man. In truth, he wrote, "Hughes emerges as the clear-headed, impressive, self-disciplined, resourceful, witty, companionable, energizing, exacting, and considerate person that all who worked with him in the various roles of his long life will recognize through their own experience."[63]

Law professor Alphaeus T. Mason criticized such statements for fostering an "idolatrous cult" about Hughes after his death. But even Mason acknowledged that Hughes was "by any standard, one of the most important public figures of this century." Why, then, is Hughes hardly remembered today? Was it, as political scientist C. Herman Pritchett suggested, that he lived too long and came to be taken for granted? Were his contributions so time-sensitive that they seem irrelevant now? Or were they such an inherent part of the transition to modernity that they have been mainstreamed and their author forgotten? The task is to understand the short- and long-range significance of someone who was so dedicated to public service, so influential in so many areas, and so determined to "be a man, not a marionette."[64]

2 | Becoming Governor, 1906–1908

Public service is the best politics.
—Charles Evans Hughes, 1906

Structural Reformer

Charles Evans Hughes was wrong. Public service may be the noblest rationale for politics, but without pragmatism it is not always the best path to political success. From this perspective, Hughes was unlikely to prevail in politics. In fact, observed British Ambassador James Bryce, leaders in a democracy were hampered by intellect and idealism. Instead, they needed verbal facility, common sense, and, above all, party loyalty. Unlike Theodore Roosevelt (TR), who believed the old adage that politics is the art of the possible, Hughes always seemed to be pursuing the impossible. Sometimes, he proved practical and politically strategic. At other times, his principles overwhelmed the demands of the moment. Moreover, he never was a "real" party man.[1]

Hughes could be eloquent and charming but aloof, hard charging, and stubborn. Time and again he defied the party establishment, leading to both victory and defeat. Lord Bryce took notice. He originally concluded that American governors were "insignificant," with "little to do and comparatively small sums to handle." However, Hughes's two terms in office renewed Lord Bryce's faith in "the power of the people to appreciate rectitude, earnestness and courage in a statesman." Hughes convinced him that much could "be accomplished by the firmness, tact and courage of a State Governor." Some might call Hughes's "rectitude" superciliousness and qualify the word "tact," but none would question his earnestness, firmness, and courage. For better and sometimes for worse, Hughes sincerely believed that "public service is the best politics."[2]

Hughes was an atypical politician, but he was not apolitical. He considered parties essential for organizing different viewpoints in a large, complex nation and firmly believed that party loyalty was "not inconsistent with independence of character." Although third parties often raised important issues, he urged young men to focus on securing change through the two major parties. As a proud, lifelong Republican, Hughes repeatedly tried to strengthen his party, albeit on his own terms. He was characteristically impatient with incompetence, intolerant of petty partisanship, and incensed by corruption. Convinced that "the people will smash any organization that is devoted to selfish interests," he wanted the party of Lincoln to become once more "a party of the people," not a party of the bosses. As governor, Hughes's political code was deceptively simple. The object was "to leave a man free and independent in the dignity of his manhood to perform the duties of office . . . unembarrassed by improper influences and unaffected by accumulated obligations." Thus, it was essential "to divorce the governorship from political entanglements" based on controlling the party machinery. "Independence of character" drove his politics and won respect, but was anathema to party politicians. Hughes welcomed the fight.[3]

The problem was not with political parties themselves. Rather, the problem was "the abuses of party organization . . . for the benefit of party managers and party workers." That system, he said, was basically a "hustle" determined by the need for money to run campaigns and buy votes. Thus, politicians were dependent on large corporations whose interests they pursued through legislation. As "the standards of efficiency are bent to the demands of favor," political parties were corrupted and respect for law undermined. Party managers used their ill-gotten gains to build support through patronage. In the process, "party machines" became "personal machines" and "the feudal system again appears with its lord, his vassals and retainers, and the common tillers of the political soil." Borrowing boss William M. Tweed's famous dare to reformers, Hughes asked, "What are you doing about it?" His answer was to challenge the bosses and reform the system from within. He was what historian John D. Buenker called "a structural reformer." As Hughes asserted in 1908, "We may accomplish needed reforms by making our institutions work as they were intended to work." If it's broken, fix it.[4]

Hughes was and remains controversial. On the one hand, his approach seemed to bolster political scientist Betty Glad's claim that he was too cautious, moralistic, supercilious, and legalistic. In addition, she considered him insensitive to the changing social needs of the times. On the other hand, biographers Merlo J. Pusey and Dexter Perkins praised Hughes for resisting entrenched politics and trying to address contemporary issues through business regulation, administrative reform, and social reform—all key components of Progressivism. They were joined by historian Robert F. Wesser who emphasized the difficulties of dealing with bossism. He applauded the governor's tenacity and willingness to learn as well as his strategy of going directly to the public for support. Hughes took risks, a key component of leadership. Fortified by the moral sense for which he was often criticized, but which permeated Progressivism, Hughes pursued an ambitious reform agenda. At the end of his service in 1910, he explained his political philosophy: "How shall we buttress Democracy? The peril of this Nation is not in any foreign foe! We, the people, are its power, its peril, and its hope! . . . Government is not something apart from us, or above us, . . . It is we ourselves organized in a grand co-operative effort to protect mutual rights and to secure common opportunity and improvement." Did he translate that ideal into reality?[5]

Hughes was governor of New York State for two two-year terms, from 1907 to 1910. Dedicated to using "the powers of government deliberately and justly," he reshaped the governor's role in keeping with Progressive principles. At first glance, he fit the profile of Mugwumps and their Progressive heirs because he was an urban, well-educated, middle-class professional imbued with Protestant moral virtues. Nonetheless, he differed from the Mugwump stereotype because he came from modest means. Rather than suffering from status decline, both Hughes and his father experienced status mobility. Hughes was only reluctantly and accidentally drawn into politics. Prior to the insurance and gas investigations, he just wanted to be a good lawyer who performs civic service. Once in the political fray as governor, he embraced the classic Progressive goals of promoting clean, efficient government, regulating business abuses, and addressing social problems. He started from the premise, as he declared in 1908, that the people "will not listen to the voice of reason if it proceeds from the mouth of the briber or the bribed." An honest, impartial, efficient government dedicated to the common good would embody the best of democratic theory and practice.[6]

Never anti-business per se, Hughes promoted business regulation "not to curtail the liberty of the people, but to protect it." For him, regulations were "not against business, but against abuses." His ultimate "objective was to secure the broadest diffusion of individual opportunity consistent with the welfare of all." That meant defending every person "against the over-reaching of any one" person. Thus, Hughes resolved "to thwart every attempt to secure or retain an improper advantage through unjust discriminations or governmental favoritism." As the New York State investigations demonstrated, the nation's new prosperity created unprecedented opportunities for the "prostitution of political power" for private gain. Now the goal was to restore "unselfish leadership" that was truly dedicated to "the public trust." However, Hughes understood that "no one can fight as a good soldier the battles of democracy who is constantly seeking cover." Citizenship and leadership required stepping up and speaking out, no matter the costs. That spirit made Hughes a "fighting governor."[7]

To be sure, Hughes developed enemies and suffered setbacks. Although his campaign for electoral reform failed, he made substantial progress in administrative reform, business regulation, labor legislation, court reform, social reform, and conservation. Time and again, his strategy of appealing directly to the public validated his faith in democracy even as democracy seemed increasingly fragile. An inveterate optimist, he once declared that "pessimists and cynics cannot develop this country." Many of his reforms became models for other states and Hughes himself was so prominent that the Republican Party considered nominating him for president in 1908 and 1912. He received the Republican presidential nod in 1916 and almost won. His name resurfaced for the nomination in 1920, 1924, and 1928. Be that as it may, his most significant political contribution was as governor. Some scholars even suggested that Hughes was "the best governor of his era."[8]

Getting Elected

Hughes's nomination as governor ushered in one of the state's most contentious, exciting, and significant gubernatorial elections. After the gas and insurance investigations, he seemed to be an island of political integrity in a sea of political corruption. But, by exposing the unsavory connections between politics and business, Hughes incensed New York State's Republican Party bosses. When his name was mentioned as a possible gubernatorial nominee, the powerful Republican Albany boss William Barnes Jr. noted, "I never spoke to this man." In other words, Hughes could not be trusted because he was not one of them. They were right, but that was precisely why TR considered him the strongest candidate.[9]

The New York State Republican Party was in a bind. The gas and insurance investigations strengthened the public contempt for politicians that had festered since the 1870s Tweed Ring only to be confirmed by the 1890s Canal Ring. Both unveiled the penchant of politicians, Democrat and Republican alike, to exploit their offices for personal financial gain. This pattern of corruption was tied to bossism, the systematic control of politics by one man. It was epitomized by "the Easy Boss," Owego County's Thomas C. Platt, who controlled other local Republican bosses throughout the 1890s. However, as Platt's power waned, Newburgh's wealthy businessman, Benjamin Odell Jr., consolidated his own power as governor from 1901 to 1904. There also were local bosses like Barnes, George W. Aldridge of Rochester, Francis Hendricks of Syracuse, Senate Majority Leader "Uncle" John Raines of Canandaigua, and Brooklyn's Timothy Woodruff, who chaired the Republican State Committee. These men became thorns in Hughes's side.

For the moment, they reluctantly backed Hughes's nomination after the president endorsed him. Platt had supported TR for governor in response to widespread pressure for political reform. Although TR worked with Platt during his 1898 to 1900 term, he was independent enough to displease Platt, resulting in his promotion to vice president and then to president after William McKinley's 1901 assassination. TR kept close tabs on local politics because he remained "a citizen of New York State and interested, as every good citizen should be, in having clean politics in Albany." Besides, he needed the support of the nation's largest state for the 1904 election. So too, in 1906, TR was worried about Republican victory in 1908, especially since New York was critical to the popular vote and the Electoral College. However, discontent within the Republican Party meant that no ordinary candidate with conventional party ties could carry the state. Therefore, TR turned to the only available extraordinary candidate, Charles Evans Hughes.[10]

At the Republican Party's September convention in Saratoga, Hughes was nominated unanimously thanks to the work of Congressman Herbert Parsons, chairman of the powerful New York County Republican Party. But the bosses only complied under presidential pressure. Hughes's initial telegram and subsequent acceptance speech confirmed their fears. Pledging to act "according to my conscience," he promised "to give the State a sane, efficient and honorable administration, free from taint of bossism or of servitude to any private interest." Emphasizing the point, he proclaimed, "It will be an unbossed administration . . . an honest administration." The challenge to the status quo was clear.

TR was delighted that his party had suddenly become "very respectable" and hoped that its new image would avoid "disaster at the polls."[11]

William Randolph Hearst embodied possible disaster. Despite opposition within the state Democratic party, Brooklyn's Tammany boss, Charles F. Murphy, got Hearst nominated for governor. It was, said Hughes, an "unholy alliance" between a wealthy, political independent with a populist message and the Tammany boss he had so often attacked. A publisher who would be president, Hearst's chain of twenty-eight newspapers reached four million readers through the sensational headlines, human interest articles, and the amusing cartoons of "yellow journalism." Hearst supported labor unions, strikes, and labor legislation. He attacked bossism, trusts, and political corruption. As New York congressman from 1902 to 1904, Hearst rarely voted but introduced bills that he knew would never pass, such as antitrust laws, shorter hours for government workers, direct election of senators, and the abolition of railroad rebates. Hearst so skillfully capitalized on the issues of the times that Progressive journalist Herbert Croly considered him "a living menace to the orderly process of reform and to American national integrity."[12]

Although Murphy backed Hearst's election to Congress, he did not support either Hearst's quest for the 1904 Democratic presidential nomination or his reelection to Congress. In anger, Hearst ran against New York City's Tammany-backed Mayor George B. McClellan Jr., who sought reelection in 1905. Hearst formed his own Municipal Ownership League, which attacked "Plunderbund" politicians who consorted with businessmen for private profit. It advocated municipal control of gas, electricity, ice, and transportation in order to kill trusts, improve services, and reduce costs. Borrowed from Europe, this idea was popular and had already been adopted by several small cities and villages in New York. Hearst ran an exciting campaign starting with a packed Carnegie Hall nominating convention followed by enthusiastic crowds at every speech and culminating in a free concert for fifty thousand supporters in Madison Square Garden just before the election.

Hearst's popularity among the working classes threated Tammany, whose voters he attracted, and the Socialist Party, whose platform he appropriated. Even independents supported him as an anti-Tammany candidate. When Tammany joined the Republicans to accuse Hearst of demagoguery, the Hearst papers ran cartoons of Murphy as a criminal in striped prison clothes. On Election Day, Tammany undercut Hearst by using repeaters, stealing ballot boxes, assaulting Hearst's poll watchers, and harassing his voters. Losing by only thirty-five hundred votes infuriated Hearst. Although everyone knew he had been cheated, his call for a recount was denied. Mainstream New Yorkers were relieved but chastened by the success of a third-party candidate promoting radical change. According to historian, David Nasaw, the lesson was that Hearst, his issues, and his followers should be taken seriously. From then on, Tammany embraced social reform in order to please its working class and immigrant voters. Hearst had changed New York politics. Proof was Murphy's endorsement of Hearst for governor in 1906.[13]

TR considered Hughes the "ideal candidate" to combat Hearst, whom he called "the most potent single influence for evil we have in our life." Because he expected Hughes to join him "in reforming the relations between the Government and the great corporations," TR envisioned that Hughes was "fighting the battle of civilization." Most importantly, he noted, Hughes did not have "the slightest tint of subservience to the great moneyed interests [but was} an honest, fearless, square man, a good citizen and a good American first, and a good Republican also." Thus, the mercurial president and the methodical litigator began a fragile political partnership.[14]

Hughes started at a disadvantage. Hearst was a seasoned stump speaker with a strong antitrust, anti-bossism message that made his newspapers "the printed protest of the poor against the rich." There were German and Yiddish editions plus a free weekly paper for farmers. Hearst offered free showings of the new talking pictures and free vaudeville as he campaigned around the state in a fancy motorcar. Hughes could not compete. However, as a college debater, trial lawyer, and concerned citizen, Hughes had speaking skills, strong opinions, and moral convictions. The challenge was communicating with the public.[15]

Hughes approached the campaign as he approached everything—with total commitment. Travelling the state by train, he often gave twenty speeches a day followed by five rallies at night. His wife worried about "the heavy strain" but believed that he would handle it in his "usual wonderful and surprising manner." He certainly surprised both conventional politicians and ordinary New Yorkers with his hearty laugh, engaging stories, warm handshakes, and genuine concern for people's problems. Such human interest reflected his concept of democracy: "We have in this country but one security. You may think the statutes are your security—they are nothing but words in a book. You may think that the elaborate mechanism of government is your security—it is nothing at all, unless you have sound and uncorrupted public opinion to give life to your Constitution, to give vitality to your statutes, to make efficient your governmental machinery."

In other words, as naïve as it may seem today, Hughes believed that democracy depended on the people. Decrying the perversion of politics "by the reckless, untruthful, and inflammatory utterances . . . of the sensational press," he was certain that "the average man" carefully weighed propaganda against the "experience of life." In 1910, even after all his struggles as governor, he urged Yale students "to put your trust, as I do, in the common sense of the people of this country."[16]

During the campaign, Hearst ridiculed Hughes and his beard as an "animated feather duster." Seemingly bemused, Hughes brushed it off, refused to retaliate, and kept his enthusiastic campaign style (see figure 2.1). However, when Hearst accused him of serving corporations, Hughes retorted that Hearst had fourteen corporations, some of which were expressly designed to avoid taxes and libel suits. Indeed, Hearst was well known for slanderous newspaper articles that deceived the public. To Hughes, nothing could have been more dishonest, disreputable, and dangerous to democracy. Despite his lack of political experience, these powerful attacks made Hughes an effective campaigner.[17]

In accepting the nomination for governor, Hughes had embraced "the duty of leadership in a contest for decent government" and promised "an honest administration" characterized by a "government efficient and economical." Above all, it would be immune to partisanship, bribery, favors, and bossism. Reflecting traditional dual federalism based on separate state and national spheres, he paid homage to TR, but issued his own call for state "laws as may be required to secure equal privileges and opportunities and to prevent any one person or class of persons from being made the victim of oppression." Hughes "promised the enforcement of the law with equal severity and equal justice to all, rich and poor, corporations and individuals." He particularly wanted "to better the condition" of workers concerning tenements, sweatshops, hours, and child labor. Opposing those (like Hearst) who tried to "make discontent serve self-interest," Hughes vowed to pursue reforms that would address and, therefore, diminish discontent. Skeptics notwithstanding, Hughes's later actions as governor and on the Supreme Court documented his sincerity. Indeed, the pursuit of "even-handed justice"

Figure 2.1. "That Animated Feather Duster," by James Creelman. *Pearson's Magazine,* September 1907, no. 1. The Miriam and Ira D. Wallach Division of Art, Prints and Photographs, the New York Public Library.

dominated his professional life and his efforts to address the challenges of modernization at home and abroad.[18]

TR appreciated being mentioned in the speech but remained nervous about the campaign. Lest Hearst carry the immigrant vote, TR urged Hughes to speak more often to Catholics and Jews. Ever sensitive to practical politics, TR also urged Hughes to include more Republican politicians on a list of prospective judges. Hughes's refusal to politicize the list signaled his first conflict with TR and a good example of his noble, but often problematic, insistence on putting principle above party, his refusal to become "a marionette." Another example was his rejection of corporate campaign contributions, which meant covering the cost of campaigning himself despite not being rich.[19]

Because Hearst was so popular with labor, Republicans sought working-class support and Hughes gave many speeches on labor issues. He also advanced the Progressive prolabor agenda that he later pursued in office. It included labor's right to organize, compensation for injury on the job, limits on child labor, an eight-hour day on government construction sites, and restructuring the state's labor department. Rarely had a New York State campaign paid so much attention to "the labor problem" even though, as historian Daniel T. Rodgers observed, these issues were already being addressed in European cities and pursued in other states. Upstate bosses remained lukewarm about Hughes throughout the campaign, but Parsons, who also worried about the labor vote, promoted his candidacy. Some unions, independents, anti-Hearst Democrats, and downstate newspapers, especially Joseph Pulitzer's *New York World* (Hearst's competitor), joined the effort. A campaign postcard gave voters the choice between "Hughes and Heaven or Hearst and Hell." But TR was still anxious. So, he sent Elihu Root to speak on Hughes's behalf. It was a sensation.[20]

Root was a highly respected New York lawyer, McKinley's secretary of war and TR's secretary of state. Because he was considered an ally of Wall Street, the speech was moved from New York City to Utica. Scheduled four days before the election, Root did not give Hearst much time to respond. Consequently, Hearst had his supporters destroy newspapers previewing the speech, ran a cartoon of "Root the Rat," and planted Tammany men in the audience to disrupt the speech. Root still made his mark. Affirming that he spoke "with the President's authority," Root attacked Hearst as a hypocrite—a rich man pretending to care about the poor, an anti-boss crusader accepting a boss's nomination, an irresponsible demagogue exploiting "the dark and evil spirits of malice and greed, envy and sullen hatred." Root may have clinched the election.[21]

Hughes carried the state by almost seventy-six thousand votes. He even prevailed in upstate cities that Hearst expected to sweep. After spending $500,000 to Hughes's $619, Hearst was reluctant to concede. However, noted Nasaw, Hearst basically defeated himself by attacking Tammany during the campaign. Murphy never liked Hearst anyway and failed to rally his followers to the polls. Upstate and downstate, ticket splitting was widespread. Independents in both parties preferred Hughes's dignified call for moderate reforms to Hearst's bellicose attacks and extreme positions. The fact that no other state Republican was elected that year confirmed TR's opinion that only Hughes had the ability and credibility to save New York's Republican Party. For now, the president was confident that "you and I, my dear Hughes, approach our work in the same spirit."[22]

Perceiving the national implications of the contest, Charles Bartholomew, a *Minneapolis Journal* cartoonist, depicted Hearst and Hughes as gardeners. Working in his "yellow garden," Hearst's flashy flowers labeled "socialism," "sensationalism," and "prejudice" grew in an "unenviable record" soil. By contrast, Hughes cultivated a "conservative cabbage patch" comprised of practical crops like wheat, lettuce, and cabbages labeled "good record," "insurance investigation," and "clean politics." Uncle Sam stood between them wondering whether "the work these fellows accomplish in this local patch may help me determine who will run the national garden for me in another season."[23]

Fighting Governor

Hughes's first term as governor had a rocky start. Opposing bossism proved much harder than expected, but he lost no time trying. After attending a postelection retreat packed with his enemies, Hughes made several symbolic moves. First, he eliminated the bosses' traditional "back door" access to the governor. From now on, they would have to enter his office by the front door and by appointment, not, as reputed, through a secret stairway. Second, Hughes began holding open "morning hour" sessions in the lavish room outside his office. Previously used only for hearings or ceremonies, it became a reception area for anyone who wanted to see the governor. On a first-come, first-served basis, politicians, businessmen, and ordinary citizens could appeal to him without fanfare. Everyone was equal under "daylight government." Hughes insisted that "when any citizen enters the executive chamber, he should feel that he has the same rights as any other man or as the temporary occupant of that chamber." The bosses were dismayed, but reformer Oswald Garrison Villard's *New York Evening Post* declared, "We have a governor again."[24]

Hughes pursued a parallel policy with the press. Following his strategy during the gas and insurance investigations, Hughes held two press conferences a day in order to clarify his policies and avoid misunderstanding. He treated every reporter equally and had no favorites. However, when one reporter claimed to have special access to the governor and misrepresented his position on a pending bill, Hughes clarified the matter. The reporter was offended and later wrote that Hughes resented "playing 'second fiddle' to Roosevelt." Hughes immediately called a special press conference to counteract the article, but the damage had been done. Tensions between the president and the governor grew.[25]

Despite facing resistance within the Republican Party. Hughes insisted that "the forceful expression of opinion, whether or not it coincides with the wishes of the party managers, is essential to keep the party vigorous and wholesome." Therefore, he became an aggressive Progressive advocating positive government defined by contempt for corruption and concern for contemporary problems. His inaugural address advocated an activist state that would improve "our charitable and correctional work" as well as "our canals, our highways, our forest preserves, the protection of the public health, the problems created by the congestion of population in our great cities." Most importantly, his standard for governmental activism would be "efficiency and not partisan advantage."[26]

Hughes confronted the conflict between party and principle as soon as he took office. His supporters were a minority in the state legislature, which had to pass all of his bills. Moreover, the legislature was divided not only between upstate and downstate, Democrats and Republicans, but also between conservative, moderate, and progressive Republicans. Even those divisions were not definitive because some of the old guard supported some of Hughes's policies and some progressives opposed others. Such a complicated scenario would have been hard for even the most seasoned politician to handle and Hughes was a novice.

In most instances, Hughes could count on support from Parsons and Timothy Woodruff, who was a former lieutenant governor, Brooklyn Republican leader, and chairman of the state Republican Party. But both were loyal party men and grew weary of Hughes's independence over time. In the state senate, his most important allies were New York City's Alfred Page, Binghamton's Harvey Hinman, and Rochester's William Armstrong, who had chosen Hughes to lead the insurance investigation. In the state assembly, he could count on a core of twenty men, representing upstate and downstate cities. These moderates and progressives agreed with Hughes that reformers should actively participate in the work of the two major parties, not withdraw from them in contempt or create independent, single-issue parties. He needed all hands on deck.

Fortunately, in 1906 the Republicans elected twenty-seven-year-old

James W. Wadsworth Jr. as assembly speaker. He reorganized the state assembly and assigned moderates and progressives as committee chairmen. A Yale graduate, Wadsworth hailed from an old, wealthy Livingston County landholding family. His father was a long-term congressman and occasional TR critic. A moderate, Wadsworth backed almost all of Hughes's proposals. He reformed the legislature by eliminating numerous no-show jobs and preventing the railroads from granting travel passes to assemblymen. Although gradually moving closer to the old guard, he initially undermined the Black Horse Cavalry, a cross-party cabal of legislators who accepted bribes for passing bills that helped special interests and killing those that hurt them. Wadsworth's support was crucial for the governor's success.[27]

Hughes faced formidable opposition from upstate and downstate machine politicians of both parties who deeply resented his anti-boss crusade. New York City's Tammany leader Thomas Grady and Kings County boss Patrick McCarren together controlled fourteen of nineteen Democratic senators. Republican Senate Majority Leader and Speaker John Raines of Canandaigua and Albany boss Barnes became Hughes's strongest adversaries. They represented the old guard and resisted any reforms that challenged their power. However, they could support changes that were less personally threatening, especially if they were popular. Both had shifted their political allegiance from Boss Platt to Governor Odell and (reluctantly) to his weak successor Governor Francis W. Higgins. After the insurance hearings, they understood the need to rehabilitate the Republican Party and disassociate it from Platt, Odell, and Higgins.[28]

"Uncle John" Raines was the elder statesman, or, in Wesser's words, the "crusty old tyrant of the state senate," which he dominated as majority leader from 1902 until his death in 1909. A smart, skillful strategist, he was praised for bills upgrading public education and imposing an alcohol tax. Although Raines worked well with four previous governors (including TR), he found Hughes distinctly cold and dangerously independent.[29]

William "Billy" Barnes Jr., whose father's corruption was exposed during the insurance investigation, became an implacable obstacle. Shortly after the election, he warned Hughes to uphold "the power of the organization" rather than push divisive reforms like racetrack gambling, ballot reform, and saloons, two of which became Hughes's major crusades. Hughes replied that he would always put the public interest first. His belief that the people were the bedrock of democracy contrasted with Barnes who once stated, "I don't believe it is the function of a leader to ask what the public sentiment is, but to direct it." Different priorities were reinforced by different personalities. Whereas Hughes was controlled, formal, and gracious, Pusey described Barnes as "a big, brazen, loud-talking" man but "keen and eloquent in a sort of bullish way." Yet Wadsworth later called Barnes "the ablest Republican leader in the state," a man who was not only an astute "student of human nature" but "absolutely honest" and "also absolutely practical."[30]

After Harvard, Barnes purchased the *Albany Evening Journal*, originally owned by his grandfather Thurlow Weed, a leader of the Whig Party and a founder of the Republican Party. Only twenty-five years old, Barnes was considered "a joke" but rapidly became "the Boy Leader" of the Republican State Committee. After working closely with Boss Platt, Barnes replaced him in 1900 as head of the state Republican Party with control over other upstate local bosses and the party newspaper, *The Argus*. Using patronage, he built a tightly controlled Albany-based machine. Saying, "I don't believe in the rule of the majority," Barnes opposed all electoral reforms. Because, wrote one historian, "every doorknob in the State Capitol had a Barnes man hanging to it," the Albany boss maintained "ironclad" power over the state Republican Party from 1900 to 1921. Hughes threatened that power.[31]

The biggest dilemma that Hughes faced as governor was how to bolster his party while reforming it—that is, how to be a structural reformer. Broadcasting his attitude toward ordinary politics, he declared, "I was not elected to play politics or to build up a political machine, and I am not trying to. I was not elected to settle grudges or to make appointments to settle grudges and I have not done so." Another dilemma involved TR. Despite wanting to remain on good terms with the president, Hughes refused to seek TR's approval for his first inaugural address on the premise that he had been elected as governor "and not as an agent" of Washington. He could not have been clearer when he proclaimed, "I shall be my own spokesman."[32]

Thus, the new governor had already offended not only the national leader of his party but also the state party power-holders. They soon showed him how politics really worked. Upholding the principle of separation of powers, Hughes refused to influence the selection of state senate committee chairmen. Raines promptly filled the key seats with Hughes's enemies and gave his friends insignificant positions. Taken aback but undaunted, Hughes responded by warning, "In any difficulty that may arise, to the people of this State I propose to appeal." Although TR had used this strategy too, the bosses did not take the new, inexperienced governor seriously. They might have won the first skirmish, but they would soon discover that Hughes meant what he said and was no pushover.[33]

Hughes knew that if he was to have any real impact, he needed competent administrators open to change. Like Progressive journalist Herbert Croly, Hughes contended that department heads should be "public servants rather than politicians" appointed and removable by the governor. As Croly explained, "There can be no efficiency without responsibility. There can be no responsibility without authority." Hughes believed that impartial administration by experts would not only improve governance but also restore public faith in government. Especially because taxes rose as government expanded, it was imperative that every employee be competent—not just "a good fellow" with connections. "We have a government of laws and not of men," he said, "but a government after all is nothing but men." In that spirit, he began challenging the party's control of critical appointments and the legislature's dominance of state government.[34]

First, he replaced Lewis M. Swasey, whom he considered "a mere tool of the machine," with a more qualified man to supervise New York City elections. Although Hughes carefully appointed someone from the party, Parsons thought Hughes was courting "hostility by party leaders" as well as party supporters, who "shiver every time he makes a speech." In addition, Hughes angered TR who had endorsed Swasey. But to Hughes, Swasey represented a system designed "to support partisan workers at the public expense. . . . Public service," he said, "is not an almshouse." In another case, TR fired Archie Sanders, an upstate federal jobholder and Wadsworth ally without consulting Hughes. TR claimed to be helping Hughes while really settling an old score with Wadsworth's father. The president seemed to be abusing his patronage powers and interfering in state affairs. When Hughes admitted that he had not approved the firing, TR looked bad. Sensational press reporting on the matter exacerbated tensions between the two men.[35]

Next, Hughes appointed State Senator Frederick C. Stevens of Attica to be superintendent of Public Works, traditionally a vast source of patronage. Stevens had earned Hughes's respect as chair of the gas investigation committee. In urging Stevens to clean up the department,

Hughes admonished him to always prioritize "the public interest," which meant not using patronage "to build any Hughes machine." However, Hughes did not know that Stevens was an enemy of Wadsworth's family. When so advised, Hughes denied intending to hurt Wadsworth and stood his ground. Although Hughes prevailed, his relationship with Wadsworth started fraying.[36]

After successfully conducting the insurance investigation and getting reform bills passed before becoming governor, Hughes was determined to follow through as governor. Unfortunately, the state insurance department was run by Otto Kelsey, an amiable, honest but ineffectual party man. Concerned about competence, Hughes asked him to resign in exchange for another job. When Kelsey refused, the bosses circled the wagons around him. Hughes dug in and used his prosecutorial skills to interrogate Kelsey during a public examination that Hughes later admitted was "an unusual course." In fact, he was so hard on Kelsey that he even offended party moderates like Wadsworth, who was already upset about Stevens and a reapportionment plan undermining his family's historic power base. The fighting governor had fought too hard.[37]

The Kelsey interrogation infuriated conservatives and strengthened their determination to defend their well-liked party loyalist. Parsons warned that removing Kelsey would discourage other decent men from political participation, but Hughes persisted. As required, he asked the senate to remove Kelsey for incompetence. When the motion was defeated, Hughes took his case to the public, speaking across the state and getting good press coverage. Appealing to the people, explained his secretary Robert H. Fuller, was "his substitute for bribery, bull-dozing, and intrigue." It was the teacher clarifying the issues, the idealist appealing to reason, and the politician building his base. When the public responded positively, Barnes accused Hughes of undercutting his own party. Journalists relished a war between the governor and the bosses. A cartoonist depicted him as a tornado chasing political corruption into a cyclone cellar (see figure 2.2).[38]

The drama now shifted to the state senate's Judiciary Committee, which was controlled by Raines and included the two downstate Tammany bosses, Grady and McCarren. The Kelsey issue became a chance to defend party rule. Aware of growing support for Hughes among the public and the press, Raines used the hearings to build an opposition. For a month, Kelsey's attorney mounted a strong defense before the Judiciary Committee while the governor's position was supported by his

Figure 2.2. "The Political Tornado," by Charles Lewis Bartholomew. *Minneapolis Journal*, October 5, 1908. Courtesy of Hennepin County Library, Minneapolis, Minnesota.

progressive allies—Armstrong, Hinman, and Page. When the issue went to the whole senate, the upstate Republican bosses cooperated with the downstate Democratic bosses to back Kelsey over Hughes. Even though Kelsey resigned after Hughes was reelected in 1908, the bosses won in the moment and Raines vowed to "fight Mr. Hughes tooth and nail for the rest of the session."[39]

The governor was down, but not out. In fact, the Kelsey issue led to a major legislative victory. In order to document Kelsey's shortcomings, Hughes sought the insurance department's records. Discovering that departmental records were generally unattainable, he concluded that executive powers should be expanded to promote accountability. Accordingly, he worked with State Assemblyman Sherman Moreland, a Progressive upstate Republican, who had been Hughes's student at Cornell and was the Assembly majority leader. Wadsworth appointed Moreland to chair the powerful Ways and Means Committee. The result was the path-breaking 1907 Moreland Act, enabling the governor to investigate state, county, and city activities.

Wadsworth opposed increasing executive power but loyally ushered the bill through the Assembly. As soon as it passed, Hughes launched an investigation of the insurance department and unearthed irregularities that comprised his second case against Kelsey. He used the act often, including to remove the borough presidents of Manhattan, Queens, and Brooklyn for incompetence, not corruption. Thus, Hughes established a new standard for officeholders. As with Kelsey, he insisted that it was not enough to be honest and popular. Public officials also had to ably discharge the public business. Manhattan aldermen defiantly reinstated their borough president and sued Hughes in court, but the court upheld the governor. It rejected what *The New York Sun* called a "marionette defense" by party loyalists.[40]

Although accused of overriding home rule, Hughes was asserting the state's interest in good government on the premise that "local government is the school of citizenship." The Moreland Act was replicated in eighteen other states and remains a key tool for governors seeking administrative reform today. In 1926, Hughes chaired a state government reorganization committee that endorsed gubernatorial control over appointments, which inspired a new state law. Thus, his fraught campaign for competence and accountability in state government was ultimately victorious. In this case, he lost the battle but won the war.[41]

The Public Interest

The most significant accomplishment of Hughes's first term as governor was the Public Service Commission (PSC) Act, which passed in 1907 so "that public privilege, under public control, shall be exercised for public benefit." It was designed to eliminate corporate monopolies and "pernicious favoritism" by monitoring the service, safety, and rates charged by state-chartered private corporations providing transportation, gas, or electricity. Because the bill was an unabashed attack on corruption, it was volatile. Getting passage tried Hughes's resolve, resiliency, and leadership skills. In rising to the occasion, he defied reality, redefined the role of governor, and revitalized democracy in New York State. He even "developed into a quick and witty platform orator." The struggle earned him prominence in the national campaign to reform state government by addressing modern problems. It was an odd metamorphosis for a scholarly, supposedly impractical, stuffy lawyer.[42]

A central part of Hughes's agenda from the beginning, the PSC Act tackled the irony of economic progress left by the Gilded Age. The development of industry and business promoted unparalleled economic growth. But monopolies and mergers undermined the very competition that originally stimulated the economy. Moreover, the benefits were not universal. Progressives like TR and Hughes were concerned about the growing conflict between private profit and public interest. Knowing that corporations were too big for individuals or groups to combat, Progressives believed that government should correct corporate abuses without totally crippling corporations. To Hughes, public utilities were particularly troubling examples of how private companies exploited "the claim of individual rights . . . to protect unlawful gains and systematic pillaging of the community through abuse of public privileges." All too often, he said, "the wolf appears in sheep's clothing."[43]

The Progressive solution was to have nonpartisan experts monitor public service rates for fairness to both the public and the companies. This approach marked a major shift from traditional governmental noninterference with business to qualified interference. Federal acts regulating railroads were largely ineffective because the railroad companies dominated the regulating bodies. Moreover, TR, the "trustbuster," feared that too much regulation would stifle economic development. In 1906, after the gas and insurance investigations, the New York State legislature enacted Hughes's recommendations for a state commission regulating gas and electricity plus bills limiting the insurance companies' ability to cheat customers and influence politics. That was a good start, but Hughes wanted to go further in order to ensure that "material prosperity will not be permitted to serve as a cover for public wrongs."[44]

Acknowledging New York State's regional divisions, the proposed PSC bill would replace all existing unreliable, incompetent, politicized railroad and rapid transit commissions with two professional nonpartisan commissions—one for upstate to address railroad issues and another for downstate to address mass transit issues. Both would oversee companies providing gas and electricity. They would be able to act whether or not a complaint was lodged, investigate a company's financial practices, set "reasonable rates, . . . require adequate and impartial services, provide for the safety of employees and for the protection of the public." Instead of discriminatory rates, rebates, and free passes, railroads would publicize standardized fares and violators would be fined. Although the bill did not cover the telephone and telegraph until 1910, the proposed commissions would be more powerful than any other regulatory commissions in the nation. In addition, they would eliminate the notoriously corrupt "strike bills," which were designed to hurt public utility companies so that they would bribe legislators to defeat them.[45]

Typically Progressive, the PSC bill required that all decisions be based on facts and reason, always a Hughes imperative. As nonpartisan experts paid by the state, the commissioners would professionalize the notoriously politicized system. Most controversial, the governor would have the right to remove senate-appointed commissioners for incompetence or malfeasance without legislative consent. The intent was to eliminate the bribes that companies gave legislators to influence legislation and administration. The bill also forbade companies from appealing the commissions' rulings in court, thus eliminating a major strategy for delaying and manipulating commission rulings.

Resistance was fierce. The steam railroads resented state interference and mounted an extensive public relations campaign to poison the proposal. These efforts, compounded by the dominance of conservative legislators, seemed certain to doom the PSC. Learning from the Kelsey affair, Hughes honed his political and communication skills. He worked closely with legislators and won Wadsworth's support. Then, he again took his case directly to the people in what Wesser called "a brilliant publicity campaign." Instead of his aggressive prosecutorial skills, Hughes drew upon his ability to explain the issues in a classroom and present his case in a courtroom. Speaking at forty meetings across the state over two months, Hughes confirmed his reputation as a dedicated public servant opposing corruption. The governor's energy and enthusiasm were inspiring; his message was compelling. Effectively targeting popular grievances, he declared, "The cry 'Every man for himself' is out of date. The demand of the future will be 'Every man for the people.'" Ironically, noted McCormick, Hughes "exploited the intense politicization of the utilities issue [to get] the question permanently out of politics."[46]

The highlight of the campaign occurred in Elmira where the governor reaffirmed his belief that administrative matters like setting utility rates were best handled by nonpartisan commissioners who would keep legislators from setting rates under corporate influence. Anticipating trouble, Hughes arranged to speak second. That enabled him to respond when the first speaker sarcastically stated that he was "under no retainer from the railroads." Hughes famously replied, "In distinction from my learned friend, I am here under a retainer. I am retained by the people of the State of New York, to see that justice is done." Denying any intention to harm business interests, he affirmed, "I stand for the people of the State of New York against extortion, against favoritism, against financial scandal, and against everything that goes to corrupt our politics." Immediately, "retained by the People" became a rallying cry.[47]

The commission idea caught fire. The press publicized the governor's speeches and Albany was swamped with mail. Accosted by angry constituents when they went home, state legislators began reversing themselves. TR added pressure. Accordingly, the PSC bill passed the state assembly unanimously and, with John Raines's blessing, passed the state senate overwhelmingly. It was an astounding victory. After only six months in office, the novice had become a skilled politician and a national political hero. Moreover, McCormick pointed out that the governor had "provided a way of adjusting the economic conflicts that nineteenth-century governments had mostly avoided."[48]

Soon after the PSC bill passed, Hughes risked vetoing popular bills for a two-cent per-mile railroad fare, a penalty for railroad shipping delays, and requirements for larger railroad crews. Being consistent, if impolitic, he explained that such policies required prior investigation by the PSC in the interests of fairness. As he explained, "Injustice on the part of railroad corporations toward the public does not justify injustice on the part of the State toward the railroad corporations." Although Hughes understood popular "dissatisfaction" with current conditions, he pointed out that "arbitrary reprisals" by the legislature would simply substitute one wrong for another. At all times, he said, "government should be fair and impartial." Because "railroads are not the enemies but the servants of the people," he insisted that they "must be subject to regulation" based on "all pertinent facts." Rates should be "reasonable" for the riders as well as the owners. As always, his standard was "fair dealing."[49]

One of the PSC bill's most important provisions was empowering the governor to appoint and remove the new commissioners. Up until then, legislators created and controlled commissions in order to decentralize authority and weaken the executive branch. In response, Progressive reformers mounted a national effort to strengthen governors, increase efficiency, and promote accountability. "The true remedy" for political corruption, proclaimed Hughes, was "to unify administration, to concentrate administrative power, and thus sharply define administrative responsibility." Combined with his advocacy of civil service reform and other political reforms, Hughes was instrumental in redefining state government for the modern era.[50]

Hughes followed through by appointing Democrats and Republicans to the PSC including several experts in relevant fields: a merchant, a lawyer, and a businessman, but, strangely, no labor representative. His friend William Willcox chaired the downstate commission. New York City's former parks commissioner and postmaster, Willcox later managed Hughes's 1916 presidential campaign. None of the new commissioners was tied to party machines. The commissioners urged the railroads to make necessary adjustments to rates and services or sought compromise solutions to those problems. Barring compromise, the commissioners often ruled in favor of the public interest. They even supported the larger railroad crews that Hughes had vetoed.

As historian Bruce Dearstyne showed, the companies gradually learned that commissions were beneficial. The PSC deflected popular anger through hearings and compromise, facilitated safety improvements, curtailed competition, and generally pursued moderate regulation. Some considered this outcome inadequate but it was just the kind of balanced, structural reform that Hughes intended. As such, it accurately reflected the basically moderate spirit of Progressivism. A cartoonist in *Judge* turned Hughes's face and beard into a broom (like a feather duster?) sweeping the grafters, lobbyists, corrupt commissions, and courts into a big dustpan. The handle was labeled "public opinion" and the caption read "A New Broom Sweeps Clean."[51]

The PSC was just the start. After the 1907 banking crisis, Hughes created an unpaid commission of six prominent New York City bankers to reassess state banking policies. Their recommendations for greater supervision of banks and trusts became twenty-one bills that Hughes endorsed and the legislature passed in 1908. With most Republicans behind Hughes, his progressive program rapidly moved through the legislature. It included bills to improve the electoral process, a controversial bill on reapportionment, and a bill providing for recounts in contested elections, as in Hearst's loss to McClellan. In addition, Hughes established the nation's first commission on probation to recommend procedural reforms for the criminal justice system. Over objections to the concept of prisoner rehabilitation, the legislature also passed a sweeping Probation Act in 1907. Altogether, Hughes achieved an outstanding record of progressive legislative accomplishment. In the insurance and gas investigations, noted one observer, he demonstrated that he could expose, "tear apart, rip up, and analyze." As governor, he developed a "creative ability" to reconstruct "a new machine out of parts of the old machine." Structural reform worked.[52]

While Hughes expanded the scope of state power on statewide issues, he used the veto to protect municipal control over local issues, a state version of dual federalism. Exacerbated by the upstate-downstate divide, home rule was (and remains) a contentious issue in New York. Hughes had ties to both regions, but his deepest allegiance was to constitutional principles. He knew an abuse of power when he saw one. Therefore, he vetoed several bills affecting the city despite the inevitable backlash. For example, when the state legislature tried to impose platoon policies on the New York City Police Department or require more jailers, Hughes vetoed the bills as unnecessary interference with local decision-making. When the legislators voted to raise New York City teacher's salaries, he pointed out that they were not only discriminating against teachers in the rest of the state but also violating the New York City Board of Education's prerogatives. Along with his veto of a mandated two-cent railroad fare, he vetoed a maximum five-cent New York City transit fare because, he said, the state legislature should not override local authority nor rule on complex matters being handled by the downstate PSC. Each of these vetoes risked offending some constituency, but Hughes stood firm. As he explained the issues, he won popular support and strengthened his national reputation.[53]

Hughes faced intense public ire over racetrack gambling. There were four different aspects to the issue. First was the popularity of horse racing. Second was anxiety over gambling, not only as immoral but also as a cause of poverty and crime. Third was the profit motive of gambling interests and of farmers whose county fairs benefitted from racetrack revenues. It actually took an organized effort of reformers and churches across the state to alert Hughes to the moral issue of racetrack gambling. Although he was always receptive to moral issues, he was actually not against horse racing per se. He considered it a "lawful sport" as long as it was not corrupted by bookmaking and legislative trickery. Oddly, bookmaking was illegal everywhere except at racetracks.[54]

Fourth was a question of law: Enter Hughes. An 1895 amendment to the state Constitution expressly forbade "any lottery or the sale of lottery tickets, pool-selling, book-making, or any other kind of gambling." A follow-up law classified bookmaking as a felony. However, the state legislature then reclassified a gambling violation as "a civil action" with "forfeiture of the money wagered" as the only punishment. Because gambling was no longer a serious crime, it flourished. Understanding that racetrack betting was popular and that it would be hard to eliminate, Hughes nevertheless resolved that "gambling shall not parade in business livery."[55]

The ensuing battle strained Hughes's resolve, especially after receiving death threats and warnings that his baby daughter would be kidnapped. Nonetheless, by 1908, he saw the gambling issue as a test of respect for law. Hughes gave the keynote speech when reformers initiated their statewide publicity campaign. He won over the powerful New York State Grange by promising state support for county fairs. To Hughes, "it is simply a question whether the people and their Constitution are supreme in this State, or whether we are ruled by gamblers and those who profit from gambling. . . . [It is] the gamblers against the people."[56]

The betting interests responded with their own statewide campaign bolstered by an alliance between Republican and Tammany legislators. Regardless, a bill restoring the original intent of the law easily passed the state assembly. The state senate was a bigger problem. In a cartoon sarcastically titled "Representation," an arrogant state senator stood astride the Anti-Racetrack Gambling Bill. Dressed like a gambler with a dollar sign hanging from his belt, he puffed on a cigar and puffed

Figure 2.3. "Representation," by Nelson Harding. *The Brooklyn Daily Eagle*, April 9, 1908.

out his chest. The governor and the people were under foot; the state Constitution was in the trash (see figure 2.3). Letters for and against the measure flooded Albany, including many fake ones. Probetting lobbyists offered bribes for votes. Barnes admitted reversing his support for the bill purely out of hatred for Hughes and made "his" senator vote no. Hughes called Barnes a dictator. Incredibly, another senator was drugged in hopes that he would sleep through the vote. He made it, but a tie vote killed the bill anyway.[57]

Forging ahead, Hughes proved to be more politically astute than expected. Following one key senator's sudden death, the governor quickly scheduled a special election for the seat and called the legislature into special session starting the day after that election. Then, he took his case to the people once more. He campaigned nonstop for the anti-gambling candidate and urged the voters to "Rise in your might" on Election Day. When he was attacked for interfering with the legislature, Hughes said he was saving democracy from the tyranny of special interests and bosses who abused power by manipulating legislation. In contrast, he said, "I have used no weapon but that of reason. I have exercised no prerogative but that of recommendation and argument." Evoking a preacher in the wilderness, the Republican bosses dismissed him as "Charles the Baptist." But, when his candidate narrowly won the election, a *New York World* cartoonist drew Hughes as an "animated feather duster" sweeping his candidate into office.[58]

Emotions ran high during the special session, culminating in an exceptional political episode. On the day before the session was supposed to end, the repeal bill passed the state assembly. Like every politician, Hughes could count votes and knew that the bill's fate hung by a thread in the state senate. Moreover, a key supporter had just undergone an appendectomy and was very weak. Hughes sent one of the bill's authors to ask the ailing senator to attend the session despite doctors' orders. Not leaving the matter to chance, Hughes had a train stop expressly to pick him up. When the ailing senator appeared, the opposition proposed three amendments to the bill in order to delay the vote and wear him out. But he hung on and ultimately cast the winning ballot. Hughes called it "a victory for law and order," but it was really a victory for Hughes. It strengthened his image as a crusader against bossism and a defender of "decent government." In the end, wrote the *New York Evening Mail*, "The house of politics is cleaner than it was thanks to the 'animated feather duster.'"[59]

Not everyone appreciated Hughes's success. Indeed, the following satirical poem criticized him as an old-fashioned moralist with an ego as big as his reform agenda. It reflected the resentments of the gambling interests and reinforced criticisms of Hughes as aloof, arrogant, patronizing, and legalistic. Based on Samuel Butler's seventeenth-century parody of narrow, contentious Puritanical politicians, it excoriated Hughes as Sir Charlie Hudibras:

As Spanish knight of old broke lance
'Gainst windmills that he met perchance,
So forth to fight a juster cause
Goes he who would uphold the laws;
And if may be it seems to him
More opportune or suits his whim,
New laws he makes for Church or State,
Like whipping child for being late;
Insurance steals, bad 'tho they be,
Worse still, race gambling, you can see
Which must be stopp'd or all to Hell
Go P-D-Q- and there may dwell.
So, lance in rest, with beard unfurled,
Like Don Quixote t'reform the world . . .
He's tall and thin, of serious mien,
His eye the sanctimonious kind
Sees far in front and well behind,
Tho' I am told can be quite blind,
Which trait is of the legal mind.[60]

The racetrack gambling fight reflected Hughes's strengths and weaknesses as a politician. He alienated some of the people some of the time but won cooperation and respect most of the time. As a "fighting governor," he was aggressive, stubborn, and moralistic. However, those potentially negative qualities were balanced by being definitive, determined, and dedicated to principle. Experience taught Hughes to be less prosecutorial and naïve, more engaging and strategic. He had not really changed but he had grown and was learning how to be a practical idealist. Time and again, Hughes was accused of being "a very narrow-minded man." In response, he said, "Well, I confess that I am narrow-minded enough to operate within the limits of the Constitution of the State!" But, he added, "at the same time, I hope that I am broad-minded enough within these limits to do anything that can be done to promote the welfare of the people."[61] He was a proud structural reformer.

To *The Brooklyn Daily Eagle,* Hughes's first term was really a contest between "the old and the new." The governor used his "legal mind" to develop a "practical working out" of modern relations between the government and the corporations. Most amazing, he "delivered to machine politics . . . if not the death blow, at least the knockout." The governor's role was reshaped in keeping with Progressive principles. Hughes believed that honest, impartial, efficient government dedicated to the common good and based on faith in the public would embody the best of democratic theory and practice. He harnessed the public anger resulting from his gas and insurance investigations to promote public political participation. McCormick concluded that by bringing issues directly to the people, Hughes's speaking campaigns "created a new kind of bond between the voters and their representatives [that] provided an antidote" for increasing public disinterest in and cynicism about democracy. Success strengthened Hughes's belief that if government acts "in the interest of the people, they will rally to its support." Progressivism prevailed; democracy was vindicated.[62]

3 | Second Term as Governor, 1908–1910

Getting Reelected

Presidential politics encumbered state politics. One reason that the racetrack gambling bill struggled was President Theodore Roosevelt's (TR's) refusal to endorse it. He did not actually oppose the bill, but he did not want to help Charles Evans Hughes because the racetrack fight was getting Hughes a lot of favorable national press. During Hughes's first term, TR became wary of him. Bitter about being overruled on Swazcy and Sanders, TR was also annoyed by the governor's insistence on total independence from the state Republican machine.

Using the same words that he would later apply to Woodrow Wilson, TR called Hughes "a thoroughly selfish and cold-blooded creature" who put his own principles ahead of practical politics. He polarized the party and alienated its leaders. The qualities that originally justified endorsing Hughes for governor were now objectionable. William Barnes Jr., Herbert Parsons, and Timothy Woodruff agreed. However, to independents like Oswald Garrison Villard, these qualities were the governor's greatest assets. In Villard's opinion, Hughes was "in every respect that which Roosevelt pretends to be, a true reformer and a real public servant . . . [who] owes his allegiance solely to the people."[1]

Regretting his promise not to run for president in 1908, TR was determined to name his successor and protect his legacy. For a moment, he considered backing Hughes but resented that "the men most hostile to me show a tendency to gather around Hughes." The governor, he said, was "a fairly good man (but not a big man) and an inordinately conceited one. He is therefore jealous of me." There is no evidence for that last claim, but there is evidence that that the governor's sterling record unsettled TR, especially because it made Hughes a presidential contender. Although he shared TR's progressive priorities, Hughes could not be controlled. Moreover, TR worried that an internally divided New York State Republican Party might jeopardize national Republican victory in 1908.[2]

Villard interviewed Hughes about the prospect of becoming president. It revealed why politicians called Hughes supercilious, why he always was divided about seeking political office, and why his relationship with TR was so tenuous. Admitting that TR did not consider him practical enough to win, Hughes declared that practical politics was "repugnant to his moral sense and . . . the worst kind of politics." He disparaged the politician who "cannot see beyond his nose or is wholly wrapped up in his own petty jealousies." In any case, Hughes said that he could not focus on the presidency because the job of governor was so demanding that "I am often at the end of my strength." Nonetheless, he would accept the nomination if offered because "no man in good health had the right to decline such an honor." Villard concluded that Hughes was admirably sincere, honest, and earnest but also "narrow, obstinate and opinionated." These intertwined attributes were assets and detriments for a politician.[3]

After wrestling with the thought of running himself, TR concluded that William Howard Taft would be his best, most loyal, and safest successor—a decision that he would soon regret. Historian Arthur S. Link called it TR's "one great mistake" and suggested that if Hughes had been chosen instead of Taft, "the future history of the United States might have been considerably different." Because Hughes was at the height of his popularity in 1908, he might have won. Hypothetically, TR might not have challenged Taft with a third party in 1912, which so divided the Republicans that a Democrat was elected president. By the same token, TR might have been just as opposed to Hughes as to Taft in 1912 and bolted the party anyway. Conjecture is fun but futile.[4]

In March 1908, muckraker Ida Tarbell published an article asking "How about Hughes?" She praised his principles, work ethic, and dedication to public service. But she also recognized that the governor's "strength with the people was his weakness with the old rank and file of the party organization." When she called Hughes "the least agitated person in the United States on the question of the presidency," Parsons contended that Hughes was actually "the most agitated person" about the nomination. Suggesting that the governor doth protest too much, Parsons thought Hughes was just as ambitious as anyone else.[5]

TR's secretary of war, Taft was a prominent lawyer, judge, former solicitor general, and civilian governor of the Philippines. He supported

TR's policies, worked closely with him in the cabinet, and was his friend. Knowing that Taft was hardly as energetic as himself (or Hughes), TR urged him to show more interest in the nomination or lose it. While graciously refusing to compete directly with Hughes, Taft gave several solid speeches, but still needed help. Accordingly, TR told him how to speak, what to say, where to stay, and what sports to play. (Golf evoked wealth; horseback riding was politically safer.) TR also used federal patronage to corral votes for Taft at the National Republican Convention. Historian Lewis L. Gould explained that "Progressive Republicans supported Taft as the President's heir; conservatives backed him to prevent another Roosevelt nomination." Hughes did not help himself by refusing to actively pursue the nomination. As one observer remarked, "He would rather be Hughes than President."[6]

After the movement to nominate Hughes spread across the country, he finally agreed to announce his availability through a major speech in New York City on January 31st. The newspapers left front-page space to cover it. However, just before Hughes spoke, TR captured that space for himself by issuing what the press called "the Hottest Message Ever Sent to Congress." TR's sensational diatribe against the nation's "unscrupulous . . . wealthy malefactors" contrasted sharply with Hughes's "temperate, sane, well-thought-out discourse." *The New York Times* understood that TR's speech was "timed to dwarf Hughes." When asked about it, TR said, "If Hughes is going to play the game, he must learn the tricks." It was more than a game. As journalist Mark Sullivan pointed out, TR was determined to remain "the pre-eminent reformer of the day" and Hughes was equally determined not to become a "minor orbit about the gigantic sun that Roosevelt was." Yet, Hughes was not quite "radiant enough . . . to set up a rival solar system of his own."[7]

The situation reflected the larger problem Hughes faced as a politician. Although there was substantial support and admiration for Hughes upstate, downstate, and in the west, Hughes remained maddeningly aloof from the political fray and squandered his opportunity to build support, an error he would repeat in 1916. Meanwhile, New York State bosses, led by Barnes, tried to block Hughes's renomination because, as Parsons put it, the party politicians "hate him like poison." Parsons even doubted that party workers would want to campaign for Hughes. Nonetheless, strong support for Hughes among independents forced Republicans to tread carefully.[8]

Parsons told Hughes that he had long admired Taft, felt that Hughes did not have enough political experience to be president, and that Taft would continue TR's policies. With key New Yorkers working behind the scenes for Taft, the state Republican Party delayed endorsing Hughes and only did so assuming that Hughes would release the state's delegates when he failed to win enough votes at the national convention. By that time, the Hughes bubble had burst and one supporter wired him: "Looks like you are deserted by everybody except God Almighty and The People." After Hughes refused to release his pledged delegates and also refused to accept the vice presidential nomination, Woodruff, Parsons, and Barnes endorsed James. S. Sherman for vice president—a conservative upstate New Yorker who was one of their own. Barnes hoped that "this is the end of Hughes."[9]

Hughes later claimed to have no regrets. He acknowledged that TR "blanketed" his speech "by a highly sensational message evidently timed for that purpose." He also understood that the former president would always try to "have a dominating influence" on policy backed by "a large following which would make the way of his successor hard." Even so, Hughes campaigned vigorously for Taft at the expense of his own gubernatorial campaign. His speech opening the Taft campaign in Youngstown, Ohio, became a major campaign document. Attacking the Democratic candidate, William Jennings Bryan, as inconsistent and unreliable, Hughes praised Taft's "sagacity, steadiness of character, firmness and sound judgement" as essential qualities for "the security of the nation." Making two more campaign trips through nine western states, often speaking a dozen times a day, Hughes impressed the public and got excellent press coverage. He also hoped to prove to critics like TR, "that I am not solicitous simply for my own candidacy."[10]

TR reluctantly supported Hughes's renomination for governor. He claimed not wanting to push "the organization" as in 1906 because Hughes "has treated them with such wanton and foolish insolence." At the same time, TR knew that Hughes "has the fanatical support of the reformers of all grades" as well as "the very ardent support of a large number of people who are not fanatical reformers" but who appreciated the governor's accomplishments. Although the party bosses fought his renomination and Barnes pushed Wadsworth's candidacy, they knew that only Hughes could carry the state and its electoral votes. Taft urged TR to support Hughes. Lacking a viable alternative, TR got Elihu Root to chair the Republican state nominating convention and secure Hughes's renomination. Root saw the irony of party discipline being used to benefit its loudest critic. Indeed, Hughes later quoted TR's comment that "the bosses, the machine leaders, took a man for whom they did not care, because he was the only man with whom they could win."[11]

Hughes actually was "disinclined" to serve a second term but felt responsible to complete the job he had begun. Being governor was exhausting and the salary was inadequate, especially since he paid for his own expenses plus his secretary and stenographers whenever he campaigned for himself, for others, and for his policies. Like Washington, he only requested reimbursement for expenses when on official state business. Rejecting a tempting offer to become president of the University of Michigan, Hughes ran for governor again because he feared that leaving office would empower the boss-controlled legislature to undo his accomplishments, especially the Public Service Commission (PSC) and racetrack gambling. However, after campaigning for Taft, he only had three weeks left to campaign for himself and was hampered by a party platform that barely mentioned his first term successes. No matter, wrote Merlo J. Pusey, "Hughes was his own platform."[12]

While Hughes was out West, his enemies were busy in New York. There were plenty of them among bosses and businessmen hurt by his policies. But there also was solid support from reformers, independents, and ordinary people across the state. Fliers recounted his legislative accomplishments regarding labor, farmers, the PSC, criminal justice, racetrack gambling, and cities. As usual, Hughes campaigned nonstop, speaking all day and well into the night. Once in October, he started at eight o'clock in the morning at a little town near Lake Erie, then traveled by train to the southern tier, speaking at every town he passed until finishing later that evening after three mass meetings in Corning. Hughes never missed an opportunity to earn a vote. Covered by the press, his speeches were so widely applauded that they bolstered the presidential ticket as well as his own. Taft was grateful, and even TR was complimentary. Barnes, Woodruff, and Parsons reconsidered their opposition.[13]

At one point, his opponent, the Democratic lieutenant governor Lewis Chanler, tried to outwit Hughes by posing ten supposedly compromising questions. Traveling by train between speeches, Hughes quickly wrote clear, compelling answers ready for the press upon arrival and turned them into a rousing speech that almost brought "the opera house down." Chanler was unable to answer the questions that Hughes posed in return. Discontent among bosses, liquor interests, gambling

Pictorial Section Part 1

The New York Times

Sunday. Dec. 29. 1907.

PHOTOGRAPHS, RECENTLY TAKEN, OF GOVERNOR AND MRS. HUGHES.

MRS. HUGHES.

Proof Positive of the Governor's Genial Side.

The Governor at his Desk.

The Office of the Governor in the Capitol at Albany.

Figure 3.1 (NYT). "Photographs Recently Taken of Governor and Mrs. Hughes," *The New York Times*, December 28, 1907. The Miriam and Ira D. Wallach Division of Art, Prints and Photographs, the New York Public Library.

enthusiasts, and insurance companies kept his final tally smaller than Taft's margin of victory in the state. Yet after covering eight thousand miles in fifty out of sixty-one counties, Hughes won with more votes than in 1906. *The New York Times* captured the governor's delight and his wife's dignity (see figure 3.1).[14]

Expanding the Agenda

Although Hughes's second term achieved several pathbreaking accomplishments, it was personally disappointing because he lost a nasty political struggle over election reform. In fact, it was so nasty that it motivated him to leave politics altogether when Taft offered him a seat on the US Supreme Court. Nonetheless, he made major contributions to Progressivism by addressing some of the most pressing problems of the day concerning criminal justice, labor, public health, and conservation. Not an expert on any of these topics, Hughes relied on organizations and individuals who had been seeking change for decades. This cooperative approach reflected his maturing leadership skills.

Reforms adopted during Hughes's second administration became national models of how state governments could promote the general good. Indeed, when he left office in 1910, reformers expressed "personal bereavement" because "the agencies for righteousness had received a damaging blow." However, they were comforted by the thought that the nation had gained "a social worker (not a politician) on the Supreme Bench." They meant it as a compliment, but others wondered whether Hughes should have been less of a social worker and more of a politician.[15]

One exception to Hughes's progressive reputation was his opposition to the proposed federal income tax, which became the Sixteenth Amendment to the US Constitution in 1913. Although Hughes was not against the principle of the tax, he objected to the way the bill was written. At issue was an open-ended grant for revenues "from whatever source derived." This clause could permit the federal government to tax state and municipal bonds, not just individual incomes. Consequently, the state's right to float bonds for economic development could be undermined and a wealthy state like New York could be exploited. He spoke both as a governor and as a lawyer. Just as he supported home rule for cities, now he protected home rule for states. In this case, he endorsed a "layer cake" concept of dual federalism, which, explained political scientist Clifford Lee Staten, presumed conflict between national and state spheres rather than a "marble cake" version, which emphasized cooperation between and interdependence of national and state governments.[16]

The narrow ground of Hughes's opposition was lost in the subsequent debate. The moneyed interests, against whom he usually fought, gleefully used his statements to attack the bill. Meanwhile, many of his supporters disagreed with him, including Root and several state progressives. Because Hughes was such an important national figure, other governors felt compelled to openly agree or disagree with his analysis. The amendment was ultimately approved in the state due to the support of Tammany, which suddenly seemed more progressive than the progressive governor. The episode reflected Hughes's legal acuity and perfectionism, stubborn spirit of independence, and willingness to accept popular disapproval for the sake of principle. Ultimately, the courts embraced his position and interpreted the amendment as taxing income, not other state revenues. Time would also reveal that Hughes was less orthodox about conflict-oriented dual federalism than he seemed.[17]

When it came to social issues, Hughes was solidly progressive. He rejected the traditional concept of minimal government and the social Darwinian emphasis on survival of the fittest. From that perspective, aiding the disadvantaged would only encourage laziness and dependence. By contrast, Hughes embraced the newer notion that "a large portion of our brethren are the helpless victims of an environment from which they cannot escape and through which they are destined to physical misery, moral impoverishment, and economic inefficiency." Therefore, Hughes considered it "our duty . . . not merely to afford temporary relief to immediate sufferers, but to change the improper environment and promote a healthier life." He warned against treating the poor "as a separate class, upon whom alms may be bestowed with lordly condescension and with the unction of self-righteousness." Private organizations were important, but government had a constructive role to play regarding work, housing, sanitation, disease, education, and even recreation. "Human Society," he declared, "cannot be stable unless it is progressive." Repeated often, these themes differentiated Hughes from conservatives like Root who, wrote biographer Richard W. Leopold, "seemed inured to the social evils of the day."[18]

Many of the problems of the industrial era were concentrated in cities. Spurred by the completion of the Erie Canal in 1825, upstate cities specialized in packaging and processing upstate and western raw materials being shipped from Buffalo to New York City. Consequently, cities along the route, like Rochester, Syracuse, Utica, Albany, and Troy, became industrial centers. In the mid- and late nineteenth century, factory and construction jobs attracted immigrants from Germany, Ireland, Italy, Greece, Hungary, Poland, and Russia. Clustering in ethnic communities near the factories, their lives were hard. Although many prospered in the long run, for the moment they found themselves in congested housing with poor sanitation, low wages, uncertain employment, debilitating illness, and rampant crime. Aside from their labor, the vote was men's most marketable asset. Urban political machines won those votes by helping immigrants with jobs and housing, plus money for rent or bail when needed. Holiday turkeys solidified the bond.

New York City had the most factories (albeit small ones), the most immigrants, the greatest congestion, poverty, and crime. It also had the most wealth, thereby creating a stark contrast between rich and poor. Hughes understood that "glaring inequalities in condition create discontent and strain the democratic relation." At three million strong, the city contained half the state's population by 1900 and its most powerful Democratic machine, run by Tammany boss Charles F. Murphy. Except for upstate cities, the vast area north of New York City was predominantly rural. In the 1880s, Thomas C. Platt's Republican machine combined upstate rural and business interests into a voting block defined by hostility to both New York City and governmental regulations. After Platt lost power, upstate was carved into several boss-run territories, with Barnes being the most powerful.[19]

By showing an interest in urban problems, the governor defied convention and courted conflict with the upstate Republican Party as well as the downstate Tammany Democrats. The former did not want to help New York City or condone active government. The latter did not want the state government to compete for popular support by providing services to the urban masses. However, the huge late nineteenth century immigrant surge altered the political landscape because Tammany could no longer meet all the needs of all of its followers. In addition, Hearst's popularity among the working classes convinced Murphy to support reform. Young Tammany men like Alfred E. Smith and Robert F. Wagner, were interested in labor issues. Consequently, most Tammany legislators supported Hughes's social and economic reforms while opposing those that threatened their personal political power.[20]

Unlike some other Progressives, Hughes sympathized with immigrants like his father. In 1907, 1908, and 1909, he called attention to their plight and warned, "We cannot afford to regard with cynical indifference the conditions and opportunities of those men who have recently come to us from foreign lands." Because all New Yorkers were "bound together by indissoluble bonds," ignoring the welfare of others was ignoring the welfare and "safety of the State." Hughes even attended meetings of the Social Reform Club, an outgrowth of reformer Henry George's 1886 mayoral run. Indeed, Hughes echoed George when he declared that the burgeoning city "presents the most complex problem of our modern times . . . the greatest wealth and the most abject poverty." Accordingly, Hughes insisted that New York State attend to the needs of its largest city where "humanity huddles in poverty, distress, and shame." However, due to upstate hostility, it took two years to get legislative approval for a new state bureau to gather data on and make recommendations concerning immigrants and work. The bureau was led by social worker Florence Kellor, who chaired the Republican women's committee during Hughes's 1916 presidential campaign.[21]

In accepting the 1906 nomination for governor, Hughes declared that he was "deeply interested in all efforts to better the condition of our working men," a concern that influenced his judicial career. Not forgetting from whence he came, he once explained, "I am a poor man's man. My people were obliged to make great sacrifices to give me an education, and I have known the hardest kind of work all my life." Therefore, Hughes consistently promoted equal opportunity for all, especially the poor. That commitment bred a reform agenda much like TR's concerning tenements, sweatshops, working hours, child labor, and workman's compensation. As historian Daniel T. Rodgers pointed out, these concerns drew upon an "Atlantic progressive connection" whereby Europe provided the United States with model corrective policies. The United States was the follower, not the leader. In 1908, TR admitted that compared to Europe, America was "backward" and "lagging" in social reform.[22]

Fluent in the general principles but ignorant of the particulars, Hughes sought more education. His teachers were the men and women who had been working with settlement houses, the Charity Organization Society, the New York Child Labor Committee, and the American

Association for Labor Legislation. It was led by economists Richard T. Ely and John R. Commons, who were inspired by European social reforms. In addition, the Consumers League and the Women's Trade Union League mobilized upper-middle-class women to protest against working conditions in retail stores and factories. Workers themselves were active through unions. Although most New York governors were uninterested in these issues, Hughes appreciated their importance for a nation struggling with the negative impacts of the Industrial Revolution. To the reformers' surprise, he sought their advice. According to lifelong reformer Herman Folks, Hughes was always open to the facts and, once convinced, he acted. Most important, said a settlement-house worker, Hughes had "a passion for humanity . . . a passion for democracy."[23]

The result was the passage of fifty-six new labor laws by 1910, previewing the legislative reform blitz after the 1911 Triangle Shirtwaist Company fire. Key New York City legislators steered the bills around urban-rural conflict and business resistance. In 1907, the state Labor Department was reorganized and professionalized with more inspectors hired to enforce existing labor standards for factories, mines, and tunnels. Several bills limited hours for railroad engineers, firemen, signalmen, plus telegraph and telephone operators. However, it took longer to pass a bill improving working conditions in stores due to the Retail Dealers Association's influence in the state senate. Even then, the 1908 bill only applied to New York City, Buffalo, and Rochester. All of these measures were limited, but they established significant precedents and documented Hughes's sincere concern for workers' welfare.[24]

Child labor was a particularly wrenching issue. In the nineteenth and early twentieth centuries, children made major contributions to New York State's industrial prominence. Their work was dangerous. As historian Jeremy Felt reported, "In the course of their labors, some fell down elevator shafts, burned to death, were mangled by machinery, worked standing in several inches of water." Outside factories, they "delivered messages to houses of prostitution, stood on their feet for twelve hours a day, sold newspapers at two o'clock in the morning, or froze to death in delivery wagons." In 1900, about four hundred thousand children, age five to eighteen, worked in New York State and only 35 percent attended school.[25]

Several organizations combined to form the New York State Child Labor Committee in 1902. Chaired by Folks. it got the nation's first child labor laws passed in 1903, but enforcement was elusive. Working with the settlement houses, the Workingmen's Federation, the Consumers League, and the National Child Labor Committee (formed in New York in 1904), Hughes pushed this issue and the legislature slowly responded. From 1907 to 1910, reform bills were passed to improve enforcement of existing laws regulating labor in mines, factories, and department stores. Children were prohibited from working in dangerous occupations or as night messengers. All of these changes made it more likely that children would finally be able to attend school, a priority for Hughes.[26]

One of the most horrifying results of progress was the high rate of industrial accidents. Work was lethal: "In one year, it was found that over 50,000 accidents had taken place in New York factories alone, in which 167 workers had been killed." Powerful, fast-moving machines lacked protective guards and could maim in an instant, making workers permanently unemployable by losing a hand, foot, leg, or eye. Cigar makers were prone to lung disease and cancer from handling tobacco leaves; pottery workers to asthma from dust; painters, plumbers, dyers, and printers to arsenic poisoning; glass workers to lead poisoning. Moreover, viral diseases quickly spread in the crowded factories. Injury or death meant the loss of wages for already marginal families. They were then plunged into desperation, even if children and women worked. Redress was impossible because the law held that workers assumed risk by taking a job and blamed all accidents on workers' negligence.[27]

Believing that "the protection of the wage earner . . . is one of the most sacred trusts of society," Hughes condemned "the shocking waste and injustice" of employer's lack of liability for work place accidents. He found it strange that we often talk about "the carnage of war, but we give too little attention to the perils of our industrial army . . . the casualties of peace." How tragic it was that the very workers who enabled America to achieve "the industrial prestige of which we boast should be subjected through ignorance or indifference to unnecessary peril." Hughes later addressed these topics on the Court.[28]

After corresponding with like-minded Boston lawyer Louis D. Brandeis in 1906, the governor raised the issue of employer liability in speeches during 1907 and 1908. He also appointed a carpenter to be commissioner of labor. In 1909, he created a commission to study the subject and improve upon an existing act for railroad workers that compensated almost no one. Hughes carefully designed the commission to reduce opposition by including businessmen, reformers, and labor representatives, a strategy he used as secretary of state. Led by State Senator J. Mayhew Wainwright, a Westchester Progressive, the commission collected data, examined existing European plans, and held hearings in New York's six biggest cities.[29]

Social reformers kept up the publicity and the pressure. Opposition came from employers' groups as well as from Samuel Gompers who thought that unions should protect workers, not the state. (Gompers opposed Hughes's presidential candidacy in 1916.) Nonetheless, in 1910 the legislature passed two bills, which were the nation's first workmen's disability compensation laws. One was for a voluntary system while the other was compulsory for dangerous occupations. After the New York State Court of Appeals declared the latter a violation of due process, the state legislature passed a revised, stronger law in 1913. Workmen's compensation also became an amendment to the state constitution. Just as New York learned from England and Germany, so twenty-eight states followed New York's example by adopting some form of workmen's compensation by 1920.[30]

Criminal justice issues were brought to Hughes's attention by Folks and social worker Lawrence Veiller, whose efforts had produced New York's pathbreaking 1901 Tenement House Law. Appealing to Hughes as a lawyer, they sought reform of the lower court system, which greatly affected the working classes. The "poor man's courts" impacted urban immigrants who were routinely discriminated against through arrests, fines, and incarceration. Veiller helped the state legislature create a bipartisan commission to study the problem. Hughes supported the resulting thirty-six reform recommendations, which were then passed by the legislature. They made the lower courts function better, doubled night court hours, and began separating children's issues from domestic conflicts. These reforms dovetailed with earlier improvements to the probation system and the establishment of the nation's first probation commission, which Folks chaired.[31]

Folks also motivated Hughes to support a public health campaign against tuberculosis (TB). Called "the white plague," TB was the city's major source of death and often struck men in their most productive years. Studies by the state Board of Health and the Charity Organization Society, plus Veiller's work on the tenements, had already documented the relationship between poverty, crowding, and communicable diseases. Knowing that more work was needed to address this crisis, in 1907 Folks obtained funds from the Russell Sage Foundation to mount a major public health campaign. Modeling Veiller's successful tenement house exhibit, Folks put together photographs, charts, tables, and free leaflets coordinated with public lectures and seminars for health providers across the state.[32]

Muckraking articles aroused public concern and cities increased medical services for TB patients. In 1908, the state required local health boards to report TB cases and prevent its spread. Due to Hughes's urging, in 1909 the legislature authorized every county to build a TB hospital. Because the state did not absorb the construction costs, the effort faltered, but six cities established dispensaries and visiting nurse services. Two cities built TB hospitals, with more planned. Minor though it seems today, this effort pushed New York State to the forefront of the nation's response to TB and its commitment to public health.

Hughes insisted that the state's 1903 Pure Food Act be properly implemented and sponsored an aggressive 1910 state Pure Drug Act in line with TR's federal 1906 Food and Drug Act. In this case, Hughes joined TR, advocating a "marble cake" form of cooperative federalism, whereby national and state governments voluntarily and informally reinforced, rather than conflicted with, each other. The state act tackled dishonest branding of drugs as well as irresponsible marketing of poisons and narcotics, practices that were common and deadly. The governor took these concerns with him to the Supreme Court.[33]

Hughes's love for the mountains, upstate lakes, and the Hudson River predisposed him to appreciate natural resources, which he considered "the property of the people." They were "priceless treasures" that must be "safeguarded and protected from spoilation." Accordingly, he held that "no selfish interest must be permitted to seize with covetous hand the public domain." Again, he was willing to learn from existing organizations, like those dedicated to preserving the Adirondacks. So many trees had been cut down by the logging industry that fires devastated a quarter of the park from 1899 to 1908. Consequently, the state passed fire protection laws in 1910, substantially increased the size of forest preserves and parks, began reforestation efforts, and professionalized the forest rangers by paying them. Hughes celebrated the new Palisades Park comprised of land donated by the Rockefeller and Harriman families. Another example of cooperative federalism, the governor reinforced the president's conservation priorities. As an advocate of public good over private greed, he understood that "private enterprise can destroy but can never replace" unique natural resources.[34]

Hughes was shocked to discover that the legislature customarily granted private companies perpetual leases on natural resources without exacting any benefits or protections for the state. Consequently, he had the Public Works commissioner calculate an initial fee and an annual rental charge for allowing a company to build a dam on the St. Lawrence River. Concerned that pollution was making "a mere sewer" out of the Hudson, Mohawk, and Susquehanna Rivers, he recommended (but failed to obtain) laws against dumping industrial and residential waste into the state's rivers. In addition, he made innovative proposals for flood control and hydroelectric power. Overall, Hughes's approach to conservation embodied his conviction that government should implement "the popular will" against "the ambition which knows no law but selfish achievement."[35]

The Direct Primary

Despite so many accomplishments, Hughes was undone by the one crusade that he considered most crucial for preserving democracy—election reform. He was convinced that "the people are tired of bossism . . . of the use of public prerogatives for private gain." The situation was particularly bad in New York City where Tammany was "notorious throughout the world." To him, the upstate "local oligarchies and despotisms" were hardly better. Taking on the politicians of both parties, Hughes generated the strongest opposition he faced as governor. He accepted the risk.[36]

Hughes recognized that "democracy, after all, is only an opportunity." It has to be guarded and nurtured in order to keep it "from being subverted to selfish ends by the astute but unscrupulous." In his opinion, the best way to protect democracy was to maximize popular participation in the selection of candidates. Giving party members a "consciousness of power" would encourage more of them to vote and would motivate men to seek office who were genuinely committed to public service. He wanted to eliminate "the worst enemies of democracy, the charlatans and demagogues, with little brain and much fluency of speech." Some were simply corrupt and sought personal profit "at the public expense." Others were "the puppets of those who would use them for their own corrupt purposes." Together, such men were the true "parasites of government."[37]

The existing system of nominating candidates for office promoted and perpetuated parasites. In his 1907 message to the state legislature, Hughes requested a bill to begin voluntary experimental direct primaries. The idea was to shift the balance of power for nominating party candidates from party managers to party members. As he explained in 1909, "Representative government depends on us having men in office who really represent the people . . . and do not owe a primary allegiance to particular men or special interests." Term limits would undercut corrupt alliances and improve public accountability. In addition, Hughes wanted the state to adopt the secret ballot and simplify the current complicated ballot so that it would be shorter and easier for voters to understand. New York City, for example, spread nineteen columns across a four-foot-wide ballot with candidates' names listed several times. The alternative was listing candidates by office rather than by party and permitting independents to challenge party nominees if they could get enough signatures. Hughes also wanted to limit campaign contributions so that poor men could run for office too. His enlightened proposals are strikingly current.[38]

Progressives across the country were trying to democratize democracy through these methods as well as through the initiative, referendum, and recall. Converting patronage jobs to civil service jobs was another strategy for undermining bossism and corruption, one that Hughes used aggressively. Muckraking articles and Hughes's insurance investigations compounded by similar revelations in other states aroused public anger against the corrupt partnership between politicians and businessmen. Consequently, by 1908, twelve states regulated lobbying, twenty-two states prohibited corporate campaign contributions, and forty-one states regulated railroads. Historian Richard McCormick pointed out that these laws changed American politics by making parties less important while making legislators, administrators, and interest groups more important. Public commissions in New York and other states placed power in the hands of nonpartisan experts and increased the power of government to regulate education, health, and conservation. Hughes championed all these developments and, in his second term, called for a mandatory direct primary system.[39]

Thirty-one states already had mandatory direct primary laws by 1908, but the idea hit a brick wall in New York. Although the state passed a law to better regulate primary elections in 1898, Republican and Democratic legislators opposed any changes to the nominating process. While liberals considered the governor's proposals too weak, the public found them too complicated. Hughes repeatedly called for reform but was preoccupied with other issues in his first term and took a hands-off strategy in the beginning of his second term. However, by adding 324 jobs to the civil service list just before the direct primary fight began, Hughes renewed his resolve to "get the best men that can be obtained" to serve the state because "we will have no government better than the men who administer it." His reward was more boss hostility and less room for negotiation. Various bills were defeated; compromises floundered; positions hardened; resentments grew.[40]

At a legislative correspondents' dinner in April 1909, Hughes was greeted by a huge banner declaring "Charlie, Quit Dreaming." His reaction was characteristic: "I may be a dreamer, but I'm not a quitter." Likewise, his forceful response to a vitriolic verbal attack by Barnes was vigorously applauded. But victory was fleeting because the election reform bill was soon defeated. Its opponents pointed out that Hughes himself was nominated by the convention system. They predicted that because candidates would have to campaign widely under the direct primary, only rich men could run. Moreover, direct primaries would allow the cities, especially New York City, to dominate the nominating process at the expense of less populated, upstate, rural districts. Wadsworth feared that it might promote other dangerous proposals, like the popular election of senators, which became the Seventeenth Amendment in 1913. Ironically, Wadsworth was New York's first popularly elected senator.[41]

Hughes's supporters formed a Direct Primary Association that sent speakers throughout the state to explain the need for reform. In 1909, forty-six assemblymen who opposed reform were defeated for reelection and several prominent Republicans lost or won by narrow margins. In 1910, the reform cause was reinforced by scandal. After John Raines's sudden death in 1909, the state senators divided over who would be the next majority leader. The options were Jotham Allds, a former Platt ally and Raines loyalist, or Harvey Hinman, a Hughes loyalist and cosponsor of the direct primary bill. Senator Root's urgent telegram from Washington supporting Hinman followed by Hughes's strong critique of legislative opposition to his program only strengthened the old guard's resistance. Allds got the job.

However, Allds did not last long because evidence surfaced that as assemblyman nine year earlier, he had been counsel to and accepted bribes from a bridge company in return for legislative favors. With Hughes's approval, the story was published in Villard's *Evening Post.* A sensational six-week investigation revealed that Allds was only one of many assemblymen on the take. Another investigation showed that an insurance company had been systematically bribing legislators and the lieutenant governor in return for favorable laws. Like the old gas and insurance investigations, these hearings exposed Albany's culture of corruption and strengthened Hughes's hand. Parsons hoped the investigations would benefit the party's image by punishing "the crooks." But Barnes's *Albany Argus* considered Allds "a burnt offering to appease the voters." The real lesson, said *The Ontario County Times*, was to reduce the temptation for graft by increasing legislators' salaries and amending the state constitution to forbid any affiliation between legislators and private companies.[42]

It was at about this time that Hughes decided not to seek a third term. President Taft worried that without Hughes the Republicans could not carry the state in 1912, thereby threatening his own reelection. However, Hughes was overworked and frustrated. In March 1910, he told Taft that he would not run again because "he had done his part" in trying to reform the state Republican Party. More than ever, he felt that "public office means a burden of responsibility—a burden of incessant toil at times almost intolerable." It was worth the effort under "honorable conditions," but by 1910, the constant struggle had taken a toll. "I do not dare run the chance of breaking down mentally," he admitted. "I must get out and make my family safe while I am able." Hughes had reached his limit. He was realistic enough and humble enough to recognize defeat. Time and again, he tried to slay the political dragon. Time and again, it came roaring back. Now he needed to return to his real calling—practicing law and performing public service as a citizen, not an official. Little did Hughes expect that a month later Taft would nominate him to become a Supreme Court associate justice.[43]

Despite the political ramifications of being a lame duck, Hughes announced his acceptance of Taft's offer in April. Supporters were shocked; opponents were delighted. Nevertheless, as long as he was in office, Hughes continued to fight. The Allds scandal reinforced his commitment to the direct primary and motivated him to support a compromise bill, which let party members select party committeemen who would then select the candidates. It increased voter influence on nominations but still let the party make the final decisions. This concession upset the reformers and reduced support. The one time he tried to appease the bosses backfired. Strengthened by Hughes's lame-duck status, they let the bill narrowly pass the senate knowing that it would die in the assembly.

Wadsworth was the key. Except for the Kelsey case, Wadsworth had supported Hughes's reforms with reservations. However, he drew the line at the direct primary bill, which he thought would destroy the whole party system, create a chaotic political free-for-all, and turn elections into popularity contests. Furthermore, he was increasingly offended by Hughes's anti-boss rhetoric and was working more closely with Barnes. After the bill was defeated, the Hughes forces campaigned against its opponents who were seeking reelection. But Hughes would not let them target Wadsworth, saying, "He is a very useful man. He's an honest man. He's a capable man and ought to be retained in public life." Nonetheless, Wadsworth's usual landslide shrank to merely three hundred votes.[44]

Hughes next tried tactics that had worked before. He called a special session to reconsider the bill and went on another speaking tour to promote it. Although there was solid support from the press and the public, it was not as strong as for the PSC. Hughes seemed less passionate than previously, but he could still clarify how the bosses' power depended on nominating candidates: "If he can select them, he can control them after they have been elected. They become his deputies." Consequently, the boss's "power is despotic and permanent. . . . The government is his government."[45]

Testifying before the state senate, Hughes admitted that the conventions never would have nominated him without pressure from TR. In truth, he said, "the high daddy with the Big Stick kept at them and swung it." Undoubtedly shocking to his audience (and TR), his conclusion was that no matter the circumstances, "it ought not to be possible for any one man to dictate" nominations. Nonetheless, Hughes sought help from Taft and even TR, both of whom reluctantly rallied to the cause. Root hedged. He condoned direct primaries in theory but questioned Hughes's proposal and called for extensive investigations before adopting it. This was his characteristically conservative fear of rapid change. Like Alexander Hamilton, Root favored representative over direct democracy lest popular passions and prejudices prevail. Hughes trusted the people. Cartoonist Charles Bartholomew saw it as a tug of war between friends (see figure 3.2). Ultimately, the compromise bill was defeated thanks to an alliance between old guard Republicans and

Figure 3.2. "When Greek Meets Greek, Then Comes a Tug of War," by Charles Lewis Bartholomew. *Minneapolis Journal,* January 30, 1909. Courtesy of the Hennepin County Library, Minneapolis, Minnesota. The title refers to an old Greek proverb concerning conflict between two powerful men.

Tammany Democrats. Savoring victory, Barnes proclaimed, "Teddy is licked to a frazzle. We no longer worship the gods; we laugh at them."[46]

In response, TR tried to reassert control over the state Republican Party but was outfoxed by the bosses. Never one to accept defeat, a month later TR declared war against bossism and special interests with his famous 1910 New Nationalism speech at Osawatomie, Kansas. Years later, when Wadsworth was senator and Hughes was secretary of state, they met in Washington, DC. Reminiscing about the old days, Hughes mused, "Wadsworth, you may have been right about direct primaries." At the time, political reform by any means seemed imperative, but maybe he had pushed too hard and too far. In the short term, bossism won again, but at great cost. Not only did the Republican Party lose the next three gubernatorial elections but, by 1914, the state had adopted both the secret ballot and the direct primary. Hughes can be faulted for staking his administration on the one issue that most threatened bossism, for failing to adequately rally the public around it and for alienating his supporters by compromising too much. Yet, Wesser suggested, he might have overcome these obstacles if only he had not publicized his Supreme Court appointment.[47]

From the gas and insurance investigations through both terms as governor, Hughes's main focus was undermining corruption and bossism in the ardent belief that "the political household needs disinfecting." Always concerned about efficiency and accountability, Hughes used his veto power to trim the state budget by over four million dollars in 1909 alone. Wadsworth once accused him of "statutory bossism" by relentlessly using legislation to actualize his priorities. However, unlike traditional bosses, Hughes made no bargains, gave no favors, wielded no patronage. As an executive in a democracy, he depended on the legislature to enact his policies. Rather than accept legislative defeat, he appealed directly to the people. Hughes upset the bosses precisely because he refused to be a boss. Coincidentally, Boss Platt died in 1910, just as Hughes was finishing his second term. Although bossism survived, it was mortally wounded.[48]

As governor, Hughes confronted all the challenges of being a structural reformer. He mastered some, but not all. Historian James MacGregor Burns explained that all leaders must be self-confident and reform leaders must be ethical. Hughes qualified on both counts. Reformers were gradualists because they sought particular changes within the existing system, not wholesale revolution. Most focused on one change, but Hughes had an ambitious, multifaceted agenda that threatened the interests of politicians and corporations. Whereas most reformers tried to build bridges within and between parties, Hughes antagonized the bosses of both parties. Consequently, he appealed beyond party to the people with substantial success. His faith in the public, the power of reason, and the importance of democracy never faded.[49]

As a "fighting governor," Hughes demonstrated qualities that earned both praise and contempt. State Assemblyman John Lord O'Brian later described "the aggressive personality, the seemingly inexhaustible energy, the unrelenting insistence, . . . the overpowering quality of his arguments during those stormy years." A paragon of ethical propriety and commitment to the public good, Hughes could be idealistic, moralistic, and hard-charging. Nonetheless, he was realistic enough to acquire the political skills needed to get bills through the legislature. He was humble enough to seek advice from and work with more experienced reformers. Reaching out to the public humanized politics and demystified policy. His program of concrete changes to (not revolutions of) the existing system was largely successful. Incensed by the fact that "selfishness and demagoguery take advantage of liberty," Hughes incurred the wrath of politicians and businessmen who would be hurt by change. Undeterred, he accepted opposition as the inherent, inevitable companion to reform. Considering the obstacles he faced, it is doubtful that a less forthright approach would have been more fruitful. For an atypical, inexperienced politician, he did surprisingly well and received a substantial amount of the ultimate political reward: public support and respect.[50]

Hughes's steely resolve, self-confidence, and sense of moral purpose were revealed when, at the close of his term, he declared, "A public officer should not wear his heart upon his sleeve, and should not take too seriously the offings of his opponents." Instead, his operating principle should be that "if he is right, he can afford to ignore them, and if he is wrong, he has no reason to complain." Even his critics had to admit that Hughes defied expectation by wielding power firmly and effectively. His supporters would add that he wielded power consistently and constructively. As one bard wrote,

O woe is me! O woe is us
That it should come to pass!
That gum-shoe King Politicus
Should go at last to grass.

It is the dee-dash darnedest thing
That ever we did see!
A Governor a-governing
At ancient Albanee.[51]

By the time Hughes left office, he had made significant contributions to the progressive concept that state governments should be expanded for the general good. Hughes advocated both layer cake and marble cake dual federalism as a politician (and on the Supreme Court). He believed that states could and should act to protect their citizens when the federal government did not but should cooperate when it did. Most important, he said, "special interests must keep their hands off the government in city, State and Nation. The common welfare must be the supreme law." Consequently, he vetoed almost three hundred special interest bills. Originally, Hughes was dismissed as "a political novice" and "a kindergartner in the geography and mathematics with which the politician is saturated to the fingertips." Growing in office, he proved to be a strong leader who could count votes. Consequently, 56.5 percent of his proposals were adopted, well exceeding Alfred E. Smith's 33.5 percent success rate. Struggles notwithstanding, Hughes upheld his independence and his principles through thick and thin. He refused to be a marionette.[52]

To be sure, Hughes learned that idealism could backfire. Criticizing members of his own party hampered his efforts and undercut his advantages. Although efficiency and accountability were generally supported by the public, they were not dramatic, compelling issues. Nonetheless, along with other Progressive governors, like Wisconsin's Robert M. Lafollette and California's Hiram Johnson (both future antagonists), Hughes proved that a governor could be a positive agent of change. His guiding principle was always to defend "public rights" against "public wrongs" and promote "just regulation" against "unjust advantage." Far from being stuck in the past, Hughes helped the nation adapt to contemporary realities. *New York World* credited him with "purifying the State government and re-establishing rule of the people." For this, wrote Villard's *New York Evening Post*, "we gratefully acknowledge that he has ennobled our public life and quickened our hope in democracy."[53]

In accepting the 1906 Republican nomination for governor, Hughes promised to meet "the duty of leadership in a contest for decent government" with a spirit of "equal justice to all, rich and poor, corporations and individuals." His two terms as governor delivered on that promise by advancing labor legislation, administrative reform, social reform, judicial reform, civil service reform, public health, and conservation. These accomplishments provided models that other states followed. Hughes's evolving political skills achieved a lot but reached their limit. Accordingly, as he said toward the end of his second term, when a leader's "appeal to his constituency fails, he should be willing and desirous to step down."[54]

Although Hughes failed to secure the secret ballot and the direct primary, he succeeded in reforming state government and expanding its agenda. Mobilizing the anger created by the gas and insurance investigations, he challenged boss rule in the interest of more efficient, nonpartisan, socially responsive priorities. It may not have been a revolution, but historians agree that it marked a significant "turning point." To McCormick, it heralded "a new political order" that expanded executive power while elevating expertise over favoritism and incompetence. The shift represented "a real departure from nineteenth century patterns of governance."[55]

Admired for his principles, persuasiveness, and persistence, Hughes embodied Progressivism and provided the aggressive leadership needed for addressing new problems in a new era. Progressivism reinforced Hughes's fundamental belief that "we have a republic only in name if those chosen to represent the people serve other interests . . . [than] public service." As he left Albany in 1910, a cartoonist depicted Hughes as an "attorney for the people" preferring to walk to Washington, DC, rather than ride in a fancy car labeled political machine and fueled by graft. Through thick and thin, Hughes maintained his integrity and his faith that "public service is the best politics."[56]

4 | Becoming Associate Justice, 1910–1916

We are under a Constitution, but the Constitution is what the judges say it is.
—Charles Evans Hughes, 1907

The Context

Immediately upon making this statement and for decades thereafter, Charles Evans Hughes was criticized for seeming to imply that judging was based on personal whim. Of course, it would have been totally uncharacteristic for Hughes to advocate capriciousness in any form at any time. However, he was so stung by the repeated attacks that he spent the rest of his life clarifying what he meant. The lasting controversy over this quote reflected a much larger debate about the role of the US Supreme Court in a democracy. It was part of the second, less quoted, half of the statement, which affirmed that "the judiciary is the safeguard of our liberty and our property under the Constitution." To Hughes, the core challenge of judging was maintaining the constitutional balance between national power, state power, and individual freedom in the context of changing circumstances. Consequently, he said, courts were "umpires" tasked with resolving conflicts fairly. The objective was not just to uphold the "dignity of the bench" but, most important, to "secure our peace and confidence" in democracy.[1]

Hughes's fundamental commitment across his careers was to "even handed justice." In that spirit, he took the judicial oath to "administer justice without respect to persons, and do equal right to the poor and to the rich." It was a delicate responsibility complicated by Hughes's conviction that there must be both continuity and "elasticity" in constitutional interpretation. Continuity secured stability while elasticity enabled the law to evolve over time. Hughes consistently advocated modernizing both international and domestic law to fit current realities. As he declared in 1922, "I have no sympathy with those who lose the spirit of the law in the worship of its garments."[2]

The main issue raised by his 1907 statement was the meaning of judicial review. Hughes was echoing Chief Justice John Marshall, who declared in *Marbury v. Madison* (1803), "It is emphatically the province and duty of the judicial department to say what the law is." Without the power to weigh legislation against the Constitution, Marshall feared that the justices would have to "close their eyes on the Constitution, and see only the law." Lacking a larger framework for judgement, they would be subservient to the legislative branch. Alexander Hamilton made a similar point in *The Federalist Papers*, number 78. Although the judiciary was the "least dangerous" branch with "neither the sword or the purse," it was the crucial "intermediate body between the people and the legislature." Therefore, wrote Hamilton, "the interpretation of the laws is the proper and peculiar province of the courts . . . as the bulwarks of a limited Constitution." So too, Hughes believed that judicial review was "of immense importance in cementing the Union" and upholding the Constitution. It was the Supreme Court's source of independence and tool for adjusting the fluid relationships between the federal government and the states, legislative, executive, and judicial branches, between the government and the individual. Democracy was complicated.[3]

However, to many people, then and now, the Supreme Court represented what law professor Alexander Bickel labeled a "counter-majoritarian force" in democracy. "Judicial review," he pointed out, "constituted control by an unrepresentative minority of an elected majority." In the process of deciding which laws are constitutional, the unelected, unaccountable Court could override the "consent of the governed" as personified by their elected president and legislators. In this sense, "judicial review is undemocratic." Hughes's statement that "the Constitution is what the judges say it is" seemed to confirm that the Court was counter-majoritarian. Thus, he became the target of much criticism even as he helped modernize the Court.[4]

Of course, Bickel understood that judicial review was important for democracy. It could correct the errors and inadequacies of legislation as well as expose the abuses of political "expediency," special interests, and corruption. Promoting national interests over "local particularism" protected democracy's "enduring values." Grounding rulings in the Constitution rendered it central to national stability. Consequently, the Constitution acquired sacred status and the Court acquired a "a mystic function" that bred a majestic image. Because the Court was removed from the electoral process, wrote Bickel, it could "correct errors of principle" along with errors of practice. Moreover, the Court acted as "a highly effective educational institution" dedicated to rational discussion in the public interest. All of these factors made the Supreme Court a perfect home for Hughes. He hallowed faith in reason, cherished democracy's "enduring values," and loved teaching. The difficulty was maintaining the Court as democracy's defender when it was seen as democracy's enemy.[5]

That dilemma pervaded both of Hughes's terms on the Supreme Court, albeit separated by fourteen years. He was the only person to serve twice on the Supreme Court and one of only five justices to resign in order to pursue other prospects. In both terms, the Court's major challenge was deciding how the Constitution should respond to changing economic, political, and social realities. Difficult as it was in his first term, when he was associate justice, the Great Depression made it even more complicated in his second term, when he was chief justice. Hughes's nomination to be associate justice in 1910, at age forty-eight, sailed through the US Senate with a unanimous vote in a five-minute executive session. However, some people feared that based on his record as governor, Hughes was dangerously liberal. By contrast, his old adversary, William Randolph Hearst, claimed that Hughes was dangerously conservative. So did William Jennings Bryan, whom Hughes had excoriated in the 1908 Youngstown speech.[6]

Hughes's initial Supreme Court appointment was further clouded by controversy over whether Taft had promised to appoint Hughes as chief justice if a vacancy arose. When the opportunity came, Taft agonized over the decision and press speculation ran rampant. Then, after abruptly cancelling a meeting with Hughes, Taft appointed Associate Justice Edward D. White, who was more experienced. Maybe Taft was influenced by other justices who resisted appointing a junior justice to be chief or by Theodore Roosevelt's (TR's) opposition to selecting Hughes. Or maybe, several historians suggested, Taft chose the older over the younger man with an eye to fulfilling his lifelong dream of someday becoming chief justice himself. In any case, Hughes assured Taft that there were no hard feelings and that he was honored to be appointed at all.[7]

Contemporaries and historians have argued about whether Hughes was liberal, moderate, conservative, or reactionary. Many contended that he was liberal in his first term but conservative in his second term. Others emphasized continuity between the two terms, especially concerning civil liberties. Hughes himself disparaged labels. When pressured about them, he responded:

> These labels do not interest me. I know of no accepted criterion. Some think opinions are conservative which others would regard as essentially liberal and some opinions classed as liberal might be regarded from another point of view as decidedly illiberal. Such characterizations are not infrequently used to foster prejudices and they serve as a very poor substitute for intelligent criticism. A judge who does his work in an objective spirit, as a judge should, will address himself conscientiously to each case, and will not trouble himself about labels.

Historian, Daniel T. Rodgers agreed that labels were deceptive. He suggested that Hughes was less attached to a particular perspective than to "public spiritedness, the dignity of public office, the need for efficiency, and dedication in the public interest." Those were also his priorities in politics and foreign policy. Because such principles were fundamentally open-ended, said Rodgers, they enabled Hughes to negotiate the changing complexities of his era in order to find a viable "middle ground." Perhaps his purported inconsistency on the Court was really a responsive flexibility. Therefore, said Rodgers, efforts to understand someone like Hughes would work "better without labels."[8]

Hughes's first term on the Court was shaped by radical economic changes that challenged conventional constitutional interpretation and laissez-faire assumptions. Despite valuing precedent and the written law, Hughes was keenly aware of and sensitive to new realities. As governor, he overcame political obstacles in order to address those changes. The Industrial Revolution altered the nature of capitalism with the rise of factories, sweatshops, labor protests, farmer unrest, monopolies, and trusts. Consequently, in 1887 the federal government established its first regulatory agency, the Interstate Commerce Commission (ICC), followed by the Sherman Antitrust Act in 1890. States also passed new economic regulations and created regulatory agencies, like Governor Hughes's Public Service Commissions.

Nonetheless, the late nineteenth and early twentieth century Supreme Court prioritized preindustrial concepts of laissez-faire reflecting classical liberalism's emphasis on individualism, private enterprise, competition, the free market, and free trade. Legal formalism applied these traditional principles to recurring controversies over due process, contracts, and property rights. Skeptical of the Progressives' belief in the benefits of active government, the justices often invalidated state efforts to address modern problems through business regulations. Although the Court upheld some state laws, others were overturned if they threatened free market competition or congressional control over interstate commerce. In 1886, the Court also defined corporations as persons covered by the Fourteenth Amendment's due process clause (*Santa Clara County v. Southern Pacific Railway*). However, law professor Mark Tushnet noted that the Court really had a mixed record and was never as reactionary or as polarized as reputed. In fact, the Court was slowly changing and recognizing that new conditions required reassessing past assumptions. Hughes played an important role in the Court's evolution.[9]

Hughes's Supreme Court opinions and other writings revealed a familiarity with and support for sociological jurisprudence and legal realism, approaches with which he is not usually associated. As advanced by jurists Roscoe Pound and Oliver Wendell Holmes Jr., among others, the basic idea was that the law should not be irrevocably wedded to the past but should respond to the present. The objective, wrote Pound, was to close "the gulf between legal thought and popular thought on matters of social reform." Rather than rely solely on written law and legal precedent, judges should consider relevant facts and circumstances as well as their social impact. Thus, law would be viewed "less as an inflexible mold" and more "as a social institution which may be improved by intelligent human effort" in pursuit of "results which are socially just." In this sense, judges were not just passively reading or "finding" law but were actively involved in modernizing or "making" law.[10]

As Hughes's controversial quote suggested, judicial review was not a stagnant process. Yet, assessing Hughes is complicated because he resisted overturning legal precedent while he advocated adjusting legal precepts. As in politics and foreign policy, he occupied a transitional position between old and new—always trying to balance past, present, and future. Hughes reflected, wrote law professor Richard D. Freidman, the "complexities of moderation" characterized by "an intricate crossweave of views," some liberal, some conservative, but all inherently and uniquely consistent. Hughes "marched to the pace of a different drummer," his own.[11]

Hughes was friendly with two key figures in sociological jurisprudence: Oliver Wendell Holmes Jr. and Louis D. Brandeis. Holmes was his closest colleague on the Court, and Hughes's opinions often echoed Holmes's writings. However, sometimes Holmes was the traditionalist while Hughes was the progressive. Hughes's friendship with Brandeis began with the gas and insurance investigations when they fought financial and political corruption in New York and Massachusetts. They remained friendly over the years and championed using facts to reconsider case law. Hughes embraced and reiterated Brandeis's statement that "our Constitution is not a straight-jacket. It is a living organism," a core Holmesian concept. Brandeis enthusiastically applauded Hughes's appointment as chief justice in 1931 and later called Hughes "the greatest chief executive genius he had ever encountered in law, in business, or in government."[12]

Holmes was chief justice of the Massachusetts Supreme Court before being appointed to the US Supreme Court by TR in 1902. His 1880 lectures at Boston's Lowell Institute became his classic book on *The Common Law.* Holmes's biographer Stephen Budiansky pointed out that for centuries, "the common law left it to judges, through their decisions in individual cases, to declare what the law was." Chastising judges who used decisions to advance their own economic biases, Holmes insisted that judges consider social and economic factors reflecting "the felt necessities of the times." In fact, he said, "the life of the law has not been logic but experience." Holmes urged judges to substitute the values of a moral man with the expectations of a "reasonable man" reflecting a "community standard."[13]

Replacing subjective with objective standards would make rulings fairer. By pointing out that "the common law is not a brooding omnipresence in the sky," Holmes rejected the idea that law was fixed. Rather, he insisted on a "living, evolving" law that changed over time in response to the times. He also advocated "judicial restraint," allowing legislators to experiment with ways to meet changing conditions. Historian Jean Edward Smith pointed out that Marshall embraced this concept in *McCulloch v. Maryland* (1819). Yet, in 1880 these ideas represented a paradigm shift from legal formalism to legal realism and sociological jurisprudence. It was also called instrumentalism or legal pragmatism, a perfect term for Hughes. Over time, Holmes became "a judicial icon."[14]

Brandeis attended the Lowell lectures and studied Holmes's work at Harvard Law School. They formed a lifelong friendship born of common commitments (see figure 4.1). As "the peoples' attorney," Brandeis defended less privileged members of society. Like Hughes, Brandeis upheld the public interest against life insurance companies. He also prevented the establishment of transit monopolies in Massachusetts and

Figure 4.1. *Holmes and Brandeis, Early 1920s*, by Handy Studios. Collection of the Supreme Court of the United States.

created a new field of privacy law. In what became the "Brandeis brief," he presented voluminous facts to challenge common assumptions while enlightening judges, lawyers, legislators, and the public. Brandeis and Hughes agreed that educating the public was the key to reform. Refusing fees in order to maintain his independence, Brandeis repeatedly won cases to improve working conditions. His most compelling principle was that "the logic of words should yield to the logic of realities."[15]

Sociological jurisprudence and legal realism paralleled Progressivism and the rejection of social Darwinism. They suited Hughes as an activist, liberal governor who promoted policies to improve the lives of ordinary people, undermine corruption, prioritize democracy, and regulate private enterprise in the public interest. Indeed, his statement that "the Constitution is what the judges say it is" implied legal realism. As Freidman observed, Hughes's "greatest contribution to modern jurisprudence was his willingness to approve the use of legislative power to deal with pressing social problems." Moreover, Hughes's "conception of law as a tool for social betterment" strongly influenced his colleagues on the Court.[16]

Like Holmes and Brandeis, Hughes believed that judicial opinions should be based not just on the written law but also on facts and the circumstances of the case. One much repeated quip was that "Hughes believed in God, but believed equally that God was on the side of the facts." Advocating "flexibility," Hughes opposed using the Constitution "to prevent the correction of new abuses incident to the complexity of our life." Also, like Holmes, he resisted judgements that were "crystallizing our own notions of policy, our personal view of economics, and our theories of moral or social improvement." Instead of blindly repeating old "formulas," Hughes thought the Court should consider "the actual effect of conduct." Slightly revising Marshall, Hughes hoped that judges would always "remember that it is an *American* constitution we are expounding. It is permeated with American ideals, infused with an American conception of liberty." American exceptionalism provided a framework for responding to, not preventing, change. As Hughes said when defending the military draft during World War I, "The Constitution marches."[17]

A Seamless Economy

Hughes resigned from the governorship a few months early in order to join the Court for its new term in October 1910. However, because he did not leave his past behind, Friedman dubbed him "a Governor on the Bench." Hughes often claimed that being objective was the gold standard for good judges, but he clearly had opinions and his experiences in New York State gave him perspective on the legislative process. He knew that laws were often vague due to the compromises needed to secure passage. As he observed, because "legislation does not execute itself, very rarely does it fully explain itself." Therefore, the courts had to interpret its meaning but, he said, not in "a technical spirit which would sacrifice the growing substance of the law to a lifeless formation." Rather, judges should view legislation as part of "the expanding life of democracy."[18]

Such was the problem posed by the interstate shipment of Dr. Johnson's Mild Combination for the Treatment of Cancer, which consisted of a liquid called Cancerine and accompanying tablets. This 1911 case (*U.S. v. Johnson*) involved the 1906 Food and Drug Act, the nation's first consumer legislation, one of TR's most significant accomplishments as president and an issue Hughes had embraced as governor. Writing for the Court's majority, Holmes narrowly interpreted the act's prohibition of "misbranding" to refer only to the list of ingredients, not claims about its effectiveness, which he considered opinion. In dissent, Hughes dismissed that argument and interpreted the act expansively. He stated that "downright falsehoods" about an item's ability to cure disease were just as dangerous as lying about its ingredients. Although technically not in the original bill, he believed that Congress intended to cover "wholly worthless" potions masquerading as medicine. Holmes hewed to the letter of the law while Hughes emphasized its spirit, a distinction first articulated by Marshall in *McCulloch v. Maryland* (1819).[19]

Sure enough, in 1912 Congress passed the Sherley Amendment to the Food and Drug Act to prohibit false claims. In 1916, Hughes wrote for a unanimous Court upholding that amendment (*Seven Cases v. U.S.*). However, he must have already convinced the brethren because he wrote a unanimous opinion for the Court in a 1915 case allowing states to ban the use of boric acid as a preservative (*Price v. State of Illinois*). Undermining nineteenth-century fears of class legislation, Hughes led the Court in exercising judicial restraint and allowing Congress to use its police powers to protect health and safety, a key Progressive concern. He promoted a pragmatic standard whereby general principles could be adapted to new circumstances.[20]

Hughes's dissent in the misbranding case illuminated the importance of dissenting itself. Despite being the junior member of the Court, his dissent not only convinced his colleagues to reconsider their approach but also influenced Congress. Unlike Holmes, Hughes was not a "great dissenter." Rather, he was "a team-work judge" who, like Marshall, tried to forge consensus, earning both praise and criticism. Although Hughes believed that "unanimity" promoted "public confidence" in judicial rulings, he cautioned that it should never involve the "sacrifice of conviction." Nor should dissenting become "cantankerousness." As someone who valued both personal and political independence, he appreciated that judicial dissents "enable a judge to express his individuality." Most importantly, he believed that "a dissent in a court of last resort is an appeal to the brooding spirit of the law, to the intelligence of a future day." Accordingly, his 1927 Columbia lectures included several examples of the Court reversing itself. Here was his characteristic faith in reason and democratic institutions, his optimism and idealism—all of which were strengthened by his pragmatism.[21]

Because of his background with the New York State's Public Service Commissions, Chief Justice Edward White assigned Hughes a formidable task. Deviating from tradition, White asked the newest, youngest justice to write the opinion for a complicated subject that none of the other justices wanted to touch and that all doubted could be resolved. Photos of Hughes's rigorous daily walk and serious demeanor reflected the discipline and determination that would define his judicial service (see figure 4.2). His penchant for work is noted in the accompanying quote.

The 1913 Minnesota rate case (*Simpson v. David C. Shepard*) plus the 1914 Shreveport case (*Houston, E. and W. Texas Railroad v. U.S.*) posed thorny questions about dual federalism in an industrialized national economy. Ranked Hughes's most important opinions as associate justice, they modernized the interstate commerce clause by providing national guidelines for navigating the changing relationships between inter- and intrastate commerce, between federal and state powers. Writing in 1916 after serving on Hughes's downstate Public Service Commission, Judge William L. Ransom considered these cases the greatest threat to national economic unity since the Civil War due to "intense rivalries between states and sections." He suggested that only someone with the former governor's practical experience and "infinite capacity" for mastering complexity could have resolved the issues.[22]

Both cases concerned the railroad, which was the connective tissue of the new economy. Industrial era concerns about trains resembled preindustrial concerns about ferries. In the landmark 1824 *Gibbons v.*

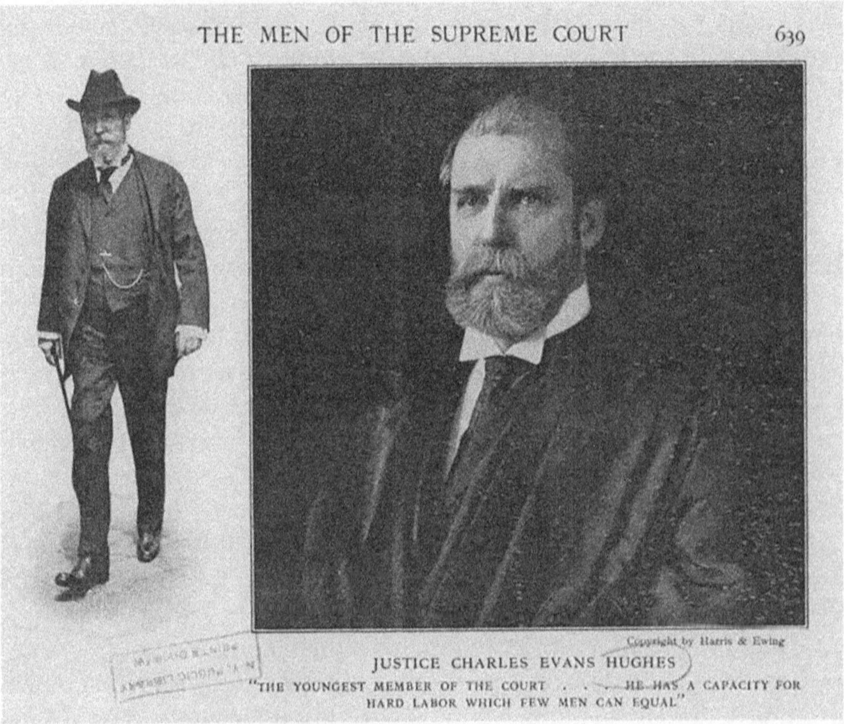

Figure 4.2. *The Youngest Member.* The Miriam and Ira D. Wallach Division of Art, Prints and Photographs, the New York Public Library.

Ogden case, Marshall ruled that Congress could regulate ferry navigation between states as part of its power over interstate commerce. In the interest of a seamless economy, "commerce among the States cannot stop at the boundary line of each State." He interpreted the doctrine of implied powers to include "the power to regulate; that is, to prescribe the rule by which commerce is to be governed." By establishing federal regulatory rights, Marshall rejected a "narrow construction [of the Constitution] which would cripple the government."[23]

Similarly, Hughes did not want regulatory power to be "contracted by construction into the narrowest possible compass." Quoting Marshall's 1824 opinion, Hughes warned against rendering the Constitution "a magnificent structure . . . to look at, but totally unfit for use." Rather, the commerce clause was originally designed to enable Congress to "meet the needs of a developing country." Accordingly, it had to move from the days of "the coach and wagon, the sailing vessel and the canal boat" into "the era of railroads, telegraphs, telephones, and . . . electric power." Hughes considered the commerce clause "a charter of freedom in interstate and foreign commerce from State interference." He understood the complexity of dual federalism in the new economy and the resulting need for flexibility.[24]

Several railroads challenged Minnesota's policies setting intrastate passenger and freight rates so low that trains crossing state borders had to lower their own rates. Consequently, the routes were unprofitable and interstate commerce was threatened. The question was whether the nation's interest in a continuous, integrated transportation system could override the state's control of railroad rates within its borders. As Hughes pointed out, federal efforts to regulate interstate commerce were fairly new developments tied to new "national needs" arising from industrialization. In his opinion, new bills like the 1887 Interstate Commerce Act, the 1890 Sherman Antitrust Act, and the 1906 Food and Drug Act had fundamentally "recast our law." The dormant commerce clause had awakened.[25]

The Minnesota rate cases highlighted the change. It required a heroic effort to wade through the exhaustive details and voluminous background materials, including four days of argument before the Court and a nine-hundred-page statement from just one railroad. Despite writing twenty-one other opinions, Hughes produced a ninety-seven-page opinion that unraveled the complicated issues involved and modernized congressional control over interstate commerce. There were no dissents and the decision became a legal landmark. The other justices were delighted and former President Taft, now teaching law at Yale, thanked Hughes for illuminating the case for his students. Ransom credited Hughes with "judicial statesmanship" akin to Marshall. So, too, Attorney General Robert H. Jackson later concluded that "Hughes's vigorous championship of federal power under the commerce clause is reminiscent of Marshall."[26]

The rate cases decisions were important because they consolidated federal power over interstate commerce while preserving state power over intrastate commerce. Hughes, wrote Friedman, had defined a "new commerce clause doctrine." To Hughes, revising while maintaining the federal-state balance of power would strengthen, not weaken, America's governmental system. As a former governor, Hughes appreciated the importance of states along with their limits. Therefore, congressional power over interstate commerce had to prevail whenever inter- and intrastate powers were so "interwoven" or "commingling" that intrastate policies created a "direct burden" or hindrance to interstate commerce. (Marshall used the word "intermingled.") Conflicting passenger and shipping rates met this test. Of course, the states still controlled intrastate rates and transportation infrastructure as well as its police power over the "health, safety, morals and welfare of its people although interstate commerce is incidentally or indirectly involved." However, if Congress set policy in those areas, federal law would override state law. The objective, he wrote, was to devise "a practical adjustment by which the National authority as conferred by the Constitution is maintained in its full scope without unnecessary loss of local efficiency."[27]

Thus, the rigid "layer cake" concept of federal versus state powers gave way to the more nuanced "marble cake" concept of interwoven powers essential for a complicated, ever-changing, seamless economy. Indeed, wrote law professor Norman Williams, the pre–New Deal Court was less committed to rigid dual federalism than reputed and increasingly accepted the overlapping character of state and federal commercial relations.[28]

In 1916, Hughes called for greater cooperation between federal and state governments, a concept that political scientist Daniel Elazar later labeled "cooperative federalism." Elazar explained that the Constitution represented an "American Partnership" of governments and the people reflecting the "independent interdependence" of the American system. Designed to avoid both "over-centralization" and "excessive localism," dual federalism "combined the possibility of national grandeur with the maintenance of liberal institutions." Fundamentally flexible, wrote Elazar, dual federalism was "the authentic American contribution to democratic thought and republican government."[29]

Significant as the rate cases decision was in affirming congressional power over interstate commerce, questions remained about the ICC's authority over intrastate commerce and the distinction between a state's direct or indirect impact on interstate commerce. These concerns were addressed a year later in the Shreveport rate case, which Hughes worked on for nine months (*Houston, E. and W. Texas Railroad v. U.S.*). The Houston and Texas Railway rates were lower between Texan cities than on a route of equal length going from Texas to Shreveport, Louisiana. The differential purposely disadvantaged Shreveport. In response to the railway's claim that internal routes were beyond ICC control,

Hughes objected to using intrastate rates in a "discriminatory manner" that impeded interstate commerce.[30]

In order to protect the national interest, wrote Hughes, Congress could regulate intrastate commerce when inter- and intrastate commerce had "such a close and substantial relation" that interstate "efficiency" and equity were at risk. He pointed out that "the Nation could not prosper if interstate and foreign trade were governed by many masters." While establishing the principle of fairness among states, Hughes strengthened federal regulatory power over states in order to avoid destructive interstate divisions.[31]

Together, the Minnesota rate case and the Shreveport case modernized federal and state roles by expanding the former without eviscerating the latter. It was, wrote Friedman, "a more flexible and dynamic conception of federal power." Law professor Paul Freund called the new formula "monumental." However, for libertarian legal scholars like law professor Richard A. Epstein, the court was embracing a dangerous principle that enabled the federal government to monopolize intrastate transportation and eventually "replace competitive processes, by hook or by crook, with state-run cartels."[32]

Hughes thought the decision redefined but maintained the balance of power between federal and state spheres, which he believed was exactly how America's dual system of government should work. The separation of powers was essential for avoiding the excessive decentralization of the Articles of Confederation, on the one hand, and the over-centralization of monarchy, on the other. As he commented, "If we did not have States, we should speedily have to create them." To Elazar, states were "the keystones of the American governmental arch." Hughes did not underestimate "the problem of many governments within one nation." However, he believed that the genius of the Constitution was a "more perfect Union" based on each state being "autonomous in its local concerns" and protected against an "unwarranted assertion of Federal power." Yet, observed political scientist Edward Corwin, the rate cases and the emphasis on a seamless economy ultimately meant more federal power and less dual federalism.[33]

While Hughes cautioned against "an unwarranted assertion of federal power," he also insisted that states should not be able "to throw out of gear the requisite machinery for unity of control in national concerns." Industrialization had so altered the relationship between government, commerce, and industry that "our dual system of government is being subjected to a new and severe strain." Therefore, it was crucial that the Supreme Court uphold, but update, the delicate constitutional balance between state and federal governments. Beyond the Court, he hoped that there would be better coordination and "accommodation" between state and federal governments. Changing realities continually required adapting the original document.[34]

Because railroads and public utilities "are clothed with a public interest," Hughes felt justified in claiming that "the commerce clause has not been enlarged; it has simply been applied." Perhaps this was one of the semantic distinctions for which he was often criticized. But Hughes considered interstate commerce "a department of practical affairs" rather than a facet of abstract economic theory. Congress was simply meeting "the needs of a growing country." For law professor and later Associate Justice Felix Frankfurter, such practicality was the most important "single quality" of a judge who tries to resolve "conflicts between national and state power." It also resembled the statesmanship Hughes would later need to negotiate foreign policy tensions.[35]

By the same token, Hughes upheld state prerogatives over intrastate commerce when there were no national standards. An example was when the Georgia legislature passed a bill requiring that intrastate trains have electric headlights (*Atlantic Coast Line v. Georgia*). The railroad invoked the commerce clause to claim that Georgia's regulation was beyond state control because it affected interstate commerce when trains crossed state boundaries. However, Hughes held that Georgia was within its right to make intrastate regulations that affected interstate commerce as long as the federal government had no competing policy and the state policy did not hamper interstate commerce. The regulation clearly met Holmes's standard of a reasonable purpose, which was public safety.[36]

These cases reflected the fact that railroads served both intra- and interstate commerce. As Hughes explained, "Train crews handle interstate and intrastate traffic indiscriminately and the practical service of the carrier is determined by the nature of the haul, not by the presence or absence of a state boundary." The whole had to remain greater than the sum of its parts. Nevertheless, Epstein pointed out that emphasizing the whole sacrificed healthy competition among the parts. The "economic nationalism" of a seamless economy bred altogether too much economic regulation.[37]

The burgeoning economy also strained traditional laissez-faire assumptions about the relationship between public welfare and private interests. During the 1905 gas inquiry, Hughes learned how easily private businesses could abuse public franchises. Therefore, it was not surprising that he supported municipal control over what were previously considered untouchable contracts protected by substantive due process. This claim was based on the Fifth and Fourteenth Amendments' provision that "no person shall . . . be deprived of life, liberty, or property without due process of law." Acknowledging that the phrasing was vague, Hughes suggested that the Founding Fathers wrote it as such because "they preferred flexibility to certainty" as long as "the general purpose" of protecting basic rights remained intact.[38]

Hughes maintained that conviction throughout his judicial career. For example, in three public utilities cases concerning street railways, Hughes asserted that, by definition, a public franchise must "be exercised for the public benefit" (*New York Electric Lines Company v. Empire City Subway Company, Louisiana Railway and Navigation Company v. New Orleans,* and *Wright v. Central of Georgia Railway*). Consequently, cities could review private franchises in order to add regulations as needed or revoke the franchises when the original contract was not properly fulfilled within "a reasonable time." According to Friedman, this "new analytical formula" affirmed that due process was not an impenetrable cloak of protection for private over public interests.[39]

Hughes opposed business combinations in restraint of trade. As a governor fighting special interests in 1908, he declared, "We desire to put an end to unfair practices, unjustifiable preferences, and oppressive proceedings by which . . . rivals are barred from equal opportunities and thrust out of the way or destroyed." Thus, in 1911, he wrote for the Court in opposing a patent medicine company that tried to dictate the prices charged for its product through private contracts between the manufacturer and the retailers (*Dr. Miles Medical Company v. Park and Sons Company*). Holmes disagreed because he prioritized conventional concepts of contract rights. By contrast, Hughes held that "a monopoly of production" cannot be used to monopolize prices (even if by private contracts) without engaging in restraint of trade harmful to the "public interest."[40]

In a similar 1912 case (*Henry Company v. A. B. Dick Company*), Holmes was in the majority protecting licensing rights and Hughes was in the minority protesting against allowing licensing to create a monopoly, which Adam Smith also opposed. At issue was a mimeograph machine company that required buyers of its patented machines to also purchase unpatented supplies, like ink. As in the *Miles* case, Hughes put public policy above private contracts. Whether in the majority or the minority, Hughes recognized the potential abuses of power under laissez-faire economics. As he wrote, "It was not the purpose or effect of the copyright law to render secure the fruits of piracy." His dissent prevailed when the Court reversed itself in 1917, after he left to run for president (*Motion Picture Patents Co. v. Universal Film Manufacturing Co.*).[41]

The new economy required new federal powers in order to protect the public good without strangling the states or private enterprise. Just as a democracy built on dual federalism was inherently complicated and fragile, so an economy based on separate units was fraught with conflict and competition. Under these circumstances, the judge's task of "saying what the law is" became harder than ever. It required, said Hughes, a comprehensive understanding of the facts in order to "secure harmony without sacrifices of any real local interest." The challenge was to weave "many governments within one nation" into a seamless "economic unity." The bottom line was that "we must have a common prosperity or none at all." Consequently, legal assumptions had to be reassessed and modernized. Hughes welcomed "a new era in the development of our law."[42]

Protecting Labor

Progressives worried that industrialism was creating "two nations" defined by the increasingly polarized upper and lower segments of society. Employer repression grew when labor boycotts and strikes multiplied. As violence and chaos threatened the progressive dream of class harmony, middle-class reformers like Hughes tried to bridge the gap. They sought, said liberal economist Richard T. Ely, to promote "social solidarity" through an appreciation of "the dependance of man upon man, both in good things and in evil things." Pursuing "a golden mean" between individualism and socialism, Progressives endorsed labor associations and laws to protect workers by regulating business.[43]

These ideas built on classical economics. In the *Wealth of Nations*, Adam Smith recognized the value of labor, criticized ruthless industrialists, and saw the laws of the market as antidotes to the concentration of wealth. Emerging from "an age of humanism and reason," wrote economist Robert Heilbroner, the *Wealth of Nations* was optimistically dedicated to "the welfare of the common man." So, too, in *The Theory of Moral Sentiments*, Smith posited that human selfishness is balanced by human sympathy and social consciousness. By contrast, Parson Malthus and David Ricardo predicted plenty for the few and misery for the many. Economics became "the dismal science." However, Heilbroner pointed out that John Stuart Mill rejected "the stifling realm of impersonal and inevitable law and brought [economics] back to the arena of ethics and morality." The key was "the ability of men to control their fate through reason." Thus, laws could be used to improve the production and distribution of wealth. Taxes, incentives, regulations, and workers' cooperatives offered "a vista of hope" based on human agency. Progressives in general and Hughes in particular echoed Mill's "gradualist, optimistic, realistic" prescriptions.[44]

While governor, Hughes learned about labor's struggles and got bills through the state legislature supporting workmen's disability compensation, maximum hours for women and children, plus prohibition of child labor in dangerous jobs and at night. He reorganized the state labor department to improve working conditions in factories, tunnels, mines, and department stores. These achievements informed his service on the Court, inclining him toward sociological jurisprudence and a more malleable dual federalism. For example, he wrote an opinion in 1913 supporting a state statute prohibiting the employment of minors in dangerous jobs and requiring employers to validate the ages of employed children (*Sturges and Burn Manufacturing Company v. Beauchamp*).[45]

Hughes authored important decisions supporting state laws for workmen's disability compensation. They overrode the employer's own "relief plans" and rejected policies that forbade compensation for injury purportedly caused by a fellow employee. Writing for the Court in 1911, Hughes held that contracts could not be used to oppress labor, especially since employer and employee never bargained as equals (*Chicago, Burlington and Quincy Railway Company v. McGuire* and *Aluminum Company v. Ramsey*). Significantly, he held that "there is no absolute freedom to do as one wills or to contract as one chooses." Instead, "Liberty implies the absence of arbitrary restraint, not immunity from reasonable regulations and prohibitions imposed in the interests of the community." According to Friedman, Hughes's opinions on this subject comprised his most important contribution to contract law.[46]

Hughes endorsed legislation that set standards to protect railroad workers. Also in 1911, he represented a unanimous Court in validating a federal maximum hours law for railroad workers (*Baltimore and Ohio Railroad v. ICC*). Such regulations, he said, were necessary for avoiding the stress of overwork that could lead to dangerous errors directly affecting interstate commerce. Using Holmes's standard, Hughes affirmed that the requirement bore a "reasonable relation" to the goal of a seamless transportation system. When the railroad insisted that it could not separate inter- and intrastate employees regarding hours policies, Hughes retorted that they could not use the excuse of the "co-mingling of duties" to evade congressional power.[47]

Similarly, in 1912, he spoke for the entire Court in upholding the Employer Liability Acts of 1906 and 1908, like the workers' compensation bill that he championed as governor (*Philadelphia, Baltimore, and Washington Railroad v. Schubert*). Here the question was whether congressional protections for job-related injury overrode previous contracts waiving such protections that the railroads made all employees sign. Hughes said that it did because congressional power to establish "uniform rules" for interstate commerce could not be undermined by prior private contracts. Otherwise, "private individuals" would control interstate commerce instead of Congress, which had the "paramount authority." These railroad cases not only challenged traditional concepts of private contracts but also endorsed a cooperative federalism whereby Congress confirmed state efforts to protect workers.[48]

Beyond railroads, industrialism revolutionized the conditions of work. Instead of small craft establishments with close employer-employee contact, work was defined by impersonal factories, mills, mines, and sweatshops using dangerous machinery six days a week, ten or more hours a day, for pitifully low wages. Health and sanitary conditions were abysmal. State laws designed to ameliorate the situation were often declared unconstitutional for violating employer's Fourteenth Amendment right not to be deprived of life, liberty, or property without due process.

The crucial 1905 *Lochner v. New York* case concerned a state law limiting bakers to ten hours a day or sixty hours a week because they were inhaling flour dust that threatened their health. To the Court, such laws were "meddlesome interferences" with the rights of employers and employees to freely engage in contracts. Dismissing the health argument, the Court feared that allowing states to regulate one condition of labor in one industry would lead to regulating all conditions of labor in all industries. In addition, noted Epstein, such regulations would disadvantage "small, immigrant owned bakeries against their larger unionized rivals." Competition and private enterprise would suffer.[49]

In dissent, Holmes articulated the basic ideas of sociological jurisprudence. He famously declared: "The Fourteenth Amendment does not enact Mr. Herbert Spencer's 'Social Statics.' A constitution is not intended to embody a particular economic theory . . . [but] is made for people of fundamentally different views." He also pointed out that liberty of contract was not specified in the amendment and that most Americans no longer endorsed strict laissez-faire theory anyway. Therefore, legislators were entitled to reflect public opinion in their laws and to experiment with new solutions to new problems. "General propositions," he wrote, "do not decide concrete cases."[50]

Holmes called for a new legal standard reflecting what "a reasonable man" would consider appropriate for the specific circumstance. Rejecting that premise and reinforcing rigid dual federalism, the Court continued invalidating state police power policies regarding labor during what is called the Lochner era (1897 to 1937). Legal scholar, Cass Sunstein, pointed out that the Court's apparent neutrality on labor laws was really an active confirmation of the status quo. Slowly, however, the Court would chip away at *Lochner*, endorse Holmes's perspective, and adopt a more cooperative form of federalism. This evolutionary process culminated with Hughes's 1937 landmark opinion in *West Coast Hotel Co. v. Parrish*.[51]

In 1908, the Court considered *Muller v. Oregon*, a path-breaking labor case shaped by Brandeis and sociological jurisprudence. Female workers were always susceptible to exploitation. Relegated to the most tedious jobs at the lowest wages complicated by sexual harassment and exclusion from male unions, they were particularly powerless. Their plight was highlighted when the Court heard arguments concerning a state law limiting women laundry workers to ten hours a day. The lawyer for the laundry claimed that men and women had equal rights to liberty and property, which entitled them to work free from legislative interference on the basis of gender.

Brandeis represented Oregon after insisting, like Hughes in the gas and insurance investigations, that he have full control of the case. He served at the behest of his sister-in-law, a leader of the National Consumers League, which was dedicated to improving women's working conditions. With only two weeks to prepare the case, she hired ten research assistants to gather background information from domestic and foreign sources about the impact of women's work on their health, morals, and family functions.[52]

Arguments before the Court were customarily based only on the law and legal precedent. By contrast, Brandeis's defense devoted two pages to the law and over one hundred pages to documenting the negative effect of excessive work on women. Like Hughes, Brandeis mastered every detail and delivered his argument without notes. Skillfully marshalling "the facts of common knowledge," he tied the poor health of overworked women to child-bearing and sickly offspring. By citing studies from the United States and Europe, said Hughes, Brandeis, used "both microscope and telescope." In fact, Brandeis was so impressive that he was allowed to speak beyond his allotted time. It was sociological jurisprudence at its best, validating Holmes's call for law based on facts and experience. "The Brandeis brief" revolutionized legal argumentation and justified legislation to address industrial problems. Amazingly enough, Brandeis convinced the skeptical, traditionalist Supreme Court, thereby marking a major turning point in American jurisprudence.[53]

Joining the Court two years later, Hughes bolstered Brandeis in cases regarding minimum wages and maximum hours for women. A 1914 case challenged an Oregon minimum wage statute that would have required a paper box manufacturer to add sixty-four cents to his female workers' eight-dollar weekly wage (*Stettler v. O'Hara et al. Industrial Welfare Commission of Oregon*). The factory owner claimed that the law not only violated his rights of substantive due process and freedom of contract but also that wages were not as directly related to work as were hours. During oral argument, Hughes cornered the factory owner's lawyer into considering that low wages might affect workers as much as long hours. That enabled Brandeis to document the desperation of young women driven to starvation, homelessness, illness, or prostitution because of poverty. Due to the absence of one justice, the Court divided evenly with Hughes supporting Brandeis. The issue was not settled until 1937 when Hughes delivered the aforementioned *Parrish* opinion upholding a minimum wage law for women.[54]

Hughes backed Brandeis again in a 1915 case concerning a California eight-hour statute that was being challenged by a hotel owner who required chambermaids to work nine hours a day (*Miller v. Wilson*). In addition to presenting the relevant facts cited in *Muller*, Brandeis emphasized the right of legislators to reflect contemporary realities and popular opinion by passing reasonable requirements in the public interest. Representing the entire Court, Hughes invoked *Muller* and its acceptance of special accommodations for women due to their "physical structure [and] maternal functions." He recycled his statement from the 1911 *McGuire* railway case that "the liberty of contract guaranteed by the Constitution is freedom from arbitrary restraint, not immunity to safeguard the public interest." Elevating public welfare over private contracts now became the prevailing legislative and judicial standard.[55]

Although these cases were praised for protecting female labor, modern feminist scholars criticized them for treating women as inferiors and limiting their options. For these liberal scholars, as well as for libertarians, "laws justified as protecting women have been a central means of oppressing them." In response, Brandeis's biographer Melvin Urofsky, professor of law, politics, and history, urged viewing these cases in the context of their own time when Lochner loomed over all labor legislation and when both genders assumed that women needed special protection.[56]

Unions raised other controversial issues. In *Adair v. U.S.* (1908), the Court overturned a congressional act forbidding employees from being fired because they joined a union. Thus, the Court upheld so called yellow dog contracts, whereby workers had to pledge not to join a union as a condition of employment. Holmes dissented because that arrangement allowed employers to exploit workers and deprive them from seeking reasonable relief through unions. To libertarian scholars, yellow dog contracts maintained a competitive system whereby workers were free to accept or change jobs. Eliminating them deprived employers of contract rights and opened the door to labor union monopolies or cartels.[57]

When the Court's majority affirmed *Adair* in *Coppage v. Kansas* (1915), Holmes reiterated his dissent and called for overturning *Adair*. Hughes joined Justice William Day in a separate dissent that avoided doing so. They claimed that *Adair* was about firing employees who joined unions while *Coppage* was about the employer's right to prevent joining unions in the first place. Yet, like Holmes, they asserted that labor unions were important to "protect those who might otherwise be unable to protect themselves." They emphasized labor's disadvantage in contract bargaining and the injustice of yellow dog contracts. Reversing the employer's Fourteenth Amendment due process claims, they pointed out that employees also deserved due process. While *Coppage* previewed Hughes's 1937 pro-union *Parrish* opinion, it also reflected his much-criticized penchant for using fine distinctions to resist overturning precedent, even when his stated positions warranted doing so.[58]

The labor cases legitimized sociological jurisprudence and progressive legislative experimentation on behalf of workers. Hughes underlined these concepts in his 1927 Columbia lectures. Decrying "the never-ending invocation of the Fourteenth Amendment," Hughes affirmed that "no one has a vested right in the common law." Nor should the Fourteenth Amendment be used to deny "a wide field of legislative discretion that is essential to the exercise of legislative power." Even if laws sometimes seemed "unwise" or "economically unsound," he said, they were not necessarily unconstitutional and the due process clause did not permit the Supreme Court to change them. Rather, the Court should exercise judicial restraint and those who opposed the laws should protest to their legislatures or seek "their remedy at the ballot box." For Hughes, the fundamental precept was that "changing social conditions require new remedies [through] the novel exercise of the police power, to care for both social and individual interests."[59]

Bolstering Civil Liberties

Hughes championed civil liberties. Just two weeks after joining the Court in 1910, Hughes confronted a case about a woman's right to sue her husband for damages caused by assault and battery, including when she was pregnant (*Thompson v. Thompson*). The Court ruled against her on the premise that although a 1901 law enabled women to own property, enter contracts, sue others, and even sue her husband for property damages, she could not sue her husband for personal damages. Hughes joined Holmes and John Marshall Harlan in dissent. They held that the law did not prohibit suing for personal damages and that the Court had no right to add a proviso to that effect. In so doing, the Court was not merely interpreting the law, but rewriting it and violating the separation of powers. Moreover, the ruling revived the concept of *coverture*, whereby a woman's rights were subsumed by her husband upon marriage, even though the 1901 law expressly abandoned that policy. The Court "must take the law as it has been established by competent legislative authority," said the dissent. "It cannot . . . make law . . . [in order to] defeat the clearly expressed will of the legislature." Supporting women's rights in this case previewed Hughes's support for women's suffrage during the 1916 campaign. Both were advanced positions for the time.[60]

Hughes continued defending civil liberties, sometimes agreeing with the majority, sometimes dissenting. In *Bailey v. Alabama,* he represented the majority's position regarding the legacy of slavery. The 1911 case involved the Thirteenth Amendment, which stated, "Neither slavery nor involuntary servitude, except as punishment for a crime whereof the party shall have been duly convicted, shall exist within the United States, or any place subject to their jurisdiction." However, an Alabama statute automatically considered it a crime when Bailey, an African American laborer, violated his contract to work for a certain period of time. He received fifteen dollars payment in advance but left without repaying the debt. Not fulfilling the contract was classified as fraud, which was a crime. Consequently, Bailey was sentenced to hard labor for 136 days and a fine of thirty dollars, a huge sum for a poor laborer.

In Hughes's opinion, the Thirteenth Amendment was not narrowly about slavery: "It was a charter of universal civil freedom for all persons of whatever race, color, or estate, under the flag." To him, the term "involuntary servitude had a larger meaning than slavery" and included other forms of compulsory labor, like the practice of "reducing slaves to the condition of serfs" on Southern plantations. Summoning the original free labor commitments of Abraham Lincoln and the Republican Party, Hughes declared, "The plain intention" of the Thirteenth Amendment, "was to abolish slavery of whatever name and form . . . to render impossible any state of bondage, to make labor free."[61]

By definition, compulsory labor was involuntary servitude and, if in payment of a debt, it was peonage, which was outlawed in 1867. The state could "impose involuntary servitude as punishment for a crime" but could not call a debt a crime in order to punish someone as a criminal. In other words, "What the State may not do directly, it may not do indirectly." Moreover, the accused was not even allowed to defend himself in court. Adding a sociological perspective, Hughes considered the law particularly egregious because of its impact on "the poor and the ignorant, its most likely victims." For all of these reasons, the law was unconstitutional and violated an "imperishable value": the freedom of labor. The case, wrote Friedman, "sounded the death knell of Southern peonage."[62]

While Hughes emphasized freedom, Holmes still focused on the sanctity of contract. According to Budiansky, Holmes had "a noticeable blind spot on racial matters" resulting in "several of the worst decisions of his career." *Bailey* was one of them. Using a narrowly legalistic argument, Holmes claimed that the labor contract was valid as a contract per se and that state law should prevail. By ignoring the fact that Southern states arrested many African American men for minor offenses and forced them into contract labor, Holmes ignored the real-life experiences that he otherwise claimed should inform legal opinions. Likewise, he supported a Kentucky law that made integrated education illegal at Berea College and an Alabama law that disenfranchised 177,000 men whose grandfathers could not vote under slavery.[63]

Whereas Hughes voted against the grandfather clause twice in 1915 (*Guinn v. U.S.* and *Myers v. Anderson*) and opposed Jim Crow as chief justice, Holmes consistently supported the 1896 *Plessy v. Ferguson* "separate but equal" clause. One 1914 case involved an Oklahoma law that allowed railroads to provide dining and sleeping cars for whites only (*McCabe v. Atchison, Topeka and Santa Fe Railway Co.*). The company claimed that low demand drove their policy. The case was dismissed for technical reasons, but, in writing for a five-to-four Court, Hughes asserted that constitutional rights should not "depend upon the number of persons who may be discriminated against." Because rights were "personal," not numerical, "substantial equality of treatment of persons traveling under like conditions cannot be refused." In a private exchange with Holmes, Hughes denounced such "a bald, wholly unjustified discrimination against a passenger solely on account of race." Although Hughes preferred to support state legislation whenever possible, he drew the line when such laws violated equal protection and harmed the underprivileged.[64]

Holmes reconsidered his position on race because of his commitment to due process. The turning point was the 1915 case of *Frank v. Magnum.* When a thirteen-year-old female worker in an Atlanta pencil factory was found bloodied and dead, the manager, Leo Frank, was accused. There was little evidence but substantial prejudice against the New York Jew. A mob packed the courtroom and surrounded the courthouse during Frank's trial. The situation was so volatile that the judge advised Frank and his lawyer to leave the courtroom before the verdict. Applause and cheers greeted the guilty verdict and Frank was scheduled to be hung. His lawyer then appealed to the Supreme Court seeking a writ of habeas corpus in order to get a new hearing. The original request went to Holmes who wrote a memo to his brethren explaining that although technical procedures had been followed, "a hostile demonstration and seemingly dangerous crowd" had probably pressured the jury into a guilty verdict and deprived Frank of due process. Months later, the Court denied the appeal seven-to-two.[65]

Holmes and Hughes dissented. The issue was not Frank's guilt or innocence but his right to a fair trial. "Mob law," wrote Holmes, "does not become due process of law by securing the assent of a terrorized jury." Such miscarriage of justice made it "our duty . . . to declare lynch law as little valid when practiced by a regularly drawn jury as when administered by . . . a mob intent on death." At great personal risk, the Georgia governor commuted Frank's sentence to life imprisonment the day before he was to be killed. In response, a furious mob stormed the prison and hanged him anyway. A former governor, a former mayor, and the current sheriff participated. Holmes was shaken by this case and increasingly valued his friendship with Hughes. As chief justice, Hughes would get another chance to oppose mob rule in the 1930s Scottsboro cases.[66]

Holmes joined a unanimous Court in another civil liberties case for which Hughes wrote the opinion. In 1914, Arizona passed a law requiring that employers hire only native-born or naturalized citizens for 80 percent of their workers if they employed more than five workers (*Traux v. Raich*). Despite the isolationist anti-immigrant climate, an Austrian immigrant sued after being fired under that law. When he was governor, Hughes showed more concern about immigrants than most politicians. In 1907, he declared that American unity "does not depend on blood relationship, whether near or remote." Rather, it is "the unity of a common National ideal" based on "the dignity of manhood . . . equal civil rights . . . [and] devotion to liberty expressed in institutions designed to give every man a fair opportunity for the exercise of his talents." The nation's strength, he said, came from "the fusion of its diverse elements" without regard to "race or creed."[67]

These convictions shaped the opinion Hughes wrote for the Court in 1915. He held that the Arizona law was designed "to deny to lawful inhabitants, because of their race or nationality, the ordinary means of earning a livelihood," which was essential to "personal freedom." Therefore, it violated the Fourteenth Amendment's equal protection clause as well as federal control over immigration. If people were entitled to immigrate, they should be entitled to work, which, claimed Hughes, was "the very essence of the personal freedom and opportunity that it was the purpose of the Amendment to secure." Furthermore, restricting employment was tantamount to restricting immigration, which invaded a congressional domain. Quite simply, "they cannot live where they cannot work." In all of these civil liberties cases, Hughes pursued an expansive vision of "life, liberty and happiness."[68]

Just as Hughes wrestled with joining the Court in 1910, so he struggled with leaving in 1916. It was the perfect job for him. As he wrote at the time, serving on the Court provided a meaningful "settled career with the great opportunity of public service." Although his legal practice was very profitable, Hughes felt that "the mere opportunity to make money would not appeal to me at all." Besides, he feared that private practice would leave him little time for public service and would create "constant opportunities for misconstruction." Precisely because serving on the Court meant "very hard work, real mental work," Hughes considered it "agreeable in every sense and with intellectual pleasure in it." Nonetheless, when drafted to run for the presidency in 1916, he felt obliged to accept. After Hughes resigned from the Court, Holmes admitted, "I shall miss him consumedly for he is not only a good fellow, experienced and wise, but funny, and with doubts that open vistas through the wall of nonconformist conscience."[69]

As associate justice from 1910 to 1916, Hughes advocated a reality-based perspective on the law. According to Friedman, Hughes valued "social purpose rather than rigid form or logic as the keystone of law." Respecting precedent but rejecting legal formalism, Hughes appreciated the socioeconomic contexts and impacts of laws. While retaining his basic commitment to the written Constitution, he helped adjust it to the new circumstances of industrialism and render it more inclusive. As he explained in 1916, the Court should support legislative efforts "to enact reasonable measures for the protection of the safety, health, morals, and welfare of the people" including "rational experimentation." This meant prioritizing public over private interests and opportunity over exploitation. Thus, Hughes played an important role in adapting both the Constitution and classical liberalism to the twentieth century, a quest that he continued to pursue as chief justice. "More than any of his brethren," said Friedman, Hughes "was attuned to the tenor of change" and skilled at building consensus for change. Both attributes would serve him well in the future. Throughout, Hughes remained a "result-oriented," practical idealist whose Progressive commitments strongly influenced his contributions as "a governor on the bench."[70]

5 | Almost Becoming President, 1916–1921

I always think of Hughes as president. . . . By far he is the strongest man before the people to-day except Roosevelt.
—President William Howard Taft, 1909

Getting Nominated

Expecting to compete against Charles Evans Hughes for the Republican nomination in 1912, President Taft offered to withdraw if Hughes agreed to run. But Taft himself had appointed Hughes to the US Supreme Court. Although the bosses were relieved when Hughes went to Washington in 1910, progressives regretted that the court appointment would remove Hughes from politics. (Some implied that such was Taft's intent.) Declaring that "the Supreme Court must be kept out of politics," Hughes refused to run. Nonetheless, one ally predicted, "If an exigency shall arise and you shall be needed, the People will pull you off the Bench for the higher position." There was no higher position than the presidency.[1]

When Hughes joined the Court in 1910, he expected to "have a long tenure—twenty or more years." He relished that prospect because, he said, "there isn't any opportunity of public service that I know of that is more important than the work of the Supreme Court." Despite the limited salary, he was eager to "devote myself unreservedly and fully for the rest of my life to the work of that Court." After being governor, he knew that political office was temporary and often immersed in pettiness. By contrast, work on the Court "was continuous and of the highest degree of importance." Once out of office, he feared becoming "a relic of the past." On the Court, he could remain relevant and might even influence the future. In the end, it would be the most meaningful form of "public service" and the best way to "sum up a life." The rub was that term *public service.*[2]

In 1916, national Republicans faced a dilemma just like the New

York State Republicans faced in 1906. The 1912 election left them divided between Theodore Roosevelt (TR) and Taft. The party needed a candidate who could not only bridge the gap but also beat the popular Democratic incumbent, Woodrow Wilson. As Hughes had rescued the state party in 1906, so might he rescue the national party in 1916. Ultimately, he answered the call when it came, thereby putting his characteristic sense of duty to the nation ahead of his equally characteristic love for the law and hatred of political infighting.

Republican prospects looked good, but the obstacles were immense. With TR complicating matters, the Republican Party was in shambles. Hughes himself had been out of office for six years, his campaign manager was inexperienced, and President Wilson was a tough opponent. Yet, Hughes almost won. Although he seemed victorious on election night, his margin shrank by morning, and three days later he narrowly lost the election. This drama was repeated in 1948 when President Harry Truman narrowly reversed an apparent early victory by another New York State governor, Thomas E. Dewey. Both elections were sobering reminders of how unpredictable politics can be.

Hughes's nomination in 1916 was the direct result of the presidential election of 1912. After handpicking Taft over Hughes as his successor in 1908, TR resented Taft's independence and disparaged his conservatism. As he had done to Hughes, TR began sabotaging Taft's reelection with a 1910 speech in Osawatomie, Kansas. There he announced his New Nationalism, a concept that was influenced by Progressive journalist Herbert Croly's 1909 book *The Promise of American Life*. The old nationalism pitted an aristocratic version of Hamiltonian strong government against a democratic version of Jeffersonian weak government. Croly advocated combining the two by using strong government for democratic purposes. Calling for a "new Federalism or a new Nationalism," Croly praised TR as an aggressive executive dedicated to progressive reform. Despite TR's earlier disavowal, the New Nationalism justified seeking the presidency again.[3]

The 1912 Republican nominating convention was so contentious that New York Senator Elihu Root thought Hughes could have been nominated to break the deadlock between Taft and TR. Nonetheless, as chairman of the convention, Root helped Taft prevail. Root served in TR's cabinet, but, like Taft, was conservative. As Taft's convention floor manager, William Barnes Jr. (Hughes's old New York State adversary) kept most delegates in line and got some TR delegates discounted. According to New York Senator James W. Wadsworth (Hughes's old ally), Barnes "had more influence than anybody there." Ironically, Taft later distanced himself from Barnes because he was a boss. TR blamed Barnes for manipulating the delegates, excoriated him in speech after speech, and won the libel suit that Barnes filed. Oddly enough, before backing Taft, Barnes urged Indiana's Progressive Senator William Borah to run as a vice presidential candidate with Hughes on a compromise ticket. Was Barnes so dedicated to the party that he would even have supported his enemy Hughes for president?[4]

After Taft won the mainstream Republican Party nomination, TR formed his own Progressive Party and created an internal party battle over activist government. TR's vice presidential running mate was Hiram W. Johnson, the dynamic, volatile, anti-boss, Progressive California governor. Like Hughes, he had secured the eight-hour day, workmen's compensation, public utilities regulation, and prison reform. Unlike Hughes, Johnson got the direct primary passed. Although Hughes praised the California governor in 1910, Johnson would be his undoing in 1916. The philosophical differences between Taft and TR were magnified by stylistic differences. Because Taft followed precedent and did not give many speeches, TR eagerly filled the gap. He had already defied tradition by attending the convention. Upon arriving, he claimed to be feeling like a Bull Moose, christening his party's nickname. For TR, politics always rose beyond policy. His quest for personal power was a moral imperative, as exemplified when he proclaimed, "We stand at Armageddon, and we battle for the Lord."[5]

The Democrats ran Woodrow Wilson, who also harbored messianic notions that motivated him to declare, "God ordained that I should be the next president of the United States." As past president of Princeton University and reformist governor of New Jersey, Wilson was a rising political star. Ironically, he ran for governor in 1910, promising to follow Hughes's example in New York. His presidential campaign reached out to Democratic and Republican Progressives while branding the Republican Party the rich man's party. Like Hughes, Wilson was an energetic, effective campaigner. However, historian John Milton Cooper Jr. considered Wilson bolder in promoting reform and combating bossism.[6]

In 1912, Wilson needed a program to compete with the New Nationalism. Luckily, he met Louis D. Brandeis, Boston's widely respected "people's lawyer" (and friend of Hughes), who believed that America must liberate private enterprise from domination by trusts. This idea became the basis of Wilson's New Freedom. He was vague about methodology but clearly criticized TR for condoning big business as efficient and for using government to regulate, not eliminate, trusts. TR countered by calling Wilson an old-fashioned, laissez-faire conservative tied to states' rights concepts of minimal government. Declaring that trusts killed competition and strangled free enterprise, Wilson promised "to set ourselves free" and prevent the 'time when the combined power of high finance would be greater than the power of the government."[7]

At this point, Wilson opposed TR's program of social justice reform, which he condemned as a paternalistic violation of a core American value—faith in individual initiative. Wilson, said Cooper, spoke as a product of the middle class concerned with opportunity and change from the bottom up. TR spoke as a member of the upper class convinced that change had to be top-down. In the end, Wilson won with barely 42 percent of the popular vote, compared to 27.4 percent for TR, 23.2 percent for Taft, and 6 percent for Eugene V. Debs, the Socialist candidate. The combined Republican total of 50.6 percent of the popular vote convinced party leaders that they could win in 1916—if they could unite.[8]

Hughes was promoted as a compromise candidate in 1912, but, being on the Supreme Court deemed it improper to run. In addition, he did not want to compete either with Taft, who placed him on the Court, or with TR, the omnipresent past president who supported him on and off as governor. Despite his expressed reluctance, presidential talk began in 1914. As in 1912, Hughes said that being on the bench meant being out of politics. He even stopped voting. Still, the Hughes boom grew and some politicians proposed a Hughes–Johnson fusion ticket to reunify the regular and progressive Republicans. But Johnson, who called Hughes a "mysterious stuffed prophet," would not abandon TR. Besides, Johnson sought the nomination himself. Considering that Hughes had been out of politics for six years, the draft was a striking development. Supporters assumed that Hughes could repeat his past performance as a fighting governor with "moral courage" and powerful stump speeches. However, Hughes refused to have his name placed on Nebraska's primary ballot in November 1915. Taft was upset because he believed that Hughes was the only man who could "save the party from Roosevelt and the country from Wilson."[9]

Increasingly pressured to run from people high and low, Hughes was undoubtedly flattered and enticed by the prospect. Nonetheless, he quickly dismissed Chief Justice White's surprising implication that if he stayed on the Court, Wilson would appoint him chief justice when the position next became available. Nonetheless, Hughes was genuinely torn and a *New York Evening Sun* cartoonist depicted him in his judicial robes weighing the scales of "patriotic obligation" against "personal inclination." Not only did he love being on the Court, but he was well aware of his previous struggles as a politician in New York State and his tendency to over work. If such had been his lot as governor, how much greater would it be as president? Hughes feared that "he may wear a crown, but it would be a crown of thorns." By the same token, he understood that his party was in crisis and that the nation faced the even greater crisis of world war. Accordingly, he warned Antoinette, "When you see me in my coffin, remember that I did not want to take this burden on myself."[10]

Hughes's ambivalence was problematic. As in 1912, he would not condone any movement on his behalf and refrained from making any public statements because he was still on the bench. However, unlike 1912, he did not definitively refuse to run and let Frank Hitchcock, Taft's 1908 campaign manager and postmaster general, organize unofficially on his behalf. Such qualified reluctance suggested that he was more ambitious than he admitted. Yet, by projecting disinterest, Hughes sacrificed the opportunity to clarify his message and bolster his appeal. Moreover, when he failed to discuss the war, TR angrily floated other possible candidates while secretly hoping to be drafted himself. A *New York World* cartoonist drew Hughes as a nightmare hovering over a sleeping TR (see figure 5.1). Taft observed that "Roosevelt of course does not want Hughes, because he does not want anybody except Roosevelt." Significantly, TR equipped one of his followers with a letter criticizing Hughes to be used at the Republican nominating convention, but it was withheld.[11]

The evening before the Republican Party convention opened in Chicago, Oregon delegates called a meeting to solidify support for Hughes. Hitchcock and New York State Governor Charles Whitman rallied the one hundred and fifty delegates in attendance. When the convention opened on June 7th, the regulars and the Progressives tried but failed to broker a peace. Behind-the-scenes machinations soon gave way to high drama on the convention floor. Whitman nominated Hughes as "a man of action, the champion of the people, the idol of the electorate, the faithful public servant, the profound thinker on national affairs."

Most important, he was "a man trained in battle for the truth" and precisely the person needed to rescue the nation in a time of peril. After an enthusiastic floor demonstration for Hughes, several other men were nominated. Root reluctantly ran on the first two ballots with support from prominent New York State Republicans, including Barnes, Wadsworth, and Charles D. Hilles, chairman of the Republican National Committee. They preferred a traditional party man whom they could control. Still resenting Root's support of Taft in 1912, TR joined others who dismissed Root as too old and too tied to Wall Street.[12]

Hughes led on the first ballot and gained on the second. Most other contenders dropped out before the third ballot, clearing the way for a unanimous nomination. The vice presidential nominee was Indiana's Charles W. Fairbanks, a former senator who was acceptable to the Old Guard and was TR's vice president in his second term. However, because Fairbanks never supported TR's domestic reform program (the Square Deal), he could not help bridge the intraparty chasm. Regardless, Ohio's Senator Warren G. Harding, chairman of the nominating convention, was sure that Hughes's "sterling integrity and unsullied private character" would spell victory. According to the *St. Louis Globe-Democrat,* "Never before has the office sought the man with such persistency; never before has it had to overcome obstacles set up by the man himself or by the circumstances of his position." The message was that "nothing less than an overwhelming public sentiment in his favor could have accomplished this result." However, Barnes warned, "We're going to be strongest on nomination day and weakest on election day."[13]

On the surface, unity suffused the hall, but it was fragile. After running sixth on the first ballot and fifth on the second ballot, TR realized that he could not win. Yet, he still believed that he could be elected because, he said, "the country recognized him as the real opponent of Wilson." Expressing lukewarm support for Hughes, TR suggested that the Progressives back his friend and foreign policy ally Massachusetts's conservative Senator Henry Cabot Lodge. Dismayed, Johnson and prominent New York Progressive Bainbridge Colby led TR's followers in nominating the former president by acclamation. Clearly, wrote historian George E. Mowry, "the Progressive Party was Roosevelt and Roosevelt was the Progressive Party."[14]

Appearing to reject their offer while leaving the door open for the Progressive Party National Committee to make the final decision, TR played his last card for the nomination. Through it all, he preached

From the New York *World*, June 4, 1916.

HIS NIGHTMARE

Figure 5.1. "His Nightmare," artist unclear. *New York World*, June 4, 1916.

unity while really inflaming the open wound that he created in 1912 and that required healing for victory in 1916. Instead, that lesion would fester and prove fatal. In the moment, TR told the press lingering at his Oyster Bay home not to take any pictures of him because, he repeated twice, "I am out of politics." He was "crestfallen." An era had closed.[15]

Upon receiving word of the nomination, Hughes's indecision evaporated. Reporters said that he smiled broadly and greeted them warmly, "unmistakably pleased" with the outcome. One wrote that "there was something so frank and so very, very human about the face of the man who has been described as the model of judicial calm and poise and coldness." At first, the reporters were taken aback, but "the easy, pleasurable smile and simple manner placed the men before him completely at ease at once." After answering their questions and shaking their hands goodbye, they concluded that he was "a very kindly . . . human being who was distinctly proud to be a candidate for the Presidency." However, Hughes was about to become embroiled in one of the most divisive presidential campaigns in US history. Because it raised fundamental issues that redefined each major political party, historian Lewis L. Gould considered it "the first modern campaign."[16]

Hughes seized the moment. After sending President Wilson a brief, formal resignation from the Supreme Court, he telegraphed the convention saying, "I have not desired the nomination. I have wished to remain on the bench. But in this critical period in our national history, I recognize that it is your right to summon and that it is my paramount duty to respond." This statement reflected his long-standing belief that it was improper to seek office because nominations should emanate from the people, not through manipulation or lust for power. One wonders if he saw the inconsistency of fighting for direct primaries as governor but refused to participate in primaries for this nomination, which was determined by conventional party politics. In any case, he appreciated the call to serve and was self-confident enough to believe that he could serve well. Revealing how much he had already been thinking about current events, his lengthy telegram accepting the nomination previewed all the domestic and foreign policy themes of his formal acceptance speech. In calling for "a united effort," he also acknowledged the major obstacle to victory.[17]

The Campaign

Hughes's nomination marked the only time in US history that a Supreme Court justice resigned to become a presidential candidate. Reactions were mixed. On the one hand, he was criticized for accepting the nomination in 1916 after proclaiming that the Supreme Court should be immune from politics in 1912. Professor Felix Frankfurter considered Hughes's nomination bad for both the man and the Court. On the other hand, many judges across the nation were supportive. Taft was relieved, independents were encouraged, and most progressives were resigned. TR waited two more weeks before officially endorsing Hughes. Publicly offering to help, privately he called Hughes "the bearded iceberg" and wished he could "put more heart into the campaign for him." Meanwhile, Hughes's old New York State allies quickly established campaign headquarters at Manhattan's Hotel Astor.[18]

Hughes narrowly failed to win even though the Republican Party was expected to carry the Electoral College. Considering how many factors undermined his campaign, it is amazing that Hughes almost prevailed. Some of the problems were of his own making; others were beyond his control. His biggest mistake was the choice of campaign manager. Out of politics for six years, still skeptical of professional politicians, and beset by division within his party, Hughes turned to a trusted friend. William R. Willcox had been president of the New York City Board of Education, New York City postmaster, and chairperson of Hughes's downstate Public Service Commission. He was not allied with either Republican faction nor as controversial as more competent political operatives like Hitchcock, Parsons, or Will Hays, future chairman of the Republican National Committee. In many ways, Willcox was like Hughes. Admired for his knowledge, efficiency, and hard work, Willcox came from upstate New York and taught school before earning a law degree from Columbia. Both men belonged to the Union League Club, a private organization of prominent men formed in 1863 to support the union, civic participation, and charity. However, never having run a political campaign, Willcox neglected the state campaigns, aggravated party tensions, and disregarded warnings when the campaign faltered. To Taft, Willcox was a "blunderhead"; to Wilson, he was a gift.[19]

The second problem was doubly complicated. Hughes not only needed to win TR's support, but also broker a peace between TR and Taft. He wrote gracious letters to TR while trying to set up a public reconciliation between the two former presidents. Whereas Taft was eager to be helpful, TR resisted. Finally agreeing to attend a meeting at New York City's Union League Club in October, TR said he would shake Taft's hand on the receiving line just as he would shake hands with Barnes or Root. But he would not make conversation with Taft or allow his image to appear with Taft and Hughes either on a campaign button or in a campaign movie. Personal pique handicapped practical politics.[20]

A third problem was the candidate himself. Hughes maintained his powerful, substantive speaking style. Always thorough and thoughtful, he was considered an eloquent orator. He could be charming and funny, but he was no TR. Nor did he follow the former president's advice that politicians should remember that "what the average voter wants is not an etching, but a poster, a statement so broad and clear in such simple language that he can thoroughly understand it." Hughes had a different approach. He believed that the public deserved an appeal to reason based on facts presented clearly, without sensationalism. Although it had worked in New York State, Hughes's faith in the people may have hampered his ability to reach them on the national stage.[21]

In 1916, Hughes faced a seasoned political adversary. At first glance, Hughes and Wilson seemed so similar that Hughes was sometimes called "the whiskered Wilson." They were both self-confident sons of preachers, well educated, idealistic, highly accomplished, nationally prominent, anti-boss, former governors of Eastern states. Both were effective speakers committed to public service and educating the public; both were considered too intellectual and aloof. The similarities were deceptive. Despite being a published scholar and president of Princeton, Wilson preferred real world politics to academic politics. He might have been as moralistic and as skeptical of ordinary politicians as Hughes, but Wilson was more politically ambitious. As governor and president, he also proved to be astute, bold, popular, and eloquent. Considered by historian Trygve Thronveit to be "the first national legislation to redistribute wealth," Wilson's New Freedom embodied constructive, responsive activism reflecting the era's progressive spirit. Hughes had met his match.[22]

The difference was clear from the start. Hughes's Carnegie Hall acceptance speech was attended by three thousand Republicans, one thousand by invitation. Curiously, TR chose this moment to end his four-year boycott of Republican Party events. His arrival sparked a demonstration with cries of "We want Teddy." *The New York Times* called it the "only episode of unusual interest at the meeting." When Hughes entered, there was another demonstration, "which, both in length and intensity, equaled but did not surpass, that bestowed upon the Colonel." Harding opened the event by noting that Hughes's "extraordinary nomination . . . has no parallel in the history of the Republican Party" and was made "notwithstanding your holding aloof from all conference and participation." Consequently, Harding predicted a "Republican restoration under your trusted leadership."[23]

Hughes's speech was typically well written, well-reasoned, substantive, and eloquent in spots but too long and too negative. Opening with a nod to the "reunion" of the Republican Party, Hughes called for true "Americanism" based on "peace . . . brotherhood . . . opportunity." His slogan "America first and America efficient" resembled the "government economical and efficient" slogan used in his 1906 gubernatorial campaign. The phrase "America First" was actually coined by Wilson in an April 1915 speech defending American neutrality. Both candidates emphasized those two words throughout the 1916 campaign, but it later was appropriated by isolationists whom neither man supported.[24]

The hall was hot and Hughes's message was sober. Strikingly negative, the bulk of the speech revolved around the assumption that "we are in a critical period, perhaps more critical than any period since the Civil War." In exhaustive (and exhausting) detail, he explained the issues surrounding Mexican relations, neutral shipping rights, and the European war. Decrying Wilson's foreign policies as "a confused chapter of blunders," he observed, "We are a peace-loving people, but we live in a world of arms." Therefore, he insisted, "Adequate preparedness is not militarism. It is the essential assurance of security; it is the necessary safeguard of peace." When Hughes purposely glanced at TR to acknowledge his campaign for preparedness, the hall erupted with cheers and applause. However, they were for TR, not for Hughes.[25]

Hughes left domestic affairs for the last third of the speech. He affirmed that unlike the Southern-based Democratic Party, the Republican Party was national and committed to "social justice." In contrast to the Democrats' free trade policy, Hughes declared that prosperity and wages depended on protective tariffs and asserted his concern for "the just interests of labor." Underlining his Progressive credentials, Hughes advocated responsible federal regulation of monopolies and policies for the "betterment of the lives of human beings" regarding health, education, working conditions, workmen's compensation, and conservation. Finally, he differentiated himself from Wilson by backing a woman's suffrage amendment, which the audience applauded. If only Hughes had put these items front and center of the speech, his campaign might have had a better start.[26]

Without mentioning his name, Hughes attacked Wilson's "incompetent administration" and pattern of "paying off political debts with public office," especially in the State Department and diplomatic corps. Hughes promised to reverse this pattern if elected and did so later. After endorsing a postwar "parliament of nations" to resolve future controversies, he ended as he began with a sense of "Americanism" under threat. Because "we live in a fateful hour," he said, we must "renew our pledge to the ancient ideals of individual opportunity denied to none because of race or creed, of unswerving loyalty." Altogether, Hughes called for a "vision of America prepared and secure, strong and just, equal to her tasks; and exemplar of the capacity and efficiency of a free people."[27]

The speech was a bad omen. Starting with and spending so much time on foreign policy was a strategic error because the electorate was (and remains) more interested in domestic issues. Hughes compounded the problem by using the same approach on the campaign trail. Although he got a rousing reception from five thousand people at his first rally in Detroit, others were disappointed. One problem, noted Gould, was that Hughes could never have met "the immense expectations that had been aroused" by his candidacy. Although his six-year absence from the political fray made him a safe nominee, it created a vacuum that was filled by glorification. After all, the speech was typically Hughes—thorough, rational, and forthright but ponderous and negative. Thus, it was criticized as too detailed and politically "flat." Only the Democrats were pleased. Journalist William Allen White complained that Hughes "was expected to produce an issue large enough to unite the Republican and Progressive parties" but descended into carping criticism instead. Moreover, he sounded like "a businessman's candidate . . . always clinging to the status quo like a sick chicken to a hot brick." After the speech, TR was swamped by well-wishers and followed to his car by such a huge crowd that he had to walk in the street.[28]

Wilson used a simpler, more positive, more congenial approach. Speaking a month after Hughes, the president could answer Hughes while establishing his own tone and agenda. He purposely delayed speaking until he could get additional progressive acts passed by Congress. Wilson was also helped by a lull in the Mexican conflict and the temporary suspension of submarine warfare by Germany. Two rousing speeches at the Democratic nominating convention established the campaign slogan "He kept us out of war." Perhaps learning from Hughes's mistakes, Wilson emphasized domestic issues and put them first. His primary objective was to undercut Hughes by luring Progressives and independents away from the Republican Party. He succeeded.[29]

Wilson had already impressed Progressives by nominating Louis D. Brandeis to the Supreme Court. During an epic confirmation fight,

Wilson defended Brandeis, who was opposed not only as a liberal but also as a Jew. The president fully appreciated the significance of the Brandeis appointment, which Cooper called "one of Wilson's greatest contributions to American public life." Moreover, Wilson had a strong record to run on. Hughes may have been a past Progressive governor but Wilson was a current Progressive president. Functioning as a true party leader, Wilson pursued the New Freedom by promoting economic stability and curtailing economic abuse through the Federal Trade Commission, the Federal Reserve, and the Clayton Anti-Trust Act. In addition, he answered the call for tariff reform by establishing a commission and, for the first time since 1801, personally appearing before Congress to promote tariff reduction. Toward the end of his term, Wilson reinvented himself by adopting the progressive mantle as his own. Just as he had developed the New Freedom to counter TR's New Nationalism, now he implemented much of the New Nationalism in order to defeat Hughes.[30]

The new bills were passed just as the campaign began. Farmers benefitted from a new Farm Loan Act, a warehouse system, and agriculture extension programs. Workers received accident compensation, strike mediation, and limits on child labor. The income and inheritance tax promoted fairness and reduced the need for tariff revenue. Now the Democrats seemed to be the real party of positive government and social justice while the Republicans were mired in an outdated, elitist past as the party of business. Progressive intellectual Walter Lippmann was impressed by Wilson's "extraordinary growth" in office. The major problem for Hughes was not that he had become more conservative but that Wilson had become more liberal. As Wilson put it, "We have in four years come very close to carrying out the platform of the Progressive Party as well as our own; for we also are progressives."[31]

Wilson defended himself on foreign affairs. He seized the moral high ground regarding Mexico and the way he had defused the latest crisis. Cleverly addressing both sides of the preparedness debate, he reaffirmed neutrality in the European war along with "reasonable" preparedness by strengthening the Army, Navy, Merchant Marine, and National Guard (all of which Hughes supported). Wilson took credit for securing Germany's suspension of submarine warfare. Most important, he offered a vision of America's postwar leadership as a beacon of "justice [and] the essential rights of men" (which sounded just like Hughes). Branding the Republicans as old and out of touch, Wilson proclaimed that "a new age, an age of revolutionary change, needs new purposes and new ideas" (another Hughes theme). Responding to Root's denigration of Democratic policy as "Little Americanism," Wilson upheld his partisans as "Americans for Big America," a nation "generous and just and to whom humanity is dearer than profit or selfish power." The speech was a resounding success. It embodied, wrote historian Arthur S. Link, an "open, unreserved and unabashed espousal of internationalism abroad and bold, nationalistic progressivism at home." Hughes was outclassed.[32]

More than outclassed, he was totally unmoored. The fundamental problem was that Hughes shared Wilson's commitment to progressivism and internationalism. But, as Wilson's opponent, he could not afford to articulate it forcefully. The more inspiring Wilson was, the less inspiring Hughes seemed. During his first term, wrote Throntveit, Wilson had developed into one of the nation's "most radical presidents" by translating progressive theory into concrete reforms. Now, he offered an international version of progressivism that applied its ethical commitments to a just world where consultation and cooperation would replace conflict. It represented the nation's first "genuinely internationalist foreign policy." Hughes would later pursue these objectives as secretary of state. For the moment, however, he was in an intellectual and political bind.[33]

The rest of the campaign followed suit. Wilson took the offensive and kept Hughes on the defensive. The president selected a superb campaign manager, personally participated in planning, and periodically delivered effective speeches from his rented home in Shadow Lawn, New Jersey. Busy as president, Wilson only traveled to the most competitive states. Secretary of State William Jennings Bryan spoke for Wilson in the West and Midwest where he was still popular and where anti-war sentiment was strong.

Previewing the modern press secretary, Wilson's secretary held two daily press briefings, distributed presidential messages ahead of time, and arranged for journalists to travel with the president. The Democratic campaign office disseminated clear, concise press releases across the country, especially through the Hearst papers. Pro-Wilson ads appeared everywhere—in newspapers and magazines, on billboards and electric street signs, in streetcars and subway stations. They demonized Hughes as a New York plutocrat and warmonger while extolling Wilson as the benign savior of peace and protector of families. Hughes knew that these ads hurt him. TR called the Democratic campaign "the most brilliant achievement in the history of American politics."[34]

Hughes tried hard, traveled widely, and spoke daily. According to Taft, he was still a good campaigner: "He is not an academic stylist like Wilson, but he is a much harder hitter." Nonetheless, the campaign was so mismanaged that Hughes's speeches were often not covered by the press. His campaign ads lacked the punch of Wilson's. For example, one ad urged voters "to *THINK* before voting for Wilson" and criticized Wilson for violating checks and balances. While Wilson appealed to emotions, Hughes characteristically appealed to reason. His ads were heavily verbal with a few stilted photographs. Attacking the president's "Prevarications, Procrastinations and Vacillations" was too cerebral and abstract. The slogan "Proper Protection Provides PERMANENT Prosperity" was alliterative but boring. Republican ads warned of economic disaster after the war when European goods would flood unprotected American markets. Because Hughes feared offending either the regular Republicans or the Progressives, he avoided bold visions and attacked Wilson on small issues. Wilson's advisor, Colonel William M. House, called him the "national scold."[35]

Hughes recognized the shortcomings of his early speeches and quickly resumed tactics that he used as governor to be funny and personable. He engaged directly with supporters by shaking hands, laughing, and kissing babies. One North Dakota farmer was surprised enough to exclaim, "Gosh, he ain't so unhuman after all." Regularly heckled by Democrats, Hughes insisted that they be allowed to speak, answered them courteously, and won over previously hostile audiences. When he traveled east at the end of October, crowds waited in the street to see him, overflowed the halls, and demonstrated wildly as he appealed to patriotism and American democratic ideals. Others applauded his oratorical skills. "Nobody shoots out thought after thought, idea after idea, with more marvelous clarity or rapidity," said a Nebraskan. "There is a rhythm to it all, a grammatical perfection and rhetorical mastery that catches the ear and transfixes the mind." The Republican press concluded that Hughes had definitively eradicated his image as "a cold man."[36]

Hughes maintained a sense of perspective about his role as a campaigner. After watching his first campaign movie, Hughes good-naturedly quipped that the film motivated him to vote for Wilson. His wife, Antoinette, helped soften his image. Ever gracious, she accompanied him on twenty thousand miles of campaign tours, the first candidate's wife to do so. During his speeches, she sat in the first row, refusing to sit on the stage lest she be distracting. When she was not urging her husband to rest, she was pouring tea for local women's groups or serving juice and cookies to journalists on the campaign train. Overcoming her delicate, shy demeanor, she attended every rally, descended into a copper mine, and climbed the Rockies. To Hughes, she was "the greatest asset of the Republican Party."[37]

Taft was supportive. Perhaps returning the favor from the 1908 campaign, he went on a speaking tour and wrote a vigorous defense of Hughes for *The Yale Review.* However, he just reinforced Hughes's old-line conservative image. In October, Root gave a rousing speech to two thousand Republicans in Carnegie Hall. In early November, Barnes surprised New Yorkers by enthusiastically introducing Hughes at a packed Albany rally. Just before the election, sixty-five thousand people marched in a parade for Hughes and fifteen thousand rallied at Madison Square Garden. His horoscope and the betting odds were favorable.[38]

TR complicated the campaign by advocating aggressive policies towards Mexico and Germany. For example, on November 3, right before the election, TR gave what Gould called "one of the most scathing diatribes any former president ever directed against an incumbent." Playing on Wilson's summer home in Shadow Lawn, TR evoked "the shadows of men, women, and children who have risen from the ooze of the ocean bottom and from graves in foreign lands; the shadows of the helpless whom Mr. Wilson did not protect." The crowd exulted but the speech antagonized many Midwestern voters, including German Americans who wanted to avoid war. TR's volatile speeches fed fears that Hughes was equally militaristic and would be TR's tool if victorious. Careful to avoid statements he might later regret and unable to control TR's torrents, Hughes repeatedly declared himself a "man of peace." He later admitted that the former president was "not altogether helpful."[39]

The Democrats capitalized on the situation with a pithy campaign slogan defining the choice between "Wilson and Peace or Hughes and War." To be sure, Wilson himself doubted that the nation could avoid war and, in 1916, secured two congressional acts designed to strengthen the Army and Navy. The slogan was ironic because, as historian Adam Tooze pointed out, Wilson was actually reversing traditional Democratic Party policies by emphasizing global interdependence and anticipating global involvement. Nonetheless, many voters clung to the promise of peace. Democratic ads reminded the voter, "You are working, not fighting; alive and happy, not cannon fodder." The press heightened public anxiety with vivid reports of every battle and every ship torpedoed with American passengers on board. Wilson tapped into American pro-British sentiment by refusing the support of an aggressively pro-Irish group. German Americans initially preferred Hughes to the pro-English Wilson but were so offended by TR's vitriol that many voted for Wilson.[40]

Hughes vociferously rejected unfounded accusations that he made secret deals with Irish Americans and German Americans. He declared, "I am an American, free and clear of all foreign encumbrances" and asserted that "We have but one country and we will not tolerate any division of allegiances." His rousing patriotic speeches inspired enthusiastic demonstrations as he proclaimed, "It is the love of country, not the love of dollars, that will make America great." Articulating one of his fundamental principles, Hughes affirmed that "you cannot strike a blow at one group without injury to all. Common justice and fair play will settle our difficulties, if suspicion and bitterness are let alone." Still, the emotional war of words over "hyphenism" and patriotism raged on. In a time of great uncertainty, both sides appealed to what they hoped would be a reassuring, if vague, sense of "Americanism."[41]

Hughes's major domestic issue was the protective tariff. It seemed like a good choice because Wilson was a free trader and protection was a standard Republican plank that might unify the party. To Hughes, protection was a prolabor policy essential for national prosperity and high wages. Although often categorized as a high protectionist, he supported a tariff commission to eliminate excessive rates and special privileges while safeguarding wages and improving the conditions of labor. Therefore, Hughes called himself a "tariff reform protectionist." He recommended an expert commission to revise the tariff "fairly, promptly, without log-rolling [or] political maneuvering, but in the interest of the American people as a whole." Careful "tariff revision" would avoid the "tariff revolution" that a Democratic revenue tariff would create. His objective was to "safeguard" American industry, its workers, and the American standard of living. Republican ads in 1916 claimed that protection was the expression of "True Americanism."[42]

Here again, Wilson undercut Hughes by creating his own commission of experts and getting Congress to lower Taft's high tariff. The lost revenue was replaced with an income tax, which Hughes had originally criticized on technical grounds, again fortifying his conservative image. Harding admitted that Wilson "has stolen some of our campaign thunder." Besides, the tariff was so standard and stale that it lacked political appeal, especially during a period of prosperity. To William Allen White, Hughes "talked tariff like Mark Hanna. He talked of industrial affairs like McKinley." Inadvertently, Hughes reinforced all the negative connotations of the Republican Party as the party of business. Because his other domestic platform—economical, efficient, honest administration—was equally uninspiring, his Progressive credentials were lost in the shuffle.[43]

Not only was Hughes unable to campaign on the Progressive program that Wilson had appropriated but he undercut his own Progressive labor record. The issue was the administration's policy concerning railroad workers as embodied in the 1916 Adamson Act. Hughes was not against limiting workers' hours or raising their wages. But he opposed capitulating to the demands of labor and rushing the bill through Congress as an emergency in order to avoid a national railroad strike after months of failed attempts at arbitration.

Hughes criticized Wilson for not using the delay to properly study the case. "We should have investigation before legislation, not legislation before investigation." So had he preached and practiced as governor when vetoing bills that arbitrarily set railroad fares prior to Public Service Commission (PSC) review. Moreover, Hughes also pointed out that the Adamson Act only affected a small class of railroad men and did not really grant them an eight-hour day. It only increased their wages, which meant higher fares for the public. Libertarians, like law professor Richard Epstein, might add that it reflected the kind of "special interest" protection of labor that was condoned by the 1914 Clayton Antitrust Act. After being attacked by labor leader Samuel Gompers on this issue, Hughes retorted with his old fervor: "Show me an abuse, and I will do my share toward cutting it out. I have done that before in public life and I have not forgotten how."[44]

Hughes called Wilson's sudden support for an eight-hour day "political expediency at the expense of public welfare," a poorly disguised effort to win the labor vote. Finally, he thought he had a good campaign issue and resolved "to press it constantly." After all, he had achieved major labor reforms as governor, including an eight-hour day for railroad workers. In addition, he had ruled for labor on the Supreme Court, including the right to organize. Hughes had a long-standing commitment to "wholesome conditions of work, adequate opportunities for education and recreation, reasonable hours of work, proper wages." The Adamson Bill and "the phrase eight-hour day," he said, was being used "to tickle the public ear in order to establish something quite different."[45]

In the end, tickling worked and criticizing the Adamson Act backfired. While alienating labor and Progressives, Hughes seemed narrowly technical and reactionary. By contrast, observed Cooper, the act was "the boldest intervention in labor relations that any president had yet attempted." Subsequent labor support for Wilson in Ohio enabled the Democrats to carry that key Midwestern state for the first time in twenty-four years and to begin building a new Democratic coalition.[46]

Further complicating matters, the Adamson Act controversy stimulated a surge of corporate contributions to the Republican Party, thereby cementing its connection to big business. As Cooper put it, "the Republican Party had been made safe for conservatism." With Republicans condemning the eight-hour law as "class legislation," Hughes was tied ever tightly to the plutocrats. To be sure, he lawyered for big business, but he also fought big business, especially their political influence. After the insurance investigations, his proposal to limit corporate campaign contributions became law in New York State and a model for fifteen other states as well as the federal government. Hughes was never as conservative as this campaign made him seem. However, it reinforced the negative image that plagued him throughout his political career, much to the delight of his 1916 opponents as well as his past and future critics.[47]

There was an even larger issue at stake. Reflecting his own convictions, the legalistic school of thought, and basic Progressive concepts, Hughes urged, "Let us get rid of class antagonisms by the spirit of justice. There is no hope for America if class is divided against class." As always, he insisted that economic policies should be based on facts with fairness to everyone—labor, management, and the public. Gould suggested that Hughes's emphasis on harmony marked a fundamental difference between the parties. It contrasted with the Democrats' newfound recognition of and commitment to mitigating class conflict through the very progressive policies that Hughes endorsed. For Gould, the Democrats' ideological reorientation defined party identity for the twentieth century—one as prolabor and the other as pro-business. Perhaps the contrast would not have been so stark if Hughes had won because he always sought balance between labor and capital. Moreover, his past support for pro-worker legislation and other social reforms revealed that he recognized class conflict. Thus, the Republican Party missed an opportunity to face reality and broaden its base.[48]

On woman's suffrage, Hughes was more progressive than Wilson and even his own party, which joined the Democrats in leaving the issue to the states. By contrast, the Progressive Party endorsed national suffrage in 1912, the first significant party to do so. Whereas Hughes (and Antoinette) supported a national suffrage amendment, Wilson, a Southerner, considered it a states' rights issue until after women's contributions to World War I. In 1916, a cartoonist depicted Hughes wooing the woman's vote while a dismayed Wilson looked on (see figure 5.2). Marking a turning point in the suffrage struggle, both major parties competed for women's votes.[49]

Seizing the opportunity, in early October the suffragists sent Inez Milholland, "the most beautiful suffragette," on a tour supporting Hughes in the West where women already had the vote. A Vassar graduate with a New York University law degree, Milholland worked with suffrage leaders Alice Paul and Harriot Stanton Blatch. They used female stereotypes of beauty to disarm their critics and draw attention to their cause while undermining those stereotypes by promoting the vote. Visiting over twenty-five cities, Milholland won extensive press coverage. Tragically, the trip exacerbated her fragile health. Although a misdiagnosed blood condition increasingly sapped her strength, Milholland pushed on. However, she never made it beyond Seattle, where she died in a hospital at the end of November and became a legend.[50]

In a less spectacular way, Frances Kellor, a prominent reformer who served in Hughes's New York State administration, led the official Republican women's committee. A separate unofficial committee of Progressive women mirrored the larger divisions in the party. The official committee was backed by a cross section of socialites, social workers, reformers, suffragists, labor organizers, and writer Mary Antin. They issued a campaign bulletin that emphasized Hughes's liberal credentials as governor and on the Court, especially concerning labor. They also sponsored a controversial campaign train trip across the country. Democrats dubbed it the Billion Dollar Special and attacked the "Hughesettes" as spoiled Eastern ladies presuming to tell poorer Western women how to vote. The press relegated the train to the society pages and it was dismissed as a symbol of "fuss, feathers, and femininity." In Chicago, hostile crowds threw eggs at the women.[51]

Figure 5.2. "The Political Debutante" by Kenneth Russell Chamberlain. *The Evening Sun*, July 24, 1916.

They fought back, listed their nonelite members, organized hundreds of meetings attended by thousands of women, rich and poor. To Kellor, this "big, courageous national experiment" revealed women's capacity for constructive political participation and livened up "a lifeless campaign." But the women were hampered by lack of support and funding from the patronizing regular Republican Party organization. Albeit well meant, the effort hurt Hughes in California and other western states where many women voted for Wilson. So, too, Jane Addams and Ida Tarbell, who promoted Hughes for president in 1908, supported Wilson because of his positions on progressivism and peace, despite his suffrage stand. Significantly, Hughes was later retained by suffragists fighting endless legal challenges from anti-suffragists.[52]

As always, race was controversial. Already having difficulty steering around intraparty division, Hughes avoided this additional conflict. His record was mixed. As governor, he promoted Booker T. Washington, spoke at Tuskegee, and supported Washington's work thereafter. However, he did not make African American appointments as governor, ostensibly because he refused to make appointments based on identity. Several of his most important opinions as associate justice condemned racial oppression and discrimination. But, in 1916, he only met with a group of prominent African American men once and addressed an African American audience once.[53]

At first, Washington's nemesis W. E. B. Du Bois, scholar and a founder of the National Association for the Advancement of Colored People (NAACP), backed Hughes. He could not ignore Wilson's ties to the Solid South nor his record of segregating government offices, restaurants, and restrooms. In addition, Wilson fired or demoted African American government workers and showed the racist film *The Birth of a Nation* in the White House. Although Du Bois regretted having endorsed Wilson in 1912, he was skeptical of Hughes.

Accordingly, Du Bois recommended not voting or voting Socialist. Meanwhile, Wilson's supporters appealed to white voters by suggesting that African Americans were migrating north not just for work but to commit voter fraud. They inaccurately claimed that as governor, Hughes had fired all African American officeholders. Most, including Du Bois, supported him anyway because, said abolitionist Charles Sumner's son, Wilson "brought Jim Crow to the national Government."[54]

To some degree, Hughes may have suffered from denial. Although supporters urged him to diversify his speeches, he was convinced that that they were being well received and that his Western trip was "a great success." However, he sensed problems and considered replacing Willcox with Hitchcock. The situation was so bad that Senator Wadsworth asked Harvey Hinman, an old New York State ally, to urge changing campaign managers. Hughes listened and even admitted that the campaign was faltering. However, he was so reluctant to confront Willcox himself that he sent Hinman instead. Deceived by victory in Maine's early voting, Hughes decided not to abandon his old friend. Once again, he revealed his limitations as a politician. He refused to be strategic if it meant being disloyal. Principle trumped pragmatism.[55]

Hughes also mismanaged his relationship with the Republican Party's Progressive wing. He initially reached out to state Progressives and insisted that regular and Progressive Republicans be balanced on all campaign committees. However, he backed off when intrastate factionalism proved too hot to handle and accepted Willcox's decision to work through the regular Republican state organizations, the official arms of the party. Of course, this policy offended Progressives, many of whom switched to Wilson. Consequently, Hughes became tethered to the Old Guard of the Republican Party against which he fought so bitterly as governor. Not only did he fail to exert party leadership personally, but he did not direct Willcox (who was not a party politician either) to use the party structure to build critical popular support.[56]

These decisions proved politically disastrous when Hughes visited California for two days in August. Making "mistake after mistake," wrote historian George E. Mowry, "no presidential candidate ever managed to alienate so many voters within so short a time." Because all efforts to balance the California factions failed, Hughes chose to remain neutral. As a presidential candidate trying to unify the Republican Party, he thought he should not take sides in state conflicts.[57]

The situation in California was particularly delicate. The regular Republicans, led by conservative railroad magnate William H. Crocker, kept Hughes away from the Progressives, led by Hiram Johnson. Facing a tough primary fight for the Senate, Johnson was more mercurial than ever. Willcox was advised to postpone the visit until after the primary but refused. So, too, Hughes was urged to endorse Johnson but refused, saying, "I should be yellow—even dishonest—if I play favorites in California simply because of Johnson's popularity . . . even if it should mean my defeat." Hoping to stay above the fray, Hughes declared in his opening San Francisco speech, "With local differences, I have no concern." To Johnson and the Progressives, however, their local struggle was an important part of the national struggle between Progressive and regular Republicans. Hughes's idealism proved impractical and counterproductive, just as Barnes predicted.[58]

Hughes also offended local labor unions when he spoke to businessmen at a restaurant where, unbeknownst to him, scabs were replacing striking waiters. Most unfortunate, he missed an opportunity to greet Johnson when they were both briefly in the same hotel. Ever cordial, Hughes would certainly have done so if he had known about it, but the Crocker forces did not tell him. Johnson knew Hughes was there but was so angry about his people being shunned by Croker that he kept his distance. When Hughes discovered the error, he telegrammed Johnson himself, sent one of his aides to apologize, and asked Johnson to chair an upcoming campaign event. Johnson rejected that offer as well as another to exchange reconciliation telegrams. He supported Hughes officially, but never mentioned him in his many Senate campaign speeches. The situation was so bad that the campaign asked Hitchcock for help but the damage had been done. Hughes vociferously denied having snubbed Johnson and even penned an addendum to his *Autobiographical Notes* emphasizing the point. Nonetheless, this disastrous trip is credited with costing Hughes crucial popular support in California.[59]

The Verdict

The election results supported that interpretation. On Tuesday, November 6, Hughes had an early lead in the industrialized, heavily Republican East and eastern Midwest. Several newspapers quickly announced his victory. But on Wednesday his margin shrank as results came in from the solidly Democratic South. Wilson also gained in the usually Republican Midwest where prosperity, recent farm bills, and peace sentiment were important. Due to delayed returns from the West, the nation was on edge until Friday. By then Wilson had won California by three thousand votes, enabling him to carry the Electoral College by twenty-three votes and the popular tally by five hundred thousand votes.[60]

Evaluating the election results must include California's Socialists, many of whom voted Democratic as did many Western women offended by the "Hughesettes" and upset by the prospect of war. Other women voted for Wilson and peace despite Hughes's support for women's suffrage. Because the Republicans overestimated their strength in the East, Hughes failed to campaign aggressively in the West, except for Michigan, which he carried. William Allen White pointed out that Western Republicans split their ticket to support Republican governors and legislators while rejecting Hughes in favor of the seemingly more progressive Democrat. In addition, labor issues and Prohibition probably cost Hughes Ohio, which had enough Electoral College votes to beat Wilson, even without California. Similarly, the tally was so close in three small states that they could have made the difference. For example, Hughes lost New Hampshire by only fifty-six votes. It was the tightest presidential election since 1896 and the most suspenseful since 1888.[61]

Wilson's victory was dramatic. It surprised everyone, including the president, particularly after the early Republican victory in Maine. Wilson was so prepared to lose that he considered appointing Hughes secretary of state, resigning from the presidency, and getting everyone else in the line of succession to resign so that Hughes could immediately take charge of the European crisis. As it turned out, Wilson won more votes than in 1912, making him the first Democrat to be reelected since Andrew Jackson.

Defections of Republican Progressives and independents were crucial. Revealing the power of ethnic politics, the Democrats carried the Irish, Catholic, and Jewish votes. They also won the German vote over the war controversy. Despite losing fourteen congressional seats, the Democrats wove the South, the border states, the West, and part of the Midwest into a new coalition. Including farmers, workers, ethnics, women, and liberals, it challenged the traditional Republican dominance of Eastern states and previewed the even broader Democratic New Deal coalition.[62]

Hughes waited for the final results to be confirmed before officially conceding on November 22nd. But he knew the die was already cast. Reflecting on the election, he took some solace from having surpassed by about a million votes the 1912 total of votes cast for Taft and TR. He understood some of the factors that led to his defeat, especially the peace theme and the Midwestern labor vote. However, he considered the California incident "inexplicable" and told Lodge that "after Johnson's success in the primary, I supposed that California would fall in line." TR agreed. Hughes admitted his own mistake concerning the "effectiveness" of the Republican campaign. "Without disparaging the zeal, integrity, and personal devotion of William R. Willcox," he later commented, "I think that if Will Hays had been the manager of my presidential campaign, it would have been successful." (Hays ran Warren G. Harding's 1920 presidential campaign.) Ironically, Hughes was undone by his Progressive faith in nonpartisan administrative expertise and appeals to reason.[63]

Most important, Hughes was unable to put the Republican Humpty-Dumpty back together again. Out of politics for six years and inactive during the 1912 election, Hughes did not appreciate the depth and complexity of Republican factionalism in 1916. Therefore, he mistakenly thought he could rise above or avoid it. Because Hughes never was fully committed to (and was contemptuous of) party politics, he lacked the desire, skills, and contacts to master internecine warfare. Moreover, his original ambivalence about running never fully disappeared. As late as July 24, 1916, he admitted in a letter, "I did not want to leave the bench and I dreaded more than I can tell you, the sort of activity in which I am now engaged." Compelled by his lifelong sense of civic duty, he had accepted the nomination and campaigned "with earnestness and enthusiasm." It was not enough.[64]

Hughes bears responsibility for the fact that so many Progressives and independents voted for Wilson. Their defection started with his uninspiring acceptance speech and grew steadily as Hughes failed to replace Willcox or articulate a powerful positive message. Just before the election, *The Nation* called Hughes "a woeful disappointment to his friends and admirers. . . . People are bewildered. . . . It is as if one of our most treasured national assets had melted away under our eyes." Explaining why *The Nation* reluctantly endorsed Wilson, Villard blamed the "utterly stupid campaign" and suggested that if the election had been held that summer, Hughes would have won. But "everywhere he went, he lost votes." In essence, wrote William Allen White, Hughes "had committed suicide."[65]

The president's ideological shift convinced ardent Republican Progressive Bainbridge Colby to campaign for Wilson, who later appointed him secretary of state. Herbert Croly, influential editor of *The New Republic,* abandoned the Republicans after Wilson adopted progressivism. In his opinion, the parties had reversed roles. Now the Democrats embraced the future while the Republicans hallowed the past. Now the Democrats were positive and specific while the Republicans were negative and vague. Now the Democratic Party was united while the Republican Party was "divided morally against itself." Under these circumstances, Croly could not "consider the nebulous reign of reason embodied in the goodwill of an ex-Justice of the Supreme Court fair compensation for the possible surrender of cherished personal convictions."[66]

Although most Progressives voted Republican, a significant minority (perhaps 15 percent) did not. They probably determined the outcome in critical states. TR wished he could have done more. Blind to his own role, he bemoaned the Republicans' internal divisions and blamed it all on weak party leadership by Taft. Significantly, Wilson expressed "sympathy" for his opponent's dilemma and recognized that Hughes "dare not have opinions [or] he would be sure to offend some important section of his following." To political scientist Betty Glad, the key variable was Hughes's personality structure, especially his puritanical disdain of politics and his "insensitivity to factions." Being cold and aloof, she said, prevented Hughes from understanding and addressing public sentiment. Be that as it may, the whole situation undermined the very forthrightness and independence that got Hughes nominated in the first place. Tantalizingly close to the highest office in the land, 1916 turned out to be the lowest point in his political career. It reduced him to being a marionette more than a man.[67]

Nor could he handle TR who was a perpetual presence in Hughes's political life, for better and for worse. After endorsing Hughes for governor in 1906, but finding him too independent, TR undermined Hughes during his first term, when he ran for a second term, when he was considered for the presidency in 1908, and during the 1916 nominating convention. Throughout the campaign, he insisted on giving bombastic, militaristic speeches that embarrassed the candidate and alienated voters. TR's true feelings surfaced after the election when he declared that the Republicans' "one chance of winning was with me." But TR just might have handed Wilson more votes. Indeed, some New York women who supported Hughes sent TR a sarcastic telegram thanking him for helping elect Wilson.[68]

Yet, TR had rallied to Hughes's support during critical moments of his governorship and they shared most policy objectives. For all the tension between these two strong, independent men, there was also a good deal of mutual respect. Hughes frequently sent TR notes of thanks and appreciation for which TR seemed genuinely grateful. When Hughes eulogized TR at a memorial service in 1919, he praised TR's "unfailing faith, courage and energy . . . constant industry and self-discipline . . . sound democratic instinct, elemental virtues and wholesome living." He emphasized TR's commitment to "social betterment," reasonable regulation, efficient government, and enlightened conservation. For Hughes, TR's efforts to balance the interests of workers and employers helped avoid "class war." Above all, he extolled TR for exemplifying "the worth of character" in public service as the antidote to "tyranny of any sort," corruption by special interests, "exploitation of the weak and all injustice." Clearly, Hughes defined TR's leadership qualities in terms that reflected his own ideals. However, in 1916, he needed more of TR's realism to win.[69]

Hughes was caught between a rock and a hard place. If he talked peace, he sounded like Wilson. If he talked war, he sounded like TR. Criticizing Wilson made Hughes seem petty. Differentiating himself from Wilson made him seem reactionary. Not commenting on Wilson's progressive legislation amounted to tacit approval and left Hughes with dull domestic issues like administrative efficiency and the tariff. These standpat items aligned him with Taft and the regular Republicans, thereby further alienating Progressives. Well might Norman Hapgood, influential former editor of *Harper's Weekly*, decry the fact that "the man with the halo" offered little but the "lawyer's criticism of detail." On balance, wrote Cooper, "the most striking aspect of the 1916 election was not that Wilson won, but that Hughes almost did." Ultimately, the combined experiences of being governor and presidential candidate convinced Hughes that he was ill-suited for the rough and tumble of politics. Fortunately, he would have other opportunities to serve.[70]

Hughes took defeat in stride. When Taft apologized for urging him to leave the bench, Hughes insisted that he had "no complaints and no regrets." Once nominated, the only "honorable alternative" was to serve. After all, it was "a high privilege to be chosen to lead" the Republican Party and possibly the nation. Hughes acknowledged that the campaign was "very difficult" and full of "so many cross currents" that "at times it seemed impossible . . . to hold together the groups whose support was essential to success." Nevertheless, he later said, "I had done my best. While of course I did not enjoy being beaten, the fact that I did not have to assume the tasks of the Presidency in that critical time was an adequate consolation." Subsequent events justified his sobering thought that "the Presidency in those war years would have killed me as it killed Wilson." Accordingly, Hughes refused all efforts to draft him as a presidential candidate in 1920, when he certainly would have won.[71]

The Rebound

Hughes lost an election, not his commitment to the common good. Consequently, he reported that public service consumed "fully one-third of my time." His new law firm, including his son, mainly defended big corporations and the wealthy, often before the Supreme Court. It was in great demand and could easily have dominated his life. However, while practicing law and serving as counsel to New York City, he agreed to be president of the New York Bar Association, the New York County Lawyer's Association, and the Union League Club. He supported the Red Cross, endorsed several politicians, and gave frequent speeches, always pro bono. As a reflection of his larger commitments, he defended the United Mine Workers in several cases and became president of the Legal Aid Society. He considered that organization essential because "without opportunity on the part of the poor to obtain expert legal advice, it is idle to talk about equality before the law."[72]

When war was declared, Hughes rallied to Wilson's side, putting patriotism above party. His son served with the 305th Field Artillery. Although Hughes believed that Wilson's "He kept us out of war" slogan cost his defeat, he wanted to be helpful. His first contribution was defending the constitutionality of the draft. Focusing on congressional powers, he concluded that "the power to wage war is the power to wage war successfully." Because "there are constantly new applications of unchanged powers," he said, the Constitution "marches." Surely, the founding fathers did not want the nation to be weak in wartime. Rather, he declared, "we have a *fighting* Constitution" so that we can "fight for the freedom of our children and that hereafter the sword of autocrats may never threaten the world."[73]

This was the type of bold statement that his campaign lacked. The nation praised Hughes's position, the Supreme Court agreed with it, and Wilson appreciated it. The speech established a new paradigm for executive and legislative powers in wartime and peacetime. Legal historian Matthew C. Waxman noted that Hughes's words have been harnessed ever since for myriad purposes, including keeping troops abroad after World War II and combatting terrorism after the September 11, 2001, World Trade Center attacks.[74]

New York State's governor promptly appointed Hughes chairman of the District Draft Appeals Board for New York City. It was a complicated job that required establishing a fair appeals system, recruiting personnel, and processing over four thousand letters a day. Hughes took the job so seriously that he personally signed every decision, which meant hundreds of letters daily in quadruplicate. His efforts were supplemented by the Legal Aid Society, which provided appeals pro bono, thereby undercutting dishonest lawyers. Although his health suffered, Hughes continued working at the Draft Board while also speaking widely. He only resigned because Wilson asked him to chair a sensitive investigation of incompetence in the nation's aircraft program, a new aspect of war. As in the old gas and insurance inquiries, Hughes insisted on independence, worked furiously, and issued a final report that was controversial but definitive.[75]

Hughes's legal work involved him in several thorny political issues. On the one hand, he refused a huge fee from the liquor industry to challenge Prohibition. Although Hughes disapproved of the Eighteenth Amendment and occasionally drank himself (only in embassies not subject to US laws), he insisted that the people's right to amend the Constitution must be respected. On the other hand, Hughes defended Michigan's Senator Truman Newberry, who was accused of accepting campaign contributions above the legal limit in a primary contest against Henry Ford (*Newberry v. U.S.*). The case seemed to contradict Hughes's gubernatorial crusades for limiting campaign contributions and democratizing primaries. However, he considered the senator innocent because he had not directly solicited or received the monies that other groups used in his primary, which was not even covered by the Constitution or federal law. As with the earlier debate over New York State railroad rates and subway fares, Hughes resisted letting just principles be used for unjust purposes. However, even Merlo J. Pusey suggested that "in trying to correct a personal injustice, Hughes had ignored a public wrong." Hughes won the Supreme Court case in 1921, but it forever tarnished his reputation as a champion of clean government. According to cartoonist Rollin Kirby, Hughes had whitewashed financial corruption and sanctified a villain (see figure 5.3).[76]

In 1919, Hughes accused Wilson of abusing executive power by continuing to impose federal controls over agriculture, mining, railroads, the telegraph, and collective bargaining. Now that the war was over, he urged the nation to "readjust" and make sure "not to use war powers to control peace conditions." Instead of presidential fiat, all proposed changes should be discussed in Congress, which should formulate "a sensible plan of regulation" and "trade agreements which are helpful alike to the manufacturer, the consumer, and the laborer." The nation had to move forward carefully. Previewing his positions as secretary of state, he observed, "We emerge from the war with a new national consciousness." It is "a consciousness of power . . . a consciousness of the possibility and potency of cooperation." But power must be used constructively at home and abroad lest the war to make the world safe for democracy undermine democracy itself. If war was intended to replace tyranny with reason and justice, we should start at home. Otherwise, he asked, "In saving the world, have we lost our Republic?"[77]

Hughes's most important postelection political effort concerned civil liberties. It was not just a case but a cause. On the eve of war in 1917, Wilson himself had predicted that the "brutality" of war would promote "illiberalism at home," making people "forget" about "tolerance, . . . free speech and the right of assembly." That was exactly what happened as the Red Scare led to government raids and arrests of any association or individual considered radical. Reflecting that repressive spirit, in 1920 the Republican-dominated New York State Assembly ejected five legally elected New York City Socialists, two of whom had served previously and all of whom had been sworn in at the beginning of the session.[78]

Although Hughes was facing a family crisis, he immediately wrote the Assembly Speaker to protest against depriving citizens of their right to elect representatives of their own choosing and then depriving those representatives of their right to serve without any evidence of crime or intention to commit a crime. In the process, sixty thousand New York City voters lost their right to representation. Broad accusations that Socialists wanted to overthrow the government were invalid, wrote Hughes, unless corroborated by hard evidence directly tied to the accused and by conviction in court. The Speaker was unmoved. So, Hughes called a special meeting of the New York City Bar Association to discuss the matter. After some debate, a lawyer's committee headed by Hughes was formed to testify before the State Assembly's Judiciary Committee, which had put the five Socialists "on trial."

After being prevented from speaking, Hughes filed a brief affirming that "if a majority can exclude the whole or part of a minority because it deems the political views entertained by them as hurtful, then free government is at an end." In fact, he wrote, there was nothing more American than peaceful political activism via the ballot. Hughes's protest became front-page news and was supported by the public, including conservative groups. Undeterred, the Assembly not only maintained the expulsions but outlawed the Socialist Party altogether. Hughes continued speaking out against "administrative caprice" and for the principle "that no one, however poor, friendless or accused, shall be deprived of

Figure 5.3. "Sanctified" by Rollin Kirby. *New York World*, August 22, 1922.

liberty without due process of law." Based on this incident, law professor Zachariah Chafee credited Hughes with helping turn the tide against the Red Scare and called him "the champion of American liberties."[79]

It was a fitting way for Hughes to end his public service as a politician. He was always strongest acting forthrightly for a lofty principle and inspiring others to follow his lead. Because he was motivated by duty and ideals, he remained steadfast, even in the face of criticism, exhaustion, and defeat. His hard-charging, hard-working, perfectionist character strengthened his independent streak. Although these qualities got him elected governor twice, they made governing complicated and contentious. Hughes met some of the greatest tests of leadership by taking controversial positions and challenging the status quo in the interests of the public good as he saw it. Overcoming significant obstacles, he managed to make major improvements in the state's administration, politics, and response to industrialism. But he never was (or wanted to be) a true party leader and remained aloof from party politicians.

The problem was that running for president placed him in the role of party leader, undermined his independence, and exposed his weakness as a conventional politician. Hughes was ambitious and welcomed power, but he was not so ambitious as to embrace the methods usually used to get and retain power. Although Hughes was dedicated to the Republican Party, he constantly criticized it and offended its entrenched leaders. Being governor significantly expanded his political skills, albeit not enough to win in 1916. That was largely why he rejected all suggestions to run again in 1920, when the nation was eager to elect a Republican after eight Democratic years. Hughes even refused to be the keynote speaker at the Republican nominating convention lest he seem to be a candidate. Instead, he endorsed Warren G. Harding and campaigned for him.[80]

In 1916, Hughes was buffeted by party politics. Outfoxed by Wilson's progressivism and outdone by TR's militarism, he floundered. The moment required Hughes to be the kind of party leader he had never been and refused to be. His political ideals were dwarfed by political realities. As internal Republican Party power struggles overwhelmed appeals to reason, Hughes proved to be an impractical idealist. Yet, he was humble enough to learn from his mistakes, push forward when possible, and accept defeat when necessary. Instead of letting failure breed embittered withdrawal, Hughes continued contributing to society in myriad ways. Always believing, as he said in 1910, that the "final test" of political leadership and statesmanship was serving "the public interest," Hughes's dedication to democratic ideals and practices kept him engaged, relevant, and prominent. Therefore, Perkins concluded that, in his lifetime, Hughes was "the most distinguished Republican in the United States."[81]

6 | Becoming Secretary of State, 1916–1921

A public officer has always got to remind himself, and he ought to say every morning as he approaches his task, "I am a servant and it is my business to see what I can do for the American people. I am not a boss, and my little authority or great authority that I happen to have for a day, is not a personal perquisite."
—Charles Evans Hughes, 1922

The Challenge

Charles Evans Hughes made this comment one year into his 1921 to 1925 term as secretary of state for Republican presidents Warren G. Harding and Calvin Coolidge. The occasion was a conference with the department's press corps, which presented him with a pair of golden shears. It was, they said, "a token of their gratitude for your kindly assistance" since assuming office. Even more, they wanted to convey their "personal esteem, regard and affection." Hughes was touched. Not missing a beat, he pointed out that they were the only people associated with a civil service department who were "appointed without examination, and for the purpose of examination and cross-examination." Symbolically, the shears were supposed to help Hughes untie the Gordian knots of diplomacy. But he planned to use them to "clip industriously" from their articles the "fair and impartial impressions" that "will keep me duly humble."[1]

This episode revealed much about Hughes, his role as secretary of state and the nature of his statesmanship. Here we see Hughes, the person, mixing formality with humor and humility. That was always his style, but now he was being criticized less harshly than when he was governor or presidential candidate. In his opinion, he had not changed. He still was motivated by a commitment to public service. He still prioritized public integrity, efficiency, and expertise. He still understood that the press molded public opinion. And he still had that twinkle in his eye. Perhaps it was just being free from guerilla warfare with New

York State bosses or the sobering legacy of six years on the bench and a bruising presidential campaign. In any case, his new job required a new style, a shift from being a "fighting governor" and discerning jurist to being a strategic diplomat. "I have a good laugh every once in a while," he admitted, "when I read about the efforts of the new Hughes." It was, he noted, "a great privilege to be pleasantly rediscovered."[2]

We also see Hughes, the public servant. In every career, he understood the possibilities and the limits of power. To be sure, he enjoyed wielding power, but he viewed it as a responsibility and an opportunity, rather than a tool for self-aggrandizement. He was not a transactional leader always making deals for personal benefit. Nor was he a transformational leader advocating major changes to the body politic. Rather, in foreign policy as in domestic policy and on the US Supreme Court, Hughes was a structural reformer using his progressive principles to modernize existing systems and traditional commitments. The question was whether these attributes strengthened or undermined his role as a statesman.[3]

What is a statesman? Eighteenth-century British philosopher Edmund Burke penned the classic definition. Because "a state without means of change is without means of its own conservation," he concluded that "a disposition to preserve and an ability to improve, taken together, would be my standard of a statesman." Accordingly, statesmen had to negotiate change and continuity, ideals and realities. They had to be both of and beyond their eras. Seeking such balance is inherently complicated and exposes statesmen to criticism, frustration, and often failure. Moreover, historian William C. Widenor cautioned that in a democracy, a "statesman could not long pursue a course counter to the public inclination without damaging the whole political fabric." Thus, a positive relationship with the public and the press was crucial for democratic statesmanship. Looking at how Hughes approached the post–World War I world reveals how well he managed to resolve these dilemmas.[4]

Political scientist Betty Glad contended that Hughes was not a statesman because he was too psychologically constrained and intellectually limited to handle the present and anticipate the future. Moreover, she claimed that he never understood twentieth-century international power politics. Similarly, historian John Chalmers Vinson praised Hughes as a good administrator but concluded that he "fell short of true statesmanship because he lacked boldness, imaginativeness, and even more, an auspicious era in which to perform." Both scholars thought Hughes's diplomacy was managerial rather than visionary and, therefore, not statesmanlike.[5]

Hughes himself defined "the highest task of statesmanship" in terms of "the constant effort . . . to diminish among peoples the disposition to resort to force, and to find a just and reasonable basis for accord." Peace was his priority, but it had to be achieved "through agreement, not through force." It demanded deft diplomacy between nations complemented by responsive, effective communication within the nation. Like his pursuit of "daylight government" in the statehouse, Hughes wanted to be "open, candid, direct . . . to the utmost practicable extent" in the State Department. He understood that because Americans "have only begun to think internationally," they were "ill-adjusted to the magnitude of our financial power" and new world role. Therefore, the secretary should help the public understand the issues at stake. "If we are to have peace." he said, "we must develop a public sentiment which will aid in. . . . facilitating the practical arrangements that make for the adjustments of peace." All his prior experiences confirmed that "misinformation is the public's worst enemy."[6]

The press could help or hurt. Recalling the 1916 election, Hughes feared that particular interest groups would try to influence foreign policy so that conflicts from "the old world are reproduced on our own soil." Extreme statements in the domestic press might lead foreigners to mistake internal conflicts for external policy thereby undermining the goodwill so essential for negotiation. He knew that "war is not only possible, but probable, where mistrust and hatred and desire for revenge are the dominant motives." As he put it, "There can be no assurance of peace, and few of the necessary and just settlements which make for peace, in a world of hate." Because the press played such a vital role is educating the public, Hughes believed that the secretary's objective "should be not to see how little he can make public but how much."[7]

Accordingly, Hughes restored the State Department press conferences that Woodrow Wilson had curtailed. Reviving a strategy he used as investigator and as governor, he scheduled two press conferences a day—the first for himself and the second either for himself or his undersecretary. Always full of solid information, always a "stimulating experience," the sessions were important. In addition to the usual foreign policy reporters, chief national political correspondents broke tradition to attend regularly. The reporters felt so comfortable with Hughes that one jokingly sent him a question written in Latin. He responded immediately, also in Latin. The teacher was in his element. However, from Glad's perspective, Hughes was just trying to manipulate public opinion to suit his own purposes and blunt dissent. His real motivations were personal ambition and a need for approval.[8]

If Hughes was primarily ambitious, he would not have rejected pleas that he run for president in 1920, when a Republican was guaranteed to win. Not only had the 1916 election convinced him that he was finished with electoral politics but he was confronting two painful parental ordeals. In 1918, his daughter Elizabeth, age eleven, was diagnosed with diabetes. At the time there was no cure and life expectancy was short. The only treatment was a low-calorie diet, under which Elizabeth shrank from seventy-five to forty-five pounds over three years. The situation seemed hopeless until 1922 when insulin was discovered in Toronto, Canada. At first, the researchers refused to treat Elizabeth but reconsidered—probably after discovering her father's identity. The first American to get insulin, Elizabeth recovered, attended Barnard, married, had children, and dedicated herself to civic causes. However, she always hid her condition and removed all evidence of it from her father's papers. Consequently, we do not know how Hughes reacted but can assume that he and Antoinette endured several years of intense anxiety.[9]

While his youngest daughter was wasting away, his eldest daughter faced an even worse crisis. After graduating from Vassar College in 1914, Helen volunteered with the Young Women's Christian Association, organized girls' clubs, and visited hospitals during the 1918 influenza epidemic. That fall, she caught the flu, got pneumonia, but recuperated and resumed work in April 1919. However, after participating in a Vassar College reunion upstate, she developed advanced tuberculosis, a disease that Hughes fought as governor. Deciding to keep Helen out of New York City, Antoinette nursed her at a rented cottage in Glens Falls, Hughes's old home.

He commuted every weekend and agonized as Antoinette's letters chronicled their daughter's decline, shedding tears over the inevitable. Helen died in March 1920 at age twenty-eight. Hughes was bereft; his "ray of sunshine" had gone dark. For him, it was "the saddest of life's ironies" that she had been "a victim of devoted services." Even in his twilight years, he acknowledged that her passing "left a wound that has never healed." Although he understood that "whoever is nominated will be elected," Hughes said he was too "heartbroken" and tearfully begged not to be considered. Perhaps in grief, perhaps combining hindsight with foresight, he solemnly predicted that the victor "will not fill out his term."[10]

Four men eagerly sought the Republican nod, including Hiram Johnson, who ran as Theodore Roosevelt's (TR's) heir. After ten ballots, the last man, Ohio Senator Warren G. Harding, moved into first place amid rumors of deals made by bosses in smoke-filled rooms. Historian Andrew Sinclair suggested that the Old Guard actually opposed Harding's nomination and that he won it himself after years of wooing friends and building bridges. A handsome, skillful campaigner who charmed the electorate, Harding carried 61 percent of the popular vote, the largest majority thus far. Restoring Ohio to its status as a president-maker, his election launched Republican domination of the presidency for the next twelve years.[11]

After being elected, Harding created his cabinet. The first senator to become president, the former small-town newspaper publisher resolved to recruit the "best minds" to his administration. Maybe he also wanted to counter rumors that he was just a tool of political power brokers. Unfortunately, several positions went to old friends, but others were solid. They included Secretary of Commerce Herbert Hoover, the World War I relief administrator; Secretary of the Treasury Andrew W. Mellon, a prominent Pittsburgh banker; and Secretary of Agriculture Henry C. Wallace, a well-known farmer's advocate and journalist. Powerful political operative Will Hays became postmaster general, a key resource for patronage.[12]

Harding's biographer insists that he never considered anyone but Hughes for secretary of state, believing that "there is nobody else who is in the same class with him." According to Hoover, the new president even "seemed a little afraid of his stiff Secretary of State." Regardless, Harding asked Hughes to help him address "the problem we have to solve in dealing with our new world relationship." Historians agree that "Hughes was the most prestigious member of the cabinet, overshadowing even the President." Hughes, said historian Warren I. Cohen, gave "the entire administration an aura of solidity that no other contemporary statesman could have contributed."[13]

Unlike TR and Wilson, Harding had a modest view of the presidency. He enjoyed ceremony and popularity but preferred to negotiate and facilitate rather than initiate. Because Harding was willing to delegate responsibility to his cabinet, Hughes had more latitude over foreign policy than most secretaries of state. Upon announcing the appointment, Harding declared that Hughes would henceforth speak for the administration on foreign policy. According to Cohen, "Harding's most valuable contribution was his sensible deference to Hughes." Most newspapers praised the appointment but some senators objected because Hughes had supported the League of Nations, albeit with reservations. After the confirmation, Hiram Johnson vowed to oppose Hughes relentlessly. So would other senators who wanted to regain control over foreign policy after years of being dominated by Wilson. Fortunately, there were enough senators, including his old New York ally James Wadsworth, who supported Hughes throughout his service.[14]

Although Harding was considered an intellectual lightweight and Hughes was an intellectual heavyweight, the two got along. Harding left policy formation up to Hughes, but Hughes always consulted the president and never acted without his approval. Both were pragmatic and aware of the complex dynamics that influenced foreign policy. In a sense, Harding was more qualified than Hughes because he had served on several Senate foreign relations committees whereas Hughes had no concrete foreign policy experience. Harding had waffled on the League during the campaign and had been a reservationist but also an internationalist. Thus, he was flexible enough to be convinced by Hughes. In turn, Hughes's cautious, reasoned approach reassured Harding, who increasingly relied on Hughes. By the same token, historian Kenneth J. Grieb suggested that Harding played a larger behind-the-scenes role in foreign policy than is assumed, especially regarding Latin America. Ostensibly an odd couple, they actually complemented each other well. That was fortunate because the nation faced many difficult postwar challenges.[15]

Hughes typically worked nonstop, mastered every detail of every problem, read and signed every letter himself. An assistant reported that "even after months of experience with him, one was startled by the breadth of his knowledge, at the penetration of his intellect, at his ability to thrust unerringly and swiftly to the heart of any matter." But brains did not suffice. Speaking to newly appointed consuls and their staffs, Hughes explained that diplomacy was not just "technical and official." Nor should the nation's representatives be "flamboyant, bombastic, boastful, unreasonable, severe, autocratic." Rather, they were urged to handle problems in a "quiet and placid" manner, demonstrating "intelligence and tact . . . integrity and efficiency." These were qualities that

Hughes always pursued himself, albeit not always successfully. Although characteristically impatient with incompetence, he was equally characteristic in mending fences with a kind remark and a "booming laugh." For his loyal staff, it was a privilege "to come into contact with his mind and to observe his courage." Not just a "mental machine," one said, "I know of no more splendidly human person, no one with a bigger heart or quicker sympathy."[16]

Much of the job was social. If Hughes preferred to be working instead of entertaining, he did not show it. Rather, he and Antoinette attended dinners with the key diplomats of every mission and invited each chief diplomat to dinner in their home. With good humor, he embraced his duty to "dine for our country." In addition, he attended numerous foreign embassy celebrations, including weddings, funerals, and royal birthdays. These events were valuable not only because conversation broadened understanding but also because courtesy built "highly prized friendships" that facilitated diplomacy. In fact, he said, "An hour of direct intercourse between responsible ministers is often worth months of written communications." Issues could be clarified, mistakes avoided, national honor preserved, and agreements achieved. "The alternative of friendly settlements," he remarked, "is resort to coercion." Peace depended on the diplomat's ability to maximize "the resources of negotiation, of reason, and persuasion." It was a challenge for which Hughes was uniquely qualified.[17]

According to Charles Cheney Hyde, his solicitor and later an international law professor at Columbia, Hughes treated everyone alike, regardless of status. After being told that charwomen were taking extra work outside the State Department against civil service rules, he refused to chastise or punish them. It was a small but significant gesture of respect for all workers. "What saved him from being terrifying or forbidding," explained Hyde, was his "passion for justice" and his abiding "goodwill." Hughes exuded "the friendliness of fairness." Therefore, the job suited him well. It harnessed his work ethic, faith in reason. penchant for policy, blend of formality and humanity. Furthermore, it enabled him to implement many of the policies that he had advocated as a presidential candidate.[18]

Hughes was always an efficient administrator. He combined the diplomatic and consular services into one foreign service in order to provide more flexible job opportunities and attract better candidates. By increasing salaries and instituting pensions, Hughes elevated the status of service. Aware that the State Department was considered “a rich man’s club,” he said, "I decry” a selection process that “discriminates against the poor man of equal ability.” Accordingly, he urged his staff to reject “archaic differentiations” so that the foreign service would be open “to a young man without means.” The 1924 Rogers Act institutionalized these reforms. They reflected Hughes’s conviction that “every American should feel ashamed that any country in the world should have a better diplomatic organization than the United States.” For him, it “is not a matter simply of national pride; it is a matter of national security.”[19]

Hughes followed in the footsteps of Elihu Root, his eminent, long-time New York State friend, fellow lawyer, and public servant. As secretary of war from 1899 to 1904 and secretary of state from 1905 to 1909, Root worked closely with TR to shape America’s emergence as a world power. He strengthened the War Department and instituted civil service merit appointments. Although Root was criticized for intervening in Cuba and repressing Filipino insurgents, he promoted self-government for both nations. Root was the first secretary of state to improve relationships with Latin America. In addition, he reached important agreements with Japan, championed increased trade with China, and strengthened relations with both Great Britain and Canada. The many treaties he secured plus his work for the arbitration of international disputes earned Root the Nobel Prize for Peace in 1912.[20]

Hughes continued Root’s policies while pursuing new strategies to confront postwar problems. He shared Root’s commitment to classical legal thought, which assumed the possibility of progress, the harmony of interests, and the perfectability of humankind. Both men recognized conflict but believed that it could be managed with a more reason-based, scientific approach. They endorsed legalism, a movement committed to modernizing international law, establishing a world court, separating international policy from domestic politics, using experts to upgrade policy formation, and educating the public about the rights and responsibilities of nations. In 1906, a group of northeastern, elite, male lawyers (no women until 1921) formed the American Society for International Law (ASIL). It was funded by the Carnegie Endowment for International Peace (CEIP). Root was president of the CEIP until 1915 and the ASIL until 1924.

Hughes succeeded him as ASIL president in 1925 while still secretary of state. That overlapping role revealed the public policy influence of the legalists behind the new field of international law, which Hughes taught at Cornell. Legalists believed that international law, impartial judges, and an appreciation for international interdependence could resolve conflicts and promote peace. As historian Benjamin Coates explaines, they rejected balance of power politics grounded in coercion or the threat of coercion. Emerging from the nineteenth-century peace movement, legalism posited that nations would voluntarily accept international law if it reflected shared values, was politically neutral, and fair to all parties. By projecting a masculine image of restraint and rationalism, legalists carefully distinguished themselves from the peace movement, which they considered too emotional, unrealistic, and feminine.[21]

Legalism dovetailed with Progressivism and American values. Advancing world order through law reinforced the nation's sense of mission to spread democracy while upholding neutrality and nonentanglement. Using the US Supreme Court as a model for a world court, legalists envisioned redeeming the world. Legal principles would also justify economic expansion and foreign trade as part of a larger civilizing mission. Like Hughes, legalists were structural reformers committed to progress based on reason and responsive to current conditions. Although they retained the basic precepts of classical thought, they emphasized modernizing it. Bridging his legal interests with his new foreign policy focus, these ideas permeated Hughes's tenure as secretary of state. Indeed, said Hyde, "Law was the language that Secretary Hughes spoke."[22]

For law professor Jonathan Zasloff, that was unfortunate. He considered legalism "the greatest disaster in American diplomatic history" because it left the West unprepared for World War II. In his opinion, legalists like Hughes, "fundamentally misdiagnosed the problem" of post–World War I geopolitics. They naïvely believed that international discord could be harmonized by turning international values into international law. To Zasloff, legalism's overlap with Progressivism was a weakness, not a strength, because of the assumption that all civilized nations would accept a "logical response to international dilemmas." As World War II proved, the "paradigm of scientific management and apolitical government" was doomed to fail without "a stable balance of power." Therefore, Zasloff concluded that "Realpolitik is not a substitute for interdependence and cooperation, but their prerequisite." Hughes epitomized this problem because, said Zasloff, he was "the period's most formidable foreign policy figure."[23]

In many ways, legalism was a new version of much older ideas advanced by Hugo Grotius, the seventeenth-century jurist, philosopher, and father of international law. Part of standard legal education and the dominant theorist of war until the 1930s, Grotius famously differentiated between just and unjust wars. While the former were motivated by self-defense and self-preservation, the latter exemplified unprovoked aggression, glory, and greed. Grotius rejected the idea that people were only motivated by self-interest. Rather, he wrote, "Mankind . . . is an uncommon animal" because he seeks "society" and "tranquil association" with others. "This concern for society . . . is the source of law" as a voluntary "obligation by contract" based on reason. Thus, law was more than "utility" because it reflected the fact that the "upright" person "approves justice and condemns injustice."[24]

Grotius, wrote political scientist Steven Forde, sought a balance between "unchanging moral principles of natural law" and "a just yet flexible code of international behavior," between idealism and realism, human rights and property rights. Although nations had their own priorities, Grotius observed that even the strongest sought alliances. They too wanted a "law of nations" to preclude the barbarism of war. The point of international law was to create enough agreement so that self-interest would give way to self-restraint, offset pure power struggles, and reduce the possibility of war. But, Grotius cautioned, international law "must have its origin in free consent" based on generally accepted notions of justice without ignoring specific national interests. Only then could international law provide the basis for a society of nations.[25]

Hughes often cited and sounded like Grotius, whose ideas dominated his key 1923 speech "The Pathway of Peace." Starting from Grotius's premise that "where the power of law ceases, there war begins," Hughes outlined his core foreign policy convictions. He understood that "war is not an abnormality" but had been "the very warp and woof of human nature," civilization's scourge for millennia. Like Grotius, Hughes considered just wars a form of "self-help . . . by which injured nations protect their territory and maintain their rights." Wars became unjust when they reflected "unrestrained selfishness" based on "the principle, each nation for itself to the full extent of its power." Such wars signified "the failure of civilization itself."[26]

Instead of the "vain attempt to compel peace by force," Hughes advocated legalist solutions—conferences, arbitration, treaties, international law, and an international court. These strategies were better suited to a world increasingly interwoven by trade and all too aware of the recent "most ruinous and horrible conflict known to history." By promoting "the prevention of war," nonmilitary methods would eliminate the need for "the regulation of war." At the same time, Hughes recognized that national interests were complex and volatile. There would always be grievances ready to be "fanned into a flame" by demagogues who were "pseudo-patriots." They would be hard to control but capitulating to them assumed a perpetual struggle for power and the inevitability of war. Therefore, "the only way to make peace secure" was "to translate controversies into voluntary, reasonable agreements" based on "fairness." For Hughes, achieving a just balance between self-interest and mutual interest was the fundamental "postulate of international relations."[27]

In 1925, as president of the ASIL, Hughes linked Grotius to legalism in a speech commemorating the three-hundredth anniversary of Grotius's book on war. The lesson of the Great War, said Hughes, was that "war is not to be ended by war, that the seeds of another conflict have been plentifully sown." He fully recognized the pull of "the old human instinct" for survival, security, revenge, and power. Nevertheless, he insisted that the only real alternative to war was "progressive self-restraint" derived from a spirit of "cooperation" solidified by international law and consensual treaties. This approach would recognize different national interests but find enough "common ground" to promote mutual interests and, therefore, mutual restraint.[28]

Toward that end, Hughes called for international conferences to modernize international law, which, by reflecting "the conscience of mankind," would open the door to peace. "The reign of law, as accepted, not imposed, may be after all the most important contribution to permanent peace." The goal, he said, was not "the mere absence of war," which was inevitably "temporary or illusory." Instead, "Our chief concern is justice [and] the peace which rests on justice." That, after all, was the central "preoccupation of Grotius." For Hughes, the message of Grotius was to pursue international peace with a steady eye on national interests so that the results would be, as he said in 1923, more lasting than "perishable parchment." Hughes ardently believed that "the only pathway of peace is that in which our peoples are walking together."[29]

These statements placed Hughes at the center of debates over foreign policy during the interwar years. As an adherent of classical legal thought, albeit updated by legalism, he was assumed to be an old-fashioned idealist who failed to appreciate the realities of international conflict. Desperate for peace after World War I, the argument went, Americans in the 1920s rejected both balance of power realities and internationalism. The premise that Americans turned their backs on the world and became isolationist was debunked by historian William Appleman Williams in 1954. Nonetheless, perceptions persisted that by refusing to join the League of Nations and pursuing international treaties without enforcement mechanisms, the twenties left the door to World War II wide open. From this perspective, Vinson concluded that Hughes's acclaimed treaties provided nothing more than a "parchment peace." US foreign policy in the twenties was hopelessly misguided, incredibly naïve, and tragically blind.[30]

As previously discussed, political scientist Betty Glad applied this interpretation to Hughes by using psychological theory to describe him as narrowly conservative, moralistic, and legalistic. She also drew upon the realist school of international politics formulated by her University of Chicago mentor Hans J. Morgenthau. For him, international relations were a constant, irrevocable struggle for power determined by national self-interest. He criticized President Wilson's 1917 assertion that Americans "prefer the interests of mankind to any interest of their own. . . . We have no selfish ends to serve." For Morgenthau, such benign internationalism was as unrealistic as isolationism, which he dismissed as the complete "negation of foreign policy."[31]

George F. Kennan was another important figure of the realist school. He served in the post-Hughes State Department from 1926 to 1950 and influenced foreign policy until his death in 2005. His small 1951 book *American Diplomacy, 1900–1950* had a huge impact. Like Morgenthau, Kennan condemned "the legalistic-moralistic approach to international problems" for creating a "legal straight jacket" that was "too abstract, too inflexible, too hard to adjust to the demands of the unpredictable and the unexpected." Treaties, international law, and the League of Nations presumed "an orderly world" based on "right and wrong." They were monochromatic solutions to polychromatic problems. Depicting the 1920s State Department as "a quaint old place," Kennan viewed Hughes and Root as idealists who missed the chance to avoid another war. Nonetheless, because "there can never be any certainty about these post-mortems on history," Kennan admitted that over time we might see the 1920s "in a more charitable light." Other historians did just that and questioned viewing the 1920s through the lens of the 1930s. Historian Melvyn Leffler urged followers of the realist school to remember that "in the 1920's, there was no threat to American security."[32]

After World War I, America's new status as the world's largest economy and most powerful nation spurred a major internal struggle over the nation's international role. These discussions were clouded by a 1920 to 1921 recession, fear of competition from cheap foreign labor, anxiety about "new immigrants," and concern about the spread of Communism. Political parties, the public, and business and agricultural groups divided over foreign policy. The entire situation made the nation a "reluctant giant" and, therefore, an "uncertain giant." The problem was how to negotiate new realities while protecting old priorities. Historian Joan Hoff Wilson called the resulting balancing act "independent internationalism." As she pointed out, the desire for peace at home depended on peace abroad. So, too, domestic economic growth required international opportunities for trade and resources. Add to the mix America's sense of exceptionalism and mission to improve the world in its own image. Historian Naill Palmer considered it "probably the most complex set of foreign policy problems yet to confront an incoming administration."[33]

Hughes understood the challenge. Sounding quite realistic, he noted that "recent developments abroad have marked the passing of the old diplomacy." Therefore, it was necessary to develop "more direct and flexible methods responsive to democratic sentiment." Changing circumstances required changing strategies. After all, "foreign policies are not built upon abstractions," he said. "They are the result of practical conceptions of national interest arising from some immediate exigency or standing out vividly in historical perspective." Equally important, he understood that "when a balance of power is deemed essential to national security, you cannot conjure it away by any form of words." Consequently, because American independence was always tied to foreign interaction, "we were not isolated and could not be." We could, however, maintain "a vigorous independent policy" that would protect national needs and pursue national ideals within the context of international realities and the desire for international peace. Discussing Hughes, historian Thomas Buckley observed that "there may sometimes be a considerable amount of realism in idealism." As Hughes put it,

> The war to end all wars has left its curse of hate, its lasting injuries, its breeding grounds of strife, and to secure a lasting peace appears to be more dif-

> ficult than ever. There is no advantage to shutting our eyes to the facts; nor should we turn away in disgust of panaceas to the counsel of despair. The pathway of peace is the longest and most beset with obstacles the human race has to tread. The goal may be distant, but we must press on.

Although contemporary problems could breed "hopelessness," Hughes insisted that "this is not the end of the world. Rather it is the beginning of a new era." Thus, he embraced "taking a new case for the people in foreign affairs." His ultimate goal was to turn the Department of State into a "Department of Peace."[34]

To be sure, time undid many of his accomplishments, but Hughes is still ranked among America's best secretaries of state. One measure of success was that despite strong resistance from a Senate jealously guarding its foreign policy prerogatives, only six of the sixty-nine treaties he submitted were rejected and four of those were approved later. His basic task was to move the nation from being an uncertain, reluctant giant to becoming a constructive leader in the postwar international system. To do so, he had to show that the United States could maintain its foreign policy independence while navigating world problems. It also required meeting domestic demands with a vision and a strategy for peace that would be acceptable at home and abroad.[35]

At age fifty-nine, Hughes had his work cut out for him. As he later reflected, "It would be difficult to imagine a worse tangle in our foreign relations than that with which the Republican Administration" was confronted. Not only was the nation "still in a technical state of war" with Germany but it faced a legacy of "suspicion and distrust" with the Far East and within the Western Hemisphere, plus vociferous domestic opposition. There were many problems and few tools to resolve them. If Hughes was to meet Walter Lippman's standard for a "true statesman," he would have to "balance . . . the nation's commitments and the nation's power" by building support at home and abroad while establishing a viable equilibrium between "ends and means." Transitioning to a new role in a new era would not be easy.[36]

The League of Nations

The debate over the League of Nations, wrote historian John Milton Cooper Jr., "elicited a breadth and depth of discussion that had not arisen before and that remain unmatched since." It preceded but influenced (and interfered with) policy decisions during the 1920s. In accepting the 1916 Republican presidential nomination, Hughes called for the creation of "an international organization" to promote international justice and "safeguard so far as practicable the peace of the world." But, he cautioned, "We cherish no illusions. We know that the recurrence of war is not to be prevented by pious wishes." Therefore, Hughes recommended an international tribunal to arbitrate conflicts supplemented by international conferences "to formulate international rules" and "adapt" international law "to new conditions." It was a typically legalist platform. Acknowledging that peace was always fragile and that the United States was at a crossroads, Hughes cautioned, "There is no national isolation in the world of the twentieth century." Instead, the nation needed to pursue "practicable measures in the common interest in order to secure international justice." Based on these sentiments, Hughes supported Woodrow Wilson's proposed League of Nations. Unfortunately, a key aspect of the plan was impracticable and the president was inflexible. The result was an intense partisan policy conflict over national identity in a radically changed world.[37]

In his January 22, 1917, "Peace without Victory" speech, Wilson proposed a deliberative international body that would foster "not a balance of power, but a community of power; not organized rivalries, but an organized common peace." It was, said Cooper, "a great speech" combining idealism with realism. As the first international peace plan offered by a US president, the League of Nations earned Wilson the Nobel Prize for Peace in 1919. Both Hughes and Wilson understood that World War I had fundamentally altered international affairs and that the United States had to assume leadership for a new world order. However, Wilson was considered a transformative leader because of his bold vision for international cooperation. By comparison, Hughes seemed to be a mediator, not an innovator.[38]

In May 1917, Hughes proclaimed his support for the League of Nations. The speech was so important to him that he quoted a section in his *Autobiographical Notes.* Hughes urged the nation to be open to the "thought that America has its obligations to the world. . . . We cannot live unto ourselves." Nor would we welcome a world in which "treaties and conventions are made only to be broken." The future, he emphasized, "offers no chance for isolation to the United States." In fact, our "vast resources and extraordinary privileges" made it impossible for us to "shrink our duty to mankind." It was a matter of "self-interest as well as a proper sense of obligation" to help erect "the structure of international justice." Above all, he said, "we should not make its establishment impossible by holding aloof." Although Hughes contributed to defeating the League, for which he was criticized, he never wavered from the basic convictions expressed in this speech.[39]

Hughes joined Root and Taft in supporting Wilson's proposed League of Nations, but with important qualifications. They worried that the League might interfere with America's autonomy regarding tariffs, immigration, and the 1823 Monroe Doctrine. The biggest problem with the League Covenant was the provision for collective security in Article X, It held that the member states would unanimously decide how to defend each other if threatened by another country. Hughes immediately recognized that although most Americans favored the idea of a league, they would resist being dragged into other nations' conflicts. It was not just that they were tired of war and wanted peace. They also cherished their historic commitment to neutrality and against entangling alliances. They still believed that two vast oceans protected them from foreign aggression. Besides, the Senate would never allow any international body to interfere with its constitutional right to declare war.[40]

As president of New York City's Union League Club, Hughes called a special meeting in March 1919 to discuss Article X, which he deemed "a trouble-breeder and not a peace-maker." Anticipating that Article X would arouse fierce opposition at home, he warned that if Congress refused to authorize troops in response in a call for collective security, the United States would be defaulting on commitments incurred by League membership. In addition, Hughes considered the League proposal too inflexible in a dynamic world where borders were perpetually contested. As if predicting his actions as secretary of state, he asked, "Why not leave the future to conference and decision in the light of events?"[41]

In July 1919, Hughes rejected Wilson's concept of collective security in favor of collective cooperation and several "mild reservations" to the League. Root and Taft agreed. In 1915, Taft founded the League to Enforce the Peace (LEP), which Hughes endorsed during the 1916 campaign. Typically legalistic, it advocated the development of a binding international legal code with violators required to seek arbitration. Taft worked tirelessly to promote the LEP and the League of Nations with reservations. Concerns about enforcement kept Hughes and Root from joining LEP's executive committee. However, all three suggested a compromise whereby mild reservations would become qualifying explanations, not actual amendments to the League Covenant. Scholars called it "Republicanized Wilsonianism." Historian Stephen Wertheim even suggested that, as president, Hughes might have endorsed the LEP or the League of Nations thereby strengthening resistance to belligerence in the 1930s and perhaps changing the trajectory of world affairs.[42]

At one point, Wilson seemed open to reservations, which could have saved the League. They did not substantially undercut the League and were widely supported. Indeed, Hughes believed that there was enough popular support for the League that, "with a leadership more sensitive to public opinion," Wilson could have prevailed. Without it, Hughes continued opposing Article X in speeches, articles, and letters. He would try to provide that kind of leadership later. Driven by a sense of mission, the president insisted that the controversial Article X, which he drafted himself, stand unchanged because he believed that collective security was crucial for international peace. According to historian Hatsue Shinohara, Wilson considered it a cooperative multilateral replacement for the old balance-of-power system based on conflict-oriented, tenuous treaties between hostile nations. The League would also promote cooperation for humanitarian causes.[43]

The president did not invite any Republican, like Taft or Root, to accompany him to the Paris peace talks. He avoided Hughes because, said Wilson, there was "no room big enough" for both of them. Hughes criticized Wilson for politicizing and personalizing the League issue. Acting "only as a party leader" and rejecting cross-party opportunities for "consultation and deliberation" kept Wilson from being a leader who "represents the sentiment of this nation regardless of party." So saying, Hughes revealed the strategy he would have pursued as president and would pursue as secretary of state. However, Wilson was not entirely at fault. Some historians blamed Hughes and other prominent Republicans for failing to explain that Article X did not require military action but left strategies open to deliberation. In fact, the European negotiators themselves considered Article X nonbinding and were willing to accept reservations. Surely Hughes must have known these facts and could have informed the public accordingly.[44]

After Theodore Roosevelt (TR) died in January 1919, Wilson's fiercest opponent was Massachusetts Senator Henry Cabot Lodge, chairman of the Foreign Relations Committee, which would determine the League's fate. Like TR and Hughes, Lodge advocated preparedness for war. Accordingly, he saw the 1916 election as crucial, campaigned vigorously for Hughes, and was devastated by his defeat. Lodge felt that by leaving the Supreme Court, Hughes "made the greatest possible sacrifice" for the good of the country. Furthermore, Lodge believed that Wilson's advocacy of "the war to end all wars" was a "nauseous hypocrisy" after opposing war for over two years and campaigning on keeping America out of war. These factors strengthened Lodge's contempt for Wilson, whom he also disliked personally.[45]

As a Republican senator strengthened by Republican victories in 1918, Lodge was determined to protect his nation, his party, and the Senate's foreign policy power. He agreed with Hughes, Root, and Taft that Article X was a threat to American sovereignty and an impractical formula for peace. According to Widenor, Lodge favored a "noncoercive" League of Nations. He was "not a true internationalist, but never an isolationist" and supported imperialism in 1898. During March 1919, Lodge circulated reservations to the League and got one-third of the Senate to support them. Acknowledging the nation's desire for peace, he also promoted a resolution to divorce the peace treaty from the League. In defiance, Wilson tied the two documents closer together hoping that the League Covenant would be carried by the peace treaty.[46]

In Paris, Wilson secured changes to the League Covenant that protected a member's right to withdraw after two years, reinforced national sovereignty over domestic issues, and, for the first time, obtained international recognition of the Monroe Doctrine. Nonetheless, Lodge still claimed that joining the League would condemn the United States to "everlasting meddling in every quarrel, great and small, which afflicts the world." Wilson underestimated Lodge who skillfully used committee hearings to stall discussion and influence public opinion. He spent two weeks reading the 368-page treaty word for word to his committee, followed by six more weeks of hearings.[47]

Fourteen senators opposed the League so strongly that they were labeled "Irreconcilables" or "bitter-enders." Idaho Senator William E. Borah was the most extreme and resolved to oppose the League even "if the Savior of mankind should revisit the earth." To Wisconsin Senator William R. LaFollette, the "monstrous undertaking" of the League would require "a great standing army . . . higher taxes, higher prices, harder times for the poor." Indiana Senator Albert J. Beveridge contended that the League was "a nest of serpent's eggs" that would "denationalize the country's manhood" while empowering "international bankers." California Senator Hiram Johnson feared that further involvement abroad would preclude Progressivism at home. All celebrated American exceptionalism and agreed with Nebraska Senator George W. Norris that it was "an honor . . . to be an Irreconcilable." A cartoonist ridiculed Borah gingerly approaching and ready to pour "cold water" on a bomb representing the Peace Treaty and the League of Nations. Other Republicans hid or ran away in fear (see figure 6.1).[48]

Twelve "mild reservationists" supported the League with moderate conditions. Twenty-three "strong reservationists," including Lodge and Harding, opposed it. As independent internationalists, they did not reject world responsibility per se but wanted the United States to decide for itself when and how to become involved. Hoping to forge "a middle ground between aloofness and injurious commitments," Hughes wrote a public letter in July 1919 proposing four moderate reservations designed to bridge the mild and strong reservations. Wilson rejected all reservations on the premise that one compromise would breed another and eventually undermine the League entirely. If the mild and moderate reservationists had combined with the Democrats, the treaty and the League Covenant could have passed the Senate. But Wilson forbade cross-party compromise and threatened to crush his opponents. His obstinance, claimed Cooper, was a disastrous "missed opportunity."[49]

Wilson considered joining the League "a moral obligation." Convinced that his idealism would save the world and his eloquence would save the day, he gave forty speeches in a three-week, eight-thousand-mile train trip across the West. Cooper pointed out that it was "the most extensive effort at public persuasion that any president has ever made on behalf of a foreign policy." The Republicans sent Johnson, their best western orator, to respond at each stop. In his final, most effective speech at Pueblo, Colorado, Wilson rejected a "middle course," excoriated those who opposed the League, and insisted that joining would not compromise American independence. He extolled the mothers who sacrificed their sons to save "the liberty of the world" and urged that the nation "not go back on those boys." Eloquence notwithstanding, the trip was disastrous. Not only did Wilson become increasingly bitter but he suffered a major stroke that paralyzed him and the rest of his presidency.[50]

After two more months of acrimony, the senators voted to end debate by invoking cloture for the first time. According to Cooper, the subsequent two days of debate were "among the most momentous encoun-

Figure 6.1. "Republican Chorus: It's a Bomb" by Nelson Harding. *The Brooklyn Daily Eagle*, July 11, 1919.

ters" in the Senate's one-hundred-and-thirty-year history, as important as "the great clashes before the Civil War and during Reconstruction." The priorities of American foreign policy were at stake and emotions were raw. On November 19, 1919, in the midst of the Red Scare, fourteen Republicans and two Democrats joined to defeat the Versailles Treaty and the League Covenant. However, there was so much public clamor for some kind of treaty that the Senate reconsidered on March 19, 1920. Mentally and physically stressed, Wilson was determined to defeat "the little group of willful men" who stood in his way. He would "get their political scalps," he said, "even if I have to give my life to it." Accordingly, he ordered the Democrats to oppose the treaty with reservations. Although about half defected, the treaty failed by seven votes. Without a treaty, the United States was technically still at war. When Congress passed a joint resolution ending the war, Wilson vetoed it because he refused to make peace without the Allies. At that point, the whole matter entered presidential politics, which would determine the League's fate and shape Hughes's challenges as secretary of state.[51]

In October 1920, Hughes signed Root's Declaration of the Thirty-One prominent men who endorsed Harding in the hope that he would support the League minus Article X. However, after Harding criticized the League during the campaign, Herbert Parsons, former New York congressman and Hughes's old colleague, resigned from the Republican National Committee and other members of the LEP followed suit. Hamilton Holt, lifelong Republican and owner of *The Independent*, secured the signatures of 121 pro-League independents opposing Harding.

Although the election may have been more a rejection of Wilson than of the League, Harding thought that the Republican midterm victory of 1918, compounded by his own sweeping success, provided a mandate to oppose the League altogether. When he proclaimed the League "deceased," Lodge gloated, "We have torn up Wilsonism by the roots." The Irreconcilables threatened to obstruct all administration proposals if Hughes dared promote the League. Under these circumstances, Hughes backed off in order to protect the new administration and prevent being replaced by a real opponent of international cooperation. According to Glad, Hughes had always been ambivalent about the League anyway and "sometimes trimmed his principles for reasons of personal or party expediency."[52]

The pro-League forces would not let up. They continued criticizing

Hughes and calling for a new international peace organization, which Harding had vaguely suggested during the campaign. Considering Senate opposition, Hughes recognized that this goal was "impracticable" and that "nothing good will come of it." Indignant at the criticism and impatient with its futility, he exchanged several testy letters with Holt and others but stood his ground. Times had changed since the declaration was signed. Then, they were expressing their opinions, not making promises. Now, "the administration had to deal with the situation as it found it upon coming into power." Although "reluctant" to abandon the League, his mild reservationist Senate allies convinced him that there was only one choice. We could perpetuate controversy and "accomplish nothing," he concluded, or "we can frankly recognize the sphere of action we can usefully fill, and accomplish something." Reality, wrote historian Selig Adler, compelled Hughes to choose "the role of statesman-politician rather than that of perfectionist." He had to become as much of a diplomat at home as abroad.[53]

Embittered by their loss, the Wilson administration turned its back on the League, withdrew all US representatives, and stopped answering League mail. Soon after Hughes took office, he had the mail answered. Yet, he was cautious about communicating personally with the League and even resisted making nominations to the World Court, a body he avidly supported. Reflecting the tensions of the moment, European diplomats were reportedly met with an atypically "icy reception" in Washington. Because the Senate had declared that "the United States shall not be represented or participate in any body, agency, or commission" of the League without explicit congressional approval, Hughes began appointing "unofficial observers." They aided the League's humanitarian work concerning disease, narcotics, relief, the arms trade, pornography, and sex trafficking. The policy of engagement without entanglement was hardly a perfect solution and never mollified either his pro-League or anti-League critics. Cartoonist Rollin Kirby underlined the dilemma by depicting Hughes telling an impoverished woman representing Europe that he sympathized but could not "associate" with her. Ironically, wrote one contemporary, Hughes had to disappoint the internationalists "in order to outwit and outflank the isolationists."[54]

Looking back on the situation in the 1940s, Hughes insisted, somewhat defensively, that US participation in the League of Nations would not have prevented World War II because the Europeans themselves were divided about Italian and German aggression. He believed that

US representatives to the League would have backed Great Britain and France, especially since the American public would never have sanctioned intervention at the time. Historian Walter LaFeber suggested that the roots of World War II derived not from failing to join the League but from the 1919 Paris Treaty's approach to boundaries, reparations, and mandates, all of which bred competition and conflict. To Leffler, being outside the League may even have given the United States more flexibility in addressing postwar problems. However, a stronger League backed by the United States may also have stiffened resistance and/or deterred aggression. Overall, concluded historian Adam Tooze, the policy of "privileged detachment" was fatally flawed.[55]

In a sense, Hughes's postwar challenge was to pursue Wilsonian ends without Wilsonian means. After all, Wilson realistically understood that the old world order was dead and wanted to create a new world order based on cooperation, self-determination, and mutual respect—objectives that Hughes and most Americans shared. Wilson envisioned the United States as a world leader motivated by a moral commitment to "make the world safe for democracy"—another goal that reinforced America's sense of mission and exceptionalism. But Wilson's formula pushed the nation farther than it was ready to go regarding involvement in world affairs and collective security. Nonetheless, said historian Frank Ninkovich, Wilson was crucial to the process of "radically redefining what it meant to be a world power." He initiated a "truly exceptional" shift from prioritizing "interest as traditionally understood over thousands of years [and] opting instead to identify . . . national security with global needs." However, because Wilson was blinded by his own imperatives, Hughes had to reshape and redirect these shared objectives into more realistic forms. By pursuing what diplomatic historian Edward Rhodes called "rational statesmanship," Hughes endeavored to steer a different ship to a similar port.[56]

Ending the War

World War I destroyed the old balance of power among England, France, Germany, Austria-Hungary, and Russia. Because the United States relied on England to maintain its strength in Europe, it warranted rescuing when threatened by Germany. Although the Allies won the war, Europe was devastated and the Far East was tense. France and England were weak and the new European nations were even weaker. Germany was defeated but defiant. Russia was wrestling with revolution; Japan was aggressive; China was vulnerable. Hughes needed to defuse all of these overlapping, volatile international circumstances.

The immediate problem was how to replace conflict with cooperation from outside the League. As Hughes commented later, "Formal international organization will provide a useful mechanism to facilitate united action in the interest of peace, but will not ensure that action." Therefore, he sought alternatives to the League that could still provide alternatives to war. Hence, the importance of international tribunals of international law, international associations, joint commissions, treaties, and international conferences. The idea was to resolve differences before they caused war. Rhodes pointed out that Hughes sought *a* pathway of peace, not *the* pathway to peace. Hughes knew that pursuing peace was a complex process requiring a variety of strategies and "constant effort." Never a fixed end in itself, peace, like democracy, would always be a work in progress.[57]

Hughes never denied balance-of-power politics but tried to mitigate and mold them. His legalist assumptions reinforced his optimistic progressive commitments to activist government and structural reform. Because the old European balance of power was dead, the United States could be instrumental in creating a new balance of power by addressing postwar reparations, debt, and the arms race. Accordingly, Hughes harnessed the nation's economic and political leverage to become the anchor of stability in a new world order. Historian Patrick Cohrs identified "an unspoken Hughes doctrine" whereby the United States became Europe's "informal—yet effectively hegemonic—arbiter." Instead of a balance of power among European countries, there would be a new balance of power between Europe and the United States cemented by a "Pax Anglo-Americana."[58]

Hughes's first challenge was securing a treaty to end the war with Germany. Somehow, the United States had to avoid endorsing the Treaty of Versailles while preserving its prerogatives concerning the postwar world as protected by that treaty. Because resubmitting the Versailles Treaty to the Senate would guarantee a new crisis, he concluded that a separate treaty with Germany was the only realistic option. In a bit of intellectual and political sleight of hand, Hughes drafted a new treaty that combined key provisions of the Versailles Treaty with the Senate's reservations in their 1921 resolution ending the war. The somewhat convoluted result gave the United States a role equivalent to the Treaty of Versailles without corresponding obligations. It epitomized "privileged detachment."

After Hughes presented the new treaty to the Senate Foreign Relations Committee, it was reported out with Borah casting the only negative vote. Overcoming opposition from Wilson and many Democrats, the Senate ultimately ratified that treaty and similar ones with Austria and Hungary, also in 1921. The process was contentious and, as always, contained a Senate reservation reasserting independence from the League and reaffirming the Senate's role in foreign affairs. Acknowledging the Irreconcilables, Hughes admitted that the treaty "was the best that could be done." But at least it was done and the war was officially over.[59]

The next agenda item was resolving claims being made by American citizens against Germany for property losses incurred by the war. Instead of a Senate sponsored process controlled by Americans and hampered by the Irreconcilables, Hughes suggested a joint American–German commission created by executive order to discuss the issue. He even convinced Borah to support the idea. Although Congress insisted that other European debts be repaid in full, Hughes, Mellon, and Hoover negotiated a flexible arrangement with Britain. Harding personally lobbied the Senate and won approval despite Johnson's claim that the deal rendered the United States "an international sucker." These initial successes reflected Hughes's desire to treat every nation with "fair and honorable dealing."[60]

Hughes applied the same rationale to the problem of German reparations. If the Senate had ratified the Versailles Treaty, a US representative would probably have chaired the Reparations Commission and could have negotiated a compromise between France and Germany. Fearing for its own security, France was determined to punish Germany with heavy reparations. Hughes had to find a way around Senate demands for full reparations, which he knew were "impracticable." After much wrangling with the French, he proposed a new international commission comprised of financial experts to depoliticize and resolve the issue. It would be chaired by Owen D. Young, a New York industrialist, and Charles B. Dawes, a Chicago banker, federal director of the budget, and later Calvin Coolidge's vice president. A typically legalist strategy, similar to one Hughes used as governor, the commission did not require Senate approval. The need was underlined when France invaded the Ruhr in January 1923 to exact revenge on Germany and demonstrate its military strength.[61]

Months later, the commission proposed the 1924 Dawes Plan, which established a practical reparations payment schedule for Germany combined with bank loans designed to stabilize the German economy. But France resisted aiding Germany. Luckily, as president of the American Bar Association (ABA), Hughes led a lawyers' delegation to Europe at this very time. It provided the opportunity to meet with foreign leaders, secure their support, and overcome French opposition. Behind closed doors, Hughes clarified that forthcoming loans to France depended on whether it agreed to the German loans and withdrew from the Ruhr. As he put it, "Here is the American policy. If you turn this down, America is through." Hughes, noted Leffler, used "financial tactics to serve diplomatic ends." He believed that crushing Germany under huge debts was counterproductive and potentially disastrous, especially since Germany was careening toward chaos. Hope lay in supporting the moderate, cooperative leaders of the Weimar Republic and reducing German resentment over the punitive Versailles Treaty. It was impossible to have anticipated Adolf Hitler.[62]

Zasloff considered the arrangement unrealistic because the old balance-of-power nations were too weak to back it up. Furthermore, he found Hughes inconsistent for claiming that the plan was an expert-driven solution that avoided balance-of-power politics but using US power to create it. To historian Jon Jacobson, however, the Dawes Plan was a significant turning point. It marked movement away from the Versailles Treaty policy of punishing Germany to rehabilitating Germany in order to stabilize Europe through "corporate pluralism and supranational integration." From this perspective, the independent commission was a clever substitute for governmental involvement. It revealed that the 1920s were not merely "an anomaly and an interlude, a pause on the road to depression and dictatorship." Rather, wrote Jacobson, the decade marked the end of "the pre-World War 1 international system" and the beginning of "new models of political organization . . . which triumphed after World War II."[63]

Hughes, Hoover, Mellon, and the business community considered restoring Europe's economy critical, not only for European political stability and a revised balance of power but also for American economic development. The Dawes Plan removed a key obstacle to postwar peace and signaled a new American international economic role. Historian

Emily Rosenberg explained that it also reflected a growing public-private relationship between government and investment banks. Prior to the Dawes Plan, the US government avoided getting directly involved in European economic recovery. Now it was actively encouraging banks to help and lobbying European governments to cooperate.[64]

After tense negotiations, J. P. Morgan Jr. corralled bankers into floating over half of the $200 million Dawes Plan loan. When the public subscribed to the rest of the loan, the United States confirmed its new role as the world's creditor and New York City replaced London as the world's financial center. Complemented by other loans, the United States made a major financial contribution to European postwar recuperation. It was a different way to accomplish Wilson's goal of peace without victory and to assert power without using force. For Norris, that was the problem. As he had opposed profiteering during the war, so he now accused the bankers of exploiting the Dawes Plan for their own self-interest.[65]

Unfortunately, the efforts to rescue Europe financially were undermined by the 1922 Fordney–McCumber tariff, which imposed the highest level of protection thus far. Although Harding recognized the need to modify protection and got some executive flexibility into the bill, he let Congress set high specific duties, which cancelled out that flexibility. Rollin Kirby captured this inconsistency in a cartoon where the tariff is a rigid steel beam under a "Notice to Foreign Salesmen—Keep Out." Consequently, it became more expensive to trade with the United States, which kept countries from selling their goods in the United States and acquiring revenue to pay their debts. This situation affected Germany trying to pay reparations, other European countries burdened by US debts, and Caribbean countries dealing with European debts. Public opinion and congressional pressures precluded voiding those obligations.[66]

Many Americans, including Hughes, still believed that domestic prosperity required tariff protection. The rapid recovery from the 1921 recession confirmed their faith in the home market. Yet, they also wanted access to world markets—that is, free trade abroad but protection at home. This inconsistency had broad ramifications. By compounding the debt crisis and stimulating retaliatory tariffs, the high tariff contributed to the international economic instability that the Dawes Plan was designed to avoid. It prolonged the Great Depression, which paved the way for totalitarianism and World War II. In this sense, the cardinal error of the twenties may have been the protective tariff.[67]

Although Hughes advocated tariff revision, he stood by his overall belief, as reflected in the 1916 campaign and long-standing Republican Party policy, that tariffs protected American workers and "infant industries" against competition from cheaper foreign labor and commodities. Here he advocated the national interest exclusively. At the same time, Hughes pursued national interests through mutual interests. He sought commercial treaties that gave the United States "equality of opportunity" in trade because it was now a major exporter of manufactured goods. As an extension of the Open Door policy and in order to end discriminatory trade deals, Hughes promulgated the unconditional most favored nation clause, which guaranteed trade equity. Thus, he managed to balance his nation's interests with other nation's interests and even won Senate support (including Borah) for the new trade policy.[68]

Similar skills were required to handle a less momentous, but still important and tricky, international situation. US prohibitionists were incensed to discover that alcohol was being served on American commercial ships. After the decline in passengers caused by the 1921 Immigration Restriction Law, shipowners upgraded third-class rooms for a newly invented tourist class. Wine was an essential lure but prohibitionists insisted that no liquor be served on US ships or brought in by any foreign ships.

While other administration officials wavered, Hughes forged a treaty policy by which foreign ships could carry liquor in US waters in exchange for helping catch smugglers. Although this policy hurt "dry" American ships, it kept trade moving and undermined smuggling. It also defused tensions with England, where American shippers were acquiring registry so that they could bring large quantities of liquor to Florida via the Bahamas. Both an accommodation to and a run-around prohibition, the resolution combined Hughes's diplomatic skill with his knowledge of constitutional and international law. It proved, as he commented in 1925, that "after all, the State Department is primarily a big international law office."[69]

Hughes did not personally support prohibition but he upheld the law. Far from being rigidly idealistic, moralistic, and legalistic, he consistently developed "practicable" strategies for working with other nations and with the Senate. Significantly, "practicable" was a word he often used to promote policies that were both realistic and actionable, cautious but constructive. Trying to navigate the treacherous post–World

War I political seas revealed Hughes's foreign policy objectives and diplomatic skills. He turned out to be flexible and creative in steering the ship of state around the nation's tempests and Europe's whirlpools. In the process, he reestablished peace and redefined America's role for a twentieth-century new world order.[70]

7 | The Washington Naval Conference, 1921–1922

Limiting Armaments

The 1921 to 1922 Washington Conference on the Limitation (not the elimination) of Armaments was the world's first "successful arms limitation conference." Also called the Washington Naval Conference or simply the Washington Conference, it was, said historian Thomas H. Buckley, "one of the most important diplomatic assemblages in all history." As the mastermind of the conference, Charles Evans Hughes won immediate acclaim but long-term blame. Was it Hughes's grandest accomplishment or his greatest failure as secretary of state? Did it make the Long Armistice (1921 to 1941) possible or did it enable Nazism, fascism, and Japanese militarism to flourish?[1]

Controversy notwithstanding, everyone agreed that the challenge of fostering lasting postwar peace was daunting and that the Washington Conference was correspondingly consequential. It was also dramatic. What could have been a routine international gathering characterized by empty formalities, endless bickering, and ambiguous resolves, was an exceptional moment of international cooperation and policy formation. By boldly confronting post–World War I realities, it began restructuring international relations for the twentieth century. Reflecting America's new status as a world power, the Washington Conference was the first international convocation located in the United States.

In 1921, cultural critic Herbert Croly, declared, "The advisor of President Harding who proposed and carried out the idea [of the conference] possessed the vision of a statesman." Likewise, in 1922, journalist Mark Sullivan credited Hughes with establishing a spirit of "cooperative responsibility" for peace in a war-torn world. The significance of the conference, added historian Frank Ninkovich, was rejecting the old diplomacy based on competitive balance of power, nationalism, and imperialism in favor of a new diplomacy based on cautious, collaborative internationalism. By contrast, reporting in 1943, journalist Walter Lippmann regretted ever having supported "the exorbitant folly" of the Washington Conference. In retrospect, he considered the whole event "tragically successful in disarming the nations that believed in disarmament" while letting the others rearm. Thus, the Allies were reduced "to almost disastrous impotence on the eve of the Second World War." While trying to solve one crisis, the Washington Conference created a worse crisis.[2]

Held in Washington's lavish Pan American Union Building for twelve weeks from November 12, 1921, to February 6, 1922, the conference embraced the formidable task of curtailing the international arms race. By calling and hosting the event, the United States became a major player in international affairs, belying its isolationist image. The time was long overdue, Croly wrote in 1909, for the nation "to assume a more definite and a more responsible place in the international system." America's new economic prominence and contributions to winning the Great War magnified the need. Now the goal was to prevent future wars. Even if the objective was idealistic, the pursuit had to be realistic. The resulting Washington Treaty System may have fallen short in long-range terms, but it ushered in a decade of peace. Moreover, in the moment, it inspired a war-weary world. Historian Selig Adler considered the conference "the crowning achievement of Hughes's diplomatic career."[3]

There already was pressure for a conference on disarmament coming from Senator Borah as well as from the British. Borah championed international disarmament believing that fewer arms would mean fewer wars. Woodrow Wilson included arms reduction in his Fourteen Points but resisted joining any discussions on the subject because the United States was not part of the League of Nations. However, Borah persisted with a Senate resolution for naval disarmament. Although it failed initially, disarmament became one of the nation's most effective public pressure campaigns. Petitions flooded Congress and peace organizations flourished. The Women's Committee for World Disarmament was supported by the National League of Women Voters and other women's organizations. The Carnegie Endowment for International Peace (CEIP) promoted World Friendship Clubs, through which five thousand public school children acquired foreign pen pals.[4]

Additional pressure came from the US Chamber of Commerce, churches, labor unions, colleges, and the press, especially *The New York Times* and *New York World.* National figures like writer Mark Twain, labor leader Samuel Gompers, and social reformer Jane Addams championed peace. The nation's new interest in foreign affairs spawned college courses, think tanks, schools, libraries, and news coverage. The 1920 to 1921 Depression increased domestic interest in lowering taxes by reducing spending on the arms race. International arms limitation would also enable Europeans to reduce taxes, spend less on arms, and buy more American goods.[5]

By the time Borah's resolution passed, the Harding administration was already pursuing a conference. Technically, Borah won, but he resented being upstaged and excluded from the Washington Conference delegation. Hughes quickly took control of the planning and dominated the actual event. From the start, he broke tradition by inviting weak nations to attend along with strong ones, thus broadening the agenda and impact of the conference. The primary aim was to reduce potential conflict by halting the ever-escalating naval competition between the United States, Britain, and Japan. Weakened by the war, England was willing to retrench, thereby relinquishing her historic role as Mistress of the Seas in favor of a stronger Anglo-American partnership. Historian Adam Tooze pointed out that "never before had an empire of Britain's stature so explicitly and consciously conceded superiority in such a crucial dimension of global power." In all three countries, the tax burden of naval competition was immense and the US Senate was sure to defeat any more defense appropriations anyway. Would it be possible to defuse naval competition without looking weak?[6]

Hughes started at home where he faced a Navy Department committed to ship-building under Wilson's 1916 Naval Appropriations Act. Of course, the admirals opposed limiting America's naval force. Helped by Harding, who actually was a strong naval advocate, and Theodore Roosevelt Jr., now in his father's old job as assistant secretary of the Navy, Hughes convinced the Navy brass to modify the 1916 expansion plan. Historian Dexter Perkins called it "an extraordinary example of the subordination of the military to the civil power." In fact, Hughes insisted that all the conference delegates be civilian, not military. The sole exception was Japan's navy minister, Admiral Tomosaburo Kato, who carefully distanced himself from the military for the conference.[7]

Further covering his domestic bases, Hughes established an advisory committee. Its twenty-one members represented important interest groups—the Army, the Navy, finance, labor, agriculture, each geographic section, each major religion, plus four women from the peace movement. Unlike Wilson, who took only Democrats to the Paris peace talks, Hughes appointed Massachusetts's Henry Cabot Lodge, Republican chair of the Senate Foreign Relations Committee, and Alabama's Oscar Underwood, Democratic leader of the Senate, as American representatives to the conference. They would become crucial congressional allies. Former Secretary of State Elihu Root, now seventy-seven years old, rounded out the delegation and proved invaluable during the conference. Through these appointments, Hughes kept the initiative for foreign policy with the executive branch while acknowledging the Senate's foreign policy prerogatives. Political scientist Betty Glad accused Hughes of excessive "sensitivity" to domestic political factors. However, as governor, Hughes had learned that "the strategist will accomplish nothing without his congress."[8]

The stage was set for action. The day before the conference was the Armistice Day ceremony, which former President Wilson attended. After laying a wreath at the tomb of the unknown soldier, President Harding delivered a moving speech honoring the dead and lamenting the "waste and folly of war." On the next day, he opened the conference by calling for "international understanding and good will" because "our hundred millions want less of armament and none of war." The American delegation anchored the head of a long U-shaped table around which the delegates sat. Three hundred correspondents from foreign and domestic newspapers attended as well. The gallery was full of prominent Americans—the vice president, the chief justice, associate justices, cabinet members, the previous secretary of state, and Theodore Roosevelt's (TR's) daughter. Hughes was unanimously elected chairman after being nominated by British former prime minister, Foreign Secretary Arthur Balfour, who would be his strongest ally throughout the conference.[9]

Hughes took over. He "looked like a statesman," wrote Buckley. "His tall, straight-backed figure, . . . his trimmed mustache and beard, now almost gray, made him appear immensely distinguished." At first, the speech seemed flat as Hughes reviewed the historical background of the conference. The tempo picked up when he deplored the costs and complications of the current arms race, which could only be stopped if naval powers made sacrifices. Yet, they could not "be expected to make these sacrifices alone." Emphasizing the classical concept of destructive competition, Hughes announced, "The time has come for action." Then he astonished the delegates with "a concrete proposition" for reducing the naval power of the five World War I Allies. Time stood still; no one moved.[10]

Outrageous as it seemed, Hughes asked the Allies not only to destroy some existing ships but also to limit new construction for ten years. He used each country's current naval strength to establish naval parity between the United States and England with Japan not far behind. The actual ratio was 5:5:3 for those three and, as specified later, 1.75 each for France and Italy. The plan would require the United States to scrap fifteen existing battleships and fifteen under construction. The British would lose twenty-three battleships and stop plans for four more. The Japanese would relinquish ten older battleships and seven new ones. Hughes concluded by declaring, "Preparation for offensive naval war will stop now." Historian William E. Leuchtenberg called the proposal "brilliant audacity."[11]

Hughes confirmed, observed Tooze, that "no other power had ever wielded such global economic dominance." The United States was now the "undisputed arbiter of world affairs." Moreover, Britain's willingness to abandon its naval dominance marked "a profound realignment" of the world's power structure and "an event unparalleled in world history." In fact, wrote historian Elizabeth Cobbs Hoffman, there was "no precedent in the history of the world" whereby nations were asked "to make themselves vulnerable to each other" by reducing arms. And remarkably enough, the world's most powerful nation offered to start the process itself. Even more amazing, the two other major political powers, England and Japan, agreed to cooperate. The plan signaled a shift from the old conflict-oriented balance of power paradigm to a new paradigm of negotiated cooperation based on a redefined (but not denied) balance of power. Wilsonian idealism survived but was translated into what Hughes hoped was "a practicable program that shall at once be put into execution." Theodore Roosevelt Jr. "felt . . . that a page had been turned in world events."[12]

At most conferences, proposals emerge at the end of painful, protracted, often secret deliberations. Exerting bold leadership, Hughes put his proposal up front for all to see, including the press and, therefore, the public. Practicing open diplomacy, Hughes allowed reporters to attend all working sessions in the belief that they would constructively influence public opinion and offset both misrepresentation and demagoguery. Of course, private negotiations were guarded closely. The strategy was to provide the delegates and the public with something tangible from the start. By precluding the usual rhetorical jockeying, Hughes hoped to create momentum and make the conference focus on implementation, not obfuscation. "It was," said Buckley, "the most dramatic occasion of Hughes's long life and has gone down in the annals of American diplomacy as the major effort of a great American statesman."[13]

Everyone was shocked but delighted. Disregarding formal diplomatic decorum, the delegates jumped up, cheered, shook hands, hugged, and slapped each other on the back. Sullivan called Hughes's speech "an immense lightning strike flashing cleanly through an atmosphere of murk." Hughes was hailed as "a national hero . . . the savior of civilization." Even Borah praised the speech as "the first great triumph of open diplomacy." Signing his note, "Your affectionate old colleague," Oliver Wendell Holmes Jr., Hughes's former and future Supreme Court companion, wrote "simply to say that I was proud of your dignity and thrilled by what you said yesterday." Balfour called Hughes "not merely a great statesman but a great artist." Across the world, the speech gave people hope for a peaceful future. It was hailed as a "master stroke . . . an experiment in practical idealism." Indeed, wrote diplomatic historian Dexter Perkins, "The striking thing about the Hughes proposal is its extraordinarily concrete character, its precision. Imaginative in its conception, it was practical in its content."[14]

After a weekend adjournment, the hard work began on what became the Five Power Treaty. France was offended. Premier Aristede Briand was not given the most prominent place at the conference table and French was ranked the second language after English. Even worse, France had the largest army in Europe but was being allotted a third-rate naval ratio. Consequently, the French requested the right to maintain a much larger navy than warranted. Conducting intense discussions in Washington and by cable to France. Hughes obtained a reasonable compromise on the number of French battleships and aircraft carriers. However, because its security concerns remained unresolved, France blocked all efforts to limit submarines and withheld approval of a treaty prohibiting submarine attacks on commercial ships.[15]

Despite several attempts, Hughes did not get limitations on other above water craft and land armaments. He understood that "Europe was not ready to limit land armament" but hoped that some of these issues would be resolved in the future, as they partly were at the 1930 London Naval Conference. Such failures underscored the difficulty of achieving agreement and the wisdom of focusing, as Hughes said, on "limited and practical aims." To Glad, such incrementalism spelled weakness and future disaster. Indeed, an unintended consequence was a new form of arms race. Nations shifted resources from big battleships to smaller cruisers and submarines while converting battleships to aircraft carriers. Hughes anticipated but underestimated this development because, at the time, battleships were still considered the key to naval power and conflict. Nonetheless, historians Harold Sproat and Margaret Sproat concluded that "freezing of the status quo" was a major accomplishment.[16]

Struggling taxpayers in all five countries were relieved. The final treaty included a ten-year ban on new battleship construction with limits set on tonnage and aircraft carriers. One observer remarked that "Secretary Hughes sunk in 35 minutes more ships than all the admirals of the world have sunk in a cycle of centuries." Root later credited the Washington Conference for paving the way to European stability as embodied the 1925 Locarno Pact, whereby seven European countries (including Germany) agreed to respect each other's boundaries. By contrast, the Hearst papers immediately attacked the conference as a "pathetic delusion" and the Socialist *New York Call* sarcastically suggested that it would only "reduce the cost of blowing each other up."[17]

Although many US naval experts considered the ship-building limitations disastrous, the Washington Conference treaties may have protected America's status as a naval power. After all, it would have declined if other nations had continued building capital ships while the United States did not. Domestic military unpreparedness in the 1930s may have resulted less from the Washington Treaty System than from congressional opposition to funding the fleet at levels allowed by the treaties. Hughes, who had advocated preparedness in 1916, warned in 1922, "It is essential that we should maintain the relative naval strength of the United States." It would, he said, be "folly to undermine our position" by allowing our shipbuilding to languish. The Senate did not listen.[18]

The Five Power Treaty resolved several other thorny issues regarding Japan. During World War I, Japan seized German islands in the Pacific and German areas of control on the Chinese coast. Japan threatened to take over China and, with the United States, had invaded Siberia in order to keep Germany from appropriating Russian supplies. But when the United States withdrew after the war, Japan remained and took over eastern Siberia. Another problem was that the Versailles Treaty seemed to give Japan control over key islands on the Pacific route from Pearl Harbor to the Philippines, including Yap, an essential cable communications center. The United States feared that Japan would fortify Yap, monopolize the cables, and threaten Guam. During and after the war, Japan had increased its naval fleet. At the conference, Japan expressed resentment at being in third place and being asked to eliminate the battleship *Mutsu*, a great source of Japanese pride. One Japanese representative likened the 5:5:3 ratio to "Rolls Royce: Rolls Royce: Ford." Hughes worked out a compromise to save the *Mutsu*, but then the British wanted to build two bigger ships to compensate. Eventually, Hughes convinced the British to accept two smaller, but still substantial, ships instead. These factors exacerbated tensions between the United States and Japan while heightening fears of a Pacific war.[19]

Working from a New York City apartment dubbed the Black Chamber, a former railway telegrapher turned World War I decoder provided Hughes with intercepted messages that strengthened his negotiating strategy with Japan. Consequently, Hughes got Japan to agree to gradually leave Siberia and grant the United States free access to Yap plus other contested islands. In return, Japan wanted guarantees that the United States would limit its fortifications of Guam, Hawaii, and the Philippines. Knowing that Congress opposed increasing military expenditures in general, Hughes conceded on Guam and the Philippines but not on Hawaii. Critics blamed the treaty for lacking an enforcement mechanism and for leaving Japan dominant in the eastern Pacific, albeit curtailed. Nonetheless, the Five Power Treaty made more progress toward world stability than anyone expected. Historian Phillip Jessup pointed out that people who criticized the conference for not doing enough forgot that it was "the only thing that has actually been done." Overall, wrote political scientist, John Braeman, Hughes's handling of Japan was "a diplomatic triumph."[20]

However, the naval limitations provisions of the Five Power Treaty would never pass the Senate unless imperial aggression in the Far East was abated. Therefore, Hughes steered the conferees to a Four Power Treaty. Short but important, it reduced US anxiety about a potential war with Britain and Japan. The 1902 Anglo-Japanese Alliance benefitted Great Britain by protecting its Pacific colonies while benefitting Japan by alignment with the Mistress of the Seas. They jointly opposed Russian expansion in Manchuria, thus ensuring a balance of power in the Far East. The Alliance badly strained US–British relations by committing

Great Britain to protect Japan, even at the risk of war with the United States, which no one wanted. Although the Pact brought Japan into World War I on the side of the Allies, the United States was troubled by Japanese expansion into Korea, Manchuria, and Shantung. Furthermore, Japanese dominance of the Pacific might close off Chinese markets.[21]

Hughes rejected the idea of joining Japan and England because it would look like an alliance and guarantee Senate opposition. Instead, he included France, which had colonized Indochina. The result was a four-way, ten-year, nonaggression treaty to respect each other's interests in the Pacific and to negotiate disputes. The French gained status and the other three nations saved face. All welcomed a new balance of power based on diplomacy rather than conflict. At one point, Harding mistakenly said the agreement would not cover the Japanese mainland, but he was quickly corrected. Although the treaty required no US sacrifice, the Hearst press labeled it the "Four Power Fraud." To Wilsonians, it was a selective agreement that undermined the League. As expected, Senators Borah, Johnson, and other Irreconcilables insisted that the treaty was a dangerous, secret foreign entanglement. From another perspective, Georgia Senator Thomas E. Watson warned that because of the treaty, "spread eaglism will be out of date. You will have caged your eagle."[22]

Faced by such strong opposition and convinced that failing to ratify the treaty "would be a national calamity," Hughes and Harding accepted a Senate reservation asserting that the United States was not obliged to militarily "join in any defense." During the 1920s, quipped one wit, "the Senate would not have endorsed the Ten Commandments without stipulating qualifications!" The Four Power Treaty was worth the compromise because it not only defused tensions in the Far East but improved US relations with England. Lodge and Underwood defended the treaty in Senate debate, which consumed two hundred pages in the *Congressional Record* and fifty roll call votes. Most Irreconcilables opposed the treaty as an alliance by another name and because of the potential for Japanese dominance in the Far East. When it barely passed, Hughes wondered how any senator could be so "reckless" as to threaten such delicate negotiations.[23]

The Five Power Treaty on naval limitation was submitted to the Senate next. The strategy worked because, with only one dissent, the Senate endorsed it. Together, the two treaties embraced a new balance of power defined by mutually agreed upon stability grounded in preventive, defensive arrangements, not aggressive, offensive competition. Grotius would have approved. Unlike those who called for enforcement mechanisms, Hughes believed that agreements based on consent would be more reliable than "the remedies of force, which are likely to prove illusory when the test comes." Besides, he knew that the Senate would never have condoned any enforcement agreement, like Article X. Hughes hoped to have brokered "an enduring peace" based on what Harold and Margaret Sproat considered "a new order of sea power" that replaced Pax Britannica. A 1922 cartoon in *The Columbus Citizen* depicted Hughes proudly taking a disarmament treaties pudding out of an oven labeled "Arms Conference" while the Senate glowered in the background (see figure 7.1). Historian Arthur Ekirch pointed out that getting Senate confirmation of the treaties was a welcome contrast to Wilson's failure with the League of Nations.[24]

Defusing the Far East

China presented more thorny issues, which were addressed in the Nine Power Treaty. It was endorsed by nations with interests in the Pacific including the main five plus China, Belgium, Holland, and Portugal. The American approach toward China was originally articulated by Secretary of State John Hay's *Open Door Notes* of 1899 and 1900. Sent to Britain, France, Germany, Italy, Japan, and Russia, the *Notes* reflected concern over spheres of influence that those nations had carved out of China. In order to protect US access to Chinese markets, Hay outlined an aspirational policy through which all nations would have access to Chinese trade with no single power dominating.

At the Washington Conference, the 1823 Monroe Doctrine's opposition to European imperialism in the Western Hemisphere was applied to the Eastern Hemisphere. (Eventually, it would be extended to the Middle East and Russia in pursuit of petroleum.) Root and Balfour helped clarify the *Open Door Notes* at the conference. For the first time, the Nine Power Treaty gave China a portion of its own tariff revenues. Most important, it delegitimized foreign spheres of influence and kept Chinese markets open. Thus, the United States gained access to those markets and the chance of war over trading rights was reduced. Although China did not get everything it wanted, it appreciated being included in ne-

By Larry Keys in the *Columbus Citizen*, February 7, 1922.

PROOF OF THE PUDDING IS IN RATIFICATION

Figure 7.1. "Proof of the Pudding Is in Ratification," by Larry Keys. *The Columbus Citizen*, February 7, 1922.

gotiations with the world's great powers. Hughes considered the Nine Power Treaty a Magna Carta for China. It was, wrote Tooze, a way to "reanimate the vision of the Open Door, creating an international space swept clean of militarism . . . which the free flow of American capital would unify and pacify."[25]

After additional difficult negotiations paralleling but technically outside the conference, the Japanese returned the Shantung Peninsula to China, with qualifications. Hughes understood that the Shantung issue had to be solved in order to secure stability in the Far East and get Senate approval for other treaties. The American public, his key advisors, and Jacob Gould Schurman, his old Cornell friend who was now minister to China, all favored China over Japan. The discussions were fraught with tension as reflected in a two-week suspension after three weeks of wrangling. At one point, John V. A. MacMurray, the US Far Eastern specialist, had to rescue the Chinese delegates from a hotel bathroom, where they were confined by Chinese students angry about negotiating with Japan. At another point, Hughes called an urgent private meeting in his home with Balfour and the Chinese delegates. As with France and the Dawes Plan, he threatened that the United States would stop supporting China if the delegates continued being uncooperative. After what Balfour called a "forceful . . . appeal" by Hughes, both the Chinese and the Japanese relented. The agreement cleared the way for Senate passage of the Nine Power Treaty without dissent. Harnessing his lawyerly skills of argument, Hughes demonstrated that he was not just about moralistic rhetoric and legalistic formulas. He meant business.[26]

Although Hughes failed to get further concessions, the Nine Power Treaty was important. Like the other treaties, it bore testimony to, as even critics recognized, Hughes's "outstanding ability and tenacious resolution." For him, the treaty's value lay in alleviating Far Eastern tensions, providing China the opportunity to stabilize itself and finally legitimizing the Open Door as international law. Hughes was especially pleased about this last development, which dovetailed with his call for modernizing international law because "new rules needed to meet new situations." Combined with the Four Power Treaty, the Nine Power Treaty signified a more realistic redefinition of America's Far Eastern policy. However, the Japanese never thought that the Open Door precluded their own activities in Manchuria, which originally caused the 1905 Russo-Japanese War. Moreover, observed historian Thomas J. McCormick, post-conference "American under-spending and Anglo-

Japanese overspending" on ships created "the very strategic imbalance the Washington Conference had sought to avoid." The lack of enforcement mechanisms ultimately mattered. Perhaps Hughes was too idealistic after all.[27]

The treaty was also criticized as a function of American economic imperialism. Hughes and Hoover assumed that public and private interests overlapped. But they never convinced American bankers like Thomas W. Lamont, partner at J. P. Morgan, to invest in China rather than Japan, which was less risky. Indeed, Hughes and Hoover undermined the Open Door policy themselves by tolerating (and sometimes encouraging) private loans to Japan. Hoover promoted the China Trade Acts, but Japan was the main recipient of American investments and loans. Moreover, when it became clear that Japan was still expanding in Manchuria, neither man protested. The inconsistency can only be explained as an effort to maintain the balance of power against Russia while protecting American investments. In any case, Hughes and Hoover were not acting like innocent players on the international field.[28]

Although his nation made sacrifices, even the Japanese prime minister considered the treaty "a blessing to all mankind." Admiral Kato praised Hughes for "his unceasing care, intense earnestness, and indefatigable industry as well as for the unalloyed sense of justice with which he discharged his duties." Historians Arthur S. Link and William Cotton called the Washington Conference "a remarkable triumph of reason over selfish nationalism." But, they added, "it was not enough."[29]

Remaining Issues

A major accomplishment of the Washington Conference was establishing a positive, working relationship with Japan. The goal was to support moderates over militarists in Tokyo (as in Germany). This development was primarily attributed to the combined efforts of Hughes, Balfour, and the Japanese Ambassador Baron Masanao Hanihara. It led to the generous material support that the United States sent Japan after the devastating earthquake of 1923. However, good feelings began unraveling in 1924 over immigration restriction. After a sabbatical in Japan, philosopher John Dewey warned that any hint of racial discrimination would unite the Japanese and strengthen the militarists. Hughes's diplomatic approach toward Japan at the conference embodied this concern. Nonetheless, in 1924 he was stymied by virulent anti-Japanese sentiment on the West Coast and in Congress.[30]

Federally condoned hostility to Asian immigrants started with the 1882 Chinese Exclusion Act, which was renewed regularly until 1943. The policy targeted Chinese laborers but enabled some Chinese businessmen and scholars to enter. Because Japanese laborers filled the gap left by the Chinese, "Yellow Peril" sentiment grew, especially in California. In 1908, Root forged an informal gentlemen's agreement that, like the Chinese Exclusion Act, restricted Japanese laborers but allowed some scholars and businessmen to enter temporarily. California and other states started passing laws limiting Japanese employment, land ownership, and access to public schools. Significantly, Japan tried to include in the Yap settlement a statement denouncing racism and guaranteeing Japanese people the right to live anywhere in peace and freedom. It echoed a 1911 Taft administration treaty that guaranteed Japanese residents the same right as native citizens to engage in business.[31]

Hughes considered the proposal extraneous to Yap but promised to reconsider it in the future. Events overtook him. Complicated by postwar hyper-nationalism and isolationism as well as the Red Scare and general anxiety cut across the country over new immigrants from Southern and Eastern Europe, immigration restriction became popular. The resulting Emergency Quota Act of 1921 set national limits expressly designed to favor the old Northern and Western European immigrants. In 1923 the Supreme Court exacerbated the situation by ruling that Asian residents were unassimilable and ineligible for citizenship through naturalization (*U.S. v. Bhagat Singh Thind*). It also legitimized California and Washington state laws prohibiting persons ineligible for citizenship to own land. Thus, observed historian Mae M. Ngai, "Asiatic" became a racial category with ominous legal and political implications.[32]

In the Immigration Act of 1924, Congress made the quotas yet more favorable to Northern and Western Europe and halved the overall immigrant limit. The smaller labor pool was offset by labor-saving devices, four million returning soldiers, and the Great Migration of African Americans from the South. For the first time, the new national origins bill planned to explicitly ban Japanese immigrants while still allowing travelers, teachers, students, and businessmen to enter temporarily. Ngai noted that passports, visas, and examination upon entry marked "a political victory for Progressive-era race-nativism as well as the isolationism of the inter-war period." Hoover and Lodge supported the policy.[33]

Hughes predicted that exclusion would destroy all the progress that had just been made to improve relations with Japan. In a letter to Washington state's Albert Johnson, chairman of the House Committee on Immigration, Hughes explained that "the Japanese are a sensitive people and would regard such a legislative enactment as fixing a stigma upon them." If they were not singled out but just given a quota of one hundred like many other nations, the number of immigrants would be reduced without insult. However, because the 1908 gentlemen's agreement was based merely on an exchange of letters, Hughes agreed to ask Ambassador Hanihara to draft a more formal policy statement.[34]

Otherwise constructive and gracious, Hanihara's statement included one unfortunate phrase. Hughes did not flag it because he did not anticipate the furor it would arouse. This time, he underestimated congressional opinion. The offending passage implied that excluding Japanese immigrants would have "grave consequences" for relations between the two nations. Incensed by what they deemed a threat, Congress doubled downed on exclusion. Johnson insisted that the legislation was not merely a response to Hanihara's letter but the outgrowth of long-standing dissatisfaction with policies that allowed an "unassimilable Japanese population" to immigrate. Exclusion was an overdue "protective" measure reflecting postwar isolationism, anxiety over Japan's naval buildup compounded by its expansion into Manchuria and Shantung. Although Hughes addressed these fears at the Washington Conference, they were revived by exclusionist claims that Japan was "the Germany of Asia."[35]

Further complicating matters, there were rumors that a member of the State Department inserted those words, a claim that Hughes and MacMurray vociferously denied. Lodge cosponsored the bill in the Senate but public opinion was divided. On the one hand, the bill was strongly supported by fourteen Western states led by California and most (but not all) of its unions. The Hearst papers amplified opposition. Issues of race and economic competition inflamed the Asiatic Exclusion League while patriotism galvanized the American Legion. On the other hand, the act was criticized on the East Coast and in the West by businessmen, missionaries, and twenty-four prominent Americans led by Lamont. Congressional hearings about the bill revealed significant opposition not just from Japanese American associations, but from people with firsthand knowledge of the Japanese. Teachers, social workers, and businessmen praised the Japanese as law abiding and industrious. Internationalists opposed the bill in the interests of peace. Nonetheless, it passed.[36]

The Japanese were furious. The government issued a formal protest and crowds besieged the American embassy in Tokyo. Consumers boycotted American goods, and Hanihara had to resign. Scholars have criticized Hughes for not protesting aggressively enough against exclusion, for doing too little too late. Perhaps, like the League fight, he appreciated the futility of opposing a determined Congress and an emotional public. Instead, he convinced President Coolidge (who was anti-Japanese himself) to request a two-year delay in implementing the bill and, when that was rejected, a one-year delay, which also was rejected.

When Coolidge signed the bill, Hughes gave up, but he long felt that "this was the most regrettable of his experience in the State Department." He feared that it "has undone the work of the Washington Conference and implanted the seeds of an antagonism which are sure to bear fruit in the future." No wonder he was "greatly depressed." Time proved him correct. Good relations with Japan survived until Japan invaded Manchuria in 1931 and abrogated the Nine Power Treaty in 1932. At least Hughes could take some comfort from the fact that the Western Hemisphere was exempt from immigration restrictions despite rising concerns over Mexican migrants and the new visa requirements that made them "illegal."[37]

Russia presented different diplomatic and domestic challenges. Hughes expanded Wilson's policy of denying formal recognition of the Bolshevik revolutionary government to include Vladimir Lenin's Soviet government. Harding was open to recognizing Russia, but, as evidenced by the Red Scare, American public opinion was strongly anti-Communist. Hughes was careful not to deny Russia's right of revolution, which was a fundamental American concept. Rather, he said the issue was "international morality." It was violated when Russia refused to pay back wartime loans, much of which came from citizen-sponsored Liberty Bonds.

Upset because Russia had confiscated private property owned by US businessmen, Hughes opposed as monopolistic a proposal made by the Standard Oil Company to join with Dutch and British interests in marketing Russian oil. Because it would violate the rights of previous property holders, Hughes considered it "a question of principle" in upholding "valid obligations and rights." His position was widely supported at the time, perhaps because it overlapped with (and camouflaged) the nation's economic self-interest. Hughes applied similar principles to Latin America.[38]

Hughes only allowed Russia to send observers, not delegates, to the Washington Conference and insisted that he would personally handle Russian concerns like Siberia, which he did. Lenin considered him patronizing. In the United States, Borah and Mellon supported recognition of Russia as an opportunity for trade and investment. But Hughes thought that the Russian economy was too weak for either. Yet, historian William A. Williams pointed out that the administration quietly promoted American investments in Russia hoping to undermine Communism and stabilize the revolutionary government.

Responding in 1923 to a women's committee seeking recognition and the forgiveness of all Russian loans, Hughes asserted, "There is no hope for the success of your gospel—our gospel—of brotherly kindness in a world of hatred and in a world which is not animated by the sincerity of good faith." According to historian Douglas Little, this hostility to Russia was embedded in the State Department. As the older generation of officers taught in the Foreign Service School, they perpetuated anti-Bolshevism, a concept to which their upper-class recruits were probably predisposed anyway. The result was "the institutionalization of anti-Bolshevism in Washington" and nonrecognition until 1933.[39]

Although Hughes supported sending $66 million for relief during the devastating Russian famine of 1921 to 1922, he remained inflexible about recognition. Noting Russia's resolve to promote revolution abroad, he feared that a Russian embassy in Washington could become a base for subversive activity and the expansion of the American Communist Party or the Workers Party, small as they were. However, he never advocated repressing radicalism itself as long as it was a homegrown expression of free speech. Accordingly, he defended New York City Socialists from being ejected by the New York State legislature in 1920 and, as Supreme Court justice, supported flying the red flag as well as joining Communist organizations.

In 1920, Hughes insisted that the best way to combat Bolshevism in the United States was to defuse discontent through a "machinery for industrial justice." That meant supporting labor's right to bargain collectively plus establishing "impartial tribunals" (with labor representatives) to address hours, wages, housing, injuries, and old age and death benefits. Significantly, America's recognition of Russia in 1933 included a promise not to interfere with US politics. At that point, the former secretary of state, now chief justice, developed cordial relations with the first Soviet ambassador.[40]

After Germany invaded Russia in World War II, Hughes joined other Western leaders in praising Russia's role in the struggle. He optimistically (naïvely?) hoped that Stalin would stabilize his country and cooperate with other countries. However, he also worried about Russia's efforts to control Poland and the new Baltic states as well as by the spread of Communism in Europe. While criticizing the "juridical tidiness" of the "legalistic-moralistic approach to international problems," Kennan shared those concerns. Sounding fairly idealistic himself, Kennan, the architect of containment, thought that the best way to combat Communism was to strengthen "the spirit and purpose of American national life." In the end, Kennan believed that the world would be "more ready to recognize and respect spiritual distinction than material opulence." Hughes would have agreed.[41]

The dilemmas concerning Japan and Russia underscored the complexity of the postwar world that the Washington Conference addressed. They also illuminated the complexity of Hughes himself and his no-nonsense approach to diplomacy. As he put it in 1922, despite being "equally harassed by the extravagant demands of dreamers and the pessimistic predictions of cynics, we were intent on certain definite and practical aims. We refused to surrender these aims either to those who were insistent on the millennium or to those who told us that the sure result of our unintelligent efforts would be to bring about another war." The strategy, he repeated, was to have "limited and practical aims" reflecting "common interests" in "peace and security." For Hughes, the key to diplomacy always was "to consider patiently and sympathetically all proposals, differences and arguments." Success depended on "avoiding extremes" and recognizing that some differences are "irreconcilable." Those differences could, however, be offset by a sincere "commitment to deal justly with every important national interest." Grotius still applied.[42]

Glad and others considered Hughes's perspective totally unrealistic and blamed him for making too many concessions. As Vinson put it, the Washington Treaty System seemed "admirable at the time," but over time it became clear that the "house of policy was built on sand." By contrast, Perkins pointed out that Hughes faced huge obstacles on both national and international stages. Successfully negotiating all of these factors was the mark of "statesmanship in a democracy," which must always be attuned to its times, even if it does not survive over time. Hyde also saw Hughes as a statesman who was able "to conciliate, as well as to convince and to persuade." For himself, Hughes held that good-faith practicality enabled the conference to avoid "irrelevancies, . . . intrigues and cabals." Most importantly, said Hughes, the "tangible results" of the treaties brought intangible rewards. The Washington Treaty System reflected "a new feeling of respect and friendship" among nations, "a new state of mind" through which "war clouds have been dispelled." That spirit justified "all the efforts of the Conference." Hughes remained proud that the Washington Conference could "scrap distrust as well as its vessels of war."[43]

Nonetheless, Hughes was disappointed that the Five Power Treaty's ban on the use of poisonous gas in warfare had not been ratified by all parties several years later. Nor had much progress been made on limiting wartime use of aircraft and submarines, especially to protect noncombatants, neutrals, monuments, and hospitals, as well as religious and cultural institutions. To him, these "humanitarian interests make the demand for the improvement in [international] law irresistible." They underlined the need for and lessons of the Washington Conference. The Washington Treaty System promulgated a new world order based on carefully crafted mutual agreements. For ten years, it stopped the vicious cycle whereby, said Hughes, the defensive buildup of "*provocative* armament" by one nation bred endless competitive buildups among nations. The treaties wove a new fabric for international peace. Nevertheless, Leuchtenberg pointed out that the accomplishments of the Washington Conference backfired by creating "excessive expectations" for peace and lulling the nation into complacency, especially regarding the Far East.[44]

Referencing Grotius, Hughes understood that peace is not "the mere absence of war" but "an opportunity" to secure international "justice." Despite different national interests and "a gospel . . . of self-determination," Hughes firmly believed that there was "much common ground" to build on in order to "continue the search for all practicable methods of settling existing disputes" and preventing new ones. The ultimate goal, he said, was to "seek justice through peace." For a lawyer like Hughes, treaties "as accepted, not imposed, may be . . . the most important contribution to permanent peace" because they addressed the obstacles to peace in concrete terms. As he explained in 1926, "Competitive armament is the outward sign of an inward distrust and will go on until confidence replaces fear and suspicion. . . . Nations must feel secure and cease to think of war" before they will disarm. Therefore, Hughes deduced that "peace is a state of mind [that] will find expression in agreements and institutions, in the willingness to assume obligations of mutual self-restraint." In this sense, the Washington Conference was an idealistic attempt to find realistic alternatives to war. To Hughes, it marked "the passing of the old diplomacy and the introduction of more direct and flexible methods responsive to democratic sentiment." Because national "interest determines national action," he knew that "common action inevitably depends upon their appreciation of common interest." Otherwise, "the best laid international plans are destined to failure."[45]

In 1929, Hughes summarized his basic philosophy in metaphorical terms. He claimed that "building the institutions of peace is the most distinctive enterprise of our time." Like initial "architectural drawings and blueprints," we are living "in a partial and frail structure with incomplete and inadequate facilities." Its "foundations . . . show pockets of quicksand in national policies, age-long antagonisms, and developing rivalries." Moreover, "the materials at our command are fragile" and may not "withstand the fierce storms of passion which are not unlikely to recur." He feared that "civilization will destroy itself as it brings the discoveries of science and the improvements of invention to the operations of war in both weapons and methods." Nonetheless, even if "we have to build and rebuild, and then mayhap rebuild again," Hughes firmly believed that "constructive processes must go on." The Washington Naval Conference exemplified that quest. Thus, diplomatic historian Edward Rhodes credited Hughes with being "the principal architect of America's liberal isolationist foreign policy and its clearest explicator." Rhodes regretted that Hughes was "now largely forgotten" because he "was one of the great political figures of his age, both in America and on the world stage."[46]

Notwithstanding the immediate success of the Washington Conference, Hughes understood that it was a start, not a solution. As he often said, "No one formula will suffice." Much hard work remained but "every single step" forward was important. Hughes hoped that the World Court, the League of Nations, international conferences, modernized international law, and sensitive, respectful diplomacy could together derail potential conflicts. For Hughes, it was essential to back broad intentions with specific agreements. Bringing nations together to define their mutual concerns and shared responsibilities was the pre-condition for peace and the establishment of "the reign of law, as distinguished from the rule of might."[47]

Meanwhile, Borah was promoting a movement to outlaw war entirely. He joined this cause partly because of his genuine opposition to war but also as a way to counter his image as a perpetual critic and to bolster his political ambitions. Another example of the moralistic-legalistic aspect of classical thought, outlawry assumed that mutual agreement could obviate balance of power politics. Initiated by France to get an alliance with the United States, outlawry became the 1928 Kellogg–Briand Pact, an international pledge making war illegal. Hughes considered the effort unrealistic because it was too grandiose and ignored different national interests. Proving his point, the Senate only agreed to join as long as the United States retained the right of self-defense and did not have to defend other signatories. Thus, they perpetuated the Article X debate and negated the whole purpose of the Pact. No wonder Hughes criticized the "delusive simplicity" of outlawry advocates who "stand in the way of the only advance that is practical [but] are ready to show you a direct road to the moon."[48]

Hughes actually was encouraged by the second clause of the Pact, which was a commitment to settle disputes by "pacific means." For him, that meant "diplomacy, arbitration, conferences, [and] judicial settlement of justiciable disputes." If pursued, such strategies could transform the Pact from a "mere declaration" of intent into a practical policy, which should include "outlawing unjustified assaults on non-combatants" as well as protecting monuments, hospitals, and religious institutions. Faced with new postwar "possibilities of widespread destruction," nations had to substitute "clear and binding agreements" for vague "discussions and declarations." The choice, he said, was "either to fight or 'live and let live.'" Despite knowing that humankind had heretofore "erected no effective barrier to war," Hughes believed that "all things are possible if nations are willing to be just to each other." Such idealism may seem as unrealistic as outlawry, but it provided a more malleable, tactical transition from a world of conflict to a world of peace.[49]

Still, it is hard to understand why Hughes dismissed a popular proposal that promoted his desire for international peace based on mutual consent. The Pact was signed by thirty-three nations in 1928, growing to sixty by 1939. It even provided the basis for indicting Nazi war criminals at the 1945 Nuremburg trails. In that sense, contended law professors Oona Hathaway and Scott Shapiro, the Kellogg–Briand Pact may have been "among the most transformative events in human history." By rejecting Grotius's assumption that "just wars" were reasonable, the Pact asserted that no war, not even supposedly "just" ones, should ever be part of international policy. It posited a new framework for world order that was ultimately embraced by the United Nations and accepted as an international principle, despite recurrent transgressions. Could Hughes have been blinded by his constant conflict with Borah or motivated by a desire to dominate foreign policy himself? Or was his criticism just a reflection of his realism and, as Rhodes suggested, a recognition that in the face of international "enmities and passions . . . such pledges would not make a difference"?[50]

Hughes's inconsistency on Kellogg–Briand did not cancel his contribution to the global transformations under way. Instead of the old conflict-oriented balance-of-power system, Hughes orchestrated a new treaty system whereby the United States assumed a preeminent role in international affairs. Not merely a power grab, it accepted the responsibility of America's new economic and political status. Hughes provided the constructive leadership that the war-torn world needed if it was to establish a new kind of stability, which everyone hoped could prevent another war.

That the Washington Treaty System lasted for ten years was a significant accomplishment; that it ultimately failed was a disaster. Yet, today's international order relies on a similar treaty system designed to mitigate balance-of-power politics. Tooze pointed out that it was "easy for self-styled realists to criticize progressive visions of interwar order as symptomatic of the delusions of liberal idealism and doleful overtures to appeasement." However, Tooze believed that "the restless search for a new way of securing order and peace was the expression, not of deluded idealism, but of a higher form of realism . . . [based on] coalition and cooperation." Therefore, he concluded that "these were the calculations of a new type of liberalism, a realpolitk of progress" that we still pursue.[51]

8 | Umpire or Empire? 1921–1925

The Dilemma

Oddly enough, Charles Evans Hughes's peak moment concerning US relations with Latin America and the Caribbean occurred three years after he left the State Department. It was a dramatic culmination of his work as secretary, replete with all its complications. Anticipating trouble, President Calvin Coolidge asked Hughes to come out of retirement and lead the US delegation to the 1928 Sixth International Conference of American States at Havana instead of Secretary of State Frank Kellogg. The President hoped that Hughes's international stature and record of goodwill toward Latin America would save the day. It was a close call.

Resentment against the "Colossus of the North" resulted from decades of US interference in Latin American affairs compounded by the ever-expanding footprint of US businesses. In 1928, these factors were exacerbated by renewed tensions with Mexico and Nicaragua as well as trade restrictions on Argentinian beef due to hoof-and-mouth disease. Hughes faced the fundamental dilemma of US policy regarding its southern neighbors. On the one hand, he wanted to improve the relationship. On the other hand, he upheld US policy prerogatives and protected US investments. It was the statesman's most difficult dilemma, which, said historians Harold and Margaret Sproat, was managing "to reconcile or to compromise conflicting national aims." As the 1928 conference demonstrated, this balancing act was particularly difficult in Latin America.[1]

The most contentious proposal made at the 1928 Havana conference was that "no state may intervene in the internal affairs of another." Clearly, the United States was the target. Hughes out-maneuvered Mexico's attempt to weaken US control of the Pan-American Union (PAU) in a subcommittee he chaired. But he could not stop El Salvador's delegate from introducing a nonintervention resolution in the final open session. Immediately, the galleries cheered and emotional anti-US speeches raged into the night. Led by Argentina, many of the delegates from the twenty-one states represented poured forth their hostility to Yankee imperialism. A Salvadorian representative spoke for small countries suffering from "the principle of the strong, of violence." Delegates outdid each other in denigrating or defending the United States.[2]

When the furor subsided, Hughes was invited to respond. According to a firsthand account, he already dominated the conference by skillfully resolving complicated issues accompanied by an effusion of courtesy that "completely disarms hostility." In this highly charged moment, wrote one reporter, Hughes rose and "glanced at the galleries with no anger, no discontent, with no reproof." At six feet tall, "he stood erect, unembarrassed, wholly unapologetic, positively commanding, and yet utterly companionable. The effect was incredible." Silence ensued. Concerned that his words might be diluted by summary, he told the interpreter to translate "sentence by sentence."[3]

Hughes spoke with emotional intensity, "dignity and fire." At one point, he put his hand over his heart, as if pledging, and affirmed his nation's commitment to "independence for every one of the American republics from the greatest to the smallest." At the same time, he asserted each nation's responsibility and "right to protect its citizens" if threatened by disorder in another state. This he called "interposition of a temporary character . . . not intervention." Explaining that the United States would only act in an emergency, he insisted that even in such cases "we have no desire to stay" and would leave as soon as possible. Although many considered that distinction semantic, it was important. By a simple turn of the phrase, Hughes made the Monroe Doctrine a limited policy of self-defense that rejected both aggression and imperialism. The speech reflected "his gift for differentiation [that] fostered the controlled evolution of doctrine," a strategy, noted law professor Paul Freund, that Hughes used often on the Supreme Court.[4]

Hughes underlined the point by stating, "We do not wish the territory of any American republic. We do not wish to govern any American republic. We do not wish to intervene in the affairs of any American republic. We simply wish peace and order and stability and recognition of honest rights properly acquired so that this hemisphere may not only be the hemisphere of peace but the hemisphere of international justice." While proclaiming that he would not "sacrifice the rights of my country," Hughes promised to work with other countries to preserve their rights through international laws that embodied "justice man to man, justice nation to nation" in keeping with "the spirit" derived "from the days of Grotius." Amid as much approval as there had been condemnation, the nonintervention resolution was withdrawn. The Argentinian delegate stormed out in disgust.[5]

To historian Elizabeth Cobbs Hoffman, a positive long-range development was taking place. By embracing a strategy of occasional intervention followed by withdrawal, the "United States became the first great power to reject colonialism." Consequently, "peacemaking in the 1920's took a dramatic turn away from restraint of aggressors toward self-restraint," which also was the focus of the Washington Conference. Deemphasizing militarism, territorial possession, and formal empires was pathbreaking. Finally, the United States was applying to foreign policy Alexander Hamilton's concept of the federal government as "an umpire or common judge to interpose between contending parties." Although still hegemonic, it marked a philosophical reorientation and concession to Latin American concerns.[6]

Hughes was hailed as the nation's "greatest living statesman." Calling it "the most significant speech of his career," *The New York Times,* often critical, said that Hughes defused hostility "by the sheer force of his personality, his eloquence and deep sincerity." However, the *Birmingham News* saw only "thinly veiled . . . imperialism" and *The Nation* accused him of just protecting private property. A cartoon in the *New York Herald Tribune,* called "Guarding the Basket," had Hughes sitting up high in a basketball hoop attached to a backboard representing "U.S. Guardianship of the Western Hemisphere." He deftly blocked the (stereotyped) Pan-American Union players from making a shot with their "No Armed Intervention" basketball (see figure 8.1).[7]

Many Latin Americans considered Hughes's subtle distinction between "interposition" and "intervention" much too subtle because it still permitted the United States to invade at will. Daring Hughes to turn words into action by withdrawing from Nicaragua and Haiti, they exposed the fault lines of legalism based on international law and Pan-Americanism. Although legalism endorsed what Hughes called, "systematic cooperation" based on "mutual interests," it barely camouflaged US domination. Indeed, international law professor Arnulf Becker Lorca explained that Latin American lawyers and legal scholars had long struggled to make international law a vehicle for recognizing true multilateralism—the equality of nations, their political and economic autonomy, and the universality of human rights. They raised these points within legalist organizations and at every Pan-

American conference. Hughes's Havana speech endorsed national sovereignty and equality, but his insistence on protecting US interests in foreign countries signaled the limits of both international law and Pan-Americanism.[8]

In this sense, Hughes's 1928 victory was delusive. Nonetheless, at a 1929 follow-up conference. a Pan-American pact requiring conciliation and arbitration of disputes was signed by all twenty-one states. Upholding legalist principles, it promised, said Hughes, "greater assurance of peace in this hemisphere" without violating any nation's "sovereign rights, . . . national honor or dignity." He viewed it as a direct "practicable" outgrowth of the Havana conference. Argentinian legal scholar Juan Carlos Scarfi disagreed. He concluded that the 1928 Havana conference was "one of the most critical moments in the history of Pan Americanism and U.S.-Latin American relations." Far from resolving issues, it exposed divisions, challenged US hegemony, and ultimately led to the replacement of US-dominated Pan-Americanism by true multinationalism in 1933.[9]

Hughes recognized some of the problems with Pan-Americanism. In a speech to the American Society of International Law (ASIL) shortly after the Havana conference, he explained that "there is no such entity as Latin America." Rather, "there are twenty states [with] distinct characteristics, aspirations, and policies" that must be respected. He understood the need to "eradicate" the belief that "the United States seeks to dominate Latin America" by acting as "a ruthless giant, without conscience and with unrestrained lust." True to Grotius, Hughes hoped to "find common ground" to offset "individual ambitions," local politics, and popular clamor. Significantly, he did not mention multilateralism, the real obstacle to Pan-Americanism. At Havana, Hughes praised a 1916 legalist resolution endorsing equality among nations and nonintervention as "a Magna Carta for the Western Hemisphere." But Scarfi pointed out that instead of admitting the disparity between theory and practice, Hughes offered a humanitarian excuse for intervention. He compromised without reconciling conflicting national aims.[10]

Hughes was ready to handle the situation in 1928 because he had spoken similar words many times before. For example, in March 1921, only ten days into his term of office, he declared, "We have and will have no ulterior purposes with respect to the Republics of Latin America." He insisted that "our interest does not lie in controlling foreign peoples. . . . Our interest is in having prosperous, peaceful, and law-abiding

Figure 8.1. "Guarding the Basket," artist unclear. *New York Herald Tribune*, February 15, 1928.

neighbors." Instead of imperialism, Hughes advocated "the fostering of friendship, and of mutually advantageous commercial intercourse."[11]

Although there was always a gap between promise and performance, the Harding administration emphasized political stability for mutual economic benefit. This theme both perpetuated and altered previous US attitudes and policies. Finding reasonable and respectful formulas for peaceful coexistence was Hughes's foreign policy goal in all theaters. Hard as it was to implement regarding Europe and the Far East, it involved different but equally difficult complications in Latin America and the Caribbean. Closer to home, these were areas where the United States was historically more entangled and where anti-US sentiment was strong.

The 1823 Monroe Doctrine was originally an aspirational declaration that Europe should stay out of the Western Hemisphere, but its meaning expanded as the United States became powerful and prosperous. Time, observed historian David Dent, gave the Monroe Doctrine "a mythic grandeur" never intended by its authors. Already by the 1820s, noted historian William A Williams, the United States was heavily involved in direct trade with Latin America as well as the carrying trade between Latin America, Europe, and Asia. By the late nineteenth century, industrialization generated more goods than the nation could consume, thereby creating a "glut theory" to explain the 1893 to 1897 Depression. The need for foreign markets plus foreign petroleum, minerals, and agricultural goods stimulated investments in nations on the Caribbean Sea, which was increasingly considered an "American Lake." These economic factors contributed to the 1898 Spanish–American War, resulting in the nation's first foreign possessions—Puerto Rico, Cuba, the Philippines, Hawaii, and Guam. However, as the nation expanded its influence in the Caribbean and the Pacific, resistance in the new territories and anti-imperialism at home created what Cobbs Hoffman called "ambivalent imperialism."[12]

Never ambivalent, Theodore Roosevelt (TR) was the first president to embrace US involvement in and leadership on the world stage. Under his tutelage, the Monroe Doctrine became overtly aggressive. In 1903, the former "Rough Rider" endorsed the Platt Amendment, which allowed the United States to intervene in Cuban financial crises in 1906, 1912, 1917, and 1920. Cuba became the nation's first protectorate. Panama was second. Also in 1903, TR fomented a Panamanian rebellion in order to secure land for the Panama Canal, an episode called "the rape of Columbia." The resulting "treaty" gave the United States total power over land for the canal "in perpetuity . . . as if it were sovereign."[13]

A Venezuelan debt crisis prompted TR to issue his famous corollary to the Monroe Doctrine in 1904. It justified America's "exercise of an international police power" whenever there was "brutal wrong-doing or an impotence which results in a general loosening of the ties of civilized society." Such circumstances "may finally require intervention by some civilized nation." And, he affirmed, "in the Western Hemisphere, the United States cannot ignore this duty." Historian Gail Bederman pointed out that TR's language reflected a gendered approach to foreign policy whereby "manly," advanced (white) nations demonstrated their masculinity by dominating and civilizing weaker, primitive (nonwhite) nations. From TR's perspective, wrote Bederman, "only by embracing a virile, racial expansionism could a civilization achieve its true manhood. This, as TR saw it, was the ultimate meaning of imperialism."[14]

TR claimed that a policing role was consistent with the original Monroe Doctrine, not a "new obligation." Nonetheless, it marked a shift from defensive to offensive, from keeping Europe out to allowing the United States in. It underlined the economic agenda of the Monroe Doctrine. For example, when the Dominican Republic faced default and a foreign debt crisis in 1904, TR authorized a US financial agent to take over the customs house, albeit with local consent but bolstered by two warships in the harbor. Most of the revenue was used to pay foreign debts with the rest left for governmental administration. As historian Cyrus Vesser showed, the customs receivership ended a decade of incompetence and exploitation by the Santo Domingo Improvement Company and inaugurated a new phase of governmental supervision of private investment in the Caribbean. The United States had acquired its third protectorate. Other interventions included Panama and Nicaragua. As "gun-boat diplomacy" facilitated economic expansion, TR encouraged the United Fruit Company to control banana production in Honduras and Costa Rica, which he dubbed "banana republics." According to international affairs professor, Noel Maurer, "The United States was now in the empire business."[15]

TR's successor, William Howard Taft, preferred financial investment to military intervention. "Dollar Diplomacy" emphasized trade, treaties, and "the substitution of dollars for bullets." Because Taft believed that governmental policy should "include active intervention to secure our merchandise and our capitalists' opportunity for profitable investment," his administration encouraged US business expansion and acquisition of property in South America and the Caribbean. Investments in Cuba alone reached $200 million by 1911. That figure multiplied geometrically over time due to the coordinated efforts of New York City bankers, financiers, and sugar brokers to buy existing sugar plantations and develop new ones. Taft believed that US bank loans would stabilize the finances of weak governments and preclude European interference. On the one hand, historian James Hudson criticized such expansion for trapping countries like Cuba in debt from loans orchestrated by Chase. On the other hand, historian Frank Ninkovich considered dollar diplomacy a new form of internationalism. It represented a middle ground between imperialism and isolationism, an alternative to the old militaristic balance of power dynamics. But it also thrust the United States ever more deeply into Latin American affairs.[16]

Financial influence inevitably led to political influence and aggravated resentments over economic imperialism. Moreover, dollar diplomacy did not preclude military involvement as demonstrated when Taft sent troops to Nicaragua in 1910, assumed control of its customs revenue, and established a fourth protectorate. Except for one year under Hughes, US troops stayed in Nicaragua until 1933. The United States repeatedly used economic crises to justify imposing financial advisors and election monitors and/or taking over fiscal operations and customs collections. The "loans for supervision" policy merely substituted informal economic empires for formal ones and enabled the United States to develop what historian Warren I. Cohen called an "empire without tears."[17]

Preaching "moral imperialism," in 1913, President Woodrow Wilson declared that the United States wanted to spread democracy, not acquire more territory. Summoning his professorial past, he declared, "I propose to teach the South American Republics to elect good men." Although Wilson later explained that he only meant helping countries that wanted democracy, historian John E. Fagg called it "a clumsy humanitarianism marred by assumptions of racial supremacy." Despite his belief in self-determination for all nations, Wilson authorized more military interventions in Latin America than any previous president. The Marines became an ever-present, often brutal reality that propped up corrupt governments. Furthermore, the 1913 Federal Reserve Act allowed US banks to open branches south of the border. New York bankers soon controlled many Caribbean economies, like Nicaragua. National City Bank's branches stretched from Cuba to Chile. As political scientist Paul W. Drake noted, "coercive democratization" was a fatally flawed oxymoron. The same could be said for gunboat diplomacy, dollar diplomacy, and moral imperialism.[18]

All of these policies increased anti-Americanism abroad and anti-imperialism at home, both of which affected the Harding administration. Hughes considered it "unsatisfactory" that "in this hemisphere, old sores were still festering." During the 1920 campaign, Harding criticized Wilson's "unwarranted interference in the affairs of the little republics of the Western hemisphere." He also "condemned the rape of Haiti and Santo Domingo by the present administration." Such aggression, he said, "made enemies out of those who should be our friends [and] discredited our country as their trusted neighbor." Although Harding and Hughes retained Wilson's goal of promoting democracy in Latin America while protecting US hegemony and economic interests, they emphasized stability and cooperation over aggression. This approach, wrote Cobbs Hoffman, made them "part umpire, part policeman, part banker." Changes notwithstanding, the Monroe Doctrine remained the central justification for US autonomous actions and preeminence in the Western Hemisphere.[19]

Hughes and Harding thought they could defuse anti-Americanism by promoting Pan-Americanism. The goal was to develop a climate of goodwill that fostered peace, cooperation, and trade across North, Central, and South America. Appreciating that Latin American states held onto their independence and equality "tenaciously," Hughes wanted to avoid conflict. He understood that Pan-Americanism was just a "moral union," not a political one. Because, Hughes said, nations were "joined together in an inescapable and constantly increasing intimacy," it made sense to "help each other." Advocating "loose associations" to promote "accord" through "understanding and comradeship," he pointed out that "there is no sacrifice of independence in cooperation," Historians Max Paul Friedman and Tom Long called this approach "benign hegemony."[20]

The Pan-American Union (PAU) originated as the Commercial Bureau of American Republics, formed in 1890 with an economic focus on customs issues. It soon was renamed the International Bureau of American Republics and renamed again as the PAU in 1910. Its original bulletin targeted "merchants and shippers" of the member nations.

The US secretary of state chaired the governing board comprised of representatives from Latin America. Elihu Root got Andrew Carnegie to fund three-quarters ($750,000) of the PAU's monumental Washington, DC headquarters while Latin American nations funded one-quarter, a telling imbalance. Completed in 1910, the lavish beaux arts building integrated architectural and sculptural elements from North and South America. It became the nation's center for diplomatic activities like the Washington Conference. The PAU was always controlled by the United States, as symbolized not only by its building but also by its hold on leadership. Efforts to make it more democratic were repeatedly diverted by the United States, including by Hughes at Havana.[21]

Latin Americans did not think US hegemony was benign. As Friedman and Long pointed out, they seized every opportunity to challenge it through "soft balancing" by using nonmilitary strategies of pressuring, asserting, and protesting through organizations like the PAU and the American Institute of International Law (AIIL), conferences, or state policies like Mexican confiscation laws. Fully aware of the contradiction between Pan-Americanism and interventionism, Latin Americans undercut US hegemony and influenced US policy by asserting their own interests. Every occupation or intervention met resistance. Every conference faced calls for multilateralism and US withdrawal. Every conference resolution was questioned or qualified. Large nations like Argentina and Mexico led the efforts while small nations like Haiti and El Salvador stood their ground. Not mere puppets, Latin American leaders used their positions to extract concessions or defy initiatives. Hegemony was never absolute.[22]

Accordingly, the new administration rejected the Roosevelt Corollary and redefined the Monroe Doctrine, Hughes championed a Pax Americana "maintained not by arms but by mutual respect and good will and the tranquilizing processes of reason." It would not replicate either the Pax Romana, based on military conquest, or the Pax Britannica, based on colonialism and naval dominance. Rather, the Pax Americana, like the Washington Conference, would promote mutually acceptable treaties reflecting "fair and honorable dealing," a phrase Hughes used often. Ideally, these relations would be based on updated international law, but Hughes knew that nations could always find ways to override international law by claiming "expediency." Legally binding treaties could reduce that possibility bolstered by economic interdependence and enshrined in Pan-Americanism. The emperor had acquired new clothes.[23]

Here, too, Hughes built on Root's legacy as secretary of state from 1905 to 1909. On the one hand, Root supported the Platt Amendment and the Roosevelt Corollary, albeit for defensive, not offensive, purposes. He also backed the expansion of US businesses in the Caribbean. On the other hand, Root set the Roosevelt Corollary in the context of Pan-Americanism and international law. He also tried (unsuccessfully) to get special tariff exemptions for Cuba and Puerto Rico in order to stimulate their economies. It was Root who soothed relations and obtained treaties with the Dominican Republic, Colombia, and Panama. He understood that "the South Americans now hate us largely because they think we despise them and try to bully them." Therefore, he resolved to seek "their friendship . . . by treating them like gentlemen. If you want to make a man your friend," he noted, "it does not pay to treat him like a yellow dog."[24]

In 1906, Root made a path-breaking goodwill tour of Latin America, becoming the first secretary of state to travel abroad. In 1907, he convened a Central American Peace Conference at which five nations agreed not to recognize any revolutionary government that overthrew a constitutional government. This Tobar Doctrine may have been intended to bolster the signatories' own power, but it was later used to justify interventions and supervise elections of rulers friendly to the United States. The 1907 conferees also established a Central American Court of Justice, which was the world's first international body for resolving disputes. Root was widely venerated in and beyond the legal profession, in and beyond the United States. Hughes endeavored to perpetuate the positive aspects of Root's record while addressing the negative legacies bequeathed by TR, Taft, and Wilson.[25]

The Empire Trap

Hughes started working on Latin American issues even before taking office and was ready to confront the first crisis of his first day. It was a border war between Costa Rica and Panama, a legacy of TR's aggressive Panama Canal policies. After studying the situation, Hughes decided that a previously arbitrated border settlement should stand. However, when Panama refused to relinquish the contested territory, Costa Rica seized it and war loomed. Upon entering office, Hughes got Harding's approval to convince the two nations to suspend hostilities by sending warships and Marines to the area. The antagonists cooled off and the original arbitration agreement was respected. In the narrow sense, the United States flexed its military might once again. In the broader sense, Hughes upheld the validity of international arbitration and avoided war. The situation highlighted the difficulties he faced and confirmed his commitment to adopt "a wise practicality" for pursuing "peace in the Western hemisphere." He was also mindful of Senate resolutions blocking formal imperialism while limiting investments in the Philippines and Cuba.[26]

Hughes balanced priorities. Because the German navy no longer posed a threat to the Panama Canal, he could be more flexible about protecting it. Responding to Panamanian complaints about tyrannical US officials in the Canal Zone, he insisted that they change their behavior. But he also claimed that the United States could not fulfill its responsibility to protect the canal and the independence of Panama without a firm boundary line. Significantly, the resulting agreement with Costa Rica granted nine million acres to American oil companies. Hughes supported another treaty compensating Colombia for land lost to the Panama Canal, but it too protected US oil and business interests. These Caribbean complications exemplified what international affairs professor Noel Maurer called "the empire trap." As he explained, "Successful intervention on behalf of overseas investors begets more overseas investment, which creates more pressure to intervene when those investments come under threat." It becomes increasingly impossible to leave. The United States was caught between its short- and long-range goals, its interests in profit and peace, its national and international priorities.[27]

Much of the credit for the shift of tone and policy toward Latin America went to Sumner Welles, chief of the State Department's Latin American Division in the beginning of Hughes's term. Welles frequently served as Hughes's special envoy to Latin America and later was President Franklin D. Roosevelt's (FDR) undersecretary of state, thus providing valuable continuity over time. In 1923, Hughes and Welles organized a Second Washington Conference on Central American Affairs to defuse tensions between Honduras, Nicaragua, and El Salvador. Along with Costa Rica and Guatemala, the Central American republics signed a peace treaty, agreed not to interfere in each other's politics, and adopted an arbitration process. The 1907 Tobar Doctrine against recognizing revolutionary governments was expanded to prohibit recognition of any government that contained any leader of a previous revolution. This clause enabled the United States to control Central American politics by deciding if a leader was acceptable, regardless of being duly elected. The United States was not a voting member but Hughes opened the conference. Although he assured the delegates that the United States had "no ambition to gratify at your expense" and offered help in securing peace, US hegemony prevailed.[28]

A year later, some of these agreements were adopted by other nations at the Fifth International Conference of American States in Santiago, Chile. Hughes did not attend because of illness, but he sent a speech that applauded the creation of a new group of jurists to codify international law. Excepting Honduras, the conferees endorsed a 1923 Pan-American Treaty, or Gondra Convention, which established strategies for arbitrating disputes among themselves and set up a commission for cooperation on other issues. These nations were substituting self-control for dependence on the United States. Going further, the Uruguayans proposed an American Association of Nations modeled on the League of Nations.

Nine Latin American states had joined the League hoping that it would protect them against US aggression. But they were largely ignored and greatly dismayed when the League endorsed the Monroe Doctrine. They also resented not being invited to the Washington Conference, even though it was held in the PAU building. Their proposed new association would have committed every Latin American state, including the United States, to mutual defense if at war with a non-American country. Considering the fight over the League of Nations and Article X, the United States was unlikely to accept such a commitment. Nor would it relinquish either its autonomy or its hegemony by making the Monroe Doctrine multilateral. After the US delegation definitively rejected the proposal, the conference ended. No one was pleased, but the Latin Americans had effectively employed "soft balancing."[29]

Although Pan Americanism suffered at Santiago, Hughes tried to strengthen it by establishing more professional standards for all troops in Latin America. In addition, every US representative was expected to speak Spanish, know about the area, and treat others respectfully. Unfortunately, Harding violated these rules by appointing a personal friend as governor of Puerto Rico without consulting Hughes. Disparaging and offensive, the new governor antagonized the Puerto Ricans until a nervous breakdown forced him to resign. Hughes immediately appointed a better replacement. Hughes also followed Root's goodwill strategy by travelling to Rio de Janeiro in 1922 for the centenary celebration of Brazil's independence. Giving four speeches, he supported the independence of Latin American states and denied that the United States had any imperialist intentions.[30]

According to historian Thomas Bender, the United States learned from its experience with the Philippines that colonization could be disastrous and resistance could be fierce. Ironically, America's ambition to civilize and democratize supposedly inferior peoples not only resulted in uncivilized war and oppression but also inspired a movement for freedom against the very nation that championed freedom. For other oppressed people across Asia, Filipino resistance was "a political earthquake," a message of "freedom, modernity, and nationhood." Seeing that colonization backfired, Hughes hoped that Pan-Americanism would replace the Roosevelt Corollary's imperialism.[31]

The 1923 centennial of the Monroe Doctrine provided a perfect opportunity to clarify shifting US attitudes toward Latin America. In two speeches, Hughes upheld the Monroe Doctrine as a fundamental "unifying principle" and "integral part" of American foreign policy. However, he asserted that it "is not a policy of aggression; it is a policy of self-defense," a component of "our proper influence to promote peace and good will." The original document was intended to deter European expansion into the Caribbean and South America in order to protect all Latin American states. Now, he said, such deterrence applied to a broader range of threats to hemispheric stability and peace, including political and financial chaos.[32]

That left a lot of room for interpretation. But, Hughes declared, "I utterly disclaim as unwarranted" statements "implying a claim on our part to superintend the affairs of our sister republics, to assert an overlordship." Again, insisting that "there is no imperialistic sentiment among us," Hughes claimed that the United States "does not attempt to establish a protectorate over Latin American States." Rather, the United States only offered "its friendly assistance to promote stability" to nations confronting "disturbed conditions involving their own peace and that of their neighbors." This rationale was really not so different from TR's. Nor did it much differ from Root's portrayal of the Monroe Doctrine as a vehicle for a collegial and humanitarian Pan-Americanism. Citing several instances when the United States sent troops after revolutions to help reestablish order, Hughes advocated a Pan-Americanism defined by cooperation and "cultivation of the interests which are distinctively American." Ironically, observed Scarfi, the Monroe Doctrine's American exceptionalism led to a doctrine of hemispheric exceptionalism that FDR's Good Neighbor policy would ultimately displace. J. Varela, minister of Uruguay to the United States, agreed that the Monroe Doctrine had protected Latin America from European threats. Nonetheless, he hoped that what he called the "Hughes Doctrine" would enable nonaggression to dominate relations between the United States and Latin America as well as within Latin America.[33]

Repeating the most often-cited part of his 1922 Brazil speech, Hughes laid the groundwork for FDR's Good Neighbor policy by declaring: "We covet no territory; we seek no conquest; the liberty we cherish for ourselves we desire for others; and we assert no rights for ourselves that we do not accord to others. We sincerely desire to see throughout this hemisphere an abiding peace, the reign of justice, and the diffusion of the blessings of a beneficent cooperation. It is this desire which forms the basis of the Pan American doctrine." At the same time, Hughes made it abundantly clear that "the United States reserves to itself" the right to decide when and how to act. Just as the United States had refused to issue the original Monroe Doctrine jointly with England, so Hughes upheld the nation's autonomous freedom of action now and urged each nation to proclaim its own Monroe Doctrine, which all would respect. To diplomatic historian Dexter Perkins, Hughes's emphasis on protecting the Panama Canal and addressing "unsettled conditions" in the Caribbean represented a new "Caribbean Doctrine" that modified both the original doctrine and the Roosevelt Corollary. For historian Joan Hoff Wilson, however, it really was a "Closed Door" policy for the Caribbean, which was gradually extended across South America.[34]

Qualifying the Monroe Doctrine made it seem less offensive, but it still was distinctly unilateral and potentially interventionist. If Hughes and Harding rejected the more aggressive aspects of Roosevelt's "Big Stick" and Wilson's "moral imperialism," they accepted their underlying implications. Hughes may have revised the dialogue to reflect his sincere commitment to peace, but he retained the faith of TR, Taft, and Wilson that American economic expansion was essential to American economic development and a boon to weaker countries. Private capital investments would reap the political profit of hemispheric stability enriched by economic profits from raw materials and trade. Although the US government would not invest directly or even condone private investments, it would protect investors, including intervening when necessary. This diplomatic sleight of hand perpetuated America's idealistic self-image while camouflaging empire.

The limitations of such an approach were captured by what was called "the Mexican problem." Wilson faced crisis after crisis south of the border, motivating him to dispatch the Marines in 1914 and six thousand troops under General John Pershing in 1916. Fatal border clashes heightened seemingly unresolvable tensions. In the presidential campaign, Hughes criticized Wilson's record by pointing out that while "decrying interference, we interfered most exasperatingly." Wilson not only brought down a duly elected president and seized Vera Cruz but imposed, removed, and reimposed an embargo, all while failing to protect our own citizens. Embarrassing as it was, Wilson withdrew the troops in 1917 and recognized a new government even though it restricted foreign investments and appropriated foreign land holdings. Mexico was asserting its national integrity against US hegemony and the imperialist implications of the Monroe Doctrine. Even more dangerous, it was establishing a precedent that threatened US investments throughout Latin America.[35]

Confronting this reality, Hughes sought Harding's approval to offer another newly elected Mexican government formal recognition in exchange for guarantees that American property rights would be upheld and that property previously confiscated would be compensated. That was basically Wilson's position. Hughes remained firm and rejected recognition for three years. However, reflecting his interest in Latin American policy, Harding pressed for compromise and sent his own representative to forge an agreement, which was signed secretly in 1923. It remained secret for decades and was never legitimized by either nation's legislature. There were good reasons for secrecy. American oil and mining companies retained their extraction rights and two commissions were created to arbitrate compensation claims. These concessions plus a clause prohibiting Mexico from developing its own oil industry technology made the treaty too contentious to publicize. Senator Norris protested against the secrecy and the benefits granted to American oil interests. Mexico continued asserting its sovereignty but welcomed the new investments. Upholding US economic interests remained central to US foreign policy.[36]

While Hughes defended US–Caribbean interventions, he tried to reduce or end them. Frequent political upheaval and constant economic crisis in the Dominican Republic convinced Wilson to send the Navy and the Marines in 1916. The imposed military government eliminated democratic institutions and a US-trained national guard undermined the power of local leaders. Opposition guerrilla forces fought against the invasion until 1921. Nonetheless, stability in the Dominican Republic, albeit imposed and oppressive, offered a chance to withdraw.

Hughes appointed a less militaristic naval officer as governor and Harding chose a competent new customs collector. After a stalemate over withdrawal, the administration sent Sumner Welles to negotiate with Dominican politicians and supervise the election (perhaps rigged) of a new president. Withdrawal began in 1924. Hughes hoped that success in the Dominican Republic would ameliorate anti-US sentiment throughout the region. That was unlikely because the United States still controlled Dominican customs, internal revenue, and public works. Moreover, when the National Guard was turned over to the Dominicans, Rafael Trujillo used it as a springboard for becoming a dictator in 1930. The desire for stability trumped democracy.[37]

Another example was Honduras, where a 1923 political crisis motivated Hughes and Harding to send warships and the Marines. Instead of occupation, they again dispatched Welles, who successfully negotiated a settlement and got British bondholders to mitigate Honduran debt. However, because the new president was a US puppet elected under questionable circumstances, anti-American resentments simmered. So too, Hughes avoided occupying Cuba despite major US business interests in sugar and trade. He postponed loans until the president promised reforms, which evaporated as soon as the money arrived. Hughes did improve relations by reining in an obnoxious US official and getting the Senate to relinquish control of one of Cuba's islands. But Norris pointed out that this seemingly benign gesture was sullied by the fact that the treaty protected a US coaling station.[38]

Much to Hughes's dismay, it was impossible to withdraw from Haiti, where the Marines controlled an abusive police force under a puppet dictatorship known for atrocities. Seeking economic stability, Hughes supported a loan to Haiti in return for allowing the National City Bank of New York to control the National Bank of the Republic of Haiti. NAACP field secretary and writer James Weldon Johnson visited Haiti and exposed the fact that the US bank had trapped Haiti in a $30 million high interest loan that no impoverished nation could ever repay. The administration looked bad. Accordingly, Hughes followed Welles's advice to switch control from the Navy to the State Department and reform the American occupation. But ongoing political unrest and fiscal mismanagement precluded withdrawal during his term of office. Norris found the whole affair shameful. Here was "one of the leading nations of civilization [taking] advantage of a poor, weak, ignorant nation." The inevitable outcome, he thundered, was justifiable scorn "all over South America." Although the US-backed president was clearly autocratic, the United States finally left Haiti in 1926, after Hughes had resigned.[39]

Six years of apparent stability and prosperity in Nicaragua encouraged Hughes to try withdrawing the Marines in 1924 after almost a quarter century of occupation characterized by oppression and protests. Political divisions, changing presidents, and questionable elections complicated the situation. Hughes sent representatives to promote electoral reforms, which were accepted by the Nicaraguan Congress but proved hard to implement. US loans did not compensate for continued control of Nicaraguan customs and monitoring of its bank. Norris deplored using the Marines "as a collection agency for Wall Street."[40]

Anxious to reduce interference in Nicaraguan politics, Hughes wavered at critical moments, earning criticism from Welles himself. A highly questionable 1924 election notwithstanding, the United States recognized the new government on the flimsy premise that the next election would be cleaner. Hughes also agreed that the United States would train a new police force to replace the Marines. These compromises enabled the United States to withdraw in 1925 but a bloody civil war led to renewed occupation in 1926. A 1927 rebellion against the Marines was led by popular guerilla leader Augusto Cesar Sandino and lasted until troops were finally withdrawn in 1933. The whole situation revealed the fault lines of US policies and the limits of Hughes's statesmanship.[41]

Money was always a two-edged sword. It epitomized the problems of the empire trap. The larger the investment, the smaller the window for withdrawal. Some countries welcomed US investments, but the massive increase of investment in the Caribbean and Central America from 1898 to 1920 bred widespread hostility. Instead of Great Britain, the United States now dominated those economies by supplying three-quarters of their imports in exchange for absorbing two-thirds of their exports. Corporations like Standard Oil, American Smelting and Refining, International Telephone and Telegraph, Firestone Tire and Rubber, United Fruit, and Anaconda Copper seized land, mineral rights, and sub-soil rights. They also tore up the countryside with roads and railroads to move goods to the ports for shipment to the United States and abroad. Following the 1920 to 1921 postwar depression, American companies further expanded through loans, branch banks, factories, and subsidiaries.[42]

Hudson criticized the rise of US "imperial banking and the internationalization of Wall Street." He explained that from 1870 to 1920, New York financial institutions established extensive networks in the Caribbean and Latin America. The banks and private investment houses, like J. P. Morgan, became agents of American foreign policy. They floated the public debts of Latin American countries, reorganized their customs collection and currency systems, and established "nominally" domestic banks. The objective was to displace European economic influence in the Caribbean and Latin America. Although there would be less purely military intervention, there would be military protection of American investors and banks. It was intervention by another name.[43]

Hughes and Hoover understood that US business expansion represented economic imperialism because it dominated the resources of other countries to benefit US private interests. Therefore, they insisted that investments would also benefit the receiving nations by developing natural resources, building infrastructure and communications networks while stimulating agriculture and industry. Knowing that a major source of political unrest was economic suffering, they linked American investments to economic and political stability. In 1950, historian and long-term foreign policy advisor Herbert Feis labeled this revised approach the "diplomacy of the dollar," whereby the pursuit of profit would be set within and camouflaged by larger diplomatic goals. Consequently, wrote William A. Williams, "economic expansion became both a means and an end for American policy-makers."[44]

Although all the key players in Harding's cabinet endorsed the liberal capitalist order, they divided over actual policies. Unlike Taft's full-throated federal support of foreign investment in the Caribbean and Latin America, Treasury Secretary Mellon thought that the government should leave private investors to their own devices. By contrast, Hoover wanted to supervise and concentrate all investment and loan decisions in his Commerce Department. Hughes fought to retain State Department control and preferred that the government distance itself, without completely abandoning, investors. However, because Hughes often agreed with Hoover in specific cases and disliked internecine warfare, the Commerce Department acquired substantial influence over investment and loan policy even as policy formation remained in the State Department. By neither promoting nor prohibiting loans officially, Hughes and Hoover exercised what historian Joseph S. Tulchin called "quiet surveillance." Instead of directly participating in loans and investment decisions, the government would offer "friendly advice" and supervise risky loans when asked by both parties. But it would refuse to discuss or accept responsibility for any business prospects.[45]

It was a delicate, perhaps deceptive, balance underlined by the State Department's loan-for-supervision policy, which involved recommending advisors to and coordinating connections between banks and interested countries. Although always avoiding direct responsibility for the loans, the State Department chaperoned more loans and seemed more involved than ever. Opposition at home and abroad mounted as banks demanded excessive interests on their loans and Hughes insisted that all diplomatic agreements protect US investments. He even got the Bolivian government to give New York banks virtual control over that nation's tax system. The difference between colonialism, investment, and supervision was blurred. In the process, wrote historian Emily Rosenberg, "the dilemmas of using private bank lending to accomplish public goals" were exposed. Somehow, the State Department had "to minimize conspicuous involvement yet maximize the appearance of security for loans considered essential to the stabilization of Central and South America."[46]

In 1921, Hughes trapped himself in a strange logistical spider's web. Amazingly enough, he agreed that potential conflicts over a bank loan to El Salvador could be referred to the US Supreme Court. That suggestion violated not only the policy of disengagement but also the separation of powers. It was a striking lapse for a former Supreme Court justice who opposed burdening the Court with administrative duties. Making matters worse, when the loan conditions were changed midstream to benefit the United Fruit Company, Hughes was dismayed but did not withdraw. In saving face, he sacrificed consistency and his prized integrity. He seemed to be Wall Street's marionette, a charge that resurfaced at his confirmation hearings for chief justice.[47]

Racism was an ugly underside of expansion. Hudson discovered that US banks held minstrel shows and used blackface waiters and singers at banquets and other social events. Racist jokes about Blacks, Jews, Asians, and Native Americans dotted bank publications. Prejudice north of the border reinforced exploitation south of the border. Hughes cannot be blamed personally for this attitude and his record suggests a nonprejudicial perspective, but some would say that his support of the banks implicated him indirectly.[48]

Investors were not always in sync with Hughes and Hoover. For example, they were unable to prevent unwise loans to Cuba, which benefitted bankers, corrupt politicians, and land owners. Some companies were so wealthy that they did not even seek government approval, which deprived Hughes and Hoover of any influence at all. For one, the United Fruit Company completely dominated the countries where it operated. In Honduras and Costa Rica, it was notorious for controlling politics and purchasing vast tracts of land, thereby destroying local life. In Chile, Peru, and Bolivia, the Guggenheims outmaneuvered the British to dominate key mineral resources like copper, tin, lead, and zinc. Rosenberg showed that reality repeatedly undermined the promise of public-private cooperation.[49]

Fully aware that American companies were greatly resented abroad, Hughes declared, "We are aiming not to exploit but to aid, not to subvert but to help in laying the foundations for sound, stable and independent government." He may have been sincere, but involvement for the sake of stability precluded leaving if instability continued or was renewed. As demonstrated by Haiti and Nicaragua, it was easy to get in, hard to get out. Except for the anti-imperialists, there was little domestic pressure to withdraw because most Americans supported American citizens' property rights and business expansion as part of the twenties' economic boom. For political scientist Hans Morgenthau, however, "indirect domination" was just replacing direct domination with "the invisible chains of economic dependence." Formal or informal, direct or indirect, political or economic, it still was an empire.[50]

As the United States moved three steps forward and two steps backward, Hughes's legacy remained mixed. Good intentions notwithstanding, the obstacles to withdrawal were immense. Each country was different, but the dilemmas were similar. The desire for political and economic stability was at once the problem and the solution. Although intervention and investment could promote stability, they stimulated resistance and resentment. All too often, the United States ended up undercutting the very democratic principles it claimed to promote. With a vested interest in the Caribbean combined with a desire for peace, profit, and prominence throughout the region, US policy was severely circumscribed and often inconsistent. Hughes never fully renounced intervention. However, he hoped to have planted the seeds for a better future. As he often asserted, "We wish to have prosperous and independent neighbors with whom we can deal in peace to our mutual advantage." With substantial limitations, Hughes moved that difficult process forward.[51]

Although Hughes was unable to achieve all of his objectives, he improved US relations with Latin America and earned a great deal of personal credibility in the process. That was why President Coolidge sent him to Havana in 1928. In addition, he was repeatedly recruited out of retirement to resolve boundary disputes like those between Panama and Costa Rica, Panama and Columbia, and Chile and Peru, as well as between Brazil, Columbia, and Peru. He even negotiated a thorny conflict between Guatemala and Honduras in 1930, when he was chief justice. The only arbiter those countries could agree upon, Hughes was still promoting the principle that the United States would be "co-workers with our sister Republics, and not masters, that our purpose is to resist aggression, not to commit it."[52]

Hughes modernized and restyled the Monroe Doctrine as a less aggressive policy committed to the sovereignty of every American state as well as hemispheric security and peace. In addition, he mitigated the protectorate policy, upgraded diplomatic standards, tried to withdraw troops, and promoted the peaceful resolution of disputes. After wrestling with the issue of business expansion and exploitation, he concluded that private investments benefitted all parties. Of course, it was unlikely that any secretary of state, especially a Republican one, would abandon US businesses investing abroad. In fact, wrote Rhodes, Hughes considered it "the obligation of a sovereign state to protect the lives and properties of residents, both nationals and aliens." Nonetheless, to Latin Americans, that policy legitimized US hegemony and contrasted with Hughes's eloquent advocacy of Pan-Americanism. In Latin America, there was a disconnect between his words and his deeds.[53]

Yet, his words were not entirely vacuous. In Latin America, as elsewhere, Hughes genuinely hoped for peace based on mutual consent as developed in conferences, ratified by treaties, codified by international law, and adjudicated by a world court. Sometimes his characteristic efforts to balance change with continuity prolonged "interposition" and bred uncomfortable compromises or disappointing retreats. Overall, said Rhodes, there was no basic "inconsistency in the policies he advanced." Hughes was caught in an empire trap that he did not create and tried to abate but actually helped perpetuate. Regarding Latin America, Perkins saw Hughes's term as secretary of state as "a transition from imperialism and offensive measures of control to the policy of the good neighbor." Not exactly, wrote Scarfi, because, unlike Pan-Americanism, FDR's Good Neighbor policy officially renounced intervention and was more multilateral, less hegemonic. In other words, Hughes began but never completed the transition.[54]

For his own part, Hughes was pleased when historian Samuel Flagg Bemis wrote in 1943 that the secretary had endeavored "to liquidate the interventions of the United States in the Caribbean and Central America, as promptly as political stability" allowed. The catch was that conditional final clause. It underlined the ultimate foreign policy dilemma, which, wrote Tulchin, was "to strike a careful balance between pressure and influence; to protect America's expanded interests in the hemisphere without having to assume formal control over another sovereign state." The struggle to simultaneously assert and limit power handicapped statesmanship. Although Hughes did not make as much progress as he wanted, he typically pursued what was "practicable" in the short term with an eye to what was desirable in the long term. He preferred being an umpire to acquiring an empire.[55]

The World Court

During the 1920s, the American public overwhelmingly supported joining the Permanent Court of International Justice, also called the World Court. So did over two hundred Chambers of Commerce, the National Association of Manufacturers, the American Legion, the American Federation of Labor, the American Bar Association, the League of Women Voters, the General Federation of Women's Clubs, all the major religious organizations, fifty business and professional groups, plus 83 percent of US newspapers. The major outliers were the twenty-two Hearst papers, *The New York Sun, The Kansas City Star, Chicago Tribune,* and *The Washington Post.* Even seventy-three senators (thirty-seven Republicans and thirty-six Democrats) were on board. The platforms of both parties endorsed the World Court in 1924. So, why was the United States unable to join the World Court until 1945?[56]

The answer was simple. The fight over joining the World Court was an extension of the fight over joining the League of Nations. It did not end until the United Nations replaced the League of Nations in 1945. The idea of an international body to arbitrate international conflicts in order to avoid war had been discussed for decades. In the United States, the Supreme Court's power to resolve disputes between states provided a model for an international body to serve, said Hughes, as an "umpire" by resolving disputes between nations. In the 1880s, Secretary of State James G. Blaine called for a similar organization to address Latin American conflicts, which became the PAU. In 1899 and 1907, the United States participated in the Hague Peace Conferences designed to promote international arbitration. However, the Senate repeatedly blocked all possibility of sharing its power over foreign policy with any international arbitrators or judges.[57]

A lifelong advocate of the World Court, Hughes was dismayed by the stalemate. He asked, "When other nations seek to promote the judicial settlement of international disputes, how can we afford to count ourselves out?" Evoking Grotius, he argued that "we cannot profess allegiance to the cause of international justice without maintaining the institutions of international justice." Hughes hoped "that after long years, peoples are emerging from the black night of hatred and distrust into a new day of reason and accord." Nonetheless, he was realistic enough to warn that "controversies will not be lacking. Economic, racial, and national interests will inevitably clash." Hughes's priority always was to recognize but replace conflict with cooperation.[58]

The 1899 Hague Peace Conference was the first time that nations from around the world met to seek ways to avoid war and improve international relations through international agreement. It established a Permanent Court of Arbitration with arbiters to be selected for disputes. But each case was handled separately with different arbiters chosen by the disputants from a certified list. There was no continuity over time and no development of consistent legal resolution principles. The Russo–Japanese War (1904 to 1905) underscored the system's shortcomings and motivated Secretary of State Root to push for a revised world court at the 1907 second Hague Conference. However, it floundered over the problem of selecting judges and the issue of arms limitation, which was postponed until the 1921 Washington Conference.[59]

In 1919, the Covenant of the League of Nations called for a Permanent Court of International Justice, which was created in 1920. Root devised a workable method for selecting the judges and helped draft the new proposal but rejected an offer to serve as judge because of his age. He wanted the United States to join even though he feared that because the World Court was originally associated with, albeit independent of, the League, it would be controversial. Hughes agreed and put off nominating justices or discussing the World Court in order to avoid antagonizing the Irreconcilables before the Washington Conference. Once it was over, he urged Harding to recommend joining.[60]

Hughes did not expect the World Court to solve all problems but considered it one of several tools to promote peace. Broad public support notwithstanding, he knew that the Irreconcilables would make joining difficult. As always, he moved carefully. Learning from the League fight, Hughes proposed reservations protecting the nation's freedom to participate in the World Court without any binding commitments. In addition, Congress would control how much money the United States contributed, and no major changes would be made to the court without US consent. Although Hughes's approach echoed his pragmatic, legalistic orientation, Glad criticized it as a prime example of his fundamentally "modest projects of reform."[61]

Be that as it may, Harding was pleased and, in February 1923, asked the Senate to ratify membership with Hughes's reservations. Joining the Court dovetailed with the president's own conviction that it is "a God-given duty to give of our influence to establish the ways of peace throughout the world." In response to claims that joining the World Court would be joining the League of Nations, the president insisted that the United States would not join the League "by the side door, the back door, or the cellar door." Popular support spurred a nationwide campaign. Even Norris approved as long as American independence was assured. However, most Irreconcilables, especially Borah, dismissed the World Court as another entangling alliance too close to the League for comfort. As with the League, Lodge delayed the issue in the Senate Foreign Relations Committee.[62]

Struggling to combat the opposition, Harding became increasingly "discouraged about the stability of popular government" when undermined by "what appears to be one half of one percent of the voters." Like Wilson, he decided to tour the country to promote the cause. On June 20, 1923, Harding, his wife, and a few cabinet members embarked on a "Voyage of Understanding" that entailed a fifteen-thousand-mile, six-week speaking tour to the Midwest, the West, and Alaska. Rejecting the idea of being a "hermit nation," Harding declared, "My soul yearns for peace. My heart is anguished by the sufferings of war. My spirit is eager to serve. My passion is for justice over force. My hope is in the great Court. My mind is made up. My resolution is fixed." The Irreconcilables were unmoved.[63]

Like Wilson, the trip proved too much for Harding's already ailing body. On July 27, he insisted on speaking at the University of Washington without a hat in the burning sun. Traveling by train to San Francisco, he suffered a mild heart attack but rebounded enough to walk to his hotel. Three days later, a final heart attack took his life. Hughes knew about Harding's physical decline and his high blood pressure but still was shocked. He immediately took charge and instructed Vice President Calvin Coolidge on taking the presidential oath of office. As the funeral train traveled back to Washington, over three million people lined the tracks and sang hymns. It was the largest national outpouring of grief since Abraham Lincoln's funeral. The nation identified with someone who symbolized the cherished American Dream that any self-made man could become president.[64]

Hughes was honored to give Harding's eulogy under the great dome in the great hall of the House of Representatives. He paid homage to "a generous and kindly spirit who counted human fellowship more precious than all the pomp and circumstance of power." He emphasized the president's charm, hatred of "strife," and commitment to international peace. By trying to meet every administrative demand and every personal request, said Hughes, "he literally wore himself out in the endeavor to be friendly." Ultimately, Harding "gave his life for his country." The message, Hughes cautioned, was that "the presidency is a super-office, but nature . . . has supplied no supermen to fill it."[65]

Harding's death left Hughes to continue the administration's fight for the World Court alone. In several strong speeches, he insisted that the Court was separate from the League and involved no entangling alliance. Responding to Borah and other critics, Hughes denied the need for enforcement mechanisms because, as at the Washington Conference, he believed that the member nations' commitment to abide by the Court's rulings was the most "practicable" guarantee of success. Although he recognized that international laws of war required revision because of "the new agencies of warfare," he advocated joining the Court without waiting for the changes. "We have an acute world need," he said, and "we shall make no progress toward the prevention of war if we adopt a perfectionist policy."[66]

No matter. Adding yet more conditions, the Irreconcilables continued depicting the World Court as an entangling alliance similar to and created by the League. Borah, who chaired the Senate Foreign Relations Committee after Lodge died in 1924, replicated his predecessor's delaying tactics. In 1926 the Senate passed a strongly conditional policy for approving judges to the World Court, which the Court members rejected. In 1927, Hughes bemoaned the Senate's intransigence. A decade later, the Senate finally voted on joining the World Court but it was narrowly defeated despite solid public support. Therefore, the United States did not join the World Court until the United Nations replaced the League and absorbed the Court in 1945.[67]

Along with the 1924 Japanese exclusion provision, the nation's failure to join the World Court represented the greatest personal disappointments of Hughes's tenure as secretary of state. Nonetheless, he was privileged to serve on the Permanent Court of Arbitration from 1926 to 1930 and on the World Court from 1929 to 1930. Significantly, he was chosen for the World Court with overwhelming support by world-wide electors, including those from Latin America. After resigning to rejoin the Supreme Court, Hughes took pains to explain how independent of the League the World Court really was. He always remained convinced that joining the World Court was not only consistent with America's "own interests" but would also do "justice to its ideals."[68]

The struggle over joining the World Court reflected the larger challenges Hughes confronted as secretary of state. It underscored the damage done by the League fight and the lasting influence of the Irreconcilables, especially Borah and Johnson, his antagonists since 1916. Their influence helped explain the stealth strategies Hughes adopted such as using unofficial observers to the League, commissions for German reparations and the Dawes Plan, plus maneuvering Senate support for various treaties. The accommodations he made to the Senate led some historians to accuse him of being too cautious and passive as a leader. This perception combined with the long-range failure of the Washington Treaty System suggested that Hughes never achieved the caliber of a statesman. In fact, wrote Glad, "In avoiding the politically objectionable, he may have left untouched the really significant problems of his time."[69]

In 1923, Mississippi's Democratic Senator Pat Harrison penned a similar critique in *The New York Times.* Although he would later support Hughes's nomination for chief justice, Harrison condemned Hughes as secretary of state. A popular, prominent senator and a dedicated Wilsonian, Harrison accused Hughes of being too "secretive," indecisive, and inconsistent, especially after signing Root's declaration. Hughes, he wrote, had shifted from being "a pro-Leaguer to a half-Leaguer to a no-Leaguer." Harrison credited Wilson for sending unofficial observers to the League and Borah for leading the arms limitation movement. Hughes only acted belatedly and under pressure. Concerning Europe, Russia, China, and Latin America, Harrison accused Hughes of simply following Wilson's policies and offering nothing new or "any definite plan of action" to solve world problems. All in all, Hughes was an "abject failure."[70]

Yet, Hughes was hardly weak and indecisive regarding treaties, reparations, the Dawes Plan, and the Washington Conference. In these cases, he demonstrated diplomatic skill, provided strong leadership, and devised innovative solutions for seemingly intractable problems. Taking control of the Washington Conference, he dominated the preparations, the agenda, and the negotiations. He certainly offered a "definite plan of action." Consequently, the conference achieved what was at the time considered unachievable—the world's first multinational agreements to curtail the arms race and address some of the most volatile conflicts of the era. Their unraveling in the thirties should not erase their significance for the twenties.

The lack of enforcement provisions was regrettable, but unavoidable, because neither the American public nor the Irreconcilables would have supported them. By definition, enforcement mechanisms embodied threats and distrust, which undermined all his efforts to build peace based on trust through mutually acceptable treaties. Moreover, enforcement mechanisms were dangerously tentative and inherently provocative. Hence, what seemed to be hopelessly idealistic may have been quite realistic. Harrison correctly pointed out the continuities between the policies of Wilson and Hughes. However, he disregarded important differences in emphasis and implementation. As Hughes often said, he sought solutions that were "practicable," meaning not only reasonable (another word he used often) but actionable.

Hughes's record was less consistent regarding Latin America. On the one hand, modifying the Monroe Doctrine was a significant departure from TR, Taft, and Wilson. On the other hand, American hegemony survived in the form of the Marines, puppet governments, protectorates, banks, private corporations, trade, and loans. Although he was divided over some of these developments, Hughes supported others and never renounced intervention, albeit temporary. However, he successfully mitigated the US presence, forestalled several border conflicts, and negotiated important treaties. At conference after conference, in speech after speech, he affirmed the goodwill of the United States and denied any imperialistic motives. His sincerity earned him much personal respect but could not overcome decades of hostility to US economic and political dominance. Nor could his good intentions compensate for political and economic chaos, some of which the United States caused, especially in the Caribbean. Hughes's success was substantial but limited—less because of his ideals and more because his idealism bowed to realism. Unlike Wilson, he did not allow his visions to obscure the need to be "practicable."

For Hughes, the different aspects of his work in the State Department comprised a cohesive whole. Upholding nonentanglement and independence, the United States rejected formal alliances but stood "ready to join in declarations of common principles." He connected the Monroe Doctrine's emphasis on stability and trade in the Western Hemisphere to US efforts to help Europe recuperate without becoming embroiled in European affairs. Impartiality after the war was an extension of neutrality long before the war. To be sure, the nation's new leadership role involved it in European affairs, but through finances and treaties, not security commitments. And the United States remained very embroiled in Latin American affairs, revisions notwithstanding.[71]

Regarding the Washington Conference, Hughes pointed to its achievements in suspending naval competition, respecting Chinese territorial integrity, expanding the Open Door, advancing humanitarian causes, and, most crucial, promoting "the peaceful settlement of international disputes." Despite the "changed conditions" that made the United States "a world power," he thought that the nation's basic objective was still "to be helpful in every way consistent with our independence." And just to be absolutely clear, he declared, "Our attitude is one of independence, not of isolation." Nationalism and internationalism could coexist.[72]

Following Harding's death, Hughes stayed on to provide continuity for Coolidge but felt entitled to resign after helping Coolidge win election in his own right in 1924. Hughes was relieved to relinquish the burdens of office after the inauguration. At age sixty-two and after twenty years of public service, he wanted to return to the law and provide for his family. At first, "the country was stunned." The press dubbed him the greatest secretary since John Quincy Adams and William H. Seward. Hughes was called "the most compelling" foreign minister of the era, one of "the foremost figures" of the day. According to *The London Observer,* "Mr. Hughes has steered world policy through the tumult and confusion of the darkest post war years into the New Era, and in that work, he has been an honor to his country and an asset to his time."[73]

In 1922, *The New York Times* conducted a survey that ranked Hughes as one of the twelve greatest Americans of the era. He was so gratified by an editorial in *The London Times* that he cited it in his *Autobiographical Notes.* It evaluated the secretary's challenges and contributions during "four anxious years." The success of the Washington Conference, it said, was not just in addressing immediate problems but in forging a new relationship with Europe. In the process, Hughes was "instilling into the American people a sober and practical view of the new realities of world politics." Unlike many public figures, Hughes was "intelligible." Faced with "a changing America and a world that was changing still more swiftly," he provided "a policy that was at once coherent and convincing to people at home and people abroad." In words that could apply to all his careers, *The London Times* appreciated that Hughes "maintained the balance. He was neither retrograde nor Utopian." This, claimed the paper, was his "chief title to fame."[74]

For Hughes, it was the tributes from the State Department that, he said, "touched me most deeply." There was the humble clerk who thanked him for so courteously acknowledging her and her colleagues every day. Then there were the Foreign Service officers. Just as the pressmen had given Hughes a pair of shears at the beginning of his term, so the officers gave him his desk chair at the end of his term. They felt that "no one else should sit in the chair where you have written so many vital state papers, in which we have so often seen you lean back and laugh with satisfaction at a happy phrase or a bit of good work accomplished."[75]

Speaking at the farewell staff luncheon in March, Under Secretary Joseph Grew conveyed "our admiration and respect, our devoted loyalty, and, what is more, our deep personal affection." Hughes, he said, had given the department "a cohesion, an enthusiasm, an esprit de corps which has never before been equaled." But his most important legacy was his "inspiring and enduring influence," which made them all "better servants of the Government, better men." The sentiment was mutual. At his New York City farewell dinner in November, Hughes said that it was "one of the greatest privileges of my life" to work with the foreign service. Underpaid and overworked, he lauded "their ability, their intelligence, their industry, their unqualified loyalty and fidelity." It was not a human icicle who publicly stated, "I think of my associates of the last four years with love and esteem."[76]

There were still more tributes, including an elaborate dinner held in the ballroom of the Hotel Astor, a place that punctuated his life. The dinner was organized by fifty of New York City's "leaders" and attended by one thousand "men in the forefront of the professions, arts, and in commerce." President Coolidge sent praise for Hughes's "accomplishment in eliminating international discord" and making "our national ideals of justice and fair dealing a living reality in international relations." Root insisted that "it is not merely what Mr. Hughes has done. . . . It is what he has stood for." He was the true public servant who never sought power or office for self "aggrandizement" and who "never abandoned or suppressed an opinion which he thought ought to be expressed in order to please anybody." These were attributes that brought "honor upon us all."[77]

When it was Hughes's turn to speak, he graciously acknowledged Root's wisdom, "inspiration and guidance." Concerned about how historians would handle complicated foreign policy issues, he quipped that at least he would not be around to see it. Rather, the key was finding "his satisfaction in the day's work and in the earnest striving to do his part worthily." Hughes discussed the importance of reorganizing the State Department and negotiating almost seventy treaties while preserving the balance between executive and legislative branches in foreign policy. To loud applause, he appealed for joining the World Court. But, he said, "Our most important service will be found not so much in any specific act as in the spirit in which we conduct our foreign relations." Instead of "old grudges" and "pseudo-patriotism," he insisted that "our greatest interest is in international friendships." Accordingly, he had tried to conduct US foreign policy in the "spirit of non-aggression, security, esteem, respect for others." As he put it, "National prestige may be associated with power, but it is never heightened by a brutal assertion of it. Indeed, our national prestige is inseparably connected with the demonstration of our sense of justice."[78]

Hughes's greatest challenge as secretary was to help the nation learn from the horrors of World War I and transition from the nineteenth to the twentieth century. Instead of withdrawing from international responsibility, he tried to use the nation's new power and wealth to avoid future wars and promote world peace. The objective was to balance idealism with realism without abandoning the nation's past commitments. These principles defined his approach in all three careers. It was a difficult task requiring him to navigate myriad domestic and foreign obstacles, build alliances, make compromises, and sometimes retreat. He valued being supported by the public and the press as well as by key domestic and foreign leaders. Nonetheless, despite immediate success, wrote Zasloff, the classical and legalist ideals that defined diplomacy in the 1920s ultimately failed because they required a stable balance of power in order to succeed. That search for stability dominated Hughes's term of office and remains today's perpetual but elusive quest.[79]

Hughes's multipronged approach to postwar peace, along with its shortcomings, moved the nation into the international role it would occupy henceforth. It meant accepting responsibility for promoting world peace by acknowledging nationalism but rejecting isolationism. To Hughes, the "highest task of statesmanship" always remained "to diminish among peoples the disposition to resort to force and to find a just and reasonable basis for accord." The words "just and reasonable" reflected his commitments as well as his constraints in Europe, the Far East, and Latin America. Overall, Cooper concluded that Hughes "wrought prodigious feats of diplomacy within the limits of normalcy" and created a "spring time of hope in the 1920's." At the State Department, reported his former assistant secretary, Hughes became "a legend."[80]

Transitions

Upon resigning from the State Department in 1925, Hughes again practiced law and was in such great demand that he earned about $400,000 a year compared to $12,000 a year as secretary of state and $10,000 a year as governor. He represented several major corporations and argued thirty-eight cases before the Supreme Court, winning twenty-one. Among his most controversial clients were the Oil Institute of America and the Duke tobacco family estate. As a lawyer, he argued for the General Electric Company's right to control a radio station, but as chief justice, he would argue against monopolizing the air waves. When he defended a controversial New York City subway fare increase as reasonable compensation for public service, he was vilified for receiving excessive compensation himself. In fact, Hughes accepted only half of the cases he was offered and followed Bar Association standards for compensation. He refused cases that were related to his previous work and, after his son became solicitor general, any cases involving the Justice Department.[81]

Although Hughes profited handsomely from his legal work, he would have profited even more had he not assumed so many uncompensated responsibilities. During this period, he was president of the American Bar Association, the New York County Lawyers' Association, the New York City Bar Association, the American Judicature Association, and the American Society of International Law. As the third president of the New York Legal Aid Society, he got the American Bar Association to form a Standing Committee on Legal Aid and Indigent Defense, which he chaired and still exists. Beyond the law, he presided over the Union League Club, was vice president of the National Municipal League, and chaired the American Committee of the World Conference on Faith and Order. Honoring his daughter, Hughes became a fundraiser for the fight against tuberculosis. In addition, he raised money for a memorial to Woodrow Wilson, a fund for the study of US history, and the Byrd expedition to Antarctica. (Byrd later had a mountain range named after him.) Hughes delivered a scathing attack on lynching and anti-Semitism. His many other speeches included lectures on the Supreme Court at Columbia in 1927, on Latin American affairs at Princeton in 1928 and Yale in 1929. These lectures were published with all stipends and profits returned to the universities.[82]

Eight months after resigning from the State Department, Hughes agreed to chair New York Governor Al Smith's 1925 Reorganization Committee. The project was opposed by bosses who feared losing power and patronage if state government was streamlined. Of course, that was the point. Typically insisting that the commission be nonpartisan, Hughes selected an impressive roster of Republican and Democratic members. Equally typical, he worked nonstop and expected everyone else to do likewise, but the members insisted on lunch breaks. Three months later, their report actualized much of his past reform agenda. Finally, the governor's removal powers were increased, the ballot was simplified, administrative departments were consolidated, and administrators' salaries were increased to obviate graft. The state legislature accepted the commission's recommendations without amendment. History gave Smith the credit for revising state government, but he could not have done it without Hughes's reform legacy as governor and skill as administrator.[83]

In keeping with his dedication to education and civil liberties, Hughes was concerned about "the ominous sign" embodied in "the growth of an intolerant spirit," which, he said, revealed that "democracy has its own capacity for tyranny." He particularly criticized "the passion for uniformity and control of opinion" embodied in a Tennessee law against teaching evolution and a Nevada law banning German language instruction. "Freedom of learning," he said, "is the vital breath of democracy and progress." To Hughes, freedom of speech and the press were essential for public enlightenment and participation in democracy. When urged to reenter politics by journalists at a Gridiron Club dinner in 1928, Hughes joked that "I have been here as a burnt offering, but now I am clad in the comfortable asbestos of private life." Being an ordinary citizen meant that "I am with you no longer as a servant, but as one of the millions of masters in this fortunate land where the Government is so organized that everyone has a chance to talk, but can do as little harm as possible."[84]

Republicans tried to draft him for the presidential nomination in 1924 and 1928, but he insisted that "I don't want the turmoil of being a presidential candidate. I had that turmoil once, and I don't want it again." In 1928, he supported the Republican candidate, Hoover, over the Democratic candidate, Smith, who now seemed too radical. Hughes was a founder of and fundraiser for the National Conference of Christians and Jews (now called the National Conference for Community and Justice), which was created in response to anti-Catholic attacks against Smith. Nonetheless, Hughes remained loyal to his party and his old colleague. He made such effective campaign speeches for Hoover that he was asked to give the final radio address before the election, a spot usually filled by the candidate himself. Ironically, as with Taft in 1908, Hughes helped make other men president more than he helped himself. Hoover was grateful.[85]

Hughes's prestige brought him many honors and responsibilities. In private life, he and Antoinette spent summers in the countryside or abroad. On the boat returning from Europe in 1926, he participated in a fundraising event to help Florida hurricane victims. The comedian Will Rogers was skeptical about working with what he assumed was "a pretty cold-blooded proposition." However, instead of ruining all his jokes, Hughes was so witty himself that all Rogers said he needed to do was pass the hat. After the third performance, Rogers concluded that "if ever a man was misunderstood in regard to being a real good fellow, it's this Mr. Hughes." But it was all too much and in 1927, Hughes barely made it through presenting a case before the Supreme Court when he suddenly lost sight in his left eye. The cumulative stress of his activities had burst a small blood vessel. He "almost suffered a breakdown." Fortunately, he followed doctor's orders to relax and reported that he soon regained his "usual vigor."[86]

Even without an official government job, the years between 1925 and 1930 were eventful. Hughes fully expected to spend the rest of his life making similar contributions alternating with summer travel. He was sixty-eight and ready to enjoy his senior years. As he put it to Antoinette after they returned to Manhattan in 1925:

We're two old birds at best,
Building another nest,
It's up a tall tree
And between you and me
Our Avenue beats all the rest.
But why speak of age
When we're only more sage!
Is not wisdom the crown of life?
My darling in truth
Has perpetual youth
Richest blessings upon my dear wife!
The years gliding by
Only strengthen the tie
That binds our hearts together.
Our love strong and true
Will pull us both through;
We're ready for any weather.

However, their lives were about to change again when he assumed his most controversial, most consequential role as Chief Justice of the United States Charles Evans Hughes.[87]

9 | Becoming Chief Justice, 1930–1941

[The chief justice of the United States] is the most important judicial officer in the world. . . . However, he is one of nine judges having no greater authority than any of his brethren in the decision of cases.
—Charles Evans Hughes, 1927

Getting Confirmed

Scholars argue over Charles Evans Hughes's judicial legacy, but they agree that his influence was great. Over the decades, he has been rated the second most important chief justice after John Marshall, except for once being third after Roger B. Taney. Although Hughes again dropped to third place when Earl Warren took second place, he still is considered one of the nation's finest chief justices. Nonetheless, Hughes had a rocky start and a tumultuous tenure during which he was constantly reminded that despite his stature, he was only "one of nine."[1]

While serving as secretary of state in President Warren G. Harding's cabinet, Hughes and commerce secretary Herbert Hoover developed a solid working relationship fortified by mutual respect and friendship. Appreciating Hughes's contribution to Hoover's 1928 presidential election, the president asked Hughes to become secretary of state again, but Hughes had just joined the World Court. Hoover then suggested becoming ambassador to England, but Hughes said that he simply did "not wish any office." Fate intervened when former president, Chief Justice William H. Taft, a Harding appointee, became critically ill and feared for the Court's future. Although Taft understood that Hughes held "a few progressive notions," he considered Hughes more reliably conservative than Associate Justice Harlan Fiske Stone. Unable to influence the president directly, Taft had others act for him. When Hoover actually made the offer, Hughes expressed concern that, being almost sixty-eight, he was too old for the job and that it might interfere with his son's career as solicitor general. Besides, he said, "I think I've earned the right to finish life in peace."[2]

It remains unclear whether Hughes accepted eagerly or reluctantly after pressure from Hoover and encouragement from Antoinette, but he agreed to serve. Law professor Richard D. Freidman suggested that because they were close, Hughes undoubtedly consulted his son, who was apparently eager to return to New York City. Hughes also asked the president to see whether his law practice as well as his political participation in presidential campaigns would be an issue because, he said, "I don't want a fight over the nomination." Hoover did not anticipate any problems. Nor did he think that a story would later surface that he only offered Hughes the job thinking that he would decline and facilitate appointing Stone. It was an awkward situation reminiscent of Hughes's initial appointment to the Court in 1910. Hughes was upset by these rumors and relieved when Hoover denied them. Yet, they persist to this day.[3]

At first, the nomination was well received by the press, Congress, and the public. Hughes was lauded as a supremely qualified "noble figure" justifying swift confirmation. Associate Justice Oliver Wendell Holmes Jr. was delighted because, he wrote, "Hughes is an old and valued friend of mine and I surmise and hope a little nearer to my way of thinking than his predecessor." Associate Justice Louis D. Brandeis urged that the "confirmation ought to be made at once and ought to be unanimous." Associate Justice Benjamin N. Cardozo called it "a great choice of a great man for a great office." However, Harvard law professor Felix Frankfurter strongly objected to the appointment because he considered Hughes too conservative. He preferred liberals like Cardozo or Stone.[4]

Nebraska Senator George W. Norris, chairman of the Judiciary Committee, sent the nomination to the Senate floor with two negative votes, including his own. Two days earlier, Norris had released without comment a list of fifty-four cases where Hughes defended rich people or big corporations. The point was clear. Hughes was the tool of Wall Street, the same claim made in 1910 and 1916. Interestingly, Norris had praised Hughes in 1916 for his record as "a humanist" on the Court. Despite knowing that Hughes's qualifications guaranteed confirmation, Norris used the occasion to dethrone the Court and pierce its aura of invulnerability, once called "Robe-ism." Norris criticized Hughes for resigning from the Court to run for president in 1916 and for endorsing other political candidates. Again, the point was clear: Hughes was too political to be a fair judge.[5]

The floodgates opened and Hughes was excoriated by senator after senator for four days. The debate was front-page news and the Senate galleries were packed. Idaho Senator William Borah enthusiastically endorsed Hughes's nomination as associate justice in 1910, but they had since tangled over foreign policy. Now Borah used the former secretary of state's defense of American private property interests abroad as proof of his pro-business bias. Ignoring Hughes's gubernatorial record and his previous Court opinions, Borah depicted Hughes as an ultraconservative corporate lawyer who would place property rights over human rights and bring "great economic oppression to the people of the United States."[6]

Other senators criticized Hughes for defending Senator Truman Newberry, despite his ultimate exoneration. Several implied that Hughes knew about the Harding era scandals but feigned ignorance. One assailed his age. Senator Burton K. Wheeler, a Montana Democrat, criticized Hughes's gubernatorial vetoes of bills for a teacher's wage increase and low transit fares. Hughes's World War I aircraft inquiry was distorted to suggest collusion rather than competence, but former President Woodrow Wilson's praise was cited in retort. When a Texas senator claimed that the 1913 Shreveport case undermined states' rights, a Louisiana senator countered that it strengthened states' rights. Finally, Hughes was accused of destroying America's battleship fleet at the 1921 Washington Conference. His entire career was assailed.[7]

Despite being Democrats, both New York senators defended Hughes's record as a progressive Republican governor known for standing up to vested interests. Robert F. Wagner, member of the 1925 New York State Reorganization Committee that Hughes chaired, conveyed "the pride of the people of the State of New York over the selection of one of its most distinguished citizens to [this] high office." Other senators pointed out that disqualifying all lawyers who represented corporations would eliminate many fine candidates, including Abraham Lincoln. Besides, in America, everyone deserved a day in court. If Hughes had defended corporations, he had also defended labor and as governor had promoted an aggressive reform agenda. On the Court, he had sanctioned state economic regulations and championed civil liberties. Altogether, his previous record revealed more balance than bias. Knowing that they had the majority, most Republicans let the opposition rail without rejoinder.[8]

During the debate, Senator Robert LaFollette, the Wisconsin Republican whom Hughes had criticized in the 1924 presidential campaign, turned sociological jurisprudence against him. Citing Holmes, LaFollette underlined the relevance of "economic and social views" to the law. Therefore, he justified questioning Hughes's leanings before confirming him, even if it made the hearings exceptionally harsh. The debate became a national drama illuminating the importance of the Court in American life. *The New York Sun* was pleased that at last "the idolatry which placed the Court above criticism has been smashed." Editor William Allen White considered the debate a boon "for the progressive cause" and an effective warning to "Republican conservative leaders that another man with less reputation and less real liberal record" would not be confirmed. In a backhanded compliment, White conceded that Hughes was "probably the best conservative that you could get."[9]

The final vote was fifty-two to twenty-six, with eighteen abstentions. Hughes's son immediately resigned as solicitor general. Because of the 1916 election controversy, California Senator Hiram Johnson refrained from speaking but voted "no." The debate was the second most contentious confirmation of a chief justice in US history. Perhaps it was less against Hughes than against the reactionary record of the Taft Court. As if anticipating the "counter-majoritarian" argument, the senators asked why nine unelected men could overrule hundreds of elected legislators. Hughes became a symbol of the "economic war . . . between the great masses of the people and these ruthless organizations of capital."[10]

Noting that Hughes was "a sensitive and proud man," his daughter Elizabeth recalled that the debate "distressed and wounded him deeply." Indeed, he later spent several pages in his *Autobiographical Notes* refuting the accusations. In the moment, however, he graciously accepted the outcome and reaffirmed his dedication to public service. Partial vindication came from a laudatory press and the fact that even his sharpest critics acknowledged his qualifications and competence. Borah himself denied impugning the integrity of "one of the most distinguished Americans of this day." Reinforcing that point, *New York Herald Tribune* ran a cartoon of Hughes as a tall figure proudly holding papers labeled "Life of Public Service" while little senators (including Borah) threw mud at him from the "Senate Political Gutter." As law professor William G. Ross observed, "No one has ever ascended the nation's highest bench with a more distinguished record of service in both public office and the legal profession."[11]

Judging

It was fitting that Hughes's old friend Holmes, the most senior associate justice, administered the oath in a simple ceremony. Becoming the nation's eleventh chief justice, Hughes returned to the Court after fourteen years with whiter hair and beard but with his strong voice and commanding presence still intact. At sixty-eight, when most men are retiring, said law professor Zachariah Chafee, Hughes "began the most important stage of his career." He was the oldest person to ever join the Court and had the broadest background of any chief justice before or since. Marshall and Taft came close. Marshall had military experience, a legal career, experience in Virginia politics, but only two years as congressman and one year as secretary of state. Taft had been a federal appeals court judge, governor general of the Philippines, secretary of war, secretary of state, and president but had less experience practicing law and never served as governor, associate justice, or World Court judge. Taft and Hughes were the only chief justices to have lost presidential elections. Despite the one being outgoing and the other reserved, they had a long, positive relationship. Therefore, Taft expected Hughes to preserve his judicial legacy. However, while Taft became more conservative over time, Hughes built upon his original Progressivism, albeit qualified by moderate tendencies. He was always hard to label.[12]

Taft and Hughes shared concerns for the efficiency and independence of the Supreme Court as well as the balance of power between federal and state governments. They differed because, as a Progressive governor and supporter of sociological jurisprudence, Hughes approved of legislative experiments that limited laissez-faire in response to modern realities. Like Taft, Hughes preferred to protect private property, if possible, but unlike Taft, he was willing to limit private contracts for larger social purposes. Like Taft, he promoted an expanded federal role in interstate commerce, but unlike Taft, he also supported unions and labor legislation. Through it all, Hughes ardently defended civil liberties, which Taft also backed, but less strongly. Although both Hughes and Taft were cautious constitutionalists, Hughes was significantly more open to change.[13]

In the wake of the vitriolic debate over Hughes's nomination, the Senate refused to confirm Hoover's next appointment. John J. Parker was a North Carolina Circuit Court judge who had opposed labor unions and African American voting rights. Accordingly, labor and civil rights groups mounted the nation's first major public campaign against a Supreme Court nominee. After six tense, emotional weeks, the Senate defeated the nomination. Hoover next nominated Owen J. Roberts, a well reputed Philadelphia lawyer and district attorney who skillfully prosecuted the Teapot Dome cases and often argued before the Court. Like Hughes, he represented corporations but also defended labor unions and clients suing corporations. As a trustee of Pennsylvania's predominantly African American Lincoln College, he was considered "a conservative with liberal tendencies." Roberts later became controversial, but in the moment, he was confirmed by acclimation. Perhaps the Senate was too worn out by the struggles over Hughes and Parker to fight again.[14]

Hughes's second term of service on the Supreme Court was more contentious than the first because the justices were more sharply divided into liberals and conservatives, with Roberts in the middle. Hughes tried to hold the Court together, also from the middle. It was hard. The polarization reflected age-old controversies over viewing the Constitution narrowly or broadly as in Thomas Jefferson's concept of strict interpretation versus Alexander Hamilton's concept of loose interpretation. Ironically, Hughes found himself maneuvering another balance-of-power situation akin to what he had navigated as secretary of state. If he had been a governor on the Court in his first term, he needed to be a diplomat on the Court in his second term. The formal headshots of the nine justices masked their differences (see figure 9.1).

Although individual justices could switch sides depending on the case, and although there was more unity on civil liberties cases than on economic ones, the broad lines of division held. One side of the pre-1937 Court consisted of the "Four Horsemen of the Apocalypse," so labeled by journalists in a Biblical reference to the forces of evil. Willis Van Devanter, George Sutherland, James Clark McReynolds, and Pierce Butler usually (but not always) voted together. As associate justice, Hughes thought that Van Devanter "was certainly not an ultra-conservative." Sutherland sometimes backed state regulatory powers over substantive due process claims. But, Hughes admitted, Butler and McReynolds demonstrated a "resolute determination to maintain their conceptions of the constitutional protection of property rights." They fit the conservative, perhaps reactionary, label.[15]

Figure 9.1. Justices of the United States Supreme Court. Top row to bottom, left to right: James Clark McReynolds, Oliver Wendell Holmes, Willis Van Devanter, Pierce Butler, Chief Justice of the United States Charles Evans Hughes, Louis D. Brandeis, Harlan Fiske Stone, George Sutherland, Owen J. Roberts. Source: "The Supreme Court," *Literary Digest*, October 3, 1931. The Miriam and Ira D. Wallach Division of Art, Prints and Photographs, the New York Public Library.

Although Van Devanter and Sutherland could be flexible, they often joined McReynolds and Butler in ruling for corporations, private property, and the sanctity of contracts. Using a literal (later dubbed textualist) interpretation of the Constitution, they opposed most federal and state reform efforts. The fact that Van Devanter, Sutherland, and Butler were self-made men from Indiana, Utah, and Minnesota, respectively, cemented their faith in individualism, private enterprise, and minimal government.

Van Devanter was a former railroad lawyer and judge who wrote many of the conservative Court opinions even though, as a former state senator, congressman, and senator, he had demonstrated some liberal leanings. According to historian, Arthur M. Schlesinger Jr., Van Devanter's "lucidity, knowledge, and sweetness of manner commanded the respectful attention even of brethren who detested his conclusions." By contrast, Schlesinger described Butler as "a bruiser, burly and contentious, untiring at his desk, bullying in conference, vigorous and dogmatic in his opinions." He came from poor, Irish immigrant roots, grew up on a farm, and was the only Catholic on the Court. A skillful cross-examiner and ardent anti-regulatory railroad lawyer, he opposed expanding civil liberties.[16]

McReynolds, claimed biographer Merlo J. Pusey, "held first honors in acidity." The Court's sole Democrat, McReynolds grew up on a plantation in a frontier region along the Kentucky–Tennessee border. As a prominent corporate attorney and Wilson's attorney general, McReynolds was committed to freedom of contract and opposed to legislative reform. He was arrogant, racist, sexist, and anti-Semitic. After opposing the appointments of Brandeis and Cardozo because they were Jewish, he refused to sit next to Brandeis for the 1924 Court portrait, did not sign the Court's farewell letter when Brandeis retired, held up papers to block his view when Cardozo delivered opinions, and declined to shake either man's hand as was customary before conference. McReynolds was the most strident conservative of the four while Sutherland was the most moderate. During his first term on the Court, Hughes and Van Devanter had become friends. Hughes had also worked with McReynolds, who even applauded his appointment as chief. Perhaps these previous associations could help Hughes pursue harmony on the Court. Indeed, from 1930 to 1936, 80 percent of its decisions were unanimous. However, the remaining 20 percent were divisive and controversial.[17]

On the other side were the liberals, who were dubbed the "Three

Musketeers," a literary reference to fighters for justice. They were Holmes, Brandeis, and Stone. After Holmes retired in 1932, he was replaced by Benjamin Cardozo. Hughes knew them all. As already discussed, he had strong relationships with Holmes and Brandeis, both of whom he valued as friends and both of whom were friends themselves. However, Hughes later admitted that Brandeis's "forceful expositions intensified opposition" from the conservatives. Cardozo was a longtime New York friend for whom Hughes's son briefly clerked in Albany. Hughes considered Cardozo "one of the outstanding jurists of his time, a rare spirit with whom it was a privilege and constant delight to be associated." In line with Holmes's work, Cardozo's writings and rulings as judge and chief judge of the New York Court of Appeals reshaped the state's common law to better reflect modernity. He held that judges must "innovate . . . for with new conditions there must be new rules." Schlesinger contrasted Cardozo's "frail and gentle personality" with his precise logic and "unassailable integrity of mind." Law professor Andrew Kaufman, considered him "one of the most distinguished judges in the history of American law."[18]

Originally from New England, Harlan F. Stone was former dean of Columbia Law School, Hughes's alma mater. Stone also served as Coolidge's attorney general while Hughes was still secretary of state. Law professor Alpheus Thomas Mason, described him as "calm and deliberate . . . modest [but] commanding," respected for his "tolerance and humanness" as well as "his eminent fairness." Skeptical at first, Stone came to endorse Holmes's concept that laws must evolve with social and economic circumstances. Stone understood that the judge "in a real sense makes law" by ruling on the constitutionality of legislation. "Tough, articulate, passionate," wrote Schlesinger, "Stone had both the energy and the will to assume the burden of the fight for progressive constitutionalism against what he deemed to be an arid fundamentalism." Although Stone was often critical, the chief respected him as "able, scholarly and experienced." Upon retiring, Hughes recommended that Stone succeed him. Was this another case, like Taft and Hughes, of a chief promoting the man who might have been chief instead of himself?[19]

The divisions among the justices not only complicated Hughes's tenure but also stimulated contemporary and scholarly debates. They were "pervaded by dichotomies," wrote law professor Mark Tushnet, that "distorted" the nature of judging. The issue was (and still is) whether judges can be truly objective. Did they base their rulings on the law or simply use the law to justify their preconceived opinions? Did Finley Peter Dunne's fictitious Mr. Dooley correctly conclude that "no matter whether th' constitution follows th' flag or not, th' supreme court follows th' iliction returns?" Government professor Robert G. McCloskey pointed out "the need for the judges to reckon . . . with the imperatives of public opinion" and dismissed the notion that judges "stop being men when they put on their robes." Mason even called "the judiciary . . . a political body, not for vote getting, but as the final arbiter of both state and national policy. And policy is politics." Citing Hughes's 1907 comment that "the Constitution is what the judges say it is," Schlesinger concluded that such "dependency . . . was precisely the problem." To him, conservative and liberal justices alike "were reading their own notions of social wisdom into a designedly ambiguous charter of government." Because they considered judging too personal and political, too susceptible to outside pressures. these scholars were called "externalists."[20]

Other scholars viewed judges as constitutionalists constantly reaffirming or reassessing legal doctrines in the context of new situations. To law professor Alexander Bickel, Supreme Court justices provided continuity and stability by virtue of being removed from political pressures. Law professor G. Edward White depicted the Court as a deliberative body. The conferences at which cases were discussed encouraged doctrinal exchange. Afterward, the draft opinion was circulated in order to invite criticisms and revisions that might avoid or mitigate dissenting and concurring opinions. Difference was respected, but unanimity was preferred. From this perspective, personal biases were checked by collegial exchange and doctrinal discussion. The justices focused on the law and tried to be apolitical in order to maintain the Court's reputation for independence and integrity. Internal dynamics outweighed external pressures. Consequently, these scholars were called "internalists."[21]

A third approach combined the two by asserting that there was no "sharp dichotomy" between doctrinal and political influences on judicial rulings. In fact, said legal historian Laura Kalman, "the 'externalist' and 'internalist' categories are useless and intertwined." Stephen L. Feldman, professor of both law and political science, saw the whole controversy as an unnecessary conflict between his two disciplines. He pointed out that "legal interpretation is never mechanical" and that judges are complex human beings. They are not only steeped in "legal rule and case precedents" but also reflect their family backgrounds, community traditions, social roles, institutional connections, and relations with the other branches of government. Factoring in their political opinions and the times during which they lived suggested that judging was multidimensional and "fluid." While acknowledging that judging is always grounded in "legal institutions [and] legal doctrine," Feldman affirmed that "law and politics . . . are connected in a strong sense . . . because politics is already part of legal interpretation" and the judge's "interpretive horizons." Most contemporary scholars now recognize that, in Kalman's words, the 'externalist' and 'internalist' labels "obscure more than they clarify."[22]

Hughes fit this third approach. He wanted the Supreme Court to provide a "reasonably continuous, non-partisan, and philosophical exposition of the Constitution." Indeed, he sometimes stretched logic in order to avoid overturning precedent. At the same time, he believed in keeping the law current as it "applied to actual cases and controversies." Although Hughes was a lifelong legal practitioner, an avid student of the law, and briefly a law professor, he never subscribed to any rigid legal philosophy. Thus, he could both respect precedent and support sociological jurisprudence, ever balancing continuity with change. Embroiled in politics as a governor, presidential candidate, and secretary of state, Hughes fully appreciated the importance of public opinion in a democracy. This mixed background precludes considering him either narrowly doctrinal or purely political. Rather, his public service background enriched his approach to the law and motivated him to balance theory with reality, past with present. Significantly, Hughes emphasized the fact that the Founding Fathers "had political ideals, but these did not run away with their practical judgement." They modeled his own practical idealism.[23]

In 1924, while serving as secretary of state and president of the American Bar Association, Hughes led the members on a trip to Europe where he lobbied for the Dawes Plan and gave a much-lauded speech encapsulating his legal philosophy. Declaring that we come "as ministers of justice in a world which needs justice and the reasonableness which makes justice possible," he praised the Magna Carta for ensuring that English law applied equally to commoners and kings. Although the colonists brought English common law with them to the New World, Hughes noted that they adapted it to their new circumstances. The result was "a structure distinctively American." Unlike England, the United States had a written Bill of Rights. "So sacred were these rights deemed to be," he said, that they were enshrined "beyond the reach of the power of legislatures." For Hughes, the key characteristic of American law was the concept of "the right to law itself, not as the edict of arbitrary power, but as the law of a free people."[24]

Americans respected precedent, he said, but did not worship "archaic forms or deny the opportunity of improvement." Quoting Holmes's statement that "the life of the law has not been logic, it has been experience," Hughes welcomed "experimentation" as long as it followed "fundamental conceptions of justice" and "freedom from arbitrariness." Sustaining these values depended not only on "the integrity and independence of our judges" but also on public participation in juries, which promoted popular confidence in democracy and provided "an education in reasonableness." Hughes underlined the importance of "learned, conscientious and fearless judges" and lawyers. Their role was to protect "the rights of the people," give "every man his day in court," maintain the separation of powers, and resist "the fluctuations of . . . political expediency." Furthermore, they should support "all efforts to improve the laws and their adjustments to new conditions and exigencies." Here were Hughes's priorities—faith in reason, liberty, justice, divided power, and precedent, but with enough flexibility to evolve and respond to change. Judging was a "delicate and difficult duty" that could breed inconsistencies as well as landmark decisions.[25]

Leading

Being chief justice was complicated by democracy. Despite symbolizing prestige and power, the position was constrained by the Court's delicate role as the balance wheel between executive and legislative branches, states and the federal government, individuals, and government. As Associate Justice Robert H. Jackson explained, the Constitution itself was the product of "a virile political philosophy" derived from the Enlightenment. Resolving constitutional conflict was inherently political because it "confirms, allocates, or shifts power." The Court, he said, dealt with "political questions in legal form."[26]

Moreover, wrote McCloskey, a system based on "We the People," compelled the justices to consider popular opinion as embodied in executive and legislative policy without capitulating to it or to temporary trends: "The Court must alter its own perspectives as history's perspectives are altered, yet must not move so fast that the idea of continuity is lost." Therefore, McCloskey concluded that the Court was most successful when it "nudged and gently tugged the nation, instead of trying to rule it." The new chief justice was acutely aware of these dynamics and his responsibility to lead the Court accordingly.[27]

Hughes was surprised to learn that his image was on the front pediment of the new Supreme Court building when it was finished in 1935. He was in good company. Of course, Marshall was there as well as Taft, who got Congress to appropriate the funds. Elihu Root was included as an exemplar of the legal profession and strong advocate of the new building. Unfortunately, Taft did not live to witness its construction. Instead, Hughes laid the cornerstone in 1932 declaring, "The Republic endures and this is the symbol of its faith." He revised the east portico motto to read "Justice the Guardian of Liberty" instead of "Equal Justice is the Foundation of Liberty." The subtle shift extolled the living law, not just its origins. Designed by New York architect Cass Gilbert, the monumental white marble building atop a wide flight of steps was a Roman temple with eighteen tall Corinthian columns. There were three blindfolded sculptures of Justice, an enthroned Liberty flanked by Order and Authority, plus other law-related symbols. Marble walls and friezes, huge oak doors, mahogany furniture, and heavy red velour drapes dignified the Court chamber. The building consecrated the mystique of the Supreme Court.[28]

It was a far cry from the Court's formerly modest trappings. Reflecting its lack of status, early requests for a separate building were dismissed by none other than Secretary of State John Marshall, who supervised the original plans for Washington, DC. Thus, the least dangerous branch occupied "a half-finished committee room meanly furnished." Its situation barely improved over time. Because there were no offices for the justices, they worked from home and convened for conference in a poorly ventilated small room. Facilities for a library, a secretary, a robing room, law clerks, and lawyers arguing cases were, wrote Hughes, "most inadequate."[29]

By contrast, the new building affirmed that the judiciary was a separate and equal branch of government, worthy of respect. Yet, Hughes admitted that the old quarters were warmer. Several justices feared that their new trappings were, in Stone's words, "inappropriate for a Court with our traditions." Brandeis and Cardozo refused to use their new offices and continued working from home. Even Hughes worked mainly from home, ever under the watchful eye of a Lincoln bust on the mantle. Critics derided the new building as a marble palace, but Hughes defended it as a fitting testament to the Court's independence and to "the national ideal of justice." In the popular mind, observed historian Jeff Shesol, the building reinforced the image of the justices as "black robed gods" and "enhanced the Court's authority when other institutions were crumbling" during the Great Depression.[30]

The chief justice was responsible for protecting the Court's authority, integrity, and status. Hughes came to the Court with solid executive experience as governor and secretary of state. In these roles as well as in his law firms and as president of various organizations, he was used to being a leader. In addition, having served for six years as associate justice and having argued many cases before the Court, Hughes was familiar with its workings. Even so, the job was difficult. According to his law clerk, Edwin McElwain, the chief justice had to master over a thousand cases a term, lead the justices in conference, preside over oral arguments, assign opinions, and negotiate conflict among the justices. Hughes also reformed the rules of procedure in civil and criminal cases.[31]

Taft's 1925 Judiciary Act had already improved efficiency by better coordinating the circuit courts through the Conference of Senior Circuit Court Judges under the guidance of the chief justice. Hughes deemphasized Taft's centralized control so that the circuit courts could handle their own administrative issues. As Frankfurter observed, he "avoided the temptations of a strong executive" to accrue more power. The result was a 1939 act creating the Administrative Office of the United States Courts to coordinate the district councils. The federal courts were woven into a more integrated, responsive, and self-reliant system. It was all in keeping with Hughes's belief in the distribution of power under dual federalism.[32]

Having confronted the need for court reform as governor, Hughes was skeptical of the lower courts' commitment to protect the poor and ethnic or racial minorities. Among the countless appeals for review by certiorari, many were written by poor defendants who could not hire a lawyer. These were often denied out of deference to the lower courts or because they were hard to understand or did not raise significant legal questions. Most did not justify the Court's time, but Hughes insisted on reading every "informa pauperis" application himself in order to ensure that justice was served. Consequently, some cases were remanded to the lower courts for retrial and the convictions reversed, which motivated more people to file petitions. Ironically, the chief who wanted to make the Court more efficient had increased its workload. It exemplified Hughes's sincere dedication to justice and, in Stone's words, the "tireless zeal for the full performance of any task which he has undertaken."[33]

Hughes understood that being chief justice provided a unique "opportunity for leadership." The Court's fundamental operating principle, he wrote, was that "every Justice has the opportunity to vote upon every question" and to express his opinions in the Saturday conferences on pending cases. Working with a small group required not only that the chief win respect but also that he promote mutual respect for each other's "courage of conviction, sound learning, familiarity with precedents," and knowledge of the cases. Ideally, such a climate would reinforce each justice's "independence, impartiality, and balanced judgement." Leading the Court demanded humility and collaboration as well as authority, a quality, said Frankfurter, that "Hughes possessed . . . to a conspicuous degree."[34]

It was important that the chief justice get along with everyone by rejecting favoritism and factionalism. However, this approach could backfire by limiting personal interaction. As in his previous careers, Hughes was gracious but distant. Consequently, he may have missed opportunities to influence colleagues and negotiate differences through casual, spontaneous conversation, a skill at which Taft excelled. Moreover, because of the heavy court workload, he and Antoinette only accepted dinner invitations for Saturday evenings. They hosted annual dinners for the justices but entertained the Four Horsemen separately from the Three Musketeers. This strategy avoided conflict but precluded better understanding. Here he seemed undiplomatic. Nonetheless, Pusey claimed that at these dinners, Hughes was relaxed, warm, and humorous. Was this another example of Hughes's ability to compartmentalize his private and professional personas?[35]

Hughes was described as a "Jovian figure" who "radiated authority" with a "majestic presence." He looked the part. As Pusey put it, "His piercing eyes and finely chiseled nose, his broad forehead, his white beard and bushy brows, standing out in contrast to his black robe, gave him the appearance of Mr. Justice himself." Tall, erect, and self-confident, Hughes, said Solicitor General Robert H. Jackson, "imparted strength to the Court . . . by his character." After arguing many cases before the Court, Jackson could report that even during heated debates, Hughes "never lost his poise. He was an ideal presiding judge." In fact, wrote Frankfurter, "to see him preside was like witnessing Toscanini lead an orchestra" (see figure 11.1).[36]

Of course, Hughes started with many advantages. In addition to his administrative background and familiarity with the Court, his prodigious memory, powerful intellect, and thorough preparation were hard to match. Frankfurter reported that Hughes could thoroughly "disembowel" any case after reading the brief and consulting the record. Throughout his political and legal careers, Hughes demonstrated his prosecutorial skills. As in the gas and insurance investigations, when he knew more about the companies than their presidents, so he often understood the implications of cases more fully than the advocates. Then he was interrogating to expose, but now he used his talents to keep the discussions moving and to clarify the issues. If a lawyer was wandering, he posed questions to refocus him. If another justice's question was evaded, he rephrased it. If a justice was being too harsh on a lawyer, he defused the moment with questions that enabled the lawyer to rescue himself. Moreover, noted McElwain, it was all done "graciously."[37]

It was also done punctually. The Hughes court was always "taut but not tense." As McElwain explained, "Court opened precisely at noon, not 11:59 a.m. or 12:01 p.m. When the hands of the Court clock were precisely together, the red drapes behind the bench would part, and there he would be." Still using the gold watch that his Columbia law students gave him decades earlier, Hughes carefully monitored the proceedings. "Courteously but nonetheless firmly," he held counsel to the prescribed time limits, even if it meant cutting someone off mid-sentence. Hughes applied his lifelong personal discipline to upgrading the dignity and efficiency of the Court. He believed, said Frankfurter, "that dignity makes for an atmosphere of respect, and that only in such an atmosphere can reason thrive."[38]

Hughes wrote that his "heaviest work" was during the initial conferences when appeals were considered and at the conferences after oral argument when cases were discussed and voted upon. To him, the conferences represented the Court's "most arduous and responsible duty." In Frankfurter's opinion, Hughes "did not rely upon his position, he fulfilled it." Of course, Hughes was always so thoroughly prepared that other justices had to be equally prepared if they wanted to challenge him. The Four Horsemen sometimes met ahead of time in order to plan strategy and the Three Musketeers may have followed suit. Roberts and Hughes belonged to neither group.[39]

In conference, Hughes spoke first but voted last. Aware of his power to set the stage, he clearly and concisely presented the facts, the arguments, and his conclusions for each case. Arriving equipped with "records, briefs and lawbooks (all with innumerable bookmarks) piled high about him," Hughes "exuded complete preparation." After discussion, each justice presented his position, starting with the junior justice in order of reverse seniority and ending with the chief justice. Roberts reported that he never saw Hughes "interrupt or get into an argument" with other justices, but his initial "treatment was so complete that little, if anything," was left to say. Indeed, Cardozo preferred waiting a day before finalizing his positions because Hughes's compelling arguments were so hard to resist. If discussions became too heated, Hughes called for a vote, thereby foreclosing both destructive and constructive argument. Contradicting depictions of Hughes as considerate and respectful of his peers, later historians suggested that Hughes "was unduly imperious." Even Brandeis, who greatly admired Hughes's efficiency in conference, once commented that the conferences could last six hours "and the Chief Justice did all the speaking."[40]

In his 1927 lectures, Hughes recounted how the conference used to be an extended, open-ended event characterized by "long arguments" that invariably became repetitious and "tedious." That was acceptable as long as the Court heard few cases. As the docket grew, it became necessary to limit discussion to two hours and then to one hour per case. Even so, Hughes believed that "a vast amount of time is unavoidably wasted in the Supreme Court in listening to futile discussion." Never one to waste time, he moved cases along at a rapid clip. Stone considered the discussion too controlled and attenuated. He called Hughes a "drill sergeant" and pointedly promoted free debate among the brethren when he became chief justice in 1941. Yet, Stone later praised Hughes as "friendly to all, partial to none. . . . He has provoked no resentments and has cherished none." Frankfurter, who often criticized Hughes before joining the Court, came to appreciate the chief's skill in focusing discussion on key issues. By "drawing elements of agreement out of differences and thereby narrowing, if not escaping, conflict," Hughes kept a fractious Court at peace and on track. Moreover, Hughes did not bear grudges over disagreements. Echoing what others said about him in his previous careers, Frankfurter suggested that Hughes's intellectual orientation and "capacity for detachment . . . saved him from crying over spilled milk."[41]

When he was in the majority, the chief justice fulfilled what he called his "most delicate task," which was deciding who would write opinions. If the chief was in the minority, the senior justice in the majority assigned the opinion. This system may have encouraged him to occasionally vote with the majority despite misgivings about the case in question. The opinions were critical because they explained the rationale of the ruling and became the basis for future judgements in related cases. Like Taft (and Marshall), Hughes sought unanimity whenever possible. Consequently, he modified his own opinions or suggested a mild revision to a draft opinion in order to address the concerns of various justices. On occasion, he would privately urge a justice to reconsider dissenting. Hughes only authored twenty-three dissents himself. However, as mentioned earlier, he considered concurring and dissenting opinions important for preserving individual integrity. He also knew that they could become the basis for overturning cases in the future, like his own dissents as associate justice in the misbranding and patent cases. Nonetheless, as chief he preferred to discourage dissents and minimize division in the interests of continuity and public confidence.[42]

Hughes wrote 283 opinions as chief justice. He often delivered the most important opinions himself, thereby adding the stature of his position to the significance of the decision. He assigned decisions carefully and let others use their expertise when appropriate. Sometimes justices were given assignments outside their specialties so that they could demonstrate breadth of knowledge. When a case was contentious, Hughes typically chose a justice who was in the middle like Sutherland or Roberts. For Van Devanter, who often struggled with writing, Hughes would gently reassign the opinion if the process was too slow. Because Cardozo became so consumed by writing an opinion that it ruined his weekend and strained his weak heart, Hughes waited until late Sunday or Monday to give him an assignment. He often gave conservative rulings to liberal justices when they voted with the conservatives and vice versa in order to offset polarization on the Court and reduce public stereotyping of individual brethren. He never liked labels.[43]

Despite trying to be sensitive, Hughes was criticized on several fronts. Within the Court, some justices were unhappy about being assigned opinions they did not want to write, especially Cardozo and Stone. Brandeis and Stone bristled at the pressure to avoid dissents, but even Stone later acknowledged that the chief "never desired unanimity at the cost of sacrifice, either for himself or for others, of strongly held convictions." Yet, there were concerns that by downplaying dissent and dominating liberal opinions, Hughes modulated them. Although political scientist Kenneth M. Holland acknowledged that "moderation" enabled Hughes to manage "a bitterly divided" Court, he concluded that "Hughes's concern with task leadership limited his ability to serve as the intellectual leader of the Court—roles played by Cardozo for the liberals and Sutherland for the conservatives."[44]

A powerful criticism came from journalist Irving Brant, who regularly communicated with Stone. Brant accused Hughes of enhancing his own image by writing liberal opinions while avoiding conservative ones, even when voting with that side. Accordingly, he "shifts back and forth with ease [being] liberal in periods of liberal pressure, reactionary when that pressure is lifted." Through it all, wrote Brant, Hughes "never deviated an inch from his policy of making America safe for reactionary business." Freidman considered this accusation "a gross distortion" of Hughes's record. Nevertheless, the question remained. Was Hughes camouflaging his basic conservatism and hypocrisy, as Brant suggested, or revealing his nonideological nature, his ability to straddle conservatism and liberalism, his rejection of labels?[45]

Regardless, wrote law professor G. Edward White, due to "sheer preparedness and forcefulness," Hughes was "a dominant Chief Justice like none since Marshall." White also implied that in his drive for unity, Hughes sacrificed consistency. Moreover, claimed White, Hughes's vision of the Court as "detached, impartial, efficient, dignified, and just" was antiquated. From this perspective, Hughes was an impractical idealist. By contrast, Holland concluded that the Hughes Court "produced opinions that in importance up to that time exceeded those of every other chief except Marshall." Clearly, Hughes faced myriad ideological, political, and interpersonal challenges as chief justice. Capturing the complexity of the man, Schlessinger suggested that Hughes was

> superbly equipped for this job. . . . His formidable personality radiated authority and distinction; and his mind, so extraordinarily quick and clear and cold and penetrating, so highly moral and, at the same time, so flecked with a profound cynicism, made him the master of law, business, and government. . . . Always aware, always disciplined, always resourceful, always urbane, he bent all his private charm, all his driving energy, all his ruthless genius toward the vindication of the Court as an institution and himself as Chief Justice.

Would these attributes be enough to meet the ultimate test of power when President Roosevelt tried to pack the Court in 1937?[46]

10 | Packing the Court, 1933–1937

The Problem

In the midst of the nation's greatest economic crisis, the Supreme Court faced the greatest threat to its constitutional integrity. The situation demanded leadership and became a contest between two leaders—the president and the chief justice—the nation's most powerful, most prestigious federal officials. Although the jovial, gregarious president seemed opposite to the serious, reserved chief justice, they were equally self-confident, pragmatic, and committed to public service. Both had been governors of New York; both were optimistic and progressive; both had prodigious memories and strong personalities. Neither was an ideologue. As New York state senator, Franklin D. Roosevelt (FDR) supported Governor Charles Evans Hughes's reform efforts and as governor, FDR agreed with Hughes that "progressive government must, by its very terms, be a living and growing thing." Yet, the court packing crisis was not just about two men. Rather, they personified much larger contests between the legislative, executive, and judicial branches, between public opinion, politics, and the Constitution, between continuity and change. It was an epic struggle.[1]

Tensions between the executive and judicial branches over legislative measures and presidential powers were not new. However, this conflict occurred during the Great Depression, which had already been raging for eight years marked by shocking levels of unemployment, hunger, homelessness, and despair across the country. President Hoover did not adequately meet the emergency despite his distinguished past supervising US relief programs for post–World War I Europe and his work as commerce secretary in alleviating Russia's 1921 to 1922 famine. To be sure, Hoover rejected Secretary of the Treasury Andrew Mellon's preference for total inaction and adopted strategies to increase public works, create a federal loan agency, and stabilize agriculture. However, Hoover still relied on local relief and private charity to handle hunger. He still expected voluntary public-private cooperation to rescue the economy, and he still feared a federal deficit. Hoover never accepted the need for bold federal intervention in the economy.[2]

FDR did. His term as governor of New York from 1929 to 1932 was a dry run for the presidency. He confronted the Great Depression's devastating impact on the state's one million unemployed men, three hundred thousand abandoned farms, and four hundred thousand people who lost their savings when banks failed. Children played eviction instead of monopoly and the homeless built Hoovervilles in Central Park using newspapers as Hoover blankets. Previewing his 1937 inaugural speech, FDR declared in 1932 that New York State could no longer "allow any individuals within her borders to go unfed, unclothed, or unsheltered." Accordingly, New York became the first state to accept responsibility for social welfare and establish programs providing direct aid to the hungry, the elderly, and farmers. Using the radio, FDR won so much public support that the Republican legislature had to cooperate. Like Hughes before him, FDR proved that positive government could work in New York. The nation was next.[3]

The 1932 election brought FDR to the White House in a landslide. It was a stunning accomplishment for a man whose meteoric political career seemed to have been cruelly canceled by polio in 1921. FDR's first inaugural speech captured the fighting spirit that enabled him to cope with his own paralysis and fortified him for confronting the nation's "fear . . . which paralyzes needed efforts to convert retreat into advance." Asserting that "this nation asks for action, and action now," FDR likened the economic crisis to a war. Whereas he "hoped that the normal balance of executive and legislative authority may be wholly adequate to meet the unprecedented task before us," he warned that if Congress failed to respond, he "may call for a temporary departure from that normal balance." In such a case, he would seek "broad executive power to wage a war against the emergency as great as the power that would be given to me if we were in fact invaded by a foreign foe." FDR promised that he would "not evade" this paramount "duty" as a leader.[4]

Drawing upon the different priorities of social workers and academics in his "Brain Trust," FDR developed his program during the harsh winter between the November election and the March inauguration. Like Hughes, FDR rejected ideological rigidity in favor of practical solutions that could reconcile diverse perspectives. Like Hughes, FDR was both liberal and conservative. On the one hand, he took a conservative approach to stabilizing the capitalist system by declaring a "bank holiday" and stopping gold trading the day after he took office. Four days later, he signed an Emergency Banking Relief Act in order to restore public confidence. The Economy Act, which cut veterans' payments and federal employees' salaries, embraced a conservative emphasis on balanced budgets. No wonder an advisor later quipped that "capitalism was saved in eight days."[5]

Yet, FDR's first inaugural endorsed several liberal, perhaps radical, economic policies. They included "direct recruiting by the government itself, alleviating unemployment, bolstering agricultural prices, halting farm foreclosures, and "unifying relief activities." In addition, he endorsed "national planning and supervision" of transportation, communications, and public utilities. These ambitious goals were translated into fifteen major bills adopted during his first one hundred days. FDR was confident that all would be upheld by the Supreme Court. As he claimed in his first inaugural, "Our Constitution is so simple and practical that it is possible always to meet extraordinary needs by changes in emphasis and arrangement without loss of essential form." However, the Supreme Court had not faced such a deluge of path-breaking, experimental legislation since Reconstruction. The justices would have to carefully consider which new laws to support and on what grounds. How "simple and practical" would the Constitution prove to be? Was it really possible to alter its "emphasis and arrangement without loss of essential form?"[6]

During the 1920s, when Hughes was secretary of state, the Taft Court invalidated more regulatory statutes than any decade before or since. It seemed like a "super-legislature" ardently adhering to the rigid version of dual federalism based on the separation of state and federal spheres. Law professor Norman Williams cautioned that the Court was less rigid than reputed and that Taft himself advocated adapting "the commerce clause to the real and practical essence of modern business growth." Although the justices did uphold some regulations, the majority resisted changes that would enable state and federal governments to weaken standard laissez-faire protections for private property, contracts, and commerce.[7]

Labor issues were particularly controversial because industrial working conditions were particularly harsh. State and federal efforts to ameliorate them were repeatedly struck down during the three decades of the Lochner era in a pro-business, anti-labor spirit. For example, in the 1918 *Hammer v. Dagenhart* case, the Court invalidated a 1916 congressional act banning interstate commerce of items produced by child labor. The five-to-four majority held that Congress could only ban interstate commerce in harmful goods and could not regulate the conditions under which the goods were made. That was a local matter for the states as reserved by the Tenth Amendment. Oliver Wendell Holmes Jr. dissented. Why could the Court condone laws banning goods considered immoral, like lotteries and liquor, but not ban "the product of ruined lives?" To be sure, the states controlled labor policies within their boundaries, but when the products of labor crossed state lines, congressional policies should prevail.[8]

Holmes dissented again in 1923 when the Taft Court invalidated the District of Columbia's efforts to establish minimum wages for women and children (*Adkins v. Children's Hospital*). As lawyer for the defense, Harvard professor Felix Frankfurter defended the law using data to document awful working conditions, like Louis Brandeis in *Lochner* and *Muller*. Writing for the five-to-four majority, George Sutherland claimed that such regulations kept employers and employees from making labor contracts freely. Moreover, general regulations ignored the specific circumstances of different workplaces. Private enterprise must be left unfettered. But Holmes pointed out that a "contract is no more exempt from law than other acts." Reprising his *Lochner* dissent, Holmes asserted that laws were valid if they reflected whatever "a reasonable man," as represented by legislators, might consider necessary, not because of the justices' personal opinions. Nonetheless, these and other cases blocked federal and state legislative regulation in the public interest.[9]

During the early years of the Hughes Court, the justices both supported and rejected state and federal regulatory laws. For example, in 1930, the Court unanimously upheld an antitrust regulation in *U.S. v. First National Pictures*. Similar to his 1915 pro-union position in *Coppage v. Kansas*, Hughes wrote for the Court supporting a workers' right to choose their own collective bargaining representatives instead of being forced to accept so called yellow dog contracts (*Texas and New Orleans Railroad Company v. Brotherhood of Railway and Steamship Clerks*). In 1931, Hughes and Owen Roberts joined the liberals to approve a New Jersey law regulating fire insurance rates (*O'Gorman and Young v. Hartford Insurance Company*). Brandeis's opinion referenced the New York State laws that emerged from Hughes's 1905 insurance investigation, which dovetailed with Brandeis's own work in Massachusetts. Such cases expanded the power of government to regulate industry in the public interest.[10]

However, in 1932, Hughes and Roberts joined the conservatives to reject an Oklahoma law requiring licenses for ice businesses because they did not involve a public interest (*New State Ice Company v. Liebmann*). Hughes was mainly concerned that the license regulation would stifle economic opportunity. In a landmark dissent, Brandeis urged that the old distinctions between public and private interests be reassessed in the context of the Great Depression "an emergency more serious than war." Moreover, each state should be allowed to "serve as a "laboratory and try novel social and economic experiments without risk to the rest of the country," a principle later called "experimental federalism."[11]

By contrast, and with only one dissent, Hughes wrote a 1933 opinion upholding the efforts of Appalachian coal producers to control prices during the Depression (*Appalachian Coals, Inc. v. U.S.*). Here he accepted the need to interfere with the free market under dire circumstances, a position he advocated in a 1932 speech justifying "adaptations to meet new conditions." These decisions revealed how votes could shift depending on the case. They challenged notions of rigid polarities among the justices. Nonetheless, politicians, the press, and the public feared that such vacillation threatened efforts to combat the Depression.[12]

Two landmark cases in 1934 suggested that the Court's liberal wing might prevail. In 1933, Midwestern farmers were so desperate that two hundred men lynched an Iowa judge who refused to stop farm foreclosures, Thousands of farmers demonstrated at the Minnesota and Nebraska state legislatures. In response, Minnesota passed a temporary mortgage moratorium law, which was challenged for breaching individual property contract rights (*Home Building and Loan Association v. Blaisdell*). Writing for the majority (including Roberts), Hughes held that the Constitution's clause protecting "the obligation of contracts" should not "be read with literal exactness like a mathematical formula." Rather, private contracts should be evaluated in the context of "public needs" and "a rational compromise between individual rights and public welfare." "The question," he wrote, "is no longer merely that of one party to a contract as against another, but of the use of reasonable means to safeguard the economic structure upon which the good of all depends." The mortgage crisis created a public emergency that justified temporary relief by the state. Making a typically subtle distinction, Hughes said that although "emergency does not create power, emergency may furnish the occasion for the exercise of power." These words recalled his approval of aggressive war powers during World War I. Drawing upon both John Marshall and Holmes, Hughes emphasized the moratorium's "legitimate end" and advocated a "rational compromise between individual rights and public welfare."[13]

Most important, Hughes dismissed the idea that "what the Constitution meant to the vision of that day, it must mean to the vision of our time." Considering the increased "complexity of our economic interests," governmental regulation was justified in order "to safeguard the vital interests of its people." By acknowledging that even contracts could bow to the greater good, he deviated from John Marshall who considered the right to private contracts equivalent to a natural right beyond state control. Perhaps as compensation, Hughes reiterated Marshall's assertion that the Constitution was "intended to endure for ages to come and, consequently, to be adapted to the various crises of human affairs." Similar to his strategy on the Monroe Doctrine, a turn of the phrase enabled him to handle a crisis.[14]

The four conservatives dissented with Sutherland contending that the contracts clause protected creditors from financial loss in economic downturns, which were too common to be considered emergencies. He rejected the idea that the Constitution could "mean one thing at one time and an entirely different thing at another time." Writing in 1934, political scientist Edwin Corwin sensed that the judicial ground was shifting. Although later quite critical, he now called Hughes's controversial 1907 quote "incisive" and relevant. He even used it to begin and end his book on the history of the Constitution. To Corwin, judges really *were* saying what the Constitution is. Through judicial review, the Court "gradually made itself morally answerable for the safety and welfare of the nation to an extent utterly without parallel in judicial annals, past or present." A New Deal supporter who influenced the court packing plan, Corwin championed a return to Marshall's concept of "national power and its supremacy" in order to ensure that "the Constitution of a progressive society . . . keeps pace with that society." For a brief moment, the scholar, the president, and the chief justice agreed.[15]

Because Hughes's opinion endorsed a "living Constitution," wrote law professor Richard D. Friedman, *Blaisdell* was "a strikingly modern decision." It signified that the Constitution would not be a countermajoritarian force rigidly resisting reality. Thus, it marked an important step towards what law professor G. Edward White called modernism. It embraced "the belief that Americans can themselves alter the course of their future by changing the shape of their government and changing the meaning of their Constitution." Drawing upon his progressive faith in human agency and his support for sociological jurisprudence, Hughes emphasized the actual "effects of individual contractual relationships on the welfare of the general public." Contracts between individuals, like mortgages, did not exist in a vacuum isolated from their social impact. Whereas Sutherland saw the Constitution, via contracts, as having "a fixed meaning," Hughes held that the Constitution was open to interpretation. Although Hughes claimed to merely be applying Marshall's concept of a Constitution that was "adapting to new conditions," White suggested that he really was advocating a Constitution that was "changing in response to those conditions." To critics, Hughes was "making law" and "the Constitution surely had become what the judges said it was." To proponents, Hughes was leading the Court in adapting to the twentieth century.[16]

The second landmark 1934 case concerned a New York State law intended to help farmers suffering from plummeting milk prices (*Nebbia v. NY*). Roberts spoke for the majority in words reminiscent of Hughes during his first term and in *Blaisdell.* A Rochester grocery owner claimed that state price controls deprived him of substantive due process. In response, Roberts affirmed that "neither property rights nor contract rights are absolute" and do not cancel the public right "to regulate in the common interest." He further rejected the long-standing principle, recently used in the *Liebmann* ice case, that regulations only applied to businesses "cloaked with a public interest." Noting milk's importance to health, Roberts redefined public interest to include "whatever economic policy may reasonably be deemed to promote public welfare." Accordingly, he wrote, "There is no closed class or category of businesses affected with a public interest." Reasonable legislative regulations to protect "the public welfare" overrode substantive due process claims. The opinion dealt a major blow to laissez-faire economics because, unlike *Blaisdell,* it was not predicated on temporary, emergency needs.[17]

In response, the four conservatives invoked *Liebmann,* called the *Nebbia* opinion much too broad, and warned that it could imperil both liberty and property whenever "an impatient majority [was] stirred by distressful exigency." To McReynolds, the milk price controls opened the door to regulating the whole economy. They were "not regulation, but management, control, dictation." Furthermore, such controls would "destroy guaranteed rights of one man with the prime purpose of enriching another." Eviscerating precedent, the ruling subjected the Constitution to "the caprice of the hour." Therefore, the new policy was unwise, unreasonable, and dangerous. Roberts understood the significance of his opinion and reportedly paced the floor before issuing it. Indeed, historian Barry Cushman called it "a revolution in due process jurisprudence." By eliminating the old public-private distinction, *Nebbia* rendered all businesses susceptible to regulation without recourse to substantive due process complaints, just as McReynolds feared. To law professor Mark Tushnet, *Nebbia* marked movement toward reinterpreting class legislation positively and accepting "interest group pluralism."[18]

These 1934 decisions suggested that Hughes and Roberts endorsed state regulation and fostered hope that the Court might support the New Deal after all. 1935 clouded the picture. The "hot oil" case was an ominous sign of things to come (*Panama Refining Co. v. Ryan*). In order to promote recovery, Congress passed the 1933 National Industrial Recovery Act (NIRA), which was administered by the National Recovery Administration (NRA). It enabled the president to establish industry-wide codes for fair practices, including wages and prices. The codes were set by industry boards appointed by the president and implemented by executive order. The board members represented industry, labor, and consumers but were dominated by industry. Violating the codes was a criminal act. The codes were initially welcomed as vehicles for stimulating the economy and improving labor conditions. The public marched in NRA parades and businesses proudly displayed posters of the NRA's insignia, the blue eagle. However, enthusiasm waned when code evasions increased and producers raised prices to offset higher wages. For one critic, the blue eagle had become a black buzzard.[19]

In this case, a company produced and shipped more petroleum than the industry code allowed, making it "hot oil." The Court had long deferred to regulatory agencies like the Interstate Commerce Commission (ICC) and the Federal Trade Commission (FTC). However, it drew the line here because, wrote Hughes, Congress had granted the president "unlimited authority" without providing any standards for the oil code or its implementation. Moreover, the industry group writing the code was not comprised of federal employees, as were the ICC and FTC. Instead, they were appointed by and answerable only to the president. Riffing on Hughes, E. G. White later observed that each code really "meant, in effect, whatever a group of industry representatives and the President said it meant." Hughes reaffirmed the Court's support for legislative "flexibility and practicality" as Congress "adapted to complex conditions." However, he held that by delegating authority with "unfettered discretion," Congress abandoned its legislative function and weakened "our constitutional system." It was not only condoning "an uncontrolled administrative authority" but granting the executive "uncontrolled legislative power."[20]

Hughes's opinion revived a rarely used nondelegation doctrine, which invoked separation of powers in order to limit presidential powers. In his 1924 Westminster Hall speech, Hughes warned that "there is no panacea for modern ills in bureaucracy." He reminded his audience of "the most precious right of democracy—the right to be governed by law and not by officials." That included "the right to reasonable, definite, and proclaimed standards, which the citizens can invoke against both malevolence and caprice." Experts, like those in his Public Service Commissions, were supposed to help, not hamper, democracy. Only Benjamin Cardozo dissented, claiming that the act did establish standards, suggesting that the separation of powers doctrine was being applied with "pedantic rigor." Although the ruling only affected part of the NIRA, the rest of the act was at risk.[21]

Another negative ruling seemed immanent when, right after "hot oil," the Court began three days of oral argument about the Gold Clause cases (*Norman v. Baltimore and Ohio Railroad Co.* and *U.S. v. Bankers' Trust* and *Nortz v. U.S* and *Perry v. U.S.*). They involved a 1933 congressional resolution, voiding clauses in public and private contracts that promised redemption in gold for all creditors, including holders of Liberty Bonds. The immediate purpose was to curtail gold hoarding and stimulate the economy. The resolution supplemented the 1933 Emergency Banking Act, which removed the nation from the gold standard. Conservatives considered it "the end of western civilization." Nonetheless, these policies had been in effect for two years, all contracts had been backed in currency (not gold), and the nation had accepted the devalued currency.[22]

The problem was that if people holding contracts, mortgages, and bonds demanded repayment in gold at the devalued rate of the dollar, they would make a sizable profit, deplete the Treasury, and cause economic collapse. That prospect generated widespread anxiety. FDR was so certain that the Court would invalidate the gold clause resolution that he prepared a Fireside Chat rejecting the ruling by appealing "beyond the letter of the law" in fulfillment of his "duty to protect the people of the United States." Fearing that a negative ruling would cause financial panic, Joseph P. Kennedy, chairman of the Securities and Exchange Commission (SEC), prepared to close the Stock Market. People talked about packing the Court or amending the Constitution. FDR was worried but did not show it when he hosted the justices at a formal White House dinner served "on the President's gold plates."[23]

National anxiety grew as Hughes repeatedly postponed the ruling. On decision day, the Court was packed. Backed by the liberals plus Roberts, Hughes spoke for the Court, holding forth for one and a half hours. First, he affirmed that the congressional power "to coin money and regulate the power thereof" enabled it to devalue currency as it saw fit. Therefore, the fundamental "question before the Court is power, not policy." Because congressional powers overrode private contracts in the national interest, gold repeal and the gold clause were constitutional. The Liberty Bonds issue was more complicated because it involved "an obligation of the United States." Hughes held that federal bonds themselves could not be abrogated. However, because the bondholder who sued had not actually been damaged, he was not entitled to an "unjustified enrichment" by cashing in the bond at the devalued currency rate. On this narrow ground, the resolution was upheld, but the bonds remained intact.[24]

Aware of the pivotal practical issues at stake, Hughes bent over backward to avoid economic disaster and support the New Deal. Roberts followed his lead. Although welcomed as the Court's "strategic retreat," the decision seemed "strange . . . and strained." Harlan Stone wrote a separate concurrence agreeing with the overall result but exposing the inconsistency of voiding private contracts while sustaining public ones. Representing the conservatives, McReynolds's oral dissent was so acerbic that parts of it were stricken from the record, including his declaration that "this is Nero at its worst. . . . The Constitution is gone. Shame and humiliation are upon us now!" To him, violating any contract was the "spoilation of citizens by their sovereign." Relieved that the economy had been saved, FDR issued a brief statement of appreciation and privately joked about being unable to deliver his "marvelous radio address." At the same time, he knew that it had been a close call.[25]

That fact was underlined two and a half months later when Roberts joined the four conservatives to overturn a mandatory Oregon railroad retirement pension law (*Railroad Retirement Board v. Alton Railroad Co.*). In the process, they invalidated the 1933 federal Railroad Retirement Act, which used the interstate commerce clause to require that employers and employees contribute to railroad retirement pensions. Roberts, previously a railroad lawyer, wrote that the law violated both the due process and commerce clauses because the payments were compulsory and because pensions were not directly related to commerce. As such, they should be left to the decisions of the railroads themselves, which could not be deprived of their resources without due process. Thus, he revived the distinction between public and private spheres that he had undercut in *Nebbia.* Dismissing pensions as "social welfare," Roberts warned that next the government could mandate free medical care, housing, food, or children's education, none of which directly affected the railroads. By implication, Congress was prohibited from regulating or promoting any such programs.[26]

In response, said law professor William G. Ross, Hughes delivered "one of his most biting dissents." As governor he had advanced enlightened labor policies and, as associate justice, he supported railroad workers' hours legislation and employers' liability for injury. Consequently, he disagreed with Roberts for the first time since they joined the Court. Backed by the three liberals, Hughes stated that, because railroads were vital interstate carriers essential to a seamless economy, the federal government could regulate whatever bore, in Holmes's terms, a "reasonable relation" to job safety or worker morale. In fact, many railroads already provided pension plans precisely for that purpose.[27]

The principle, said Hughes, was that "industry should take care of its human wastage, whether that is due to accident or age." It was simply part of "the reasonable demands of justice." Endorsing the progressive concept of legislative experimentation, he held that legislation did not have to "be perfect." Rather, the Court should exercise judicial restraint and grant Congress "broad discretion . . . even of mistakes." These statements reinforced Hughes's long-standing expansive view of the commerce clause and sociological jurisprudence. However, if he was consistent, Roberts was not and his starkly conservative position made FDR nervous. The president and his advisors revisited strategies to curb the Court.[28]

The Crisis

Black Monday came merely two weeks later on May 27, 1935, a day considered as disastrous as the original Black Monday of October 28, 1929, when the Stock Market crashed. In three unanimous decisions, the Court invalidated two laws and one executive action. The cumulative effect was shocking.

The least damaging Black Monday ruling was the Court's decision that the 1934 Federal Farm Bankruptcy Act violated the Fifth Amendment protection against losing property without due process (*Louisville Joint Stock Land Bank v. Radford*). Designed to benefit farmers, the act prevented banks from foreclosing on farms after a five-year moratorium. Brandeis's opinion called this policy an illegal confiscation of the banks' property as mortgage holders without due process or just compensation. The law was sponsored by two Progressive North Dakota Republicans and pushed by FDR's Louisiana critic, Governor Huey Long. Aware of its origins and its poorly drafted form, the president had signed it reluctantly. Its invalidation did not really hurt the New Deal.[29]

By contrast, FDR was very upset when the Court reversed his decision to fire an obstreperous member of the FTC who was blocking all efforts to regulate unfair business practices and turning the FTC into a protector of corporations rather than a defender of consumers (*Humphrey's Executor v. U.S.*). Sutherland's opinion pointed out that the FTC was an independent agency outside the executive branch and that, therefore, the executive could not remove its members, especially not on political grounds. The ruling was an important reaffirmation of the separation of powers. However, having been advised by lawyers that he would win the case, FDR was taken aback. According to administration lawyer and future associate justice Robert Jackson, "That damn little case made him madder at the Court than any other decision." He took it "personally."[30]

The last Black Monday case had the largest implications. *Schechter v. U.S.*, called the "sick chicken" case, followed up on the "hot oil" case to definitively kill the NIRA. Knowing how important it was, Hughes wrote the unanimous opinion himself. The case involved a small kosher chicken market in Brooklyn, New York, whose owners were accused of violating the live poultry industry code by selling diseased chickens. They ignored wage and hours policies as well as other requirements. The poultry business was notorious for racketeering and cutthroat competition as well as filthy working conditions. Moreover, New York City was known as "a national dumping ground for diseased poultry." The Schechters were found guilty for violating the codes, fined, and briefly jailed.[31]

When the Schechters' appeal reached the Supreme Court, their conviction was overturned. Hughes pointed out that the NRA code did not apply. Although the chickens arrived from out of state, they were only sold within the state. Therefore, they did not affect the flow of interstate commerce either directly or indirectly and the federal government had no authority over them. To Stone, the distinction between direct and indirect effects was "too mechanical, too uncertain in its application, and too remote from actualities to be of value." Indeed, Hughes was widely criticized for straining reason and being inconsistent. Law professor Alpheus Thomas Mason called it "one of the most reactionary judicial pronouncements of this century."[32]

However, Hughes thought this case was unlike an earlier case in which poultry industry racketeers controlled transportation to and prices in other states. It also differed from his 1914 Shreveport ruling where one state's regulations discriminated against another. Hughes had not abandoned his expansive view of the interstate commerce clause but did not consider it relevant here. What did apply was his long-standing commitment to a cautious dual federalism that required carefully balancing national and state prerogatives. Otherwise, he said, "there would be virtually no limit on federal power, and for all practical purposes, we should have a completely centralized government." Oddly, just after recognizing the interwoven, marble cake nature of state and federal commerce in his *Nebbia* dissent, Hughes seemed to revert to an old layer cake version of dual federalism in *Schechter.*[33]

Beyond interstate commerce and dual federalism issues, the case involved presidential powers. Refining what he wrote in *Blaisdell* about emergency powers, Hughes explained that "extraordinary conditions may call for extraordinary remedies, but extraordinary conditions do not create or enlarge constitutional power." The NRA code was, as he held in "hot oil," an excessive delegation of congressional authority to the executive branch without standards, guidelines, or possibility for review. Congress had given the president "an unfettered discretion to make whatever laws he thinks may be needed or advisable for the rehabilitation and expansion of trade or industry." Every justice agreed that the codes violated democracy's sacred separation of powers. Even Cardozo, who had dissented in "hot oil," issued a concurrence joined by Stone. Although urging that the distinction between direct and indirect effects remain flexible, they deplored the codes as "delegation run riot." A cartoon in *The Kansas City Star* titled "Still Supreme" depicted Hughes, the teacher, instructing FDR, his Brain Trust, and key senators about the meaning of the Constitution, especially concerning executive authority and the codes (see figure 10.1).[34]

Figure 10.1. "Still Supreme," artist unknown. *The Kansas City Star*, May 28, 1935. Courtesy of the Folklife Center, Crandall Public Library, Glens Falls, New York.

Despite the fact that the NRA was already controversial and would soon expire, the ruling stung. The president could not believe that he had lost the support of the three liberals for a bill he had once called "the most important and far-reaching legislation in the history of the American Congress." Distraught, he demanded to know how Brandeis,

Cardozo, and Stone had voted. In each case, his lawyers responded that they stood with the majority. FDR was incensed but waited four days to respond.[35]

As reporters crowded around his desk, the president delivered a ninety-minute disquisition on the Court. With great drama, he read telegrams from small businessmen across the country begging for federal help. To him, the *Schechter* ruling was as disastrous as the 1857 *Dred Scott* decision. Killing the NRA, he said, meant "that the United States Government has no control over any national economic problem." It would resurrect "the horse and buggy definition of interstate commerce" and prevent the nation from helping its people during crisis. Although FDR declined to give any opinion about the Court's future, he reported receiving many suggestions: "They go all the way from abolishing the Supreme Court to abolishing the Congress, and, I think, abolishing the president." Laughter filled the room.[36]

Of course, it was no laughing matter, especially if it spelled the New Deal's demise. Popular furor surged and the government stopped enforcing other NRA codes. However, to New Deal critics, like Hughes's old foe Senator William Borah, the ruling was a blessing because checking executive power meant that "the Constitution is reestablished." So was cutthroat competition. Wages dropped; working hours rose; child labor grew; prices plummeted; commodity and stock markets fluctuated. In Congress, Democrats (minus states' rights Southerners), floated bills to regulate working conditions and curtail the Court, including one by Senator George Norris, another Hughes foe. Some called for a constitutional convention. Others preferred amending the Constitution, but FDR concluded that it would take too long and lacked public support. Likewise, court packing was discussed but seemed unwise because the justices had been unified in *Schechter*. FDR would bide his time.[37]

1936 changed everything. Month after month, with only one exception, a divided Court ruled against federal and state regulatory acts designed for economic rescue and reform. That was only possible because the two swing votes, Hughes and Roberts, frequently joined the four conservatives. Their positions angered contemporaries and have confounded historians ever since. Public dismay was exacerbated by a sensational book published in December 1936. Written by journalists Drew Pearson and Robert S. Allen, it castigated *The Nine Old Men* of the Supreme Court who were comfortably ensconced in their marble palace arrogantly over ruling the people's will. Together, they were "more omnipotent" than the legislative and executive branches "combined." Hughes was particularly culpable as he "swung like a man on a flying trapeze" in futile efforts to harmonize the justices. Mixing metaphors, Hughes was compared to "a setting hen trying to get eight unruly chicks under his wing." The chaos on the Court rendered Hughes "a tragic failure" as chief justice. This widely read book strengthened calls for court reform and confirmed the general sense, in Bickel's later term, that the Court was a "counter-majoritarian force" in democracy.[38]

January 1936 began badly when the Court invalidated the Agricultural Adjustment Act (AAA) in *U.S. v. Butler*. A hallmark of the New Deal, the AAA was FDR's major effort to help farmers, whom he had always championed and who were being decimated by low prices due to overproduction and underconsumption. Through the AAA, farmers who agreed to reduce production received subsidies financed by taxing farm product processors, including canners, meat processors, millers, and textile manufacturers. Understanding that the act "carved a new and untrod path," the president worked hard to get it passed. He pressured key senators, made compromises, extended farm credit, and created a Home Owners' Loan Corporation to refinance nonfarm mortgages. Once implemented, the AAA not only improved farm prices and farmers' incomes but also generated fifteen hundred lawsuits protesting excessive federal control. Despite knowing that the AAA had "imperfections," FDR wanted "to do something to increase the value of farm products, and if the darn thing doesn't work, we can say so quite frankly, but at least try it."[39]

The Court focused on those imperfections in a six-to-three decision written by Roberts for Hughes and the Four Horsemen. An old friend of Butler's lawyer, Roberts echoed his argument that the program was compulsory, not voluntary. Evoking Marshall in *McCulloch v. Maryland* (1819), Roberts said that "the power to confer or withhold unlimited benefits is the power to coerce or destroy." In addition, he contended that the tax on processors was less about raising revenue than about achieving social change by taking "money from one group for the benefit of another." Ironically, that was McReynolds's point when he criticized Roberts in *Nebbia*.[40]

As governor, Hughes had asserted state control over agriculture, a position that Roberts now affirmed by claiming that Congress could not use the taxing power to override the Tenth Amendment's reserved rights of states. Otherwise, congressional power to regulate would be limitless. In seeming contradiction, Roberts endorsed an expansive Hamiltonian interpretation of the power to tax for the general welfare. That section was pressed by Hughes, who later called it "the most significant and important ruling" of the case. It was central to his vote and marked the first time the Court adopted such a broad position on taxation. Hughes later claimed that *Butler* set the precedent for the Court to uphold the Social Security Act in 1937 (*Helvering v. Davis*). Strangely, the endorsement of a broad taxing power appeared in a case that ruled narrowly on that very power. That disparity made Hughes look as inconsistent as Roberts.[41]

Stone had concerns about the AAA but rebuked the Court for its "tortured construction of the Constitution." Joined by Brandeis and Cardozo, he dismissed Roberts's fear that Congress might regulate everything. The real problem was that, after this ruling, Congress would be unable to regulate anything. Most important, Stone criticized the majority for abandoning judicial restraint and rejecting the legislature's reasonable effort to use its taxing power to address economic problems. By wading into policy, the Court was exalting its own role and undermining the separation of powers. "Courts," he wrote, "are not the only agency of government that . . . have the capacity to govern." Agricultural processors and the conservative Liberty League applauded the decision as well as 59 percent of the public who already opposed federal regulation of agriculture before the decision. Yet, other farmers regretted losing federal assistance and, in Iowa, the six majority justices were hung in effigy. Roosevelt's anger mounted.[42]

In mid-February, the Court gave the New Deal a temporary reprieve by partially endorsing the TVA (*Ashwander v. Tennessee Valley Authority*). The eight-to-one opinion, with McReynolds dissenting, narrowly focused on the legality of one TVA contract to sell excess power derived from Alabama's Wilson Dam in Muscle Shoals. The ruling rejected the notion that by selling and distributing electric power, the federal government was illegally competing with and undermining private power providers. Hughes affirmed the TVA's right to build dams to improve interstate waterways as part of federal control over interstate commerce. The TVA, he said, was just distributing excess energy, not starting a business. The TVA director was grateful. Nonetheless, he was well aware that the Court had not ruled on larger questions posed by the TVA's bold experiments in rural electrification, soil reclamation, and flood control. These were the kind of national planning associated with socialism. For the moment, however, Tennesseans celebrated and *The New York Times* suggested that maybe those nine old men were really not "bent on imposing their will on Congress and writing their private prejudices into the Constitution." But *The Nation* warned that such optimism was premature.[43]

The Nation was right. Over time, the Hughes Court endorsed five important New Deal measures plus the gold clauses. However, from late February to May 1936, the justices split sharply in over-ruling several other federal and state regulatory efforts while upholding only one. They also narrowed the role of the SEC and negated part of the Federal Homeowners' Loan Act. Hughes and Roberts often joined the Four Horsemen, but sometimes Hughes sided with the Three Musketeers, including their protest against voiding the 1934 Municipal Bankruptcy Act. Again, he looked inconsistent, if not reactionary. Moreover, the Court itself looked bad with dissents from one side sounding as acerbic as from the other side. Although with a twinkle in his eye, Hughes felt compelled to assure the American Law Institute that "the Supreme Court is still functioning." Divisions within the Court, he claimed, were as natural as they were "in theology, philosophy and science." Thus, controversy was a sign of health because the law should never be frozen in "icy certainty." That hardly seemed to be a danger.[44]

An April 1936 case revisited the power of administrative agencies. *St. Joseph Stockyards v. U.S.* dealt with maximum rates for services set by Secretary of Agriculture Henry A. Wallace. The company called the rates an arbitrary confiscation of its property and requested a hearing, which was denied. The Court agreed that the charges were not confiscatory but disagreed about the process used. In his majority opinion, Hughes insisted that there had to be a fair hearing in which the company could present its case in court for judicial review. Its rights required protection against potentially arbitrary administrative decisions, a position he advocated as governor and in his 1924 speech.

Brandeis suggested leaving personal rights to the courts and property rights to administrators. But Hughes held that both deserved the protection of judicial review lest administrators "go beyond the limits of constitutional authority." That was a real possibility because of the current "multiplication of administrative authorities." Stone and Cardozo dissented. Not only did the decision allow rich companies to challenge regulations but it also encumbered the courts and undercut all regulations. Although FDR considered hearings unnecessary delays,

Hughes's position that all rights deserved judicial review was affirmed by the Court in 1938 (*Morgan v. U.S.*). To political scientist Kenneth M. Holland, Hughes's insistence on equitable procedure represented "one of his most important contributions to public law."[45]

Learning from the *Schechter* case, FDR's lawyers redrafted parts of the NIRA. One result was the 1935 Bituminous Coal Conservation Act, also called the Guffey Act after its Pennsylvania Senate sponsor. In May, the Court invalidated the act by a complicated five-to-four vote (*Carter v. Carter Coal*). The act was premised on the generally accepted belief that bituminous (soft) coal was a key national industry with broad implications for prices, wages, and hours beyond any single state. Cutthroat competition and persistent strikes made the whole industry so chaotic that it deepened the Depression and motivated Congress to seek stability. Supported by the United Mine Workers but hotly debated in Congress, the act set production quotas and minimum prices. In a separate section, it set minimum wages and maximum hours. Workers acquired the right to organize and bargain collectively. Mines that complied were given a tax break; detractors faced an excise tax.

Writing for the majority, Sutherland held that mining itself was a local productive industry beyond the reach of congressional power over interstate commerce. However, unlike Schechter's chickens, 97 percent of the Carter Company's coal was shipped beyond West Virginia after being mined. Moreover, seven coal producing states informed the Court that federal regulations were needed to save the industry. No matter. The Four Horsemen plus Roberts held that neither coal production nor labor strikes that paralyzed production were directly related to the flow of commerce. They also argued that treating prices separately from wages and hours (with separate federal commissions) was irrelevant because, like "hot oil," the commissions were comprised of unaccountable private industry representatives. The excise tax was dismissed as an illegal penalty that deprived mine owners of their property without due process.[46]

The three liberals dissented with Cardozo insisting that Congress could act "in the face of price wars and wage wars so pregnant with disaster" for the entire nation. Unlike "hot oil," Congress set standards and could regulate intrastate prices that directly impacted interstate prices. Cardozo cleverly invoked Hughes's Shreveport opinion linking intrastate railroad rates to interstate commerce. Surely, coal was similar.[47]

Reflecting the difficulty of being in the middle, Hughes wrote a separate opinion agreeing with the majority that the excise tax was illegal and that mining was local production. However, he shared the minority position that the federal government could regulate unfair competition and prices if coal was sold interstate. Hughes referenced *Nebbia*'s expansive definition of businesses having a public interest but stopped short of including intrastate productive industries like coal mining. Nor did he resolve the inconsistency of equating Schechter's local market with Carter's national market or of supporting federal regulation of railroads, but not coal.

To Stone's private complaint that Hughes strained reason, Brandeis suggested that the chief was "deeply unhappy [because] he has no control over the Court." At best, Hughes's position was Solomonic; at worst it was contrived. Such ambiguities, suggested law professor James F. Simon, undercut Hughes's exalted image. Perhaps his dissent captured the difficulty of moving from the old rigid dual federalism to the more flexible one. In any case, the ruling itself dealt a death blow to the NIRA and, by implication, other New Deal acts. How could the nation go forward?[48]

The last case of the term was even more controversial. It infuriated the public and was the straw that broke FDR's back on court packing. Delivered on June 1st, the case overturned a well drafted New York State law setting minimum wages for women and minors (*Morehead v. NY ex rel. Tipaldo*). Joseph Tipaldo was jailed for refusing to pay his laundry workers the state-required minimum wage for women. Despite his *Nebbia* opinion upholding New York State milk prices, Roberts opposed this law, raising new questions about his reliability. He joined the Four Horsemen, who had voted against a similar 1923 Washington, DC, minimum wage law (*Adkins v. Children's Hospital*), which Pierce Butler's majority opinion cited as precedent. He asserted that "arbitrary" mandated wage standards violated freedom of contract and substantive due process. Butler also dismissed concerns that employers and employees, especially women, were inherently unequal in making wage agreements. Combined with *Carter Coal*, the *Tipaldo* decision meant that neither federal nor state governments could regulate wages.[49]

Hughes dissented. Always reluctant to overthrow precedent, he claimed that *Tipaldo* differed from *Adkins* by emphasizing a "fair wage" instead of just a "living wage." This dubious distinction enabled him to dismiss *Adkins* as irrelevant and convey his disapproval without overturning it. He reiterated his opinions from two 1911 cases (*McGuire* and

Ramsey) that freedom of contract was not absolute but must be measured against the realities of the case. The circumstances here were plain. Female employees were not equal to male employers in making wage contracts. Furthermore, poverty wages benefitted employers and forced society to compensate by providing relief. As an advocate of sociological jurisprudence, he declared, "We are not at liberty to disregard these facts." As a former Progressive governor concerned about working conditions, he feared that the decision would strangle state reform efforts.[50]

Backed by Brandeis and Cardozo, Stone wrote a stronger dissent, which advocated overturning *Adkins* and letting legislatures decide what wage policies were best. Stone renewed his (and Holmes's) previous complaint that the majority justices were ruling on the basis of their "own personal economic predilections." Privately, he scorned Hughes's constant search for a middle ground that would minimize conflict on the Court and lamented "that such an imposing façade rests, at times, upon such a slender foundation." Stone considered Hughes a weak leader whose narrow interpretations rendered the current court term "the most disastrous in its history." Yet, Mario J. Pusey pointed out that "of the twelve decisions upsetting New Deal statutes thus far, six were unanimous, and in two others the vote was eight to one." Maybe the Court was not as polarized or as reactionary as it seemed. Certainly, Hughes was not the only decision-maker and his record was more nuanced than Stone suggested. Opposing seven but supporting five of twelve key New Deal measures, Hughes still resisted labels.[51]

Tipaldo was universally condemned as "a new *Dred Scott* decision." Democrats were livid and the national press was overwhelmingly critical. A Californian decried the "JUDOCRACY" where one man can "nullify the progress of half a century along humanitarian lines." Even conservatives were embarrassed by being made to look inhumane. As *The New Republic* commented, "The liberty of contract" was now equated with "the liberty to starve." When the Republican National Convention met on June 2nd, its platform supported minimum wage laws and its nominee, Alfred M. Landon, called for a constitutional amendment to let states legislate on maximum working hours. Even Herbert Hoover thought Congress should restore the states' regulatory rights. Although most women's groups opposed the ruling, some praised it for treating women as citizens, not inferiors needing protection. Rather than comment directly on the case, FDR recommended that people read the three opinions to better understand how the justices had created a "no-man's-land where no government can function." When a reporter asked FDR how he would "meet the situation," he responded, "I think that is about all there is to say about it." In a few months, he would have plenty to say.[52]

The Solution

First, FDR had to get reelected. He ran a solid campaign but expected the returns to be close. Instead, he won a resounding victory in November 1935 with the largest popular plurality in history to date and the strongest Electoral College vote since 1820. Most important, he strengthened the Democratic Party with a new coalition that advanced interest group pluralism by including cities, farmers, labor, the elderly, ethnic minorities, African Americans, and women. Running on his first term record, he carried every state, except Maine and Vermont. In addition, the Democrats acquired commanding majorities in both the House and the Senate. To FDR, the results represented a mandate because, he said, "there's one central issue in this campaign. It's myself, and people must either be for me or against me." Although he avoided explicitly attacking the Court, he alluded to it by proclaiming, "Better the faults of a Government that lives in the spirit of charity than the consistent omissions of a Government frozen in the ice of its own indifference."[53]

Hughes administered the oath of office to FDR for the second time, enjoining him to "preserve, protect, and defend the Constitution of the United States." Although the president repeated the words faithfully, he later admitted that he really wanted to add, "Yes, but it's the Constitution as I understand it, flexible enough to meet any new problem of democracy—not the kind of Constitution your Court has raised as a barrier to progress and democracy." Having considered the options for court reform for two years, he knew what he was going to do. For the moment, however, he turned on the charm and engaged Hughes in lengthy banter at the annual judiciary dinner held two weeks after the nation's first January inauguration. Nor did he tell the cabinet and congressional leaders until he called an emergency meeting a few days later. News spread quickly in the halls of Congress and through the press. The justices found out while hearing a case.[54]

Reforming the Supreme Court was not a new idea nor was the number of justices fixed by the Constitution. It had shifted between six, seven, nine, and ten until finally settling on nine in 1869. During his 1912 presidential campaign, Theodore Roosevelt (TR) advocated popular referenda to overrule unpopular court decisions. President Taft appointed Hughes as associate justice in 1910 in order to rectify the "outrage" of a Court comprised, he said, of "those old fools" who refused to retire, particularly "the four men on the bench who are over seventy." FDR enjoyed learning that, as Wilson's attorney general, McReynolds suggested expanding the lower federal courts if judges insisted on serving beyond the age of seventy. In 1921, the American Bar Association endorsed the idea of increasing the Court by three justices.[55]

During his 1927 Columbia lectures, Hughes mentioned an 1869 act offering full pay to federal judges who chose to retire at seventy after serving at least ten years. Although some judges stayed too long, Hughes believed that "the community has no more valuable asset than an experienced judge." Far from causing "fossilization," Hughes thought that "the work of the court tends to keep a man keen-witted and earnest." It certainly did for him. He considered drawing the line at age seventy-five but rejected all limits as arbitrary. For proof, he offered eighty-five-year-old Holmes, who was still working "with the same energy and brilliance that he showed twenty years ago." Alexander Hamilton also had rejected age limits for men who "served their country long and usefully" based on "arbitrary" criteria and "the imaginary danger of a super annuated bench."[56]

Knowing that the topic was sensitive, FDR asked Attorney General Homer Cummings to design a proposal secretly. On February 5, 1937, FDR presented the resulting Judicial Procedures Reform Act. It contained provisions for expanding lower federal courts and promoting efficiency. But the central feature was adding up to six new Supreme Court justices for every justice who did not resign within six months of turning seventy. Exactly six of the current justices fit the bill—the Four Horsemen, Hughes at seventy-four, plus one of FDR's strongest supporters, Brandeis at eighty. Resenting the Court's recent rulings and regretting his inability to appoint even one Supreme Court member, the president justified reform as necessary to avoid catastrophe.

The problem, he said, was that "aged or infirm judges [with] lower mental or physical vigor" were slowing the work of the courts and preventing it from understanding "complicated and changed conditions." Consequently, "new facts become blurred through old glasses fitted, as it were, for the needs of another generation." Even worse, the Court was acting like a "policy-making body" by preventing Congress from "meeting squarely our modern social and economic conditions." Because life tenure had created "a static judiciary," it was essential to establish a method by which "a constant and systematic addition of younger blood will vitalize the courts." FDR accurately predicted that his public announcement would land had like a "bombshell." He loved surprises, but the impact of this one was not what he expected. Indeed, observers predicted that the president's message would stimulate as much controversy as the fight over the League of Nations.[57]

What was more surprising? The plan itself or the president's lack of planning? How could such a superb politician have neglected to get his political ducks in a row before acting? Why did he so badly misread the public and underestimate the chief justice? Was it hubris derived from his recent victory or a reflection of "his instinct for the dramatic"? Or was it a genuine response to still seeing, as he said in his 1937 second inaugural speech, "one-third of a nation ill-housed, ill-clad, ill-nourished."[58]

For historian James McGregor Burns, court packing was "a miscalculated risk." However, legal historian Laura Kalman concluded that far from folly, court packing had precisely the results FDR sought—a more liberal, pro–New Deal Supreme Court. Much of the ensuing debate revolved around the president's own assessment that he "lost the battle but won the war." He may have won in the short term but, wrote Burns, he lost in the long term by damaging his image and dividing his new Democratic coalition. Leuchtenburg added that the plan alienated Republican Progressives who had provided bipartisan support for the New Deal. Meanwhile, Hughes doubled his resolve to protect the Court in any way possible and wryly remarked, "If they want me to preside at a convention, I can do it."[59]

The Senate was eerily silent while the clerk read the text of the Court reform bill. Taken aback, Republicans immediately condemned it as a prelude to dictatorship. As with the League of Nations, Hiram Johnson and William Borah prepared to fight court packing together. Some Democrats made tentative statements of approval. But Vice President John Nance Garner of Texas, stood just outside the cloakroom holding his nose and giving a very visible thumbs-down. It only took a few days for the vast majority of both liberal and conservative newspapers to oppose the plan. *Brooklyn Daily Eagle* pointed out that previous presidents disagreed with the Court but none tried to override it. FDR had "unleashed a terrible sword" that would kill democracy. Thousands of angry telegrams flooded congressional offices. The legal profession vehemently resisted any tampering with the judiciary. Senate moderate Democrats resented not having been consulted. Southern Democrats predicted that a packed FDR court would undermine segregation. Progressives feared presidential tyranny. The more that Democrats fought among themselves the less Republicans needed to say.[60]

FDR was concerned enough to ask his son James to lead a strategy board that would lobby the hill and tally votes. The president himself pressured senators without much luck. Although some labor and farm organizations supported the proposal, most did not. Gallup polls indicated that public opposition was solidifying. It cut across religious and party lines as Catholics, Protestants, and Jews alike feared that the plan would make the Court too political and too susceptible to popular passions like the religious persecution raging abroad.

Others feared the concentration of executive power and the decimation of the Constitution. Newspaper publisher Frank Gannett formed the National Committee to Uphold Constitutional Government, which distributed over five hundred thousand fliers and thousands of related materials. A Constitutional Democracy Association organized opposition in small cities and rural areas. Both organizations mobilized public anger at the president's assault on an institution they cherished. A cartoon from *The Washington Post* depicted the six potential new justices as FDR clones.[61]

All was not lost. In mid-February, Senator Robert La Follette, a Progressive from Wisconsin, defended the bill on the radio. Attorney General Cummings followed a week later. Key Democratic senators, Arkansas's Joseph Robinson and Arizona's Henry Ashurst, supported the bill in debate. However, they were over shadowed by Montana Senator Burton Wheeler who lambasted court packing for threatening the separation of powers. His defection was ominous because he was among the first Progressives to endorse FDR in 1932 and was a solid New Dealer. At a Democratic victory dinner on March 4th and in a subsequent fireside chat, FDR fought back by calling for action "NOW" to "meet the needs of the nation." He compared the three branches of government to a three-horse team that must work together to get democracy's field plowed. Clearly the Court was not pulling its weight. Quoting Hughes, he blamed the problem on the fact that "we are under a Constitution, but the Constitution is what the judges say it is." Therefore, it was necessary "to save the Constitution from the Court and the Court from itself."[62]

On March 10th, attention focused on the Senate Judiciary Committee, where the bill was considered before being sent to the whole body. Because so many people wanted to attend, Chairman Ashurst relocated the hearings to the large Senate Caucus room, which was quickly filled by four hundred spectators and numerous reporters. Following the initial supportive arguments, Wheeler presented his own surprise. It was a letter from the chief justice. Hughes was willing to testify in person, as Wheeler originally proposed, but consulted Brandeis, who considered it improper. They settled on a letter, which Wheeler gave Hughes two days to write. When he finished, he got approval from Brandeis and Van Devanter, the senior liberal and conservative justices. Although he was later criticized (especially by Stone) for not asking others, Hughes, the pragmatist, probably anticipated that extended consultation would have meant debate and delay. Besides, he was sure that all the justices opposed the plan. When Wheeler picked up the letter, Hughes smiled and said, "The baby is born."[63]

Mincing no words, Hughes undercut FDR's claim that he was just seeking efficiency. "The Supreme Court," he wrote, "is fully abreast of its work. . . . There is no congestion of cases upon our calendar." In fact, adding justices would make the Court less efficient: "There would be more judges to confer, more judges to discuss, more judges to be convinced and to decide." Unfortunately, he also claimed that "the Constitution does not appear to authorize" the Court to divide into panels, which being much larger would demand. This statement looked political, a danger that other justices might have flagged. Frankfurter thought the whole episode reeked of hypocrisy as the Court played politics while claiming to be apolitical. Freidman and Kalman questioned the long-range significance of the letter in the court packing debate. For the moment, however, Hughes hit his mark. Labeled "Bulls Eye," a cartoon in *The Christian Science Monitor* depicted the letter as a cannonball landing on FDR's proposal. All in all, concluded Burns, "Hughes's political leadership and shrewdness matched Roosevelt's."[64]

Providing another angle on the controversy over New Deal acts, Hughes told Wheeler privately that "the laws have been poorly drafted, the briefs have been badly drawn, and the arguments have been poorly presented." Ashurst admitted that the early New Deal bills were written too quickly to even correct the grammar never mind address basic constitutional issues. This was particularly true of the NIRA, the Guffey Coal Act, and the AAA—all acts about which FDR harbored doubts himself. Historian Arthur Schlesinger Jr. observed that the initial laws were marked by "loose draftsmanship and emotional advocacy" while the later laws "were masterpieces of the lawyer's art." Consequently, when the constitutional questions were finally answered, the Court upheld revised versions of five of the bills it had voided. The 1937 Wagner Act, for example, was considered "a beautifully drafted statute." Apparently, doctrinal and technical issues, not just political expediency, influenced the Court's decisions.[65]

The Judiciary Committee continued calling witnesses for six more weeks, intentionally dragging the bill to a slow death and replicating Lodge's approach toward the League of Nations. Divisions within the labor movement and violent strikes increased public anxiety about destabilizing the Court. Meanwhile the justices were rendering the reform bill moot by a series of decisions endorsing the New Deal, which actually began before the court packing plan was announced. In November 1936, the Court upheld by five-to-four, without a written opinion, a New York State unemployment insurance plan designed to implement the Social Security Act (*Chamberlin v. Andrews*).[66]

In December, with only one dissent, it supported broad presidential discretion regarding arms sales to foreign nations (*U.S. v. Curtiss-Wright Export Corp.*). This landmark decision compensated for previous decisions curtailing executive power. Sutherland wrote the opinion, but Hughes undoubtedly influenced him and the other justices due to his expertise and strong belief in executive authority over foreign policy. He would have wanted to support FDR because the president was encountering Senate pressures for neutrality similar to the isolationism Hughes faced as secretary of state. Much of Sutherland's language echoed Hughes's statements on the subject.[67]

In early January 1937, Hughes wrote a unanimous opinion ratifying a 1934 act banning interstate commerce in convict-made goods (*Kentucky Whip and Collar Co. v. Illinois Central Railroad Co.*). Holding that the goods could be prohibited even though they were harmless in themselves, Hughes contended that the competition of convict labor with free labor made them harmful. Furthermore, he affirmed that Congress was "as free as the States to recognize the fundamental interests of free labor." This opinion accepted cooperative federalism. It contradicted his position in *Carter Coal,* when he distinguished between direct and indirect impacts on interstate commerce. Then he had kept local and federal realms separate, as in traditional conflict-oriented dual federalism. It also contradicted the 1918 *Hammer v. Dagenhart* decision, which rejected banning interstate commerce of harmful goods made by child labor. Hughes refrained from over-ruling the precedent, something he always tried to avoid. However, that strategy won over the Four Horsemen and secured a unified Court, something he always tried to obtain. This decision previewed his 1941 support of the Fair Labor Standards Act in *U.S. v. Darby.*[68]

A week after Hughes's letter, the Court handed down several rulings that further undercut court packing. March 29, 1937, was White Monday, in contrast to Black Monday, when three New Deal Acts were invalidated. It was a big day. Authored by several different justices, the Court handed down twenty decisions, among which were three unanimous rulings supporting the New Deal. The Railway Labor Act expanded labor's organizing rights (*Virginia Railway Co. v. System Federation No. 40*). The National Firearms Act used the taxing power, not just for revenue but to cripple firearms sales (*Sonzinski v. U.S.*). The Federal Farm Bankruptcy Act was affirmed in an opinion written by Brandeis, who had authored the 1935 Black Monday decision against the original act (*Wright v. Vinton Branch of the Mountain Trust Bank of Roanoke*).[69]

Hughes saved his own opinion for last. It was momentous but not unanimous. McReynolds broadcast his opposition by abruptly leaving just as Hughes began speaking. The case concerned a chambermaid whose employer paid her less than Washington state's minimum wage for women (*West Coast Hotel Co. v. Parrish*). When she asked for $216.19 in back pay, the company offered seventeen dollars. She sued and the case reached the Supreme Court in mid-December 1936. With Stone absent due to illness, the Court split four to four. Rather than report without an opinion, Hughes waited for Stone to tip the scales. FDR's supporters accused the chief of "playing politics" in response to the court packing plan. In fact, Hughes understood that Stone would support the Washington law, thus enabling the Court to finally overrule *Adkins* and *Tipaldo,* the two cases preventing federal and state economic regulations.[70]

Long in favor of minimum wage and maximum hours laws, Hughes dissented in *Tipaldo* and avoided overturning *Adkins,* despite clearly disagreeing with it. However, now the situation had changed. Hughes knew that Roberts was going to support the Washington law, thereby reversing his controversial *Tipaldo* vote. Hughes's role in Roberts's decision remains unclear. But Hughes and his wife visited the Roberts's farm in the summer of 1936, shortly after *Tipaldo*. Much to their wives' dismay, the two men spoke privately (and intently) for hours. According to Pusey, when Roberts later informed Hughes that he would uphold the Washington law, "the Chief had almost hugged him."[71]

The *Parrish* case involved the fundamental constitutional dilemmas of the modern era with which the Court had been wrestling for decades. Efforts to confront economic change challenged conventional dual federalism and concepts of laissez-faire, especially regarding federal and state regulatory powers, private property, and contracts. For Hughes, it was a conflict between public and private interests, a key concern ever since the New York State gas and insurance investigations three decades earlier.

Now he asked, "What is this freedom?" He answered that instead of enshrining "freedom of contract," the Constitution "speaks of liberty and prohibits the deprivation of liberty without due process of law." However, as he said in 1911 as well as in *O'Gorman*, *Blaisdell*, *Nebbia*, the Gold Clause cases, and *Tipaldo*, liberty itself was "not an absolute right." Nor was it "uncontrollable" because "the liberty safeguarded is liberty in a social organization which requires the protection of law against the evils which menace the health, safety, morals, and welfare of the people." Therefore, "reasonable" regulations "adopted in the interests of the community is due process." Without offending Roberts by directly attacking *Tipaldo*, Hughes undercut the claim that substantive due process protected freedom of contract. He elevated the public good over private prerogatives.[72]

Applying this definition to the issue of minimum wages for women, Hughes then asked, "What can be closer to the public interest than the health of women and their protection from unscrupulous and overreaching employers?" Significantly, that was a quote from Holmes's dissent in *Adkins*. Once again, Hughes pointed out that women were easily exploited in the labor contract bargaining process and, consequently, were underpaid. By definition, private contracts were tailored to private, not public, interests and could be unjust. Because employer paternalism could mask exploitation, minimum wage legislation on behalf of the disadvantaged was reasonable. Although those laws were often dismissed as special interest legislation, they really rewarded the employer's "selfish disregard of the public interest." For all these reasons, *Adkins* "should be and is overruled." The time had come to reject precedent. That decision, said Ross, was "a watershed" because it ended the "zigzagged" pattern of Court rulings regarding substantive due process as a barrier to economic regulation. For Hughes, it was the culmination of decades supporting sociological jurisprudence and worker's rights. As Robert Jackson remarked, the chief justice's voice "was one of triumph. He was reversing his Court, but not himself."[73]

Sutherland's dissent was steeped in barely veiled personal attacks on Roberts, Stone, and Hughes combined with sweeping, reactionary pronouncements. Condemning judges who responded to political pressure, he denied the legitimacy of legislation attuned to the needs of the times. As in the 1934 *Blaisdell* case, Sutherland insisted that "the meaning of the Constitution does not change with the ebb and flow of economic events." If that hallowed document was found wanting, he declared, it should be changed by amendment, not by legislation or court packing.[74]

The majority opinion was widely praised and many people credited Hughes with effectively besting FDR again. By contrast, Mason objected that Hughes "was praised to the skies" because, he said, Stone was the real leader on this issue. Stone himself claimed that his *Tipaldo* dissent was the basis for Hughes's *Parrish* opinion. On April 1st, the *Pittsburgh Post-Gazette* published a cartoon of the justices playing baseball with Hughes as pitcher, Stone as catcher, Roberts at bat, and everyone else eager to catch the ball. As Uncle Sam and FDR watched, the former asked the latter, "Are these your nine old men?" FDR ruefully responded, "They April Fooled me, Uncle."[75]

Nonetheless, Hughes and Roberts were both criticized as pawns of political pressure, which Hughes vigorously denied. As the only justice to have changed sides, Roberts became the focus of "the switch in time that saved nine." After all, *Parrish* came only nine months after *Tipaldo.* He was accused of being a flip-flopper more concerned with his public image than with constitutional principles. Roberts suffered under the assault but did not respond for years, and then only through a private memo to Frankfurter. Hughes resented the relentless impugning of his colleague's integrity. Speaking to the American Law Institute in May, he reinforced the need to maintain "an independent judiciary" and preserve our "democratic institutions" by endorsing "the processes of reason as opposed to the tyranny of force," a familiar theme for the former secretary of state. To the Court's critics, however, radical reforms like packing seemed better than depending on one undependable justice. The difficulty, said Rhode Island's Senator Theodore Green, was that once "again we learn that the Constitution is what Mr. Justice Roberts says it is."[76]

Law professor F. D. G. Ribble thought that the *Parrish* decision epitomized Hughes as a "diplomatic chief." However, law professor Richard A. Epstein thought the decision epitomized the way "progressives rewrote the Constitution" and redefined liberty. He disputed the progressive faith that expertise and impartial government would offset economic inequity and democratize the workplace. Epstein saw an opposite trend. Beginning with *Muller,* Progressives opened the door to limitless governmental regulations and enabled unions to monopolize market forces. Consequently, the nation's commitment to classical liberalism, competition, and economic freedom suffered. To Epstein, the healthy free market had been replaced by inflexible regulations and government sanctioned "cartels" on both sides of the labor-management divide.[77]

In April, merely two weeks after *Parrish,* the Court handed down another big surprise. Mrs. Hughes's presence in the courtroom heightened anticipation. Few people expected the justices to uphold the 1935 National Labor Relations Act, also called the Wagner Act after its author, New York Senator Robert F. Wagner. It granted workers the right to organize and bargain collectively with their own representatives. A National Labor Relations Board (NLRB) would monitor unfair labor practices and resolve labor disputes. The question was whether congressional power over interstate commerce violated employers' substantive due process rights by interfering with labor disputes. Of the five cases discussed on April 12th, a bus company and the Associated Press were unanimously considered interstate (*Washington, Virginia, & Maryland Coach Co. v. NLRB* and *Associated Press v. NLRB*). Three companies manufacturing commercial trailers, clothing, and steel were also judged interstate but by five to four votes (*NLRB v. Fruehauf Trailer Co.* and *NLRB v. Friedman-Harry Marks Clothing* and *NLRB v. Jones & Laughlin Steel Corp.*).[78]

These rulings had broad implications for the interstate commerce clause, substantive due process, dual federalism, labor law, and, therefore, the New Deal. Hughes supported the NLRB's jurisdiction over labor strife and workers' efforts to join unions in companies that shipped their products out of state and were, therefore, part of "the stream of commerce." The clothing and trailer businesses fit because their raw materials came from out of state and their finished products were sold out of state. Both companies repressed labor organizing. "It is the effect on commerce," Hughes asserted, "not the source of the injury" that matters. Reprising the old Minnesota rate and Shreveport cases, Hughes said the key was whether intra- and interstate commerce were so "interwoven" that intrastate commerce created a "direct burden" on interstate commerce. That rationale was a stretch when applied to these small businesses, especially after failing to apply it to the much larger, clearly interstate, Carter Coal company. Consequently, law professor Edward Corwin called Hughes's rulings in *Schechter, Carter Coal,* and these cases fundamentally inconsistent. He concluded that the latter cases represented a major reversal, a doctrinal revolution, that was stimulated by earlier dissents from Stone and Cardozo. Like Mason, Corwin gave them the credit for the Court's shift, not Hughes.[79]

The Jones & Laughlin Steel Company presented a stronger interstate commerce argument because it possessed out-of-state coal, ore, and limestone extraction facilities, plus warehouses, shipping facilities, and nineteen subsidiaries. Exuding confidence with his booming voice, Hughes delivered another landmark opinion. Unlike Schechter's poultry market, he said, a company organized "on a national scale" was inherently part of interstate commerce. A labor crisis in one location could easily spread to others and stop the flow of interstate commerce. The result "might be catastrophic," perhaps even leading to "the paralyzing consequences of industrial war." It was not just a matter of the goods produced or where they were produced. "Burdens and obstructions," Hughes pointed out, "may be due to injurious actions springing from other sources," like strikes.[80]

Again summoning sociological jurisprudence, Hughes declared that we should not "shut our eyes to the plainest facts of national life" and "actual experience" lest we function "in an intellectual vacuum." Because, as he said in 1916, "interstate commerce itself is a practical conception," the "fundamental right" of labor to organize is "often an essential condition of industrial peace." Thus, the conflict between liberty of contract and freedom of association was finally resolved in favor of the latter. Liberty was not just for employers but also for workers; not just for private-property owners but also for the general public.[81]

Hughes later linked this decision to his 1911 *McGuire* opinion that contracts do not grant "immunity from reasonable regulations and prohibitions imposed in the interests of the community." Holmes's reasonableness standard and call for judicial restraint prevailed. Although Hughes again avoided reversing *Carter Coal*, he reinforced his expansive, pragmatic approach to the general welfare and interstate commerce clauses in the interest of a seamless economy. Unlike Mason and Corwin, Friedman concluded that Hughes's position in *Jones & Laughlin* was consistent with the overall thread of his commerce opinions and that *Carter Coal* was an anomaly, one that Hughes regretted.[82]

While validating the NLRB's role in resolving labor conflicts, the Court not only undermined substantive due process claims but weakened traditional "layer cake" dual federalism. The distance between federal and state authority shrank when the national government was allowed to interfere with intrastate business in the context of interstate commerce broadly defined. As historian Michael E. Parrish observed, this was the first time that the Court applied its evolving interstate commerce concepts to industries beyond railroads. Emphasizing the overlapping, intertwined nature of commerce, it endorsed the "marble cake" version of federalism. Ironically, although Hughes began this transition as associate justice, now he cautioned that it might "obliterate the distinction between what is national and what is local." Even as he championed a seamless economy, part of him remained a governor on the bench.[83]

Speaking for the conservatives, McReynolds emphasized this danger. He called the steel company's impact on interstate commerce indirect and beyond federal control. Fearing an ever-expanding federal government, he asked, "Are our states obliterated?" Furthermore, said McReynolds, the decision allowed unions to take away a business owner's "power to manage his own property," which included labor. For him, substantive due process claims still outranked social concerns. So too, the reserved powers of states outranked federal powers to deal with national economic problems. McReynolds bemoaned the "momentous" significance of a decision that posed such great "possibilities for harm" to the republic. His law clerk predicted "the end of an era in the law, and the death of an entire way of thinking."[84]

Others were ecstatic. *The Nation* called it "nothing short of a miracle." When one lawyer declared, "Chief Justice Hughes has saved the Supreme Court," another replied, "I think he has saved the United States as well." Jackson credited Hughes with restoring "John Marshall's concept of nationalism." Many people thought Hughes had mortally wounded court packing. While portraying the NLRB ruling as "purely" political, FDR privately called Hughes his "most dangerous, implacable enemy." FDR would soon claim to be the real victor, but in the moment, he declared that the Court's legislative "no man's land" had been replaced by "Robert's Land." *The New Republic* asked, "Who knows when Mr. Justice Roberts will do another flop?" Court packing was still necessary.[85]

The Resolution

Actually, the plan was rapidly becoming less necessary. In the wake of the April 12th NLRB decisions, Wheeler declared, "The Court bill is dead." Such rumors, Mark Twain would have said, were greatly exaggerated. However, the bill was doomed to die by July 22nd and literally kill a key senator in the process. Everything depended on Arkansas's Joe Robinson, Senate majority leader. Along with many other senators, he was lukewarm about court packing but supported it because FDR promised him the first Supreme Court seat if the bill passed. Accordingly, Robinson began working on a legislative compromise the day after the NLRB decisions.[86]

The problem was that neither its main proponent, the president, nor its main opponent, Wheeler, was open to compromise. Both expected to win. FDR's optimism was grounded in his electoral victory six months earlier and confirmed when a vacant Congressional seat was filled by Lyndon Baines Johnson, a Texan who ran as a "Roosevelt man." FDR remained certain that "the people are with me." However, the all-important Senate was not and Gallup polls registered steadily declining popular support. Despite FDR's disapproval, Robinson drafted a compromise bill raising the retirement age to seventy-five and limiting new appointments to one per year. It convinced several wavering senators.[87]

Meanwhile, Wheeler and Borah pursued another angle. In March, Congress finally passed a new pension plan for Supreme Court justices enabling them to retire at full pay. It had languished for two years but was finally pushed through in protest against court packing. Both Van Devanter, age seventy-eight, and Sutherland, age seventy-five, wanted to retire, but not under the old half-pay pension plan. Now Wheeler and Borah, Van Devanter's friend, suggested that he wait to announce retirement until the Senate Judiciary Committee voted on court packing. Ironically, observed Ross, the whole fight could have been avoided if the pension bill had been passed earlier so that justices could retire and be replaced through the normal presidential nominating process.[88]

May 18th was significant. The Judiciary Committee registered its initial vote against court packing, with half of the Democrats in opposition. Van Devanter promptly announced his retirement and Sutherland followed six months later. These developments were good and bad news. Although the committee vote was sobering, FDR was delighted at finally being able to make a Court appointment. The downside was that he wanted to appoint a liberal and Robinson was a conservative Democrat. As FDR delayed making the appointment, Robinson became distraught. In response, FDR soothed him with a two-hour long, reassuring (but typically noncommittal) one-on-one conference. Robinson renewed his resolve and redoubled his efforts to please the president even as calls for scrapping court reform got louder every day.[89]

The Court was busy too. On May 24, 1937, it delivered four important decisions. Key sections of the Social Security Act were upheld in two cases, one 5–4, the other 7–2. Roberts supported both cases while Sutherland and Van Devanter voted "no" on the first case but "yes" on the second case, again defying their conservative images. Cardozo wrote both opinions. The first case legitimized a payroll tax on employers who received a federal tax credit in return for contributing to their state's unemployment fund (*Steward Machine Co. v. Davis*). Unlike *Carter Coal*, this tax was not considered coercive or harmful to state sovereignty. In fact, it would help states pay for unemployment benefits and ensure, wrote Cardozo, that the country's "people were not to starve." Broadly interpreted, the federal taxing power could be used for the general welfare. The conservatives dissented, but Sutherland and Van Devanter concurred with most of the opinion. Butler and McReynolds condemned it as a gross violation of state sovereignty and an unwarranted, potentially unlimited form of "public philanthropy."[90]

The second case upheld the provision for old age benefits over a similar dissent by Butler and McReynolds (*Helvering v. Davis*). Again Cardozo justified the need for a broad interpretation of the federal spending power for the general welfare. Noting that about 75 percent of people over seventy-five could not support themselves, Cardozo explained that "the hope behind this statute is to save men and women from the rigors of the poor house as well as from the haunting fear that such a lot awaits them when journey's end is near." In both cases, national problems justified national solutions.[91]

A third opinion, delivered by Stone on the same day, upheld an Alabama unemployment compensation law 5–4 (*Carmichael v. Southern Coal & Coke Co.*). McReynolds objected to the whole concept, but Butler, Sutherland and Van Devanter couched their opposition on narrow technical grounds, not overall intent. A fourth 5–4 case, written by Brandeis, upheld a Wisconsin law forbidding the use of injunctions against peaceful union picketing (*Senn v. Tile Layers Protective Union*). These two cases confirmed that the Court had finally been converted to the principle of judicial restraint and deference to state legislatures, as first articulated by Holmes in 1905.

Distinctly Progressive, all four cases contradicted claims of a rigidly conservative, counter-majoritarian Court and further undermined court packing. The Court, concluded historian Jeff Shesol, "was building a new constitutional order." Much of the credit went to Hughes's leadership. However, Frankfurter, not yet on the Court, was skeptical about the Court's new liberalism. Castigating Hughes, he complained to Stone that "a synthetic halo is being fitted upon the head of one of the most politically calculating of men." And journalist Irving Brant feared that with an evenly divided Court, "more than ever before, . . . the Constitution in the immediate future will be what Mr. Chief Justice Hughes says it is."[92]

Other factors now came into play. On June 13th, Vice President Garner suddenly left Washington for a fishing vacation. During thirty years of service, he had never taken a break while Congress was in session. It was an unsubtle abandonment of the president and court packing, which Garner opposed from the start. A day later, the Senate Judiciary Committee, to which Borah belonged, issued a devastating report on court packing. Declaring that the Constitution "is in our hands to preserve or destroy," they condemned the bill as a dangerous attempt to control the Court. Deceptively clothed in the language of reform, it was really a plot to emasculate "an independent Court, a fearless Court." It would "make this Government one of men rather than one of law and . . . make the Constitution what the executive or legislative branches of the Government choose to say it is." Accordingly, the committee declared, the proposal "should be so emphatically rejected that its parallel will never again be presented to the free representatives of the free people of America."[93]

Seven Democrats signed the report and the rest did not submit a minority report. FDR feigned disinterest, but, said a key advisor, it was "the worst public humiliation he had ever had." As usual, he rebounded quickly and allowed Robinson to pursue the compromise bill, cleverly demonstrating some flexibility even as he refused to back down. Meanwhile, he tried another strategy. In what Kalman called "a master stroke" of political maneuvering, on June 15th, FDR welcomed Democratic congressmen (no women) to a lavish picnic on an island in Chesapeake Bay where he hoped to win support through fun, food, and fraternity.[94]

At about the same time, Hughes delivered two speeches for his grandsons' graduation ceremonies at Brown and Amherst. Carefully avoiding court packing, he made his position clear enough. On the subject of age, he declared, "We come to you with youthful spirits, with spiritual arteries not yet hardened." He extolled liberty and "reasonable methods" as the bulwarks of "democratic principle" and crucial antidotes to "a regime of force." For Hughes, there was "no conflict" between "liberty and progress" in a society where free individuals were "not mere puppets of the State." Regarding executive power, he cautioned that "the question is no longer one of establishing democratic institutions but of preserving them. The question is not one of the adequate power of government . . . but how that power shall be used." His harshest words were for "the arch-enemies of society . . . who know better but by indirection, misstatement, understatement and slander, seek to accomplish their concealed purposes." By implication, court packing was anathema to a government based on freedom, "balanced judgement," and the separation of powers. The speeches were essential Hughes.[95]

The closing scenes of the court packing drama came in July. Just before the floor debate began on July 6th, FDR called Wheeler to the White House in a final, unsuccessful attempt to win over his major Democratic Senate opponent. Robinson opened the debate in his typically emphatic way, "pounding his desk with his fist, slashing the air with his arm, and bellowing at his opponents." He explained the compromise bill, attacked the Court, and battled with his opponents, especially Wheeler. After he invoked Senate rules to prevent a filibuster and limit amendments, the vicious debate and personal attacks intensified. Order broke down. Republicans stood back while Democrats fought against each other. Hughes was criticized as "a supremely clever politician." Roberts was condemned as a weakling who would inevitably "backslide." Through it all, FDR insisted that "the people are with me," but his leadership skills were faltering. One critic's poem concluded with: "I ruined their country, their homes, and then / I placed the blame on the NINE OLD MEN."[96]

On July 9th, Wheeler gave a vitriolic three-hour speech demolishing every argument in favor of the bill. He railed against dictators like Hitler and Mussolini who totally controlled their own courts. Other senators predicted all sorts of disasters if the bill passed. The emotional onslaught affected Robinson. He looked sick and ate little. On Monday, July 12th, he suffered sharp chest pains, seemed faint, was revived with soda water, and went home. He felt ill the next day but attended a movie with a friend who was concerned enough to stay the night because Robinson's wife was away. The senator returned to the office in the morning to have a charcoal portrait drawn and meet with thirty colleagues about the bill. However, he left early. The next morning, July 14th, the maid found Robinson dead on the bedroom floor with his glasses and the *Congressional Record* by his side.[97]

Mourning barely replaced debate. Beyond praising Robinson, the eulogies bore the bill's vitriol. Republicans blamed FDR for forcing Robinson to sacrifice his life for a bill that no one really supported, including Robinson. Democrats criticized Republicans for prolonging the acrimonious debate, thus causing Robinson's demise. FDR issued a condolence statement and attended the brief, formal funeral held in the Senate. However, he refused to withdraw the bill and did not accompany the funeral train to Arkansas. Packed with politicians, it became a hotbed of debate. Hostility rode the rails. Garner joined them in Little Rock and quickly sensed the acrimony. Upon returning to DC, he told the president, "You are beat. Capt'n. You haven't got the votes." Adding insult to injury, Herbert H. Lehman, current New York governor and FDR's former lieutenant governor, issued a public disavowal of court packing. It was another embarrassing defection.[98]

The final curtain call was a roll call vote on July 22nd. Republicans demanded it in order to force Democrats to vote their conscience against the compromise bill or their loyalty to the president. The bill went down 70–22, with fifty-three Democrats voting "no." It was then sent back to the Judiciary Committee where it was relegated to legislative purgatory. In partial compensation, the original bill's lower court reforms were adopted and reluctantly signed into law by the president.

Despite strategically refraining from criticizing the report, FDR's bitterness surfaced on Constitution Day that fall. Without mentioning the

Court, he decried having to wait "while the law catches up to life." As it turned out, he did not have to wait long. Three weeks after his original bill died, FDR began turning defeat into victory. At last, he could appoint his first Supreme Court justice followed by six more over the next four years due to the passing of Cardozo and Butler plus the retirements of Sutherland, McReynolds, Brandeis, and Hughes. Because the new Court did not invalidate any New Deal acts, FDR really seemed to have lost the battle but won the war. In essence, he had packed the Court.[99]

That was the prevailing opinion for decades. FDR contributed to his own vindication by asserting that he just wanted to make the Court more liberal, not dominate it. Many observers and historians gave him credit for using court packing to scare the justices into supporting the New Deal. Kalman pointed out that there was significant congressional support for adding two more justices during much of the debate and that a compromise bill could have prevailed if FDR had been amenable. Nonetheless, his "constitutional hardball" tactics successfully pushed the Court toward legal liberalism. Accordingly, the *Parrish*, *NLRB*, and Social Security decisions marked a judicial revolution, an actual "switch in time that saved nine." It achieved the long-awaited predominance of legal realism over legal formalism, of a responsive over a resistive attitude to progressive legislation.[100]

Historian Samuel Hendel suggested that Hughes was pushed by events to "reluctantly" participate in this revolution despite his basic conservatism: "He stood thus as a kind of heroic and, in a sense, tragic figure, torn between the old and the new, seeking at first to stem the tide, but relentlessly caught up and moving with it." Or was he, as Leuchtenberg contended, a careful, clever "tactician" who held "the center" to protect the Court and gradually forge coalitions out of conflict? Rather than demonstrating a tragically compromised conservatism, Hughes's actions underlined his long-standing commitment to a progressivism that dovetailed with sociological jurisprudence and legalism. These factors, plus his political background, predisposed him to practical reforms and structural changes that respected the past but responded to reality and moved the nation forward.[101]

Historian James Henretta offered a third perspective. While intending to promote liberal democracy "by enhancing the powers of government and administrative bureaucracy," Hughes really undercut liberal democracy by promoting a "bureaucracy-rich national administrative regime" responsible for the stifling "statism" of modern political life.

In fact, Hughes had often warned that bureaucracy could create its own problems. But he believed that if used selectively and with proper oversight, it could replace the culture of corruption with a progressive culture of nonpartisan expertise, efficiency, fairness, and rational deliberation. Accordingly, noted Holland, Hughes was well "ahead of his time" in insisting on more openness and accountability for bureaucratic administrative agencies.[102]

Analysis is complicated by labels. The justices often divided along conservative-liberal lines but they could also act in unison. Despite strongly supporting the New Deal, the liberals joined the conservatives to invalidate several acts. Moreover, there sometimes were splits within the conservative-liberal divides. Just as Sutherland and Van Devanter were more flexible than Butler and McReynolds, so Brandeis, Cardozo, and Stone did not always agree. Roberts and Hughes often pursued their own paths, but the chief voted with the three liberals in eight of the twelve key New Deal cases. In addition, noted Ross, "Hughes never provided a critical fifth vote for a major decision invalidating regulatory legislation."[103]

The key variable was Roberts and the central question was why he shifted so abruptly after *Tipaldo*. For those who emphasized the importance of external influences on judges, the answer was the 1936 election, political disapproval of *Tipaldo*, congressional calls for reform, and labor unrest, compounded by the threat of court packing. To be sure, Hughes may have influenced Roberts and was always attuned to the public pulse himself. However, Roberts was hardly an empty intellectual vessel and his contradictory opinions may have reflected genuine struggle with the serious constitutional issues at stake as well as political sensitivity.[104]

Scholars now suggest that the judicial revolution was really a judicial evolution over decades of responding to major socioeconomic changes resulting from the Industrial Revolution and magnified by the Great Depression. Maybe the Court really began to change in 1930 to 1932 when Hoover appointed Hughes, Roberts, and Cardozo, thereby ending the stranglehold of judicial conservatism on the Court. Maybe Hughes's apparent vacillation between liberal, moderate, and conservative rulings reflected not only his lack of doctrinal rigidity but also the transitional nature of jurisprudence in the first half of the twentieth century. After all, the reconsideration of traditional approaches to regulatory legislation, administrative agencies, the commerce clause, substantive due process, and liberty of contract were already under way by the early twentieth century and continued into the 1940s.[105]

Thus, Cushman rejected the idea that "laissez-faire constitutionalism was summarily jettisoned for political reasons in the course of a couple of months in the spring of 1937." Rather, it was a "more complex story" of how conventional legal constructs "gradually unraveled over the first forty years of the twentieth century." Reassessing one doctrine led to reassessing others resulting in "structural ripple effects" across the legal landscape. The shift may have been partly, but not entirely, about immediate political pressures. Kalman agreed with the internalists "that, doctrinally speaking, the constitutional revolution preceded 1937 and lasted beyond it." However, she also agreed with the externalists that political factors, including FDR's shrewdness, skill, and persistence, were critical to the ultimate realignment of the Court.[106]

Neither as liberal as the Three Musketeers nor as conservative as the Four Horsemen, Hughes epitomized this evolution. His strained distinctions, inconsistencies, and reluctance to overturn precedent reflected his constant search for a practical balance between continuity and change. This quest was further complicated by his administrative desire for as much unity as possible. While cherishing precedent and dual federalism, he weakened both by joining Holmes and Brandeis in modernizing convention to incorporate changing realities. As he said in *Tipaldo* (and basically reiterated in *NLRB*), "We are not at liberty to ignore these facts." He later pointed to his 1911 *McGuire* and 1912 Minnesota rates opinions to suggest that his post-packing opinions did not represent a sudden shift. More evidence can be found in his 1916 ABA speech and 1927 Supreme Court lectures, plus numerous written opinions and dissents, including *Nebbia* and *Blaisdell*, both in 1934, which preceded court packing.[107]

Nonetheless, the 1936 election and the court packing plan may have pushed Hughes faster than he would have moved otherwise. Indeed, Ross remarked that only a profound threat would have motivated Hughes to write his letter and "break the magisterial silence" of the Court regarding politics. Yet, observed Friedman, Hughes never assumed an aggressive political role (as Taft might have done) in lobbying Congress to pass the retirement bill or urging Van Devanter to retire, both easy solutions to the court packing crisis. Rather, his "influence against the bill was at once less conscious, more subtle, and more powerful." By maintaining his "dignity," avoiding "rancor," and treating the

New Deal with "scrupulous fairness" despite all the attacks against him and his Court, concluded Friedman, he "seemed to grow in stature." Looking back, Hughes considered the court packing plan ultimately beneficial because it highlighted public support for "the independence of the Court" and demonstrated "the actual independence of the Justices." Here he spoke as chief, but he practiced as a judge whose primary commitment was, like Grotius, to justice itself.[108]

However, "justice" was a complicated, ever-moving target, an abstract concept with concrete ramifications. Still evoking Progressivism, Hughes pointed out that being just required "patience and fairness, . . . weighing of evidence in scales with which prejudice has not tampered, of reasoned conclusions satisfying a sensitive conscience." It also required "firmness in resisting both solicitation and clamor." Hughes spent his life negotiating that complexity in domestic politics and foreign policy as well as during both terms on the Court. At different times and in different circumstances, he could seem liberal, moderate, or conservative; antiquated or modern; reluctant or bold; theoretical or practical. The court packing crisis revealed all of these characteristics and proved that labels never adequately captured the whole Hughes.[109]

You could say that Hughes won the war with FDR in his own cautious, incremental way. Bolstered by shrewd strategy and diplomatic skill, he maneuvered the Court away from antiquated constitutionalism toward a more Progressive, more functional approach, albeit with crucial help from the three liberals. As chief justice during one of the Court's most perilous periods, Hughes not only protected but enhanced its independent status and confirmed that the Constitution is what the justices say it is.

FDR lost the immediate struggle over court packing at some cost to his personal reputation and political support. However, he won by getting the policy endorsements he sought when the Court adopted judicial restraint and abandoned the nondelegation doctrine. Leuchtenburg concluded that the Court fight represented a "huge success" by legitimizing "a vast expansion of the power of government in American life." To Homer Cummings, short-term "mistakes of tactics" paled by comparison to the long-term "reform" that "managed to reverse the constitutional trends of twenty-five years." That meant, wrote Corwin, replacing "the laissez-faire, noninterventionist conception of governmental function" by a more "feasible approach to the problem of adapting the Constitution to the needs of the Twentieth Century." Indeed, despite all their disagreements and political jockeying, the president and the chief justice agreed on the most fundamental proposition of all: that America needed a living Constitution. Thus, the nation was the ultimate victor.[110]

11 | Reorienting the Court, 1937–1941

The New Court

The last three years of Charles Evans Hughes's tenure as chief justice were significantly less conflict ridden than the previous eight because President Franklin D. Roosevelt (FDR) appointed five new justices, all solid New Dealers. Although the new court was often called the Roosevelt Court, it remained the Hughes Court until his retirement in 1941. He was in more control than ever. FDR's new appointees changed the Court and guaranteed that no New Deal legislation would be invalidated henceforth, an outcome that Hughes largely supported.

At the same time, by expanding civil liberties, the Court went well beyond FDR's own agenda to realize many of Hughes's fondest dreams. Because it did so in ways that evolved from the pre-1938 Court, there was continuity as well as change over time. Hughes himself saw a strong connection between his positions as associate justice and as chief justice regarding civil liberties. Decisions in this area previewed the civil rights judicial revival of the 1950s and 1960s. In that sense, the Hughes Court engineered two constitutional revolutions—one on economic issues and power relations plus a second on civil liberties. Accordingly, historian Michael E. Parrish viewed "the Hughes era as the true birthplace of modern, twentieth-century judicial constitutionalism."[1]

The likelihood that the Court would advocate judicial restraint increased with each new confirmation. All five justices appointed before Hughes retired were strongly committed to legislative and executive activism. Willis Van Devanter's 1937 replacement was Alabama's Hugo L. Black. A self-educated man from modest origins, he became a lawyer, county prosecutor, and Progressive senator, except on anti-lynching bills. His prosecutorial style and avid defense of labor legislation made him controversial. Frankfurter even warned FDR that Black was not equipped to "beat the C. J. [chief justice] in some of his shenanigans." Senator Black voted against Hughes's nomination as chief and for court packing, but they developed a positive relationship based on mutual respect. Although Black's prior, if brief, membership in the Ku Klux Klan marred his appointment, he became a proponent of civil liberties on the Court and Hughes let him write opinions to demonstrate that fact.[2]

Also in 1937, George Sutherland's seat went to Stanley F. Reed. A doctor's son who earned bachelor's degrees from both Kentucky Wesleyan and Yale, he passed the Kentucky Bar exam despite lacking a law degree. Reed served Herbert Hoover and FDR as general counsel to two federal agencies and became FDR's solicitor general in 1935. In that role, he defended court packing before the Senate Judiciary Committee. On the Court, Reed advocated judicial restraint while supporting labor rights and civil liberties.[3]

It was fitting that in 1938, Benjamin Cardozo was replaced by Felix Frankfurter, thereby maintaining the "scholar's seat" originally held by Holmes. Like Cardozo, Frankfurter was Jewish and scholarly but more aggressive than his soft-spoken predecessor. The son of immigrants from the Lower East Side, Frankfurter graduated from the City College of New York and Harvard Law School, where he became a professor. Mentored by Holmes (as was Cardozo), Frankfurter corresponded with FDR, Louis Brandeis, and Harlan Stone before joining the Court. He championed liberal causes, defended radicals after World War I, helped create the American Civil Liberties Union, and was an avid Zionist. As a liberal and a Jew, he was subjected to hostile testimony and ruthless scrutiny in the nation's first public hearing for a Supreme Court nominee but was confirmed unanimously. Stone expected him to be a counterweight to Hughes and was disappointed when Frankfurter, who criticized Hughes before joining the Court, subsequently befriended and praised him.[4]

It was yet more appropriate that Brandeis was succeeded by William O. Douglas in 1939. A legal realist and passionate civil libertarian, Douglas developed a social conscience from growing up poor after his father died when he was five. Working his way through Whitman College and Columbia Law School, he taught at both Columbia and Yale Law Schools before FDR appointed him to the Security Exchange Commission (SEC), which he soon chaired. A loyal New Dealer, Douglas backed governmental activism and championed civil liberties. At age forty, he was one of the youngest people to join the Court and, upon resigning thirty-six years later, had served the longest. He. might have become president if the 1944 Democratic convention had honored FDR's wish that Douglas be his vice-presidential candidate.[5]

Ironically, Pierce Butler, the arch-conservative, was replaced in 1940 by Francis W. Murphy, who, wrote law professor William G. Ross, may have been "the most liberal—even radical—justice ever to sit on the Supreme Court." He resembled Butler in having Midwestern, Irish Catholic roots. The difference was Murphy's profound commitment to improving the lives of ordinary people. That objective defined his terms as Detroit's mayor, Michigan's governor, and governor-general of the Philippines. As FDR's attorney general, Murphy strengthened the Justice Department's protection of labor organizers and African Americans while also creating a Civil Rights Division.[6]

The new justices solidified the Court's shifts regarding judicial restraint, taxing policy, and administrative agencies. Concerning labor, they condoned various National Labor Relations Board (NLRB) policies, upheld the Fair Labor Standards Act, and the Norris–LaGuardia Anti-injunction Act. Union picketing and secondary boycotts were supported unless violent. Ruling that membership in a union could not disqualify workers from being hired further undermined yellow dog contracts. Hughes usually voted with the majority except when too much deference to legislators seemed to undermine judicial review and dual federalism. Although Owen Roberts often joined Hughes's dissents, he and Sutherland wrote several opinions for the majority. Butler and James McReynolds dissented frequently. Perhaps feeling more comfortable with the new majority, Hughes wrote fewer opinions himself; perhaps he also was winding down.[7]

The opinions that Hughes did write referenced or clarified previous positions. In 1938, he drew upon his *Jones & Laughlin* ruling to apply NLRB labor standards to a fruit company that employed over one thousand people and shipped 37 percent of its goods out of state (*Santa Cruz Fruit Packing Co. v. NLRB*). Typically, he avoided overruling *Carter Coal* even as he emphasized *Jones & Laughlin*, thereby inviting criticism from Butler and McReynolds in dissent. Also in 1938, Hughes defended the authority of the SEC to compel public utility holding companies to meet registration and disclosure requirements, a throwback to his New York State Public Service Commissions (*Electric Bond and Share Co. v. SEC*).[8]

In 1939, he used the 1913 Shreveport principle to justify federal regulation when "intrastate and interstate transactions are commingled in the tobacco market" and when "new conditions" required flexibility (*Currin v. Wallace*). In 1941, he held that even though Consolidated Edison produced and sold all its electricity in New York State, labor conflicts in New York could cut off electricity to other states disrupting vast transportation and communications networks. Consequently, as he held in *Jones & Laughlin*, the NLRB had jurisdiction over the company's labor relations (*Consolidated Edison v. NLRB*). In all these cases, Hughes remained sensitive to the interwoven nature of the modern economy and the resulting need to expand executive and legislative functions.[9]

However, Hughes never endorsed limitless federal powers because he never completely relinquished his commitment to dual federalism. For example, his 1938 opinion supporting the revised Municipal Bankruptcy Act (*U.S. v. Bekins*) evoked his dissent from the 1936 case about the original act (*Ashton v. Cameron County Water Improvement*). The new act improved on the original by requiring that municipalities seek state approval before declaring bankruptcy. Thus, it better protected state sovereignty, a priority for the former governor. The act recognized that shrinking municipal tax revenues during the Depression forced some cities into bankruptcy. Thus, congressional support for state sponsored municipal bankruptcy did not undermine the state but helped it "retain control of its fiscal affairs." By reinforcing the principle of coordination among federal, state, and local governments, it condoned cooperative (marble cake) federalism.[10]

As Hughes explained in *Santa Cruz* in 1938, he was committed to "maintaining the balance of constitutional grants and limitations [through] the gradual process of inclusion and exclusion." But, because that balance changed over time, noted government professor Samuel Hendel, Hughes was always "safeguarding the old . . . while accepting the new." In the process, said law professor Richard D. Friedman, Hughes "continued to roll back the old constitutionalism without acknowledging he was doing so." Hughes's national stature, wrote future justice Robert Jackson, conveyed "a sense of steadiness in spite of rapid movement" and reassured the nation that he sought "the amendment of doctrine rather than . . . destruction of institutions. The Chief Justice was himself a symbol of stability as well as of progress." Visual artist Al Hirschfeld caricatured a thoughtful chief justice engrossed in his role (see figure 11.1).[11]

First Amendment Rights

Hughes's role in the court packing crisis may always be controversial, but his contribution to civil liberties has never been questioned. In fact,

Figure 11.1. *Charles Evans Hughes, 1937*, by Al Hirschfeld. ©The Al Hirschfeld Foundation. https://www.AlHirschfeldFoundation.org.

it may have been the most revolutionary legacy of the Hughes Court. The whole subject was a legal and political quagmire best symbolized by the 1857 *Dred Scott v. Sandford* case, which Hughes considered the Court's worst "self-inflicted wound," a term he coined. It created "a public calamity" that "undermined confidence in the Court" for decades. Fortunately, the Court recuperated and, Hughes claimed, achieved "a rank second to none among the judicial tribunals of the world." He intended to keep it that way.[12]

Hughes understood that protecting civil liberties was delicate but firmly believed that, as he said in his 1927 lectures, "it is the duty of the courts to be watchful for the constitutional rights of the citizen, and against any stealthy encroachments thereon." Hughes referenced Chief Justice Taft's 1921 statement in *Traux v. Corrigan* that the "specific guaranty" of the Fourteenth Amendment "was aimed at undue favor and individual or class privilege, on the one hand, and at hostile discrimination or the oppression of inequality on the other." Furthermore, "it sought an equality of treatment of all persons, even though all enjoyed the protection of due process." During Hughes's term as chief justice, the Court applied this principle by using the Fourteenth Amendment to extend the entire First Amendment as well as parts of the Fourth and Fifth Amendments to the states. Already by 1934, a journalist observed that Hughes demonstrated "a greater fondness for the Bill of Rights than any Chief Justice this country has ever had."[13]

At issue was the dual federalism that Hughes cherished. The Bill of Rights only protected civil liberties from violation by the federal government. However, the 1866 Fourteenth Amendment stated, "Nor shall any State deprive any person of life, liberty, or property without due process of law, nor deny to any person within its jurisdiction equal protection of the laws." Hughes agreed with Taft that, although due process was mentioned in the Fifth Amendment, the Fourteenth Amendment expanded it. Rather than just providing negative, minimal procedural protection, said Hughes in 1927, the post-Reconstruction Constitution served to "guaranty" a broad "equality of treatment of all persons" free from "hostile discrimination or the oppression of inequality." Yet, due process was most often used to protect property holders from governmental regulations and labor demands. After World War I, the meaning of due process began shifting from protecting property to protecting life and liberty, from private to public priorities. Rigidly bifurcated dual federalism was evolving into a more integrated, cooperative, holistic federalism.[14]

To Hughes, the advantage of originally lacking a clear definition of due process was that vagueness left room for growth. In his words, "Its meaning was unsettled, but it was not meaningless, nor was it limited by anything short of the general purpose to afford immunity from any violation of fundamental rights." If the Constitution was to remain useful and relevant, it should never be frozen in time. In fact, he said, the Article Five amendment provision was expressly designed to encourage the healthy "development of American law" by applying constitutional precepts to "new obligations." The Fourteenth Amendment was "the affirmation of individual rights deemed to be fundamental" to America's "conceptions of justice" and "freedom from the exercise of purely arbitrary power." It embodied "the essentials of liberty."[15]

This subject was so important to Hughes that he not only discussed it in his 1916 ABA speech and his 1927 lectures but also in the only legal memorandum included in his *Autobiographical Notes.* At all times, he insisted that the Constitution be "flexible." Quoting a nineteenth-century justice, he affirmed that "the Constitution of the United States . . . was made for an undefined and expanding future, and for a people gathered and to be gathered from many nations and of many tongues." Therefore, "we should expect that the new and various experiences of our own situation and system will mold and shape it into new and not less useful forms." Hughes wanted to replace "archaic" concepts of the Constitution with a commitment to its "elasticity." Characteristically, he pursued change within the context of continuity and resisted overturning precedent. Yet, he moved faster and further on civil liberties than on other issues. If he helped the Court embrace judicial restraint regarding economic legislation, he led the Court in adopting judicial activism regarding civil liberties.[16]

Three cases in 1931, his first year as chief, highlighted his commitments to freedom of speech, press, and thought. The first case involved a nineteen-year-old camp supervisor who was an American citizen of Russian parentage (*Stromberg v. California*). She had her young charges salute a red flag depicting Soviet symbols and the insignia of the Young Communist League, to which she belonged. California convicted her of violating its criminal syndicalism law against displaying the red flag because it suggested opposition to organized government and could be "a stimulus to anarchic action" or sedition. Despite his opposition to Russia as secretary of state, Hughes protected the right of free speech for Communists as a domestic, democratic matter.[17]

In a landmark seven-to-two opinion, Hughes contended that California's law was so vague that it prohibited the use of any banner criticizing government. It violated freedom of speech that "did not incite to violence and threaten the overthrow of organized government by unlawful means." Such banners, he said, were forms of symbolic speech, a category he now added to the rubric of free speech. To Hughes, "the opportunity for free political discussion is essential to the security of the Republic [and] a fundamental principle of our constitutional system." Its repression was "repugnant to the guarantee of liberty contained in the Fourteenth Amendment." In other words, noted law professor Mark Tushnet, the Court was beginning to emphasize the government's positive role in protecting the use, not just preventing the abuse, of First Amendment rights.[18]

Hughes confirmed the principle of applying or incorporating the First to the Fourteenth Amendment as posited by the Taft Court in *Gitlow v. New York* (1925). However, he rejected the *Gitlow* principle that speech was punishable if it had a "bad tendency." Instead, he endorsed Holmes's dissents in *Gitlow* and *Schenk v. U.S.* (1919) saying that speech should not be prohibited unless it presented "a clear and present danger." For Hughes, that meant as long as it did not directly incite violence, crime, or overthrow of the government. Van Devanter joined the majority. McReynolds and Butler dissented on technical grounds without questioning that the Constitution protected peaceful protest. There was basic agreement across supposedly polarized perspectives.[19]

Freedom of the press was next. In *Near v. Minnesota*, the state banned a small newspaper as "a public nuisance" for making "malicious, scandalous and defamatory" accusations that Jewish Minneapolis politicians colluded with organized crime. Another landmark opinion by Hughes protected freedom of the press from prior restraint and censorship. "The object of the statute," he declared, "is not punishment . . . but suppression." For the first time, the Court explicitly included the First Amendment's press freedom as part of the Fourteenth Amendment's protection of liberty in the states. Nevertheless, press freedom could still be limited by concerns about national security, obscenity, and inciting violence. Representing the conservatives, Butler contended that the state law was justified by the vicious nature of the press attack and the inadequacy of libel laws.[20]

Hughes noted that the importance of freedom of the press went back to English legal scholars and Parliamentary rulings as well as to America's colonial struggle against the crown. Reaffirming his belief in the importance of the press as governor and secretary of state, he pointed out that "a vigilant and courageous press" with the right to criticize authority was particularly important in modern times as government became increasingly complex and susceptible to "malfeasance and corruption . . . especially in great cities." Although some publishers might abuse their rights, he insisted that suing them for libel would be better than censoring a constitutional right. He also warned that repression could backfire and cause "violent reactions." The *Near* case marked a turning point for condemning prior restraint and protecting press freedoms.[21]

In the third civil liberties case of 1931, Hughes wrote a powerful dissent (*U.S. v. Macintosh*). The immediate issue was the right of conscientious objection as a function of religious freedom. The case involved a Canadian born Baptist minister who taught theology at Yale. His application for citizenship was denied because, without foreswearing all wars, he would not promise to defend the United States in what he considered an unjust war. The case must have touched Hughes, who was the first Baptist to serve on the Court and whose father was a Baptist minister. In addition, as secretary of state, he promulgated Grotius's concept of just versus unjust wars.

This case interrogated the naturalization oath's requirement to "support and defend the Constitution and laws of the United States against all enemies, foreign and domestic, and bear true faith and allegiance to the same." The applicant also had to be "well disposed to the good order and happiness" of the nation. Speaking for a five-to-four majority, Sutherland emphasized the need for "good order" and unity, especially in wartime. Accordingly, he claimed "that unqualified allegiance to the Nation and submission and obedience to the laws of the land . . . are not inconsistent with the will of God." He referenced a 1929 case that denied citizenship to a Hungarian-born avowed pacifist (*U.S. v. Schwimmer*). Butler's opinion for the majority in that case focused on Congress's right to compel military service and the possibility that pacifism could undermine nationalism. In dissent, Holmes (with Brandeis) pointed to America's historic tolerance for the pacifist Quakers and famously stated that free thought meant not just "free thought for those who agree with us, but freedom for the thought that we hate."[22]

Joined by Holmes, Brandeis, and Stone, Hughes's *Macintosh* dissent echoed America's long tradition of allowing conscientious objectors to serve in wartime without bearing arms, which the oath did not explicitly require. The nation's history, he said, demonstrated that "the battle for religious liberty has been fought and won with respect to religious beliefs and practices which are not in conflict with good order." Surely, the nation could maintain an "orderly government without demanding that either citizens or applicants for citizenship shall assume by oath an obligation to regard allegiance to God as subordinate to allegiance to a civil power." Despite such strong words, Hughes refused to recommend overruling the *Schwimmer* precedent. Nonetheless, his dissent was used when both *Schwimmer* and *Macintosh* were finally overturned in 1946, after he left the Court.[23]

These three cases set a pattern for the rest of Hughes's term as chief justice. Although we will emphasize his own contribution, it was definitely enhanced by the new justices. The old justices maintained fairly consistent roles. Butler and McReynolds usually opposed judicial restraint for economic laws but could split on civil rights cases. Stone's Footnote Four from his opinion in the 1938 *U.S. v. Carolene Products* case promoted protecting civil liberties. Usually deferential to legislation, here Stone qualified judicial restraint by distinguishing between economic statutes and those "directed at particular religious . . . or national . . . or racial minorities." The latter, he wrote, justified "more searching scrutiny" of "prejudice against discrete and insular minorities." They represented "a special condition, which tends seriously to curtail the operation of those political processes ordinarily to be relied upon to protect minorities." In other words, civil liberties required extra protection.[24]

This footnote was credited with turning the Court away from its focus on economic issues towards civil liberties. But, as just discussed, the shift started well before 1938. There is some confusion about who wrote the footnote. Some scholars suggest that Hughes wrote the first paragraph. Others claim that the whole first draft was penned by Stone's law clerk. In any case, when it was circulated after conference, Hughes suggested strengthening the wording about violating free speech and press. Stone agreed and revised the text accordingly but also added words encompassing the entire Bill of Rights. Stone got full credit for Footnote Four even though he himself recognized that "the groundwork had been laid by the earlier opinions of Holmes, Brandeis . . . Hughes [but] the real pathbreakers were Cardozo and Holmes." Meanwhile, historian Barry Cushman pointed out that Footnote Four was not considered revolutionary until after World War II and was not cited widely until the 1970s. Regardless, it was a significant reflection of the Court's new direction.[25]

The Court continued incorporating the First into the Fourteenth Amendment. Freedom of the press was upheld in 1936 when Sutherland spoke for the Court in voiding a Louisiana law designed to eliminate press criticism of Governor Huey Long (*Grossjean v. American Press Co.*). In 1938 Hughes broadened press protections to include "pamphlets and leaflets" as well as "every sort of publication which affords a vehicle of information and opinion." The issue arose when a Georgia town required the approval of the city manager before its residents could distribute any literature (*Lovell v. City of Griffin*). That kind of regulation, wrote Hughes, "strikes at the very foundation of the freedom of the press by subjecting it to license and censorship." After all, he noted, it was Tom Paine's pamphlet that definitively shaped American history.[26]

In 1937, Hughes wrote a landmark opinion incorporating freedom of assembly into the Fourteenth Amendment for the first time (*De Jonge v. Oregon*). The Court held that Oregon could not use its anti-syndicalism statute to issue a seven-year prison sentence for speaking at a Communist Party meeting protesting police abuse of strikers. Guilt by association was unacceptable and "the holding of meetings for peaceful political action cannot be proscribed." Nor can peaceful participants "be branded as criminals." Hughes insisted that "the right of peaceful assembly . . . is equally fundamental" as the freedoms of speech and press. If they are "abused . . . in order to incite to violence or crime," state legislatures could address the transgression. However, curtailing peaceful free assembly violated the due process clause of the Fourteenth Amendment, which was now being used to protect civil liberty, not just private property.[27]

Hughes's approach in this case resembled his 1920 protest as a private citizen when five duly elected Socialists were expelled from the New York State Assembly, not for any specific violation but simply for their party affiliation. Building on his own long-term convictions and on 1920s dissents by Holmes and Brandeis, Hughes asserted that the best strategy for preventing revolutionary activity was "to maintain the opportunity for free political discussion." The objective was to keep government "responsive to the will of the people and that changes, if desired, may be obtained by peaceful means." Again, he avoided overturning precedents but underlined the importance of free assembly and discussion. "There lies the security of the Republic, the very foundation of constitutional government." The decision was unanimous.[28]

The Jehovah's Witnesses compelled the Court to clarify religious freedom. Although previous cases implied that First Amendment freedom from religious establishment and for religious exercise should be covered by the Fourteenth Amendment, it took until 1940 to make it official. In *Cantwell v. Connecticut*, Roberts pointed out that the "freedom to believe" was intertwined with the "freedom to act" and should be protected by the states unless a "clear and present danger to public peace and order" was involved. Thus, Jehovah's Witnesses were entitled to seek converts, even by playing an offensive anti-Catholic record in a Catholic neighborhood, so long as they did not incite violence. Roberts recognized that some people might abuse this privilege. But, in the interest of an "enlightened" citizenry, controversial opinions should be debated rather than repressed.[29]

Also in 1940, the Jehovah's Witnesses challenged Pennsylvania's requirement that all public school children salute the flag because it involved worshipping a graven image (*Minersville School District v. Gobitis*). In conference, Hughes admitted, "I come up to this case like a skittish horse to a brass band." Two of his fundamental commitments were in conflict—freedom of religion versus the social order needed to protecting that freedom. Ultimately, he decided that the case was really about inculcating good citizenship. It represented "educational self protection" similar to "the physical self-protection of the "familiar red traffic light." Hughes assigned the opinion to Frankfurter who valued public schools in shaping his own assimilation and success. In addition, noted law professor Brad Snyder, Frankfurter was profoundly concerned about events abroad. Thus, he concluded that the "time and circumstances" justified requiring the salute in order to promote "the binding tie of cohesive sentiment," which formed "the basis of national security."[30]

Pointing out that the school policy applied to everyone equally, Frankfurter held that choosing to send their children to public schools obliged parents to follow state law. This position confirmed his belief in judicial restraint and deference to state legislation, both of which dovetailed with Hughes's faith in dual federalism. Recognizing "the conflicting claims of liberty and authority," Frankfurter nonetheless held that because "the flag is the symbol of our national unity," states could use it to promote civic education. "Religious convictions" should not trump "political responsibilities." Moreover, said Frankfurter, the Court was in no position to be "the school board for the country." In his only vote against civil liberties, Hughes agreed with Frankfurter that promoting good citizenship was essential for the social stability required to protect freedom in wartime. For him, the issue revolved less around religion than around "ordered liberty." For others, the case just proved how susceptible the Court really was to external political circumstances.[31]

Harkening back to Footnote Four, Stone's dissent emphasized the need to protect religious freedom and avoid making the flag salute coercive. As he put it, "There are other ways to teach loyalty and patriotism" without sacrificing "the liberties of small minorities to the popular will." Ironically, that was Hughes's point in the 1931 *Macintosh* case, but it was decided in peacetime. Chastened by the subsequent persecution of Jehovah's Witnesses school children, Black, Douglas, and Murphy reconsidered their positions and the Court overturned *Gobitis* in 1943 (*West Virginia State Board of Education v. Barnette*). Parrish called it "one of the most stunning turnabouts in the Court's history."[32]

This time, Frankfurter spoke for three dissenters. Hughes rarely reacted to Court decisions after retiring, but he wrote Frankfurter to reaffirm his support. In *Macintosh,* Hughes had separated refusal to wage an unjust war from overall loyalty, but here he focused on loyalty as the predicate for religious freedom. He may also have been revisiting his previous positions on preparedness, the draft, and "just wars." As a former secretary of state, he would be concerned about unity in wartime. As such, Hughes was consistent. However, he was inconsistent regarding his belief that religious liberty was not an abstract concept but had "practical implications" for equality before the law. Society, he said in 1922, was "ever in danger of being made the instrument of the mistaken zeal of those who would deny to others the right to think as they chose." His position on the flag salute cases strained that commitment.[33]

So, too, Hughes seemed inconsistent in a 1930 opinion concerning a Louisiana state law providing nonreligious textbooks to private, including parochial, schools (*Cochran v. Louisiana State Board of Education*). He considered the law constitutional because the books were serving the larger public purpose of educating all children and because taxes used to buy the books did not expressly separate private from public institutions. Furthermore, secular books did not help establish religion. Thus, "its interest is in education; its method comprehensive." By claiming that the books helped the children, not the school, Hughes established a new "child benefit theory." It was controversial because it could support other forms of public aid to parochial schools like bus service, which the Court validated in 1947 (*Everson v. Board of Education*). Although Hughes's ruling reflected his lifelong commitments to education and state sovereignty, it complicated his other commitment to the separation of church and state. By not offering any standards by which such policies should be assessed, it also conflicted with his insistence on implementation standards for New Deal policies regarding codes for hot oil and sick chickens.[34]

Before retiring in 1941, Hughes wrote a unanimous opinion rejecting a Jehovah's Witnesses' protest against a New Hampshire law requiring a license for any "parade or procession" on a public street (*Cox v. New Hampshire*). Again, he upheld the need for "public order without which liberty itself would be lost in the excesses of unrestrained abuses." To him, there was no conflict between civil liberties and such a basic "social need," especially when regulations were applied to everyone equally, as Frankfurter held in *Gobitis*. Familiar themes emerged with Hughes generally championing individual freedoms but sometimes limiting them in the interests of local autonomy and social order. He tried to balance individual interests with social interests as long as public policies were not discriminatory.[35]

Racial Discrimination

It was a different matter when public policies did discriminate. In 1944, Swedish sociologist Gunner Myrdal identified race as the central American dilemma. Hughes confronted this issue by inviting Booker T. Washington to a Baptist Social Union dinner in 1906, speaking at the Tuskegee Institute in 1908, and condemning lynching in 1918. As associate justice, he wrote for the majority in voiding Alabama's peonage laws as involuntary servitude. In his 1927 lectures, he traced the origin of the 1865 Thirteenth Amendment abolishing slavery and involuntary servitude back to the 1787 Northwest Ordinance, which banned slavery from the new territories. Hughes considered it "a charter of universal freedom for all persons, of whatever race, color, or estate." Under his leadership, the Court not only pursued that promise but opened the door to future advances. The need was underlined by the resurgence of the Ku Klux Klan during the twenties.[36]

In 1931, nine young African American men were accused of rape by two white women on a freight train near Scottsboro, Alabama. The circumstances were murky. Apparently, there was a fight between African American and white drifters and the whites jumped or were thrown off the train. They complained to the local sheriff who sent a posse to intercept the train and arrest the African Americans, ages thirteen to twenty.

The women then accused them of gang rape. They may have been protecting themselves from arrest as prostitutes crossing state lines in violation of the 1910 White Slave Traffic (Mann) Act. No evidence of rape was found on either woman during medical examinations and, after consulting the Reverend Dr. Harry Emerson Fosdick (Hughes's pastor), one recanted. Nevertheless, the young men were divided into groups. Each group got a separate trial, one after another on the same day but with different juries. They were quickly convicted and sentenced to death by electric chair, a standard punishment in Alabama for African American men accused of raping white women. The case was appealed to the State Supreme Court, which confirmed the lower court with one powerful dissent.[37]

Although applauded in the South, the verdict inspired national and international protests against a widely perceived miscarriage of justice. It has been called "the most famous rape case of the twentieth century." Consequently, wrote poet Langston Hughes, the town of Scottsboro would always be known for "its court too weak to stand against a mob, its people's heart too small to hold a sob." Mainly due to the work of the Communist affiliated International Labor Defense Committee (ILD), with some help from the National Association for the Advancement of Colored People (NAACP), three separate cases rose on appeal to the Supreme Court—one in 1932 and two in 1935. A fourth case was dismissed by the state supreme court because the defendant was only thirteen years old, but he remained incarcerated under local law until 1937.[38]

Using a fair hearing standard, the remaining cases enabled the US Supreme Court to make landmark decisions regarding Sixth Amendment rights to a fair trial, counsel, and an impartial jury. These cases were a wake-up call about discrimination in the Southern legal system and a siren call for reforming criminal justice throughout the nation. To be sure, their immediate impact on Southern legal process was offset by a concerted backlash. However, law professor Michael J. Klarman suggested that the Scottsboro cases may have had significant long-range influence on African Americans' awareness of their rights and the utility of protest. In addition, they upset liberal whites and set the stage not only for future Court rulings but also for the civil rights movement.[39]

During the 1932 conference discussion on *Powell v. Alabama,* Hughes emphasized the inadequacy of counsel at trial. He then asked Sutherland to write the opinion as a conservative voting with the majority along with Van Devanter. The ruling was strong. Competent counsel, said Sutherland, is always important because defendants are unfamiliar with legal procedure and unable to represent themselves. This was especially true for young, illiterate men who were too poor to hire a lawyer, even if they had been so advised, which they were not. It "would be little short of judicial murder," said Sutherland, to deprive defendants of effective counsel when facing the death sentence. Indeed, the attorneys were unfamiliar with capital cases, were appointed at the last minute, had no time to prepare, and barely met the defendants before trial. Moreover, held Sutherland, the desire for a speedy trial could not be used to deny the right to effective counsel, especially when the court went "forward with the haste of the mob." That was not a euphemism because, like the Leo Frank case, a hostile crowd surrounded the courthouse and dominated the courtroom. Unlike Leo Frank, the defendants were placed under military guard to avoid lynching.[40]

The next step was, for the first time, to make a clear connection between the rights of the accused covered in the Sixth Amendment and the Due Process Clause of the Fourteenth Amendment as applied to the states. Accordingly, Sutherland suggested that "it is possible that some of the personal rights safeguarded by the first eight Amendments against National action may be safeguarded against state action, because a denial of them would be a denial of due process." Without definitively incorporating the Bill of Rights into the Fourteenth Amendment, the Court paved the road for full nationalization of the rights of the accused in the 1960s.[41]

Perhaps the justices wanted to offset their conservative economic rulings with a more liberal civil liberties ruling that could mollify their critics. McReynolds and Butler were not so inclined. Objecting to the Court's newly expansive view of the Bill of Rights, they claimed that the more limited, more customary use of substantive due process would have sufficed without threatening state sovereignty. Their dissent acknowledged that the Court's ruling was path breaking.

In 1935, Hughes wrote the landmark opinion for the second case.

He had already spoken for the court in 1931 affirming the right of a lawyer defending an African American to question prospective jurors about their positions on racial prejudice (*Aldridge v. U.S.*). Not only were such queries essential to "fairness," he said, but not taking prejudice into account when selecting jurors was guaranteed "to bring the processes of justice into disrepute." Social reality could not be swept under the procedural rug. McReynolds considered the issue too vague and too complicated for courts to pursue. The *Aldridge* case previewed the second and third Scottsboro cases, which focused on the issue of jury selection. Meanwhile, the ILD organized a steady stream of worldwide letter writing campaigns, rallies, and press releases. They sent Ada Wright, two of the defendants' mother, on a six-month European speaking tour, accompanied by an ILD official.[42]

On appeal, the second and third Scottsboro cases were moved to other counties where all eight defendants were again ruled guilty and condemned to death. Final appeals brought both cases to the Supreme Court in 1935 (*Norris v. Alabama* and *Patterson v. Alabama*). In *Norris,* the defense claimed that the systematic exclusion of African Americans from juries deprived the accused of an impartial jury as protected by the Sixth Amendment and compounded by the due process and equal protection clauses of the Fourteenth Amendment. No Alabama law specifically prevented African Americans from serving on juries, but there was no county record of any ever being considered as jurors.

Moreover, because handwriting analysis revealed that local court officers had forged the names of African Americans on the jury rolls, the case qualified as "intentional discrimination." The rationale was that none were qualified to serve. Indeed, the county jury commissioner testified in *Norris* that no African American was "honest and intelligent, . . . [of] good character and sound judgment, who is not an habitual drunkard, who isn't afflicted with a permanent disease or physical weakness . . . and who can read English, and who has never been convicted of a crime involving moral turpitude."[43]

Hughes indignantly declared it "impossible to accept such a sweeping characterization," especially since the records showed that there were many African Americans in the county who were qualified. The issue, he wrote, was whether a constitutional right, like having a jury of one's peers, was not only "denied in express terms but also whether it was denied in substance and effect." McReynolds did not participate and Butler did not dissent. However, the Southern press vowed that the ruling "can and will be evaded." Patterson's case was dismissed on technical grounds. But, by sending it back to the lower court, Hughes managed to get him a new trial and prevent his execution. Ultimately, charges were dropped for four of the defendants, but the other five served long prison sentences replete with escapes, parole violations, and reimprisonments. Releases began in 1943 until the last man was finally pardoned in 1976.[44]

Although the Scottsboro boys served too many years in prison, including time in solitary, publicity protected them from severe abuse. They were never tortured, but three Mississippi sharecroppers were (*Brown v. Mississippi*). After a white planter was killed, the men were arrested, convicted, and condemned to death based on nothing beyond confessions obtained under horrific conditions. Their backs were mercilessly whipped with the buckle end of leather belts. The most recalcitrant man was strung from a tree and beaten. The rope marks on his neck were visible when he appeared in court. The abuse continued until they all agreed to sign detailed confessions as demanded by a mob. The deputy sheriff did not deny participating in the abuse and testified that the whippings were not "too much for a negro." In dissent, one brave Mississippi Supreme Court judge emphasized the racial disparity between the torturers and the tortured. To him, "the transcript reads more like pages torn from a medieval account, than a record made within the confines of a modern civilization which aspires to an enlightened constitutional government."[45]

In a decision authored by Hughes, the Supreme Court unanimously overturned the three men's death sentences in 1936. In order not to overturn precedent, Hughes conceded that states retained control over most criminal procedures. However, they could not "substitute trial by ordeal" for trial by jury nor "the rack and torture chamber . . . for the witness stand." Repeating his concern about the Leo Frank trial, he insisted that "the State may not permit an accused to be hurried to conviction under mob domination—where the whole proceeding is but a mask—without supplying corrective process." Even more, he proclaimed, "it would be difficult to conceive of methods more revolting to the sense of justice" than those used in this case. Technical arguments made by the state were invalidated as "a clear denial of due process." This was the first time that the Court identified forced confessions as violating self-incrimination in the Fifth Amendment as well as due process in the Fourteenth.[46]

In 1935, the Court sent a case back to California for retrial because a man was convicted after a prosecutor knowingly used perjured testimony (*Mooney v. Holohan*). Hughes declared that depriving a defendant of due process "by the action of the State" deprived him of a fair hearing and violated "the fundamental conceptions of justice which lie at the base of our civil and political institutions." Klarman pointed out that because the public generally supported the Court in these cases, it was not counter-majoritarian after all.[47]

Two related 1937 and 1940 cases further highlighted the Court's vigilance against racial injustice. In *Chambers v. Florida,* Black condemned the "dragnet methods" used to arrest and coerce confessions of murder from four African American tenant farmers. In *White v. Texas,* the Court sent an alleged rape case based on a tortured confession back to the state three times. After Bob White was finally acquitted, he was killed point blank in the courtroom by the alleged victim's husband. These cases did not nationalize all rights of the accused, but they exposed racism and protected civil rights, not just property rights. In the 1960s, the Court built upon these cases to assert that the rights of the accused must be protected by the states.[48]

Another landmark 1938 case presaged the pivotal 1954 ruling against segregated public education (*Missouri ex rel. Gaines v. Canada*). Recently graduated from the state-supported, African American Lincoln University, which lacked a law school. Lloyd L. Gaines was academically qualified to attend the all-white University of Missouri law school. But its registrar, Silas W. Canada, rejected him solely because of his race. In a test case, Gaines sued after refusing to apply for a state scholarship that would pay his tuition at an adjacent state's public law school open to African Americans.

To defend Gaines, the NAACP chose Charles Hamilton Houston, the African American dean of Harvard Law School, who would become the key lawyer in the pivotal 1954 public school desegregation case (*Brown v. Board of Education of Topeka*). The premise was that Missouri's policy violated the Fourteenth Amendment's equal protection clause as well as the 1896 *Plessy v. Ferguson* requirement of "separate but equal" facilities. Hughes and five other justices agreed; Butler and McReynolds disagreed. (Cardozo's death left one seat vacant.) The dissenters claimed that, considering the realities of southern race relations, Missouri made a "fair effort" by providing the out-of-state option. To McReynolds, abrogating not only state control over education but also the "settled practice of separate schools" would "damnify both races." Significantly, he turned his back on Hamilton during oral arguments, a tactic that he also used to demonstrate contempt for the Jewish justices.[49]

Following Houston's strategy of using rather than trying to overthrow *Plessy*, Hughes said that Missouri had to provide equivalent legal education for African American and white students. According to the *Plessy* standard, Missouri could have established a law school for African Americans but had not done so and did not plan to do so. Sending Gaines to another state was an unacceptable evasion of the state's responsibility to provide equal, albeit segregated, educational opportunities in Missouri. "The equal protection of the laws," he wrote, "is a pledge of protection of equal laws . . . within its own jurisdiction." Referring back to the 1914 *McCabe* railroad car case, Hughes reiterated that providing separate but equal facilities did not depend on the number of people seeking them because the right is "a personal one" regardless of race or numbers. "Equality of right" was due to each individual, even if only one person seeks it.[50]

In response, the Missouri state legislature allotted minimal funds for Lincoln University to establish a law school. It opened in 1939 with four professors and thirty students, but not Lloyd Gaines. He disappeared, never to be heard from again. That strange development prevented testing the school's legitimacy in court. The *Gaines* case was celebrated in the North and condemned in the South. Independent scholar Richard Kluger called it "an enormous milestone" that could "serve as the basis for suits against any jurisdiction that failed to provide equal public school facilities for Negroes anywhere along the educational ladder." In fact, said Ross, "Hughes had signaled a new approach to separate but equal that would later bear fruit." Focusing on and "raising the standards of equality" forced the states to reassess or retrench their segregation strategies and led to the 1954 declaration that segregated public school facilities were inherently unequal. Consequently, Parrish concluded that "no opinion of the Hughes Court era held greater significance for the nation's racial future."[51]

With a more liberal Court behind him, Hughes issued another important challenge to "separate but equal" in 1941. Among his last opinions, *Mitchell v. U.S.* reinforced the continuity between his two terms on the Court. Like the 1914 *McCabe* case, the issue was segregated railroad cars. An African American congressman from Illinois purchased a first-class ticket going from Chicago to Arkansas. He sat in the integrated first-class Pullman car until forced to move to a segregated second-class coach car when the train entered Arkansas, which mandated racial segregation. The congressman promptly claimed a violation of the Interstate Commerce Act, which forbade "any undue or unreasonable prejudice or disadvantage in any respect whatsoever." Giving the "equal" part of the *Plessy* formula as much importance as the "separate" part, Hughes held that the railroad had to provide equivalent first-class cars for both races, even if only one person requested it. Based on his own rulings in *McCabe* and *Gaines*, Hughes again insisted that failing to provide equal facilities was "an invasion of a fundamental individual right which is guaranteed against state action by the Fourteenth Amendment." Such discrimination, he wrote, was "palpably unjust." Without directly challenging *Plessy*, Hughes emphasized the Court's responsibility for monitoring racial discrimination. He was systematically (and characteristically) undermining *Plessy* while avoiding overturning it.[52]

The issue of voting rights revealed the difficulties of forging new ground. After the Taft Court invalidated the Texas state-run white primary in 1927 (*Nixon v. Herndon*), the state shifted control of primaries to its political parties, which limited membership to whites. In 1932, Hughes joined the majority in declaring this arrangement a violation of the Fourteenth Amendment's Equal Protection Clause (*Nixon v. Condon*). However, three years later, the Court ruled unanimously that the Texas white primary was constitutional as long as it was run by a private organization, like a political party, and not by the state (*Grovey v. Townsend*). Similarly, in 1937 the Court ruled unanimously that Georgia's one dollar poll tax was constitutional because it fell on all people equally (*Breedlove v. Suttles*). But in 1939, it invalidated Oklahoma's second effort to have a literacy test exclusively for African Americans because it established "onerous procedural requirements" that were intentionally discriminatory (*Lane v. Wilson*). Going further, in 1941 the Court reaffirmed Congress's right to regulate party primaries and protect ballot counting from partisan manipulation (*U.S. v. Classic*). Hughes did not participate in this case because it overturned *Newberry v. U.S.*, when he had defended Senator Newberry partly because the Constitution did not explicitly grant Congress control over primaries. Finally, in 1944, after Hughes resigned, the Court overturned *Grovey* and declared white primaries unconstitutional (*Smith v. Allwright*). It was an extended, if convoluted, process that, like the evolutionary process regarding New Deal legislation, reflected the justices' doctrinal struggle to modernize without weakening the Constitution.[53]

Hughes did not write any of these opinions or any dissents. Nonetheless, he stated his overall position on civil liberties in 1940 when receiving an award from the National Conference of Christians and Jews as a cofounder committed to interreligious and interracial cooperation. For him, the intolerance and prejudice that bred hatred and hostility were the "deadly enemies of true democracy, more dangerous than any external force because they undermine the very foundations of our democratic effort." In that spirit, the Hughes Court gave new life to the concept of equal protection under the law.[54]

It did so, wrote Tushnet, by developing "an affirmative theory of the first Amendment" whereby "fundamental freedoms were now based in the Bill of Rights, not due process." A major shift in its own time, this reformulation left a lasting legacy. By exposing inequities, broadening their constitutional context, and underlining the sociopolitical aspects of the judicial system, these civil liberties rulings motivated reformers and helped stimulate the civil rights movement. As law professor Merle Loper pointed out, many of the basic civil liberties legal principles established by the Hughes Court "still stand undisturbed today."[55]

The Constitution Marches

McReynolds's law clerk correctly concluded that the 1937 NLRB–Wagner Act cases represented "the end of an era in the law, and the death of an entire way of thinking." That transition process was reflected in two cases that bookended the Court from post-court packing in 1938 to Hughes's retirement in 1941. They marked the definitive acceptance of Holmes's reasonableness standard, judicial restraint, and sociological jurisprudence. They also formalized Hughes's efforts to expand the interstate commerce clause, recast substantive due process, redefine contracts, and prioritize public over private interests. While bridging Hughes's role as a prominent private lawyer with his two terms on the Court, they illuminated his own doctrinal development as well as the Court's. It was another evolutionary revolution proving Hughes's 1917 declaration that "the Constitution marches." Hughes chose not to write either opinion. Although he had some reservations about the specifics, he appreciated the larger significance of the cases and was comfortable enough with the new Court to play a secondary, albeit still important, role. Perhaps he was also paving the way for the next chief justice.[56]

The unlikely subject of this important process was a product called "filled milk." In 1923, Congress passed a Filled Milk Act prohibiting the interstate shipment of an inexpensive version of condensed milk that substituted coconut oil for butterfat. The product looked, tasted, and smelled like regular condensed milk. However, without the vitamin A so essential to infant development, it could be deemed harmful. The act was supported by dairy farmers but opposed by filled milk producers as a violation of their due process rights to sell their product. Furthermore, they said that filled milk did not violate the 1906 Food and Drug Act because all contents were clearly labeled and no false claims were made. A challenge to the act came before the Court in 1938 in *U.S. v. Carolene Products Co.* According to Barry Cushman, *Carolene* marked a major milestone in constitutional federalism that was cemented in 1941 by the more famous case *U.S. v. Darby Lumber Co.* Both opinions were assigned to Stone, probably because, as a private lawyer, Hughes argued a related 1919 case (*Hebe Co. v. Shaw*) and because, as usual, he resisted overturning precedent.[57]

The *Hebe* case upheld an Ohio law prohibiting the sale of filled milk. With Hughes defending the filled milk company and Holmes opposing it, the situation reversed the 1911 misbranding case when Hughes exposed the fraudulent claims of Cancerine and Holmes supported the company. Maybe the difference for Hughes was that the Hebe company's marketing was technically honest. Or maybe, his critics would say, Hughes was getting a big retainer. Speaking for a six-to-three Court, Holmes pointed out that accurate labels were irrelevant because most consumers never read them, especially if the price was right. Due process claims fell before the state's right to legislate in favor of nutrition and against deception.[58]

The case was about more than milk. Hughes was not on the Court for the 1918 *Hammer v. Dagenhart* case when it accepted a manufacturer's substantive due process suit against the 1916 Child Labor Act, which prohibited the interstate sale of goods made by children. The Court ruled five-to-four that the act improperly invoked the interstate commerce clause to punish manufacturers and control labor conditions within a state indirectly because it could not do so directly. As previously discussed, Holmes dissented on the premise that congressional power over interstate commerce superseded its effect on individual states. Otherwise, Congress could never establish national standards for anything, as it already had done for the sale of obscene literature, lottery tickets, and other goods. But precedent held that the goods must be harmful to interstate commerce or to people in other states. Because the products of child labor were not in themselves harmful, the majority held that the child labor bill exceeded the scope of the commerce clause. Substantive due process prevailed along with rigid dual federalism and states' rights.[59]

The *Hammer* decision was controversial. When the 1923 filled milk bill was debated in Congress, opponents used *Hammer* to assert that filled milk was neither harmful nor fraudulent. The bill's supporters used *Hebe* to call filled milk harmful to children's health because it lacked vitamin A but was marketed as wholesome. During the Depression, thirty-four states passed their own laws banning filled milk in order to aid dairy farmers. The Carolene Products Company, a filled milk producer, campaigned to overturn these laws in the 1930s and succeeded in eight states. After the federal government sued the company for illegally shipping filled milk from Illinois to Missouri, the company challenged the legality of the 1923 act. When the case reached the Supreme Court in 1938, the 1923 Filled Milk Act was upheld eight-to-one, with McReynolds dissenting.[60]

Stone's *Carolene* opinion was path-breaking. First, he reasserted the long-accepted principle of the 1895 Lottery Act and the 1906 Food and Drug Act that the interstate commerce power included the right to prohibit items considered "injurious to the public health, morals, or welfare." It could only be limited through the Fifth Amendment due process clause. However, those claims could be negated by legislation that "rests upon some rational basis within the knowledge and experience of the legislators." It was up to Congress, not the courts, to decide whether and how to regulate. As Holmes's "rational basis" became the standard for judicial restraint regarding legislation, the arena for federal activism grew. Furthermore, the commerce clause now outweighed the due process clause, which had been the bulwark of anti-regulatory legislation for decades. The next step was to overrule *Hammer*, something Hughes had painstakingly avoided in his 1937 *Jones & Laughlin* opinion.[61]

By 1941, Hughes had changed his mind. In considering *U.S. v. Darby Lumber*, his commitment to precedent fell before his interests in improving labor conditions and expanding the interstate commerce clause. The *Darby* case challenged the 1938 Fair Labor Standards Act, the last major New Deal reform legislation. It set minimum wages and maximum hours for adults working in interstate commerce or producing goods for interstate commerce. Employing children under sixteen was prohibited. During Senate negotiations, some jobs were exempted for political purposes, particularly those held by African Americans. The new act was intended to reverse the Taft Court's 1923 *Adkins* case invalidating a DC minimum wage law for women and children. It would also offset the 1935 *Schechter* decision, which killed the NIRA's labor protections in the process of killing the NRA's industry codes.[62]

Hughes assigned the unanimous *Darby* opinion to Stone as a follow up to *Carolene.* Law. Professor Alphaeus T. Mason claimed that Hughes reluctantly joined Stone's opinion, but Friedman pointed out that Hughes's misgivings only referred to one phrase, which Stone amended. Although Hughes "preferred not to write," he based his conference presentation on Stone's *Carolene* reasoning and told Stone that the case upheld "the general principles" of the Court concerning "the exercise of the commerce power." Stone's *Darby* opinion was consistent with his own Shreveport opinion. In return, Stone referenced Hughes in *Kentucky Whip* when he could have but did not overturn *Hammer.* Now, Stone explicitly declared that *Hammer* "could not be reconciled" with *Darby.*[63]

Building on Marshall's 1824 *Gibbons v. Ogden* advocacy of an expansive commerce clause "as complete unto itself," plus Holmes's dissent in *Hammer* and his own opinion in *Carolene,* Stone rejected narrow definitions of "business affected with a public interest." Rather, he affirmed that Congress could ban from interstate commerce any items considered "injurious to the public health, morals or welfare" of states which receive the goods, even though those states had not banned them. As Hughes wrote in *Kentucky Whip,* that applied to harmless as well as harmful goods. Now, Stone said it also encompassed "substandard labor conditions" that were "detrimental to the maintenance of minimum standards of living necessary for health and general well-being." Unregulated harmful conditions, including child labor, would spread in the ruthless competition for low prices, thereby disadvantaging states with fair labor practices.[64]

Finally, Stone dismissed the claim that congressional regulation violated the Tenth Amendment's protection of states' rights under dual federalism. That Amendment, he wrote, was nothing but "a truism that all is retained [by the states] which has not been surrendered to the federal government." However, if the federal government had limitless power to regulate interstate commerce, then the Tenth Amendment was irrelevant and dual federalism was significantly narrowed.[65]

Together, *Carolene* and *Darby* cemented a long line of judgements expanding the meaning of the interstate commerce clause, ending the use of substantive due process to block legislative regulations, and endorsing the policy of judicial restraint. These cases demonstrated how the evolution of legal doctrine created the revolution of constitutional interpretation that characterized the Hughes Court. Like democracy itself, the Constitution was always a work in progress and, said Hughes in 1927, the Court was always engaged in "the gradual process of judicial inclusion and exclusion."[66]

The Court's metamorphosis reflected the complexity of constitutional interpretation, especially as it moved into uncharted judicial territory. Industrialism posed new economic, social, and political problems while World War I raised new civil liberties issues, and the Great Depression created unprecedented challenges to the Court's priorities and identity. An inherently cautious institution tied to precedent, the Court often seemed to take five steps forward and two steps backward. Time and again, the justices weighed the importance of state experimentation against the need for federal regulation, the sanctity of private property against the sovereignty of individual rights. Hughes believed that dual federalism was central to the nation's strength, but he also understood that it could obstruct reasonable change and necessary "elasticity." Thus, he often supported cooperative over conflict-based federalism. The challenge was to balance continuity with flexibility and power with liberty in order to promote, he said, "the progressive development of legal ideas." New York State Supreme Court Justice Joseph M. Proskauer, observed that Hughes's objective was not only to uphold "the fundamental principles" of democracy but "to make these principles function . . . to make the processes of government work."[67]

That spirit permeated both of Hughes's terms on the Court. Being result-oriented was a logical extension of his service in Albany and at the State Department. Accordingly, Associate Justice Hughes advanced the legal process of facing reality by expanding the interstate commerce clause, supporting the rights of labor, and promoting civil liberties. Ironically, he helped alter the dual federalism he cherished for the sake of a seamless economy and legislative experimentation in changing times. The Minnesota rate and Shreveport cases along with the railroad, labor, and contracts cases found him adapting past economic assumptions to new economic circumstances. By expanding the meaning of the interstate commerce clause and adjusting concepts of due process,

Hughes elevated the public good over private interests. He endorsed a shift from narrowly doctrinal rulings to those that reflected actual conditions. The same pattern prevailed regarding labor issues and civil liberties. Sociological jurisprudence suited his blend of idealism, legalism, humanitarianism, and pragmatism.

Hughes served as chief justice during a difficult decade when the need to ensure that the Constitution responded to contemporary realities was compelling and complicated. Over his eleven-year tenure, Hughes dominated the Court, increased its efficiency, and improved its image. In addition, he strengthened the federal judicial system and judicial procedure. Whether by evolution or revolution, the philosophy of judicial review was solidified in the court packing crisis but circumscribed by the principle of judicial restraint. While supporting federal activism in some cases, Hughes opposed federal power in other cases. He struggled to both condone and constrain the New Deal while coping with deep divisions on the Court and intense pressures from outside the Court. Hughes's approach to FDR reflected not only his dedication to the integrity of the Court and the separation of powers but also his political acumen. Was he always just a governor on the bench?

Chief Justice Hughes firmly believed that stability and continuity strengthened the Court. Thus, he resisted overturning precedent even as he embraced change. This tendency has been interpreted as conservatism. Critics assume that whenever Hughes voted against a New Deal measure, he was motivated by fear of class conflict and the emerging welfare state, that he preferred a weak central government based on classical concepts of decentralized power and the harmony of interests. Evidence could include the 1906 governor's race against William Randolph Hearst, whom he accused of exploiting class division. He also opposed the Adamson Act during the 1916 presidential contest and criticized Wilson's postwar use of wartime powers. To be sure, Hughes hoped for harmony. But he recognized class conflict in his gubernatorial policies as well as his judicial opinions limiting substantive due process while supporting labor unions, better working conditions, workmen's compensation, and pensions. His civil liberties rulings demonstrated an acute awareness of the inequalities embedded in gender, class, race, and ethnicity.[68]

During the court packing crisis, Hughes affirmed that a strong, independent Supreme Court was essential for a working democracy. As the anchor of the separation of powers, the Court's mission was "the true and firm administration of justice," which, he said, was "the primary concern of civilized society." Still evoking Grotius, Hughes envisioned that a people dedicated to reason, tolerance, and fairness would cherish the institution best suited to promote and protect those values. Despite often sounding unrealistic, Hughes strategically used his skills to promote his vision and save the Court. In the end, he could take comfort from the fact that the public and Congress supported the Court over the president. The least dangerous branch had been most important in upholding the Constitution.[69]

Commemorating Hughes in 1948, Nathan Miller, former New York State governor and chairman of the New York State Bar Association, explored the comparison of Hughes to John Marshall. The latter, he said, "breathed . . . life into the Constitution by the doctrine of implied powers." Hughes gave it new life by "demonstrating its adaptability to the needs of a complex society at a time of unusual stress and strain." Whereas the original Constitution was "a compromise between state sovereignty and centralized authority," Hughes led the Court in carefully rebalancing that relationship. Miller considered Hughes's commerce clause rulings as associate justice consistent with his rulings as chief justice. The link was expanding federal power without obliterating state power. Hughes's contribution, said Miller, was recognizing that because contemporary problems were national, they required national solutions. Consequently, Hughes proved that the Constitution was not "outmoded" but could and should mature with the nation, just as Marshall would have wanted.[70]

There were additional connections between Hughes and Marshall. As law professor Joel Richard Paul pointed out, Marshall had a more diverse background than Hughes because he came from poor origins and was a soldier. But otherwise, the similarities were striking. Both were successful lawyers, politicians, diplomats, and chief justices. Both faced hostility from the executive and legislative branches. Neither was ideologically rigid. Like Hughes, Marshall was a consensus builder who prevailed "by sheer personality and intellect." So, too, Marshall "was a consistent voice for moderation, compromise, and pragmatism in the face of ideologues and adversaries." Most important, Marshall considered the Constitution "a living document that responded to the needs and demands of a growing nation." Accordingly, he favored loose over strict construction and a strong over a weak federal government. Marshall's major accomplishment was articulating "virtually every foundational doctrine of constitutional law that has guided the United States for two centuries." In the process, he asserted the supremacy of the Court to interpret the Constitution and become a truly coequal branch. As historian Jean Edward Smith put it, "Marshall transformed the Constitution from a compact of states into a charter of national life and created a political role for the Supreme Court at the very center of the nation's development." No one can compare with Marshall's contribution.[71]

Why then was Hughes so often ranked as the second or third most important chief justice after Marshall? Could it be because of the critical role he played in preserving and updating Marshall's legacy? Like his predecessor, Hughes's major concern was keeping the Constitution relevant while maintaining the integrity and dignity of the Court. In fact, wrote law professor Paul A. Freund, "Hughes's stewardship brought the Court through a crisis matched only by that of Marshall's period." Hughes's personal prestige, like Marshall's, helped validate the many landmark opinions he delivered. His pursuit of consensus and stability often led him, again like Marshall, to make compromises, side with the conservatives, and write key opinions himself in order to control rulings and steer the Court forward—sometimes incrementally, sometimes boldly. His "calm and deliberate" demeanor, executive background, and lawyerly skills enabled Hughes to steady a deeply divided, politically threatened Court.[72]

According to Freund, both men were "magisterial, resourceful, powerful in dialectic, possessed of zealous regard for their Court as an institution." These qualities, said Hendel, characterized the constructive leadership needed "in a period of reexamination of many of the foundation principles of constitutional law." Thus, Hughes had "long-range influence," especially regarding procedural due process, substantive due process, the contract and commerce clauses, civil liberties, and judicial restraint. Like Marshall, Hughes was cautious and pragmatic, sometimes inconsistent, but always profoundly committed to the nation he served. Most observers would say that Marshall faced the greater challenge, but both men met the needs of the moment because they possessed visions beyond the moment. At least one citizen mistook Hughes for Marshall and sent the current chief justice a letter addressed to the former one. Reporting on the incident at a conference of circuit justices, Hughes was pleased that citizens considered the Court important enough to contact. However, he admitted, "I have been in a quandary as to where I should forward this letter, as I do not know the ultimate destination of our distinguished predecessor."[73]

In a 1932 speech preceding the New Deal, Hughes explained his approach to the Constitution and judicial review. His primary objective was "in maintaining the constitutional balance between State and Nation and in enforcing the principle of liberty which the Constitution safeguards against arbitrary power." The point was not to do so "in a narrow, technical spirit" or to "forbid flexibility in making adaptations to meet new conditions." Thus, the Court must acknowledge "appropriate state power as well as federal power." Above all, The Court should use judicial review as a tool for correction, not repression. Power holders had to face "limitations . . . in the interests of liberty" and protect rights considered "fundamental" by the Founding Fathers. Quoting James Madison, Hughes upheld the judicial branch as "the guardian of those rights . . . an impenetrable bulwark" against abuse by the other two branches. "Perennial debate" over rights was inevitable but did not diminish "the great guarantees of individual liberty."[74]

It was this multifaceted, multilayered, interwoven fabric that made the Constitution uniquely American. The complexity of its design defined Hughes's own judicial philosophy, which often invited criticism precisely because it was neither simplistic nor linear. Yet, it was the outgrowth of a coherent concept of the Constitution as an enduring but malleable document. Only a living Constitution would keep democracy from dying. For Hughes, preserving democracy depended on the judge's understanding of how precious that fragile framework really was.

The Supreme Court's role, he said, was to demonstrate "a statesmanlike appreciation of past, present, and future through which alone the Judge can meet his responsibilities as the interpreter of legislation in the expanding life of democracy." Therefore, it was crucial that every judge demonstrate a dedication to "justice, a rectitude of purpose, a clarity of vision and a capacity for independence, impartiality and balanced judgement." Such was the typically high standard that Hughes set for himself and others when he declared, "We are under a Constitution, but the Constitution is what the judges say it is."[75]

Conclusion, 1941–1948

The only reason I have lived so long is because I have never been absorbed in the past, brooding over disappointments. I have pushed what is done out of my mind and gone on to new activities.
—Charles Evans Hughes, 1937

Charles Evans Hughes's lifelong, optimistic spirit of moving forward and welcoming new challenges resulted in one of the nation's most exceptional, most diverse public service careers. But it could not last forever. In late February 1939, Hughes had a strange medical episode. Suddenly overwhelmed with weakness, he turned ashen. Fortunately, the other justices had just left the conference room and he was alone with his clerk, who quickly helped him to a couch. Refusing to let the clerk get a doctor, Hughes lay there until he felt well enough to go home. He insisted on doing so alone, lest being accompanied raise any suspicions. Characteristically determined to forge ahead, he pushed himself to keep up with the Court's demanding schedule over the next week.[1]

March 4th marked the commemoration of the Supreme Court's 150th anniversary. Of course, the chief justice would speak. However, Hughes was so weak that he hardly made it to the podium and paused several times, once seeming unable to continue. Somehow, Hughes summoned the strength to deliver one of his shortest, most eloquent, most significant speeches (without notes as usual). Celebrating the survival of democracy over time despite vast changes and challenges, he focused on the unique concept of power embodied in the US Constitution.

Hughes urged the representatives of the three branches in attendance to remember that "we are here not as masters, but as servants, not to glory in power, but to attest our loyalty to the commands and restrictions of our sovereign, the people of the United States." Because power was temporary and derivative, it must be wielded with "wisdom and restraint." Because power was divided, it required constructive cooperation among equal "partners." The object, he said, was to achieve "through the very limitation of power the promotion of the wise use of power." That involved a healthy blend of "stability and rational progress" reflecting "the good sense of the American people." Only then could the nation really protect the promise of democracy—life, liberty, and the pursuit of happiness. Here were his operating principles—limited power for good government (not personal aggrandizement), faith in reason, belief in and responsiveness to the people, the pursuit of both continuity and change. In one form or another, Hughes pursued these convictions throughout his life.[2]

After the ceremony, weak as he was, Hughes presided over the regular Saturday conference for six hours. He had never postponed one yet and refused to start now. Similarly, he hosted a big dinner that evening at his house. Then, he finally went to bed. On Monday, the doctor discovered that Hughes had a duodenal ulcer and had lost a lot of blood. (A duodenal ulcer is caused by bacterial infection, not by compulsiveness, as Betty Glad claimed.) It took Hughes a month to recuperate enough to return to the Court. A slight relapse caused two days of bed rest in June.[3]

Otherwise in good health, Hughes was unsettled by these developments. He had already asked his family to advise him if they thought he was getting senile. That never was an issue, but it was becoming harder to maintain his intense pace of work. He felt and looked older. Nonetheless, his humor remained intact. After Franklin D. Roosevelt's (FDR) fourth inauguration in 1941, Hughes joked that he had been tempted to follow the oath with, "Franklin, don't you think this is getting to be a trifle monotonous?" The president sent him a seventy-ninth birthday wish that April 11th, saying, "You are not a day older—mentally or physically than I am—just 59!" Hughes responded, "Your extraordinary appraisal of my youth has almost turned my head. While I am old enough to know better, I am young enough to like it."[4]

In his 1927 Columbia lectures, Hughes acknowledged that "some judges have stayed too long on the bench." However, the key variable for retirement, he said, should not be age or even illness but "decrepitude." Although Hughes hardly fit that description, he felt that it was time to go and tearfully admitted to the brethren, "I have always had a fear of continuing in office under a delusion of adequacy." Despite not needing the money, he retired rather than undermine the Court's new full pay retirement policy by resigning without compensation. Hughes was the only chief justice since John Jay to leave the position in good health. As when governor and secretary of state, Hughes gave up power when he believed that he had done his best and run his course. He recommended that FDR appoint Harlan F. Stone to replace him. As the senior associate justice, Stone was the logical choice. Perhaps Hughes was also rectifying Hoover's decision to appoint him chief instead of Stone in 1930.[5]

Hughes's retirement was treated as a national calamity. FDR immediately telegrammed the "great shock" that he and "the whole nation" felt. Praise poured in. The brethren thanked him for his "generosity, kindness, and forbearance." Frankfurter predicted that Hughes would long be remembered as "the voice of law." Journalist William Allen White wrote, "I wanted you to know how proud I am to have lived in the generation with you." Former secretary of state Henry Stimson called Hughes "one of the great pillars of integrity and morality in public life." His work as chief justice earned comparisons to John Marshall and predictions that he would go down in history as the "ablest Chief Justice" and one of the Court's "great figures." In a cartoon called "That's the Question," Uncle Sam held two big shoes as Hughes was getting ready to leave. Scratching his head, Uncle Sam asked, "Where will I ever find another to fill these shoes?"[6]

Retirement was a new kind of career and, as with all of his endeavors, Hughes wanted to make the most of it. Painfully aware of the personal time lost with Antoinette and his family due to the demands of public life, Hughes focused on private life. Therefore, he politely rejected all attempts to hold celebratory dinners and declined all invitations to give speeches. Wanting to be spared "the fatigue of public performance," and knowing that, being out of office, his words would lack impact, he decided "to leave to others the effort to inform, clarify and persuade." Those three words captured his approach to public service—the teacher as politician, statesman, and judge.[7]

The only request he could not refuse came from Secretary of State Cordell Hull, who was helping draft the United Nations charter in 1944. Deeply committed to international cooperation and always regretting the nation's failure to join the League of Nations or the World Court, Hughes made several suggestions that became part of the final document. They avoided the mistakes of the League of Nations while building on lessons learned from the Washington Conference and the Pan-American Union. Thus, he urged avoiding strict commitments, including small nations in the Security Council, attending to French sensitivities, recognizing the Monroe Doctrine, and utilizing the World Court to resolve disputes. He also repeated the warning that he had

Figure 12.1. *Chief Justice and Mrs. Charles Evans Hughes Attending a Judiciary Reception at the White House, January 4, 1940,* Harris and Ewing. Library of Congress, Prints and Photographs Division.

given concerning the League. Although the UN could provide "a beacon in a darkened world," he noted that organizations are not solutions in themselves "unless they are infused by good will and permeated by a spirit of reasonableness." The practical idealist spoke.[8]

Hughes wanted to put his own life in order. While collecting his papers, working on his autobiographical notes, and spending many hours with biographer Merlo J. Pusey, his primary occupation was as a family man. Above all, he relished every moment with Antoinette. They took walks, traveled, and lived for each other. When she underwent surgery in 1941, he was driven to and from the Johns Hopkins hospital daily. On every anniversary, he declared his love in a note or a poem. For their fifty-fifth in 1943, he wrote: "Dearest—How precious are these years! Each one draws us closer together as in loving companionship. . . . *You are all in all to me.*" For her eightieth birthday, he penned a poem in appreciation for having "climbed the hill together" and "now that we are going down on the other side, we find the slope gentle and beautiful." He fully expected that they would "go hand in hand—in the eighties" (see figure 12.1).[9]

It was not to be. During the summer of 1945, Antoinette experienced heart spasms that led to debilitating weakness and fainting spells. One collapse required hospitalization for several weeks, after which she was nursed at home. By October, Antoinette could not feed herself or speak. By November, the situation was dire and she died on December 6th, a day after their fifty-seventh anniversary. The moment was heartbreaking. When the nurse told Hughes that Antoinette was fading, he rushed upstairs, found her unconscious, and, for the third time in his life, lost control of his emotions. Overcome and barely able to speak, he called his daughter and all three children arrived right away. After regaining his composure, Hughes made funeral arrangements and issued a statement to the press. Reflecting his stature, the Pennsylvania Railroad provided a special funeral car and a separate car for the family on the trip from Washington, DC to New York City. Antoinette was buried in Woodlawn Cemetery, a setting, he said, that "was fit for a queen, and she was a queen."[10]

Antoinette's passing created a void that could never be filled. Their living room remained untouched and he was often depressed. When his children urged him to move to New York City to be closer to them, he explained, "I prefer to live here. It is your mother's memorial." Yet, Hughes was resilient and insisted that "you can always make yourself think of something else." Daily newspapers were supplemented by books in history, philosophy, and biography. He still quoted Shakespeare, Goethe, and Schiller. And he still wrote silly poems. When someone asked him for a lock of hair, he told his daughter, Catherine:

> Well, here is a true friend,
> He wants a lock of my hair.
> But I am sorry to say
> I have none I can spare.
> So much love, Father.

Winters were spent in Florida with one daughter; summers on Cape Cod with another. There he delighted in his five-year-old granddaughter Tibby. They took walks, played make-believe, created stories, and sang songs. Letters to his other children were inscribed "from Tibbyland." Once at bedtime, she announced, "I'm the Chief Justice now, and I'm not going to bed." Taken aback, Hughes firmly responded, "I'm sorry, young lady, but I'm still the Chief Justice and you are going to bed."[11]

When Hughes turned eighty-five on April 11, 1947, his son, who now argued cases before the US Supreme Court, hosted a family birthday party and President Harry Truman called with congratulations. Hughes knew he had been "the luckiest man in the world. I've had everything. I've drunk the wine of life to the bottom of the glass." However, he sensed that "now only the dregs are left." Six months later, his duodenal ulcer started bleeding again. Recuperating for all of January, he could not go to Florida until February. By then, he was twelve pounds lighter and suffered from a weak heart. His system did not tolerate the appropriate medications. When he returned to Washington in April, he needed to stay in bed with two nurses on hand. His children were attentive and he appreciated every kindness for "the old relic." That summer he insisted on going to Cape Cod by train against doctor's orders, accompanied by one nurse. When Hughes learned that the doctor secretly sat in a separate car, he protested against "babying." However, he soon developed uremic poisoning and congestive heart failure. An oxygen tent brought temporary relief but could not prevent the inevitable. Charles Evans Hughes fell into a coma and passed away on August 27, 1948.[12]

Flags were lowered to half-mast in Washington, DC, and New York State. Again, the Pennsylvania Railroad provided private cars for the coffin and the family as they traveled back to New York City. The memorial service was held in his old religious home, Riverside Church, presided over by his old pastor, the Reverend Dr. Harry Emerson Fosdick. The church was filled to capacity by sixteen hundred dignitaries. True to Hughes's penchant for efficiency, the service was only twenty minutes long. Nonetheless, it captured his spirit and legacy. The Reverend Fosdick proclaimed Hughes "integrity personified," a man who, unlike his stern image, was so "warm and friendly" that "we admired him but loved him too." Above all, he was a man to whom "real nobility meant service; real religion meant to do justice with love and mercy and to walk humbly with his God." The coffin was followed by Governor Thomas E. Dewey, Chief Justice Fred M. Vinson, Associate Justices Frankfurter, Roberts, Black, and Jackson. Hughes was buried beside Antoinette in Woodlawn Cemetery.[13]

In addition to his children and his secretary, Hughes's bequests reflected his lifelong commitments to education and the law. They included Amherst, Barnard, Brown, Colgate, and Vassar, plus the New York City Bar Association, the New York County Lawyers Association, and the Legal Aid Society. Barnard named a building after him and Colgate created the Charles Evans Hughes Chair of Government and Jurisprudence, representing two of his careers. Similarly, the National Conference of Christians and Jews marked his importance as a founder by establishing the Charles Evans Hughes Gold Medal for "courageous leadership in governmental, civic and human affairs." His daughter, Catherine, maintained a lifelong commitment (derived from both parents) to overcoming racial prejudice through work at the United Negro College Fund and the NAACP. In addition, the family formed a Charles Evans Hughes Memorial Foundation, which recently sunset after an impressive seventy-five-year run. The foundation promoted human rights, education, other social causes, and the Legal Aid Society. It honored Hughes's conviction that "when we lose the right to be different, we lose the privilege to be free."[14]

The many testimonials offered in Hughes's memory reflected each of his careers. Called "one of America's greatest public servants," he was lauded as an exemplary lawyer, determined reformer, efficient administrator, skilled diplomat, and outstanding chief justice. Admirers represented the many organizations with which he was affiliated on local, national, and international levels. They included legal associations, universities, unions, civic and reform organizations plus foreign delegations from Africa, Europe, and Latin America. Contradicting Hughes's cold image, several spoke of him as a kind, considerate friend. According to the New York State Bar Association, "An outward appearance of austerity was relieved by his graciousness and warmth of his human understanding and sympathy." Everyone extolled his dedication to justice and world peace. Walter White, executive secretary of the NAACP, recalled his 1918 speech opposing lynching. Judge Learned Hand praised him as "one who helped keep alive and pass on that ordered freedom without which mankind must lapse into savagery." Herbert Hoover commemorated "so magnificent a mind, so elevated a character, and one so determined to serve."[15]

When Hughes retired from the Supreme Court, New York Senator Robert F. Wagner observed that "every phase of this great transitional era bears the mark of your labors." Indeed, as governor, secretary of state, and Supreme Court justice, Hughes wrestled with the most compelling national and international problems of the first half of the twentieth century. Yet, he did not seek any of his positions, resigned when he felt his job was done, made other contributions while out of office, and returned to office when summoned. Not consumed by power and self-aggrandizement, Hughes was a public servant in the best sense of the term. In his 1931 eulogy of William H. Taft, Hughes revealed what law professor Paul Freund called "a mellow humanity." Accepting the fleeting nature of human enterprise, Hughes acknowledged that "the best endeavors, striking as they may be in their immediate aspect, will soon form the background of another picture." Nonetheless, he said, "without illusion and with steady will, we continue our task."[16]

Edwin McElwain, his former law clerk, suggested that Hughes (and therefore the nation) benefitted from his unique professional trajectory because each career broadened his understanding and sharpened his skills for the next career, culminating as chief justice. In their 1941 letter, the brethren thanked Hughes for that "tireless . . . single-minded devotion . . . that unflagging energy and painstaking care with which you have guided our deliberations with thoroughness and dispatch." They recognized that his leadership was the result of "all the resources gained from many years of eminent public and professional service" to the country. Similarly, law professor William G. Ross concluded that "the political acumen that Hughes acquired as governor, secretary of state, and presidential nominee, served him well during the court packing crisis."[17]

Hughes faced both success and failure. Accordingly, his struggles, accomplishments, and defeats tested the vitality of democracy and reflected the hazards of change. In New York State, Hughes exposed corruption, fought bossism, and pursued governmental accountability. His bold, ambitious agenda addressed many of the negative results of industrialism involving workers, public health, cities, criminal justice, and conservation. However, as governor and as presidential candidate, his political independence proved problematic. In 1916, he lacked the requisite political skills and crusading message that made him a "fighting governor." In that role, however, he proved that governors could be progressive and effective in addressing modern problems.

As secretary of state, Hughes used treaties to secure postwar peace and achieve the world's first voluntary arms limitation agreement. It lasted for a decade but could not prevent another war. He modernized the Monroe Doctrine and promoted Pan-Americanism, albeit qualified by practical problems and economic entanglements. Nonetheless, his tenure marked significant redefinitions of American foreign policy resulting from its new role as the world's wealthiest, most powerful nation. He negotiated not only the domestic tensions created by resistance to that expanded role but also the complications of postwar international relations. Although many of the problems he confronted were not and still have not been resolved, Hughes moved American foreign policy into the twentieth century with principles and strategies that remain relevant today.

On the Supreme Court, Hughes was instrumental in the shift from legal formalism to legal realism, especially regarding the interstate commerce clause, due process, contracts, and civil liberties. Despite his concern for stability and continuity, he supported sociological jurisprudence, judicial restraint, and cooperative federalism as part of adjusting the Constitution to contemporary conditions. At the same time, he deflected history's most serious threat to the separation of powers, FDR's court packing bill.

In every career (including 1916) efficiency was Hughes's mantra—a reflection of his progressivism as well as his perfectionism. But it was perfectionism with a heart and a sincere desire to improve the lot of humankind. In all three careers, he pursued structural reform in order to meet the needs of a rapidly changing, complex nation in a rapidly changing, volatile world. In all three careers (except 1916), Hughes took strong, often controversial, positions, managed opposition, and secured significant change. He wielded power without succumbing to its temptations.

Of course, Hughes's efforts to cope with reality were often circumscribed by reality. Bossism, financial corruption, domestic isolationism, international antagonisms, economic imperialism, and constitutional conservatism complicated and sometimes prevented progress. So did his refusal to play party politics, his support of US economic interests in Latin America, and his reluctance to overturn precedent. Hughes was never unrealistic about these limitations. Rather, he made conscious choices based on his principles and strategic assessments, which always defied neat labels.

Obstacles and disappointments notwithstanding, Hughes rejected "brooding" about the past and kept embracing "new activities." He grew over time. After excelling as a prosecutor, he acquired the political skills needed to implement his progressive political agenda as governor. Although they failed him as presidential candidate, he went on to develop the diplomatic skills essential for healing a divided world and leading a divided Court.

Through it all, Hughes's progressive commitments testified to his faith in reason, belief in democracy, and respect for law as the bulwark of civilized society. A perennial teacher, his spoken and written style reflected a no-nonsense emphasis on clarity and core principles. According to New York State Supreme Court Associate Justice Joseph M. Proskauer, "The adjective and the adverb were sparsely used; the verbs and nouns stood erect." Neither radical nor reactionary, Hughes was a practical idealist, a structural reformer who valued continuity as well as change. For him, improving existing systems was the best way to strengthen them.[18]

Not being tied to any single panacea, strategy, or doctrine enabled Hughes to bolster his idealism through realism and flexibility. Accordingly, his perpetual search for balance between past, present, and future, between the desirable and the "practicable," was a source of strength, not weakness. As one eulogist put it, "He was thinker and doer, scholar and politician. Absolute master he was of the law, both as law written in books and law as lived through functioning social institutions." Across three different careers, "his efficiency was superb, but it was tempered by a zealous humanitarianism." Most important, Hughes "knew when to reform as well as when to preserve. His understanding encompassed the ultimate possibilities as well as the practical probabilities."[19]

On the centennial of Hughes's birth in 1962, the US Postal Service issued a commemorative stamp in his honor and a memorial plaque was unveiled at his birthplace, Glens Falls, New York. At Columbia Law School, over six hundred people attended the dedication ceremony of a bust. Chief Justice Earl Warren praised Hughes for "creative statesmanship" in defusing the court packing plan and redefining "the role of the court in the new social and economic climate" that shaped its future. Speaking at Colgate later that day, Warren highlighted Hughes's influence on "the administration of justice to rich and poor" and to upholding the highest judicial standards. Hughes set equally high standards for politics and international relations (see figure 12.2).[20]

Because Hughes's three careers placed him at the center of the nation's responses to industrialism and world war, they gave him the responsibility and opportunity to redefine policy priorities in a pivotal pe-

Figure 12.2. Commemorative postage stamp, 1862–1962, United States Postal Service. Gift of Jeanne Robeson.

riod. As governor, secretary of state, and Supreme Court justice, Hughes understood the need for change. He was instrumental in the quest for clean, responsive state government, international leadership, and constitutional flexibility. In the process, he wrestled with party politics, dual federalism, isolationism, hemispheric hegemony, and legal precedent. Sometimes cautious, sometimes bold, sometimes inconsistent, his complexity reflected the complexity of the transitional era in which he lived and led. Hughes's successes and failures exposed the complications of America's maturing identity in the twentieth century.

Hughes's shortcomings did not eradicate his significance then or now. If his contributions were set within and limited by the context of one man and one era, they also endured beyond both. After all, we still seek more democracy, justice, accountability, and inclusiveness in our politics, judicial system, and world community. We still try to balance change with continuity, reason and the rule of law with humanitarianism. We still try to adapt our principles to fluid realities, to be practical idealists and structural reformers. Nobody ever said it would be easy, particularly not Charles Evans Hughes. That is why he was so widely admired in his own time and offers a model for constructive leadership in our time. His contributions to the modernization of politics, foreign policy, and the Constitution reflected not just the challenges of his era but the remaining challenges we face in the perennial pursuit of democracy, peace, and justice.

Notes

Abbreviations

PEOPLE

RHF	Robert H. Fuller
CEH	Charles Evans Hughes
WGH	Warren G. Harding
HCL	Henry Cabot Lodge
HP	Herbert Parsons
FDR	Franklin Delano Roosevelt
OWH	Oliver Wendell Holmes Jr.
TR	Theodore Roosevelt
ER	Elihu Root
WHT	William Howard Taft

NEWSPAPERS

BDE	*The Brooklyn Daily Eagle*
NYS	*The New York Sun*
NYT	*The New York Times*
WH	*The Washington Herald*
WP	*The Washington Post*
WT	*The Washington Times*

MANUSCRIPT COLLECTIONS

CUOHP	Columbia University Oral History Project, Rare Books and Manuscripts Library
LC	Library of Congress
NYPL	New York Public Library

PUBLISHED WORKS

AN	Charles Evans Hughes, *The Autobiographical Notes of Charles Evans Hughes*, ed. David J. Danelski and Joseph S. Tulchin (Harvard University Press, 1973).
AP	Charles Evans Hughes, *The Addresses and Papers of Charles Evans Hughes, 1906–1916* (G. P Putman's Sons, 1916).

CEHABH Alpheus Thomas Mason, "Charles Evans Hughes: An Appeal to the Bar of History," *Vanderbilt Law Review* 6 (Dec. 1952): 1–21.
CEHADS Dexter Perkins, *Charles Evans Hughes and American Democratic Statesmanship* (Greenwood Press,1956).
CEHCJ Richard D. Friedman, "Charles Evans Hughes as Chief Justice: The Complexities of Moderation," PhD diss., Oxford, 1978.
CEHI Betty Glad, *Charles Evans Hughes and the Illusions of Innocence* (Urbana: University of Illinois Press, 1966).
CEHMP Merlo J. Pusey, *Charles Evans Hughes* (Columbia University Press, 1963). Originally published 1951.
CEHP Robert F. Wesser, *Charles Evans Hughes: Politics and Reform in New York* (Cornell University Press, 1967).
CEHS William Lynn Ransom, *Charles Evans Hughes, The Statesman* (E. P. Dutton, 1916).
CEHSC Samuel Hendel, *Charles Evans Hughes and the Supreme Court* (Columbia University Press, 1951).
CP Charles Evans Hughes, *Conditions of Progress in Democratic Government* (Yale University Press, 1910).
OWHDH Mark Tushnet, *The Oliver Wendell Holmes Devise History of the Supreme Court*, vol. 11 (Cambridge University Press, 2022).
PP Charles Evans Hughes, *The Pathway of Peace: Representative Addresses Delivered during His Term as Secretary of State, 1921–1925* (Harper & Brothers, 1925).
SC Charles Evans Hughes, *The Supreme Court of the United States* (Columbia University Press, 1928).

Introduction

1. Felix Frankfurter, "The Impact of Hughes," *NYT*, November 18, 1951. See also Joel Richard Paul, *Without Precedent: Chief Justice John Marshall and His Times* (Riverhead Books, 2018), 2.

2. Frankfurter, "Impact of Hughes"; *AN*, xxviii–xxix; Lewis L. Gould, *The First Modern Clash over Federal Power: Wilson Versus Hughes in the Presidential Election of 1916* (University Press of Kansas, 2020), 42; *CEHADS*, 171.

3. Melvin I. Urofsky, *Louis D. Brandeis, a Life* (Shocken Books, 2009), x.

4. James T. Kloppenberg, *Uncertain Victory: Social Democracy and Progressivism in American and European Thought, 1870–1920* (Oxford University Press, 1986), 4–6, 153, 162, 194, 267, 361–362, 413; James T. Kloppenberg, *Toward Democracy: The Struggle for Self-Rule in European and American Thought* (Oxford University Press, 2016), 4–10.

5. *CEHMP*, vi–ix; Laura Kalman, *FDR's Gambit: The Court Packing Fight and the Rise of Legal Liberalism* (Oxford University Press, 2022), 281; Edward S. Corwin, "Review of *Charles Evans Hughes* by Merlo J. Pusey," *American Political Science Review* 46 (Dec. 1952): 1167–1173; Fred Harvey Harrington, "Review of *Charles Evans Hughes* by Merlo J. Pusey," *Hispanic American Historical Review* 32 (Aug.

1952): 426–427; Samuel J. Konefsky, "Review of *Charles Evans Hughes* by Merlo J. Pusey," *Yale Law Journal* 61 (May 1952): 765–775; *CEHABH*, 18–19; Arthur S. Link, "Review of *Charles Evans Hughes* by Merlo J. Pusey," *Annals of the American Academy of Political and Social Science* 280 (March 1952): 172–173.

6. *CEHABH*, 6; *CEHS*, 10–13; CEHSC, 64–67; Aaron I, Abell, "Review of *Charles Evans Hughes and the Supreme Court* by Samuel Hendel," *Review of Politics* 13 (Oct. 1951): 516–518.

7. *CEHADS*. xiii, xvii, 139, 190; William E. Leuchtenburg, "Review of *Charles Evans Hughes and American Democratic Statesmanship* by Dexter Perkins," *Mississippi Valley Historical Review* 43 (Dec. 1956): 512–513.

8. *CEHABH*, 1–19; *CEHI*, 1–7; James MacGregor Burns, *Leadership* (Harper & Row, 1978), 60–63; Richard W. Leopold, "Review of *Charles Evans Hughes and the Illusions of Innocence: A Study in American Diplomacy* by Betty Glad," *Political Science Quarterly* 83 (June 1968): 301–302; Thomas Buckley, "Review of *Charles Evans Hughes and the Illusions of Innocence: A Study in American Diplomacy* by Betty Glad," *Journal of American History* 54 (June 1967): 187–188; Arthur A. Ekirch Jr., "Review of *Charles Evans Hughes and the Illusions of Innocence: A Study in American Diplomacy* by Betty Glad," *History of Education Quarterly* 8 (Spring 1968): 139–140.

9. *CEHP*, 340–347; Burns, *Leadership*, 69–181; Leonard Dinnerstein, "Review of *Charles Evans Hughes; Politics and Reform in New York, 1905–1910* by Robert F. Wesser," *New York History* 49 (Jan. 1968): 100–101; J. Joseph Hutmacher, "Review of *Charles Evans Hughes: Politics and Reform in New York, 1905–1910* by Robert F. Wesser," *American Historical Review* 73 (June 1968): 1667–1668.

10. *AN*, xi–xxix. See also *CEHABH*, 1–21; Edwin W, Tucker, "Review of *The Autobiographical Notes of Charles Evans Hughes* by David J. Danelski and Joseph S. Tulchin," *American Historical Review* 79 (June 1974): 896–897.

11. *AN*, xxix, 2. See also *CEHABH*, 1–21.

12. "Hughes Asks Nation to Join World Court," *NYT*, November 11, 1925.

13. John A. Garraty, *Henry Cabot Lodge, a Biography* (Alfred A. Knopf, 1953), vii.

Chapter 1: Becoming Hughes, 1862–1906

1. *CP*, 24–25. See also *AN*, 1–14, *CEHMP*, 1–12.
2. *CEHMP*, 12.
3. *CEHMP*, 3.
4. *CEHMP*, 3–4.
5. *AN*, 11 and 11n22.
6. *AN*, 27. See also *CEHMP*, 11–16.
7. *AN*, 24, 27, 28. See also *CEHMP*, 17–33.
8. *CEHMP*, 38–39. See also *CEHI*, 21–27.
9. *AN*, 34–35; *CEHMP*, 38. See also "Home," Delta Upsilon, accessed September 23, 2024, https://www.deltau.org.
10. *AN*, 35; *CEHMP*, 55.

11. *CEHMP*, 48–49, *AN*, 45. See also *CEHI*, 21–47.

12. *AN*, 28. See also *CEHI*, 11–20, 21–43, 92–95.

13. Richard D. Friedman, "Charles Evans Hughes as a International Lawyer," *American Society of International Law* 90 (1996): 144; Richard D. Friedman, "Governor on the Bench: Charles Evans Hughes as Associate Justice," *Harvard Law Review* 89 (March, 1976): 961.

14. *AN*, 29–48; *CEHMP*, 30–38, 42, 43–52, 54, 61–62; *CP*, 11.

15. *AN*, 49–52; *CEHMP*, 59–66.

16. *CEHMP*, 60.

17. *AN*, 53–54.

18. *AN*, 57–74; *CEHMP*, 69–73; Edwin McElwain, "The Business of the Supreme Court as Conducted by Chief Justice Hughes," *Harvard Law Review* 63 (Nov. 1949): 6n2.

19. Ida M. Tarbell, "How About Hughes?" *American Magazine*, March 1908, 450–464, CEH Manuscript Collection, NYPL, box 5, 462. See also *CEHMP*, 75–76; McElwain, "Business," 6–7, 17.

20. *AN*, 80–81; *CEHMP*, 83–88.

21. *OWHDH*, 15; *AN*, 88–89; *CEHMP*, 88, 94–96.

22. *AN*, 95n15; *CEHMP*, 104.

23. *CEHMP*, 101–103.

24. *AN*, 100; Burton J. Hendrick, "Governor Hughes," *McClure's Magazine*, March 1908, 521–536, 670–681; CEH Manuscript Collection, NYPL, box 5, 527; McElwain, "Business," 10. See also *CEHMP*, 115–118.

25. Tarbell, "How About Hughes?" 463. See also *AN*, 114–118; *CEHMP*, 118–131.

26. *CEHMP*, 371, 775.

27. CEH, "Oliver Wendell Holmes at His Ninetieth Birthday," *Phi Beta Kappa Key* 7 (May 1931): 781–783; Stephen Budiansky, *Oliver Wendel Holmes: A Life in Law, War and Ideas* (W. W. Norton, 2019), 448.

28. *AN*, xii, xix–xx; *CEHMP*, 105, 118, 125, 406, 414; Felix Frankfurter, "The Impact of Charles Evans Hughes," *NYT*, November 18, 1951; Erman J. Ridgway, "Hughes," *Everybody's Magazine*, March 1908, 356, CEH Manuscript Collection, *NYPL*, box 5; *CEHADS*, xv.

29. *CEHI*, 108–114. See also *CEHMP*, 94–95, 105, 120, 125.

30. *CEHMP*, 98–99, 120–131, 778.

31. Robert H. Fuller, "Hughes as Governor," 344, *AN*, 112, 113, 344; *CEHMP*, 117; Lloyd C. Griscom, *The Reminiscences of Lloyd C. Griscom, CUOHP*, 90, 94.

32. Frankfurter, "Impact"; Felix Frankfurter, "The Administrative Side of Chief Justice Hughes," *Harvard Law Review* 63 (Nov. 1949): 1–4.

33. *AN*, xxi; *CEHMP*, 189, 635; Ridgway, "Hughes," 354–363, 356; L. T. Michenor to C. I. Long, September 5, 1908, Chester I. Long Manuscript Collection, Kansas Historical Society.

34. *AN*, xii–xiii, xviii, xxix, 3–11; *CEHMP*, 175, 221, 415; *CEHI*, 108–110; Griscom, *Reminiscences*, 85–89; Hugh R. Wilson, *Diplomat Between Wars* (Longmans, Green, 1941), 162.

35. *AN*, xix; *CEHI*, 109; Herbert Hoover, *The Memoirs of Herbert Hoover: The Cabinet and the Presidency, 1920–1933* (Macmillan, 1952), 58.

36. H. Stuart Hughes, "They Don't Make Them like That Any More," *New York Review of Books*, May 30, 1974.

37. William T. Gossett, "The Human Side of Chief Justice Hughes," *American Bar Association Journal* 59 (Dec. 1973): 1413.

38. *AN*, 25–26; *CEHMP*, 57.

39. *CEHMP*, 110–112; *AN*, 111–113; CEH, "Roger Williams," *PP*, 267–273.

40. *AN*, 110–113.

41. CEH, "Address at the Union League Club Meeting," February 22, 1908, *AP*, 108–113.

42. *CEHMP*, 605; Hendrick, "Governor Hughes," 527.

43. CEH, "Speech before the Middlesex Club, Boston," February 12, 1907, CEH Manuscript Collection, NYPL, box 1. See also *AN*, 112–113; *CEHMP*, 110–111, Hendrick, "Governor Hughes," 527.

44. Michael E. McGerr, *A Fierce Discontent: The Rise and Fall of the Progressive Movement in America* (Oxford University Press, 2003), 183.

45. CEH, "Speech at the Meeting in the Interest of Tuskegee Institute," January 17, 1908, *AP*, 292–298; "Mrs. Hughes Dies," *NYT*, December 7, 1945.

46. CEH, "Address at Union College Commencement," June 10, 1909, CEH Manuscript Collection, NYPL, box 2.

47. CEH, "Address at the Jamestown Exposition," July 5,1907, *AP*, 238; Thomas T. Thalken, "The Papers of Charles Evans Hughes," *Quarterly Journal of Current Acquisitions* 11 (Nov. 1953): 6. See also *CP*, 32, 120.

48. *CP*, 11–15.

49. *CP*, 12–15.

50. *AN*, 110.

51. *AN*, 120; *CEHMP*, 134.

52. *AN*, 132–139; *CEHP*, 28–32; Richard L McCormick, *From Realignment to Reform: Political Change in New York State, 1893–1910* (Cornell University Press, 1979), 194–197.

53. *CEHMP*, 142. See also *AN*, 121–131; *CEHP*, 41–48.

54. Mark Sullivan, *Our Times, the United States, 1900–1925*, vol. 3 (Charles Scribner's Sons, 1933), 55; Tarbell, "How About Hughes?" 455.

55. Hendrick, "Governor Hughes," 531; *CEHP*, 45.

56. *CEHMP*, 161; Oswald Garrison Villard, *Fighting Years: The Memoirs of a Liberal Editor* (Harcourt, Brace, 1939), 184; "The Pied Piper of Life Insurance," *BDE*, December 8, 1905.

57. Ridgway, "Hughes" 58; CEH, "Reply to Committee Appointed to Notify Him of His Nomination for Mayor of New York City," October 9, 1905, *AP*, 49–54. See also *CEHMP*, 148–151; Richard l. McCormick, *The Party Period and Public Policy: American Politics from the Age of Jackson to the Progressive Era* (Oxford University Press, 1986), 197–202.

58. McGerr, *Fierce Discontent*, 174. See also *CEHMP*, 165–168; McCormick, *Realignment*, 212–218; Zechariah Chafee Jr., "Charles Evans Hughes," *Proceedings of the American Philosophical Society* 93 (June 10, 1949): 267–269.

59. McCormick, 217; McGerr, 174. See also Richard L. McCormick, "The Discovery that Business Corrupts Politics: A Reappraisal of the Origins of Progressivism," *American Historical Review* 86 (April 1981): 260–264; Richard L. McCormick, "Prelude to Progressivism: The Transformation of New York State Politics, 1890–1910," *New York History* 59 (July 1978): 270.

60. CEH, "Speech before Middlesex Club. See also Melvin I. Urofsky, *Louis D. Brandeis, a Life* (Shocken Books, 2009), 159–161; Michael E. Parrish, "Review of *The Autobiographical Notes of Charles Evans Hughes*," *American Journal of Legal History* 19 (Jan. 1975): 83.

61. "Hughes, the Man," *BDE*, November 12, 1905; *CEHMP*, 165, 170.

62. Hendrick, "Governor Hughes," 536.

63. Frankfurter, "Impact."

64. *CEHABH*, 4, 6; C. Herman Pritchett, "Review of Charles Evans Hughes by Merlo J. Pusey," *Virginia Quarterly Review* 28 (Spring 1952): 203.

Chapter 2: Becoming Governor, 1906–1908

1. "Hughes Keynote: Action, not Finesse," *NYT*, November 24, 1906; James Bryce, *The American Commonwealth*, vol. 1 (Commonwealth Publishing, 1908), 84–92; Robert F. Wesser, "Theodore Roosevelt, Reform and Reorganization of the Republican Party in New York, 1901–1906," *New York History* 46 (1965): 231.

2. Bryce, *The American Commonwealth*, 84–92; James Bryce to CEH, June 15, 1907, James Bryce to Alton B. Parker, February 14, 1911, CEH Manuscript Collection, *LC*; *CEHMP*, 189–190.

3. CEH, "Speech at the Banquet of the Albany Republican Organization," February 27, 1907, *AP*, 204–208; CEH, "Speech at the Dinner of the Republican Club of the City of New York," October 18, 1907, *AP*, 77–79; *CP*, 75.

4. *CP*, 90, 92, 98, 100–101, 109; John D. Buenker, *Urban Liberalism and Progressive Reform* (W.W. Norton, 1973), 2; CEH, "Address at the Union League Club Meeting in the Auditorium at Chicago," February 22, 1908, *AP*, 120.

5. *CP*, 8. See also *CEHMP*, 268–270; *CEHI*, 66–86; *CEHADS*, 3–28; *CEHP*, 344–347.

6. CEH, "Address at the Jamestown Exposition on Jefferson Memorial Day, July 5,1907," *AP*, 239; CEH, "Address at the Union League Club Meeting in the Auditorium at Chicago," February 22, 1908, *AP*, 123. See also *CEHI*, 92–93; *CEHP*, 102–106; Robert F. Wesser, "Charles Evans Hughes and the Urban Sources of Political Progressivism," *New York Historical Society Quarterly* 50 (Oct. 1966): 365–400; Wesser, "Theodore Roosevelt," 230–252; Richard Hofstadter, *The Age of Reform from Bryan to F.D.R.* (Random House, 1955), 131–173, 174–198; J. Joseph Hutmacher, "Charles Evans Hughes and Charles Francis Murphy: The Metamorphosis of Progressivism," *New York History* 46 (1965): 25–40.

7. CEH, "Address Before the Republican Club of the City of New York," January 31, 1908, *AP*, 91–92; CEH, "Speech to the Buffalo Chamber of Com-

merce," April 18, 1907, *AP*, 172–173, 175; CEH, "Address to the City Club," February 2, 1908, CEH Manuscript Collection, NYPL, box 1; CEH, "Address at Jamestown Exposition on Jefferson Memorial Day," *AP*, 234–235, 239; *CP*, 28; *CEHMP*, 181.

8. CEH, "Address, Union League Club," *AP*, 117; Richard I. McCormick, *From Realignment to Reform: Political Change in New York State, 1893–1910* (Cornell University Press, 1979), 227.

9. *CEHMP*, 172.

10. TR to HP, December 20, 1905, HP Manuscript Collection, CUOHP, box 1. See also Wesser, "Theodore Roosevelt," 230–252.

11. CEH, "Speech in Response to Formal Notification of His Nomination as the Republican Candidate for Governor, at the Republican Club, New York City," October 3, 1906, *AP*, 54–64; *CEHMP*, 173. See also *CEHP*, 61–69; Robert H. Fuller, "Governor Hughes and the Bosses," CEH Manuscript Collection, NYPL, box 1; TR to HP, September 17, 1906; CEH to HP, September 27, 1906; TR to HP, October 14, 1906, HP Manuscript Collection, CUOHP, box 3; HP to Dr. Parkhurst, December 16, 1906, HP Manuscript Collection, CUOHP, box 6; "A Nomination by Unanimous Vote," *BDE*, September 26, 1906.

12. *CEHMP*, 173–174; Herbert Croly, *The Promise of American Life* (Capricorn Books, 1964) 163–167. See also David Nasaw, *The Chief: The Life of William Randolph Hearst* (Houghton Mifflin, 2000), 186–190.

13. Nasaw, *Chief*, 194–201; McCormick, *Realignment*, 206–209; Irwin Yellowitz, *Labor and the Progressive Movement in New York State, 1897–1916* (Cornell University Press, 1965), 188–196.

14. CEH, "Speech at the National Arbitration and Peace Congress, New York City," April 15, 1907, *AP*, 203–220; TR to CEH, October 5 and 25, 1906; TR to HCL, October 16, 1906, *Letters of Theodore Roosevelt*, ed. Elting Morison et al. (Harvard University Press, 1951–1954), 443–444, 459–460, 468–469.

15. Nasaw, *Chief*, 196, 205–210.

16. *CP*, 22–23, 30.

17. *CEHMP*, 176; *CEHP*, 86–89. See also Maury Thompson, *The Animated Feather Duster* (Maury Thompson, 2018).

18. CEH, "Speech in Response to Nomination," *AP*, 55–61–63.

19. TR to ER, August 8, 1906; TR to CEH, October 4, 1906; TR to HCL, October 16, 1906; *Letters of TR*, 369, 442–444, 459–460; CEH to TR, October 7, 1906; TR to HP, October 8 1906, HP Manuscript Collection, CUHP, box 3; TR to CEH, October 4 and 5, 1906, CEH Manuscript Collection, LC; Lewis L. Gould, *The Presidency of Theodore Roosevelt* (University Press of Kansas, 1991), 89–90; Lewis L. Gould, "Theodore Roosevelt, Woodrow Wilson, and the Emergence of the Modern Presidency: An Introductory Essay," *Presidential Studies Quarterly* 19 (Winter 1989): 44.

20. "Political Postcard," 1906, LC, Prints and Photographs Division Digital ID 19038. See also *CEHMP*, 176–178; *CEHP*, 89–93; Daniel T. Rodgers, *Atlantic Crossings: Social Politics in a Progressive Age* (Harvard University Press, 1998), 112–130, 130–159; TR to HP, September 17, 1906; CEH to HP, September 27, 1906; TR to HP, October 10 and 14, 1906; HP to TR, October 15, 1906, HP

Manuscript Collection, CUOHP, box 3; TR to CEH, October 2, 1906; CEH to TR, October 4, 1906; CEH to TR, October 7, 1906; TR to CEH, October 17, 1906, CEH Manuscript Collection, *LC.*

21. *CEHMP*, 178–180; *CEHP*, 96–98; Nasaw, *Chief*, 210–212; Philip C. Jessup, *Elihu Root*, vol. 2 (Dodd Mead 1938), 113–123; HP to TR, October 15, 1906, HP Manuscript Collection, CUOHP, box 3; Croly, *The Promise of American Life*, 163–167.

22. *CEHMP*, 180. See also *CEHP*, 98–101, 222–227; Nasaw, *Chief*, 212–213; Yellowitz, *Labor*, 204–215; "Hughes Wins," *NYT*, November 7, 1906.

23. "Looking for a Gardener Himself," *Minneapolis Journal*, September 30, 1906.

24. *CEHMP*, 181–186; CEH, "Speech at the Amen Corner Dinner, Fifth Avenue Hotel," February 2, 1907, CEH Manuscript Collection, NYPL, box 1. See also *AN*, 140.

25. *AN*, 147–148; *CEHMP*, 194–197, 234–235; *CEHP*, 163–166.

26. *CP*, 76; CEH, "Inaugural Address, Albany, NY, January 1, 1907," *AP*, 63–69. See also *AN*, 134–135; *CEHP*, 108–113.

27. *CEHP*, 148–152; Martin L. Fausold, *James W. Wadsworth, Jr., the Gentleman from New York* (Syracuse University Press, 1975), 41–55, 56–67, 71–74; Peter Eisenstadt, ed., *The Encyclopedia of New York State* (Syracuse University Press, 2005),1647; James W. Wadsworth, The *Reminiscences of James W. Wadsworth, 1952, CUOHP*, 54–64; Burton J. Hendrick, "Governor Hughes," *McClure's Magazine*, March 1908, CEH Manuscript Collection, NYPL, box 5, 506–508; TR to HP, December 20, 1905, HP Manuscript Collection, CUOHP, box 1.

28. *CEHP*, 7–17, 113; McCormick, *Realignment*, 69–84.

29. *CEHP*, 113, 131–132. See also Charles F. Milliken, *Ontario County, New York, and Its People: Geneological and Biographical*, vol. 7 (Lewis Historical Publishing, 1911), 338–340.

30. WB to CEH, November 26, 1906; CEH to WB, December 3, 1906, CEH Manuscript Collection, LC; *CEHP*, 105–106, 257; Wadsworth, *Reminiscences*, 89–91; See also Hendrick, "Governor Hughes."

31. Howard N. Fuller, "Albany County," in Charles Elliott Fitch, *Official NY from Cleveland to Hughes*, vol. 3 (Hurd Publishing, 1911), 56–63; Robert A. Slayton, *Empire Statesman: The Rise and Redemption of Al Smith.* (Free Press, 2001), 109; Frank S., Robinson, *Machine Politics: A Study of Albany's O'Connell's* (Transaction Books, 1977), 8–13. See also Hendrick, "Governor Hughes," 506–508; Eisenstadt, *Encyclopedia*, 151.

32. CEH, "Speech at Amen Corner;" *CEHMP*, 181; *CEHP*, 102–104.

33. *CEHMP*, 185.

34. Croly, *Promise*, 336–337; *CP*, 41, 51. See also Jeffrey M. Stonecash, Mark D. Brewer, R. Eric Peterson, and McGee Young, "Politics, Alfred Smith, and Increasing the Power of the New York Governor's Office," *New York History* 85 (Spring 2004): 153–158.

35. *AN*, 135–136, 147–148; HP to RHF, April 1, 1907, Parsons Manuscript Collection, CUOHP, box 5; *CP*, 46–47. See also *CEHP*, 116–119, *CEHMP*, 181–182, 186–189; Fausold, *James W. Wadsworth*, 60–61; HP to CEH, December 4,

1906; CEH to HP, December 6, 1906, HP Manuscript Collection, CUOHP, box 3; RHF to HP, April 2, 1907, HP Manuscript Collection, CUOHP, box 5.

36. *CEHMP*, 188–189. See also *CEHP*, 114–123, 163; Fausold, *James W. Wadsworth*, 61.

37. *AN*, 137.

38. Robert H. Fuller, "A Close View of Hughes," *Collection of Campaign Bulletins*, no. 4 (Aug. 30, 1916), 6–7 (Women's Committee of the National Hughes Alliance, 1916). See also *CEHP*, 126–133; HP to CEH, March 14, 1907; CEH to HP, March 18, 1907, HP Manuscript Collection, CUOHP, box 4;

39. *CEHMP*, 195–196. See also *AN*, 137–138; CEH, "Speech at the Banquet of the Utica Chamber of Commerce," April 1, 1907, *AP*, 158–168; *CEHP*, 134–140; Fausold, *James W. Wadsworth*, 62–67.

40. "President Ahearn's Defense," *NYS*, September 15, 1907; "Aldermen Reelect Ahearn," *NYS*, December 20, 1907; "More Than Honesty," *Binghamton Press*, December 12, 1907; Robert H. Fuller, *Hughes Administrative Scrapbook Newspaper Clippings*, NYPL.

41. CEH, "Address to City Club." See also: *CEHP*, 140–145; McCormick, *Realignment*, 231–233.

42. CEH, "Speech at the Glens Falls Club," April 5, 1907, *AP*, 159; CEH, "Message to the State Legislature, Jan. 2, 1907, Recommending the Passage of a Public-Service Commissions Law," *AP*, 135–145; Hendrick, "Governor Hughes," 670. See also *AN*, 141–142; CEH, "Speech at Banquet, Utica," *AP*, 145–158; *CEHADS*, 14–15; McCormick, *Realignment*, 239–241, 267–269; Stonecash, Brewer, Peterson, and Young, "Politics," 158–161.

43. *CP*, 14.

44. CEH, "Jamestown Exposition, July 5. 1907," *AP*, 233. See also Mark Sullivan, *Our Times, The United States, 1900-1925* (Charles Scribner's Sons, 1933), vol. 3, 67; Gabriel Kolko, *Railroads and Regulation, 1877–1916* (W. W. Norton, 1965), 107–126.

45. CEH, "Message to State Legislature, Jan. 2, 1907," *AP*, 139; CEH, "Speech at Banquet, Utica," *AP*, 145–158; McCormick, *Realignment*, 235–238; *CEHP*, 153–156; *CEHMP*, 201–202.

46. *CEHP*, 169; CEH, "Speech at the Jamestown Exposition, on New York Day (Oct. 10, 1907)," *AP*, 270; McCormick, 237.

47. CEH, "Speech before the Elmira Chamber of Commerce" (May 3, 1907), *AP*, 179–187.

48. McCormick, *Realignment*, 235. See also *CEHMP*, 204–209, 216; *CEHP*, 153–170; "Editorial," *Independent*, May 9, 1907, CEH Manuscript Collection, LC.

49. CEH, "Veto of the Two-Cent Fare Bill," June 11, 1907, *AP*, 192–199; "Veto of the Bill to Require an Extra Brakeman on Freight Trains," June 15, 1907; CEH, *The Public Papers of Charles Evans Hughes, 1907–1910* (J. B. Lyon, 1908–1910); CEH, "Address at Union League Club," *AP*, 124–125.

50. Hughes, "Speech at Glens Falls," *AP*, 167–168. See also Stonecash, Brewer, Peterson, and Young, "Politics," 153–162; Richard L McCormick, "Prelude to Progressivism: The Transformation of New York State Politics, 1890–

1910," *New York History* 59 (July 1978): 270–272; McCormick, *Realignment*, 250; *CEHP*, 340–347.

51. Bruce W. Dearstyne, "Regulation in the Progressive Era: The New York Public Service Commission," *New York History* 58 (July 1977): 331–347; "A New Broom Sweeps Clean," *Judge*, February 2, 1907.

52. Erman J. Ridgway, "Hughes," *Everybody's Magazine*, March 1908, CEH Manuscript Collection, NYPL, box 5, 354–363, 363. See also *CEHP*, 172–179, 184–188, 327–330; "Editorial," *Bankers Magazine*, June 15, 1908, 819–820, CEH Manuscript Collection, LC; "Bank Probers Are Ready," *New York Evening Post*, November 14, 1907; "Radical Changes in Bank Laws," *Albany Argus*, March 16, 1908, Fuller, *Hughes Administrative Scrapbook*.

53. *CEHP*, 179–180; Brooklyn Young Republican Club, "Governor Hughes and Personal Liberty," 1908, CEH Manuscript Collection, LC.

54. CEH, "Message to State Legislature on Race Track Gambling," June 8, 1908, CEH, *Public Papers*.

55. CEH, "Message to State Legislature on Race Track Gambling"; *CEHMP*, 226–232; CEH, "Address at Union League Club," *AP*, 111, 115. See also *CEHADS*, 19–21; *CEHP*, 189–208.

56. CEH, "Speech at the Dinner of the Northside Board of Trade at Ebling's Casino, Bronx, NY," March 6, 1908, CEH Manuscript Collections, NYPL, box 1.

57. *CEHMP*, 226–229; *CEHP*, 192–204.

58. *CEHMP*, 221, 229; CEH, "Speech to the Ulster County Republican Club at Kingston," March 10, 1908, CEH Manuscript Collection, NYPL, box 1; "Still Animated," *New York World*, May 14, 1908. See also Robert H. Fuller, "Hughes as Governor," *AN*, 345; Chase Mellen to CEH, April 4, 1908, HP Manuscript Collection, CUOHP, box 8.

59. *CEHMP*, 232.

60. Harry Roy Sweny, "A Political Poem Entitled Sir Charlie Hudibras, Being a Truthful History of Political Events in the Race-Track War of 1908," 2nd ed., 1909, CEH Manuscript Collection, NYPL, box 5.

61. CEH, "The City and the State," Address to the City Club of New York, February 25, 1908, NYPL pamphlets, 10.

62. "Race Track Gambling Bills Passed," *BDE*, June 11, 1908; "Gov. Hughes and the Legislature," *BDE*, June 26, 1907; McCormick, *Realignment*, 230–231; CEH, "Speech at Banquet, Albany," *AP*, 205. See also *CEHP*, 202–208.

Chapter 3: Serving a Second Term, 1908–1910

1. *CEHMP*, 235; John Milton Cooper Jr., *The Warrior and the Priest: Woodrow Wilson and Theodore Roosevelt* (Harvard University Press, 1983), 317; Oswald Garrison Villard, *Fighting Years: The Memoirs of a Liberal Editor* (Harcourt, Brace, 1939), 183. See also *CEHP*, 200–201; Henry C. Beerits, "Renomination and Reelection as Governor," 2–3, CEH Manuscript Collection, LC.

2. TR to Kermit Roosevelt, January 17, 1908, in, *Letters of Theodore Roosevelt*, ed. Elting Morison et al., vol. 6 (Harvard University Press, 1951–1954), 916.

See also *CEHMP*, 233–236; *CEHP*, 209–213; Doris Kearns Goodwin, *The Bully Pulpit: Theodore Roosevelt, William Howard Taft and Golden Age of Journalism* (Simon & Schuster, 2013), 508–509, 524–525.

3. Villard, *Fighting Years*, 186–187. See also "Being Governor with all his Might," *BDE*, April 22, 1907.

4. Arthur S. Link, *Woodrow Wilson and the Progressive Era, 1910–1917* (Harper & Row, 1954), 3. See also Goodwin, *Bully Pulpit*, 508–510.

5. Ida M. Tarbell, "How about Hughes?" *American Magazine*, March 1908, 450–464, CEH Manuscript Collection, NYPL, box 5; HP to Ida Tarbell, Dec. 31, 1907, HP Manuscript Collection, CUOHP, box 6.

6. Lewis L. Gould, *The Presidency of Theodore Roosevelt* (University Press of Kansas, 1991), 284; *CEHMP*, 233–234. See also *CEHP*, 209–225; Mark Sullivan, *Our Times*, vol 4. (Charles Scribner's Sons, 1933), 296–297, 304–307; Philip C. Jessup, *Elihu Root*, vol. 2. (Dodd Mead 1938), 123–131; TR to WHT, November 5, 1906, *Letters of Theodore Roosevelt*, vol. 5, 486–487; WHT to TR, October 31, 1906, TR, LC; WHT to HP, January 23, 1908, HP Manuscript Collection, CUOHP, box 7; "Is the President Hostile to the Hughes Boom?" *Literary Digest*, November 30, 1907, 814–816.

7. *CEHMP*, 238; Sullivan, *Our Times*, vol. 3, 287–288, and vol. 4, 298–304; *CEHP*, 220. See also CEH, "Address before the Republican Club of the City of New York," January 31, 1908, *AP*, 87–107; Goodwin, *Bully Pulpit*, 535–536; "Big Stir in Washington over Hughes' Candidacy," *BDE*, January 22, 1908.

8. HP to John B. Townsend, December 27, 1908; HP to CEH, March 3, 1908, HP Manuscript Collection, CUOHP, box 7. See also HP to Charles A Dana, April 13, 1908, HP Manuscript Collection, CUOHP, box 8; Stewart L. Woodford to CEH, March 28, 1908, CEH Manuscript Collection, LC.

9. A. B. Humphrey to CEH, April 24, 1908, CEH Manuscript Collection, LC; *CEHMP*, 233–239. See also *CEHP*, 220–225; Hughes Committee of 25, Republican Club of NYC, January 14, 1908; HP to Charles D. Hilles, January 23, 1908; HP to John B. Townsend, January 27, 1908; HP to CEH, March 3, 1908, HP Manuscript Collection, CUOHP, box 7; CEH convention telegram to HP, June 15, 1908, HP Manuscript Collection, CUOHP, box 8.

10. *AN*, 145–148; *Hughes's Reply to Bryan*, Speech at Youngstown, Ohio, September 5, 1908, *AP*, 300–314; *CEHMP*, 236; *CEHP*, 245–247. See also WHT to TR, September 4, 1908, WHT Manuscript Collection, LC.

11. TR to ER, August 3 and 8, 1908; TR to HCL, August 8, 1908, *Letters of Theodore Roosevelt*, vol. 6, 1150, 1160–1161; *AN*, 149–151. See also *CEHMP*, 240–246; *CEHP*, 226–238; Jessup, *Elihu Root*, 123–133; Martin L Fausold, *James W. Wadsworth, Jr., The Gentleman from New York* (Syracuse University Press, 1975), 68–70; Beerits, "Renomination and Reelection," 1–6, CEH Manuscript Collection, LC.

12. *AN*, 148–149, 157n40; *CEHMP*, 246. See also Robert H. Fuller, "Governor Hughes and the Bosses," 14–15, CEH Manuscript Collection, NYPL, box 1; CEH, "Speech at the Rink in Brooklyn, NY, Accepting the Republican Nomination for Governor," September 26, 1908, CEH Manuscript Collection, NYPL, box 2; "Tiger at the Gate," *Jamestown Post*, October 9, 1908; Robert H. Fuller, *Hughes Administrative Scrapbook Newspaper Clippings* (n.p., 1907).

13. Brooklyn Young Republican Club, "What Has the Hughes Administration Done for the People?" and "Governor Hughes and Personal Liberty," 1908, CEH Manuscript Collection, LC; WHT to CEH, July 15, 1908; TR to CEH, October 14 and 20, 1908; CEH to TR, October 26, 1908, CEH Manuscript Collection, LC; Beerits, "Renomination and Reelection," 8–10, CEH Manuscript Collection, LC; John Lord O'Brian, "Remarks," *Proceedings of the Bar and Officers of the Supreme Court of the United States, November 4, 1949. Proceedings before the Supreme Court of the United States, May 8, 1950, in Memory of Charles Evans Hughes* (Washington, DC, 1950), 42.

14. *CEHMP*, 248–249; *CEHP*, 242–251; Richard L McCormick, *From Realignment to Reform: Political Change in New York State, 1893–1910* (Cornell University Press, 1979), 234–235; "'Hughes and What He Stands for: the Career, Personality and Platform of the Governor of New York,' by A Newspaper Man Who Knows Him," *World's Work*, March 1908, 10036–10041, CEH Manuscript Collection, NYPL, box 5; "Chanler's Catechism," *Troy Times*, October 21, 1908; "A Critical Hour," *Syracuse Journal*, October 21, 1908; "The Chanler Fiasco," *Albany Evening Journal*, October 23, 1908; Fuller, *Hughes Administrative Scrapbook*; James Bryce to CEH, November 4, 1908; TR to CEH, November 5, 1908; ER to CEH, November 21, 1908; CEH to ER, November 26, 1908, CEH Manuscript Collection, LC; Beerits, "Renomination and Reelection," 8–15, CEH Manuscript Collection, LC; "Hughes, Too," *NYT*, November 4, 1908.

15. Warren Ferris to CEH, October1, 1910, CEH Manuscript Collection, LC; *CEHP*, 326.

16. Clifford Lee Staten, "Theodore Roosevelt: Dual and Cooperative Federalism," *Presidential Studies Quarterly* 23 (Winter 1993): 129–130.

17. John D. Buenker, "Progressivism in Practice: New York State and the Federal Income Tax Amendment," *New York Historical Society Quarterly* 52 (April 1968): 139–160; Henry C. Beerits, "Second Term," 23, CEH Manuscript Collection, LC; *CEHI*, 120.

18. CEH, "Speech to the Charity Organization Society," Carnegie Hall, November 19, 1907, CEH Manuscript Collection, NYPL, box 1; Richard W. Leopold, *Elihu Root and the Conservative Tradition* (Little, Brown, 1954), 20.

19. *CP*, 7.

20. Joseph Hutmacher, "Charles Evans Hughes and Charles Francis Murphy: The Metamorphosis of Progressivism," *New York History* 46 (1965): 25–40.

21. *CEHP*, 322–323; CEH, "Speech at the Jamestown Exposition on New York Day," October 10, 1907, *AP*, 268, 265–266. See also *CEHMP*, 109.

22. CEH, "Speech in Response to Formal Notification of His Nomination as the Republican Candidate for Governor, at the Republican Club, New York City," October 3, 1906, *AP*, 62; Erman J. Ridgway, "Hughes," *Everybody's Magazine*, March 1908, 362, CEH Manuscript Collection, NYPL, box 5; Daniel T. Rodgers, "An Age of Social Politics," in *Rethinking American History in a Global Age*, ed. Thomas Bender (University of California Press, 2010), 258.

23. Tarbell, "How About Hughes?," 464. See also *CEHP*, 302–312, 316, 325; Daniel T. Rodgers, *Atlantic Crossings: Social Politics in a Progressive Age* (Harvard University Press, 1998), 84, 110, 149, 236.

24. *CEHP*, 309–313; *CEHMP*, 212; CEH, "Speech to Charity Organization Society," 1.

25. Jeremy Felt, *Hostages of Fortune: Child Labor Reform in New York State* (Syracuse University Press, 1965), 1, 17–18, 31–37, 96–127.

26. *CEHP*, 306–313; Felt, *Hostages*, 28–31, 63–95; Robert H. Bremner, *From the Depths: The Discovery of Poverty in the United States* (New York University Press, 1966), 213–229; Walter I. Trattner, *Crusade for the Children: A History of the National Child Labor Cttee and Child Labor Reform in America* (Quadrangle Books, 1970), 93–116.

27. Phillip S. Foner, *History of the Labor Movement in the United States*, vol. 3 (International Publishers, 1964), 20–23. See also Crystal Eastman, *Work-Accidents and the Law* (Russell Sage Foundation, 1910), 3–15.

28. CEH, "Speech at the Exposition of Safety Devices and Industrial Hygiene," January 28, 1908, CEH Manuscript Collection, NYPL, box 1.

29. *CEHP*, 308, 316–322.

30. *AN*, 153; *CEHP*, 314–321; *CEHADS*, 25; Eastman, *Work Accidents*, 269–295; James Weinstein, *The Corporate Ideal in the Liberal State, 1900–1918* (Beacon Press, 1968), 40–61; Robert F. Wesser, "Conflict and Compromise: The Workmen's Compensation Movement in New York, 1890–1913," *Labor History* 11 (Summer 1971): 348–360; Rodgers, *Atlantic Crossings*, 245–254.

31. *CP*, 38; *CEHP*, 322–330, Trattnor, *Crusade*, 85–103; Walter I. Trattner, *Homer Folks, Pioneer in Social Welfare* (Columbia University Press, 1968), 85–103.

32. Trattner, *Homer Folks*, 152–166.

33. Trattnor, *Crusade*, 161–167, *CEHP*, 330–335; Bremner, *From the Depths*, 149–151; Staten, "Theodore Roosevelt," 129–130, 134.

34. CEH, "Address before Republican Club," *AP*, 99; CEH, "Address at the Union League Club Meeting in the Auditorium at Chicago," February 22, 1908, *AP*, 124; CEH, "Message on Saratoga Springs," May 29, 1909, *The Public Papers of Charles Evans Hughes, 1907–1910* (J. B. Lyon, 1908–1910). See also *CEHP*, 336–338; Snarky Aardvark Films, *My Native Air: Charles Evans Hughes & the Adirondacks*), YouTube, August 26, 2023, https://www.youtube.com/watch?v=GNvTc18_nW8.

35. *CP*, 18; CEH, "Speech at the Jamestown Exposition on New York Day," *AP*, 268. See also *CEHMP*, 213–214, 335–338; Edward H. Hall, ed., *The Hudson-Fulton Celebration, 1909* (J. B. Lyon, 1910), 400–403; Phillip C. Terrie, *Contested Terrain* (Adirondack Museum and Syracuse University Press, 1997), 115.

36. CEH, "Speech before the New England Dry Goods Association, Boston," March 10, 1908, CEH Manuscript Collection, NYPL, box 1; CEH, "Speech before the Young Republican Club of Brooklyn," February 20, 1909, CEH Manuscript Collection, NYPL, box 2. See also Beerits, "Second Term," 1–22, CEH Manuscript Collection, LC.

37. CEH, "The Fate of the Direct Primary," *National Municipal Review* 10 (1921): 23–31.

38. CEH to Nicholas Murray Butler, January 15, 1909, CEH Manuscript Collection, LC. See also *AN*, 151–153; *CP*, 57–58, 115–116; CEH, "Speech Before Young Republican Club," CEH Manuscript Collection, NYPL, box 2;

CEHMP, 183, 260; Francis S. Barry, *The Scandal of Reform: The Grand Failures of New York's Political Crusaders and the Death of Nonpartisanship* (Rutgers University Press, 2009), 72–77.

39. McCormick, *Realignment,* 240–241; Richard L. McCormick, *The Party Period and Public Policy: American Politics from the Age of Jackson to the Progressive Era* (Oxford University Press, 1986), 235–241; Richard L. McCormick, "The Discovery that Business Corrupts Politics: A Reappraisal of the Origins of Progressivism," *American Historical Review* 86 (April 1981): 266–270.

40. CEH, "Address to the National Civil Service Reform League Annual Meeting, Buffalo," November 7, 1908, CEH Manuscript Collection, NYPL, box 1. See also *AN,* 151–153; *CEHP,* 252–273; William Barnes to ER, January 27, 1909, ER Manuscript Collection, LC.

41. *CEHMP,* 262–263; James W. Wadsworth, "The Reminiscences of James W. Wadsworth, 1952," 70–73, CUOHP; Fausold, *James W. Wadsworth,* 71–74

42. HP to Josiah T. Newcomb, February 14, 1910, HP Manuscript Collection, CUOHP, box 13; "Sustained," *Albany Argus,* March 10, 1910; Fuller, *Hughes Administrative Scrapbook.* See also *CEHP,* 270–280; Hendrick, "Governor Hughes," 495–500; Villard, *Fighting Years,* 201–215; "Senator Allds," *The (Utica) Observer,* March 16, 1910; "Senator Allds Is Guilty," *The Buffalo Commercial,* March 31, 1910; "A Needed Amendment," *Ontario County Times,* March 6, 1910; Fuller, *Hughes Administrative Scrapbook.*

43. Unsigned (Fuller?), "Notes of a Meeting with Lloyd Griscom and George Agnew," February 9, 1910, CEH Manuscript Collection, NYPL, box 4; CEH, "Speech at Dinner of Republican Club," in *AP,* 75–76; *CEHMP,* 267–268.

44. Fausold, *James W. Wadsworth,* 71–74. See also *CEHP,* 288–295; O'Brian, "Remarks," 44.

45. CEH, "Bosses and the Direct Primary," n.d., CEH Manuscript Collection, NYPL, box 5. See also CEH, "Memo to the State Legislature Calling for an Extraordinary Session on the Direct Primary," June 20, 1910, CEH, *Public Papers*; "Ballot Reform Problem," *Buffalo Express,* September 19, 1907; "True Ballot Reform," *Troy Press,* December 2, 1908; "The Massachusetts Ballot," *Geneva Times,* November 12, 1908; Fuller, *Hughes Administrative Scrapbook.*

46. CEH, "Speech, and Testimony before the New York State Senate, Albany," April 15, 1909, CEH Manuscript Collection, NYPL, box 5; *CEHP,* 299. See also *CEHMP,* 262–267; Burton J. Hendrick, "Governor Hughes," *McClure's Magazine,* March 1908, CEH Manuscript Collection, NYPL, box 5, 509–512; Jessup, *Elihu Root,* 169, 238, 290; Leopold, *Elihu Root,* 9, 20; Lewis L. Gould, *The William Howard Taft Presidency* (University Press of Kansas, 2009), 112–113; "People Must Have More Power," *NYT,* February 26, 1909; "Leaders Puzzled by Root's Speech," *NYT,* February 27, 1909.

47. Wadsworth, "Reminiscences," 94; *CEHP,* 301. See also Goodwin, *Bully Pulpit,* 539–544;

48. Abstract of speech at the Merchants' Exchange Banquet, New Rochelle, March 29, 1910, CEH Manuscript Collection, NYPL, box 2. See also "State Appropriations," *The (Rochester) Post Express,* January 11, 1910; Fuller, *Hughes Administrative Scrapbook.*

49. James MacGregor Burns, *Leadership* (Harper & Row, 1978), 169–181.

50. O'Brian, "Remarks," 413; *CP*, 7.

51. *CP*, 52; *CEHMP*, 189. See also McCormick, *Realignment*, 249.

52. CEH, "Address at the Union League Club," *AP*, 121–123; Hendricks, "Governor Hughes," 670; *CEHMP*, 269. See also "Hughes and What He Stands For," CEH Manuscript Collection, NYPL, box 5; *CEHP*, 341–345; *CEHADS*, 27–28; Jeffrey M. Stonecash, Mark D. Brewer, R. Eric Peterson, and McGee Young, "Politics, Alfred Smith, and Increasing the Power of the New York Governor's Office," *New York History* 85 (Spring 2004): 153–162.

53. CEH, "Inaugural Address," Albany, New York, January 1, 1907, *AP*, 66–67; *CEHMP*, 269.

54. CEH, "Speech in Response to Notification of Nomination as Governor," *AP*, 55, 63; *CP*, 88.

55. McCormick, *Realignment*, 235, 250, 254, 266–269.

56. CEH, "Address at Chautaugua," *AP*, 251; "No Thank You, I'll Walk," 1910, Miriam and Ira D. Wallach Division of Art, Prints and Photographs: Print Collection, The New York Public Library; "Caricatures and Cartoons," New York Public Library Digital Collections, Digital ID 1801055. See also O'Brian, "Remarks," 412–413; Hendricks, "Governor Hughes," 521, 673–676, 681; *CEHP*, 340–347; Hutmacher, "Charles Evans Hughes and Charles Francis Murphy," 26; "Service to Public Won Hughes Fame," *NYT*, June 11, 1916.

Chapter 4: Becoming Associate Justice, 1910–1916

1. CEH, "Speech Before the Elmira Chamber of Commerce," May 3, 1907, *AP*, 179–181; *AN*, 143–144; *SC*, 87–88; *CEHSC*, 10–13.

2. *AN*, 143–145; *CEHMP*, 74, 422; *SC*, 197.

3. James F. Simon, *What Kind of Nation: Thomas Jefferson, John Marshall and the Epic Struggle to Create a United States* (Simon & Schuster, 2002), 186; "Publius, No. 78," in Alexander Hamilton, James Madison, John Jay, *The Federalist Papers* (New American Library, 1961), 465, 469; *SC*, 88, 95.

4. Alexander M, Bickel, *The Least Dangerous Branch: The Supreme Court at the Bar of Politics* (Bobbs-Merrill, 1975), 16–18.

5. Bickel, *Least Dangerous*, 18–33.

6. *CEHSC*, 13–15.

7. *AN*, 159–160; *CEHMP*, 278–281; Paul A. Freund, "Charles Evans Hughes as Chief Justice," *Harvard Law Review* 81 (Nov. 1967): 4–5; Lewis L. Gould, *The William Howard Taft Presidency* (University Press of Kansas, 2009), 128–129; Jeffrey Rosen, *William Howard Taft* (Times Books, 2018), 110–111.

8. *AN*, 300; Daniel T. Rodgers, "Living Without Labels," *Law and History Review* 24 (Spring 2006): 173–178. See also James A. Henretta, "Charles Evans Hughes and the Strange Death of Liberal America," *Law and History Review* 24 (Spring 2006): 141–153, 161–178; James A. Henretta, "In Defense of Traditional Stories and Labels," *Law and History Review* 24 (Spring 2006): 210–213; William S. Murray, "Review of Charles Evans Hughes and the Supreme Court

by Samuel Hendel," *University of Pennsylvania Law Review* 99 (May 1951): 1045–1047.

9. Les Benedict, "Law and the Constitution in the Gilded Age," in *The Gilded Age: Essays in the Origins of Modern America*, ed. Charles W. Calhoun (Scholarly Resources, 1996), 289–307; *OWHDH*, 1–7.

10. Roscoe Pound, "The Scope and Purpose of Sociological Jurisprudence," *Harvard Law Review* 25 (April 1912): 506–510, 516; Andrew L. Kaufman, *Cardozo* (Harvard University Press, 1998), 200–203.

11. *CEHCJ*, 2–3.

12. Melvin I. Urofsky, *Louis D. Brandeis, a Life* (Schocken Books, 2009), 169, 580, 675; CEH, "Address before the New York State Bar Association, Jan. 14, 1916: Some Aspects of the Development of American Law," *AP*, 343, 350, 352. See also Stephen Budiansky, *Oliver Wendell Holmes: A Life in Law, War and Ideas* (W. W. Norton, 2019), 448–449; Richard D. Friedman, "Governor on the Bench: Charles Evans Hughes as Associate Justice," *Harvard Law Review* 89 (March 1976): 963–967.

13. Budiansky, *Oliver Wendell Holmes*, 11, 169, 172, 175, 232, 294.

14. Budiansky, 169, 172, 232, 293–295, Michael E. Parrish, *The Hughes Court: Justices, Rulings, and Legacy* (ABC-CLIO, 2006), 52; Jean Edward Smith, *John Marshall, Definer of a Nation* (Henry Holt, 1996), 445.

15. Urofsky, *Louis D. Brandeis*, 155–180, 200–206. See also Alpheus Thomas Mason, *Brandeis: A Free Man's Life* (Viking, 1956), 630.

16. Friedman, "Governor," 962–963.

17. *CEHMP*, 370, 692–693; *SC*, 165–166. See also Friedman, "Governor," 964–966; Bickel, *Least Dangerous*, 106–107; Joel Richard Paul, *Without Precedent: Chief Justice John Marshall and His Times* (Riverhead Books, 2018), 341.

18. Friedman, "Governor," 961–962, 976–982; CEH, "Address before NYS Bar," *AP*, 354–355.

19. *CEHS*, 101–104.

20. *CEHMP*, 292; *CEHS*, 104–106; *CEHSC*, 26–27, 50–51; *OWHDH*, 40–42.

21. *CEHS*, 10; *SC*, 66–69, 208–213; *CEHMP*, 293.

22. *CEHS*, 11–19. See also *CEHMP*, 303–309; *CEHADS*, 35–37; Friedman, "Governor," 976–985; Montgomery N., Kosma, "Measuring the Influence of Supreme Court Justices," *Journal of Legal Studies* 27 (June 1998): 357; Aaron I. Abell, "Review of Charles Evans Hughes and the Supreme Court by Samuel Hendel," *Review of Politics* 13 (Oct. 1951): 516–517.

23. J. E. Smith, *John Marshall*, 477–479; *SC*, 142–144; Paul, *Without Precedent*, 364–372; Simon, *What Kind of Nation*, 288–291.

24. *SC*, 142–145.

25. CEH, "Address before NYS Bar," *AP*, 333–334, 343; *SC*, 29, 143, 150–151.

26. *CEHS*, 11, 15–49; Robert H. Jackson, "The Judicial Career of Chief Justice Hughes," *American Bar Association Journal* 27 (July 1941): 410. See also *AN*, 175n33; *CEHMP*, 306–307.

27. Friedman, "Governor," 976; *CEHS*, 27–29; Paul, *Without Precedent*, 369; *SC*, 147–148. See also *CEHSC*, 55–63.

28. Norman Williams, "The Commerce Clause and the Myth of Federalism," *UCLA Law Review* 54 (August 2007): 1847–1852, 1896–1898.

29. Daniel J. Elazar, *American Federalism: A View from the States* (Harper & Row, 1966/1984), ix–x, 1–3.

30. *CEHS*, 52; *CEHMP*, 307–308.

31. *CEHMP*, 307–308.; *CEHSC*, 60.

32. Freund, "Charles Evans Hughes Chief Justice," 37; Friedman, "Governor," 982–985; Richard A. Epstein, *How Progressives Rewrote the Constitution* (Cato Institute, 2006), 52–53.

33. CEH, "Address before NYS Bar," *AP*, 337, 340–341; Elazar, *American Federalism*, 1; Edward S. Corwin, *The Twilight of the Supreme Court: A History of Our Constitutional Theory* (Yale University Press, 1934), 48–51.

34. CEH, "Address before NYS Bar," *AP*, 337, 341–343.

35. *SC*, 142, 220; CEH, "Address before NYS Bar," *AP*, 338–340; *CEHSCH*, 61.

36. *CEHS*, 53–56.

37. CEH, "Address before NYS Bar," *AP*, 338–339; Epstein, *How Progressives*, 8. See also *CEHADS*, 37.

38. *SC*, 187.

39. *CEHS*, 165; Freidman, "Governor," 991. See also *CEHSC*, 39–40.

40. *CEHS*, 174; Arthur M. Allen, "The Opinions of Mr. Justice Hughes," *Columbia Law Review* 16 (Nov. 1916): 568–570.

41. *CEHS*, 180–185.

42. CEH, "Address before NYS Bar," *AP*, 333, 340–347.

43. Michael E. McGerr, *The Decline of Popular Politics: The American North, 1865–1928* (Oxford University Press, 1986), 54, 64–69.

44. Robert L. Heilbroner, *The Worldly Philosophers: The Lives, Times and Ideas of the Great Economic Thinkers* (Simon & Schuster, 1961), 33, 40, 54, 57, 70–84, 110.

45. *CEHSC*, 26; *CEHS*, 131.

46. *CEHSC*, 24–25, *CEHS*, 132–134; Friedman, "Governor," 987–988, Jackson, "Judicial Career," 410.

47. *CEHSC*, 48–49.

48. *CEHSC*, 49–50; *CEHS*, 57; Friedman, "Governor," 987–988.

49. Robert G. McCloskey, *The American Supreme Court* (University of Chicago Press, 1964), 102–104; Epstein, *How Progressives*, 48. See also Alpheus Thomas Mason, "The Case of the Overworked Laundress," in *Quarrels that Have Shaped the Constitution*, ed. John A. Garraty (Harper & Row, 1964), 177–178; Budiansky, *Oliver Wendell Holmes*, 292; Stephen M. Feldman, "The Rule of Law or the Rule of Politics? Harmonizing the Internal and External Views of Supreme Court Decision Making," *Law & Social Inquiry* 30 (Winter 2005): 103–105.

50. Budiansky, *Oliver Wendell Holmes*, 294–295

51. Budiansky, 295; *CEHADS*, 38–39; Cass R. Sunstein, "Lochner's Legacy," *Columbia Law Review* 87 (June 1987): 875–881.

52. Urofsky, *Louis D. Brandeis*, 212–215.

53. Urofsky, 215–224; Mason, "Case," 176–190; Bickel, *Least Dangerous*, 237.

54. *CEHMP*, 312–313, 702–703; *CEHS*, 136–145; *CEHSC*, 125–126; Urofsky, 224–226; *CEHADS*, 180–181.

55. *CEHS*, 162–163. See also *CEHMP*, 312; *SC*, 195, 204–207; *CEHADS*, 180–181.

56. Richard A. Epstein, "Liberty and Feminism," *Independent Review* 4 (Summer 1999): 13; Epstein, *How Progressives*, 90–93; Urofsky, *Louis D. Brandeis*, 222–227; Freidman, "Governor," 969–970.

57. *CEHSC*, 27–28; Budiansky, *Oliver Wendell Holmes*, 302, 348; Epstein, 45, 49–51.

58. *CEHSC*, 28–29; *CEHMP*, 311–312, 758–759; *CEHADS*, 40–41.

59. *SC*, 195.

60. *CEHS*, 154–160.

61. *CEHS*, 242–243. See also Eric Foner, *Free Soil, Free Labor, Free Men: The Ideology of the Republican Party before the Civil War* (Oxford University Press, 1970), 11–39.

62. *CEHS*, 244–246: *SC*, 175–176; *CEHSC*, 19–22; Friedman, "Governor," 993–994; *CEHMP*, 288–289.

63. Budiansky, *Oliver Wendell Holmes*, 112–114.

64. *CEHSC*, 33; *CEHMP*, 291. See also Budiansky, 414; Friedman, "Governor," 993–994.

65. Budiansky,.

66. Budiansky, 351, 348–353. See also *CEHMP*, 289–290; *CEHS*, 191–204, Friedman, "Governor," 995.

67. CEH, "Address at the Dedication of the Monument to General Franz Sigel," New York City, October 10, 1907, *AP*, 276–277.

68. *CEHMP*, 290–291; *CEHSC*, 33–34; *CEHS*, 248–261; *CEHADS*, 43; Friedman, "Governor," 991–992.

69. Undated, unsigned note, CEH Manuscript Collections, NYPL, box 1; *CEHMP*, 284–285.

70. CEH, "Address before NYS Bar," *AP*, 351; Friedman; "Governor," 961–967. See also *CEHMP*, 314; *CEHSC*, 64–67; *CEHADS*, 46–49; Henretta, "Charles Evans Hughes and Strange Death," 141.

Chapter 5: Almost Becoming President, 1916–1921

1. Archie Butt, *Taft and Roosevelt. The Intimate letters of Archie Butt, Miliary Aide.* (Doubleday, Doran 1930), 223. See also *CEHMP*, 267, 278, 301; Lloyd C. Griscom, "The Reminiscences of Lloyd C. Griscom, 1951," 93, CUOHP; CEH to ER, June 21, 1912, CEH Manuscript Collection, LC; Henry C. Beerits, "Second Term as Governor," 36–39, CEH Manuscript Collection, LC; Jonathan Lurie, *William Howard Taft* (Cambridge University Press, 2012), 122–126.

2. CEH, Undated statement, CEH Manuscript Collection, NYPL, box 1; Unattributed notes (by Robert Fuller?) of conversation between Taft and Hughes at Governors' Conference, February 20, 1910, CEH Manuscript Collection, NYPL, box 5.

3. Herbert Croly, *The Promise of American Life* (Capricorn Books, 1964), 168–175. See also Arthur S. Link, *Woodrow Wilson and the Progressive Era, 1910–1917* (Harper & Row, 1954), 18–20; Lewis L. Gould, *Four Hats in the Ring: The 1912 Election and the Birth of Modern American Politics* (University Press of Kansas, 2008), 17.

4. James W. Wadsworth, "The Reminiscences of James W. Wadsworth, 1952," 89–91, CUOHP; *CEHMP*, 301. See also Lewis L, Gould, ed., *Bull Moose on the Stump: The 1912 Campaign Speeches of Theodore Roosevelt* (University Press of Kansas, 2008), 11, 14, 36, 52, 67, 99–100, 109, 182, 206; ER to CEH, June 30, 1912, CEH Manuscript Collection, LC; Phillip C. Jessup, *Elihu Root*, vol. 2 (Dodd Mead 1938), 172–204.

5. *CP, 79;* Link, *Woodrow Wilson and Progressive Era*, 13–20; Gould, *Four Hats*, 1–21, 22–44, 45–75, 126; Michael P. Weatherson and Hal W. Bochin, *Hiram Johnson, Political Revivalist* (University Press of America, 1995), 37–62, 65–72; John Milton Cooper, *The Warrior and the Priest: Woodrow Wilson and Theodore Roosevelt* (Harvard University Press, 1983), 143–163.

6. Gould, *Four Hats*, 77; Cooper, *Warrior and Priest*, 5, 8, 124, 131–139.

7. Cooper, 162–167; Trygve Throntveit, *Power Without Victory: Woodrow Wilson and the American Internationalist Experiment* (University of Chicago Press, 2017), 76–79; Alpheus Thomas Mason, *Brandeis: A Free Man's Life* (Viking, 1956), 374–385; Patricia O'Toole, *The Moralist: Woodrow Wilson and the World He Made* (Simon & Schuster, 2018), 54–55.

8. *CEHMP*, 269; Link, *Woodrow Wilson and Progressive Era*, 20–24; Gould, *Four Hats*, 76–102, 151–183; Cooper, 164–186, 186–205, 206–221; Melvin I. Urofsky, *Louis D. Brandeis, A Life* (Schocken Books, 2009), 340–347.

9. *CEHMP*, 301, 315–320; Richard Coke Lower, *A Bloc of One: The Political Career of Hiram W. Johnson* (Stanford University Press, 1993), 68–75. See also Lewis L. Gould, *The First Modern Clash Over Federal Power: Wilson Versus Hughes in the Presidential Election of 1916* (University Press of Kansas, 2020), 50, 71–72; Lewis L. Gould, *The William Howard Taft Presidency* (University Press of Kansas, 2009), 74–78; CEH to ER, June 21, 1912; ER to CEH, June 30, 1912; Oswald G. Villard to CEH, May 8, 1916, CEH Manuscript Collection, LC; "They're Off at the Hughes Headquarters," *NYT*, June 18, 1916.

10. "Patriotism Wins," *NYS*, May 25, 1916. See also *AN*, 178–181.

11. Lurie, *William Howard Taft*, 182n17.

12. *CEHMP*, 326–329, 337. See also Gould, *First Modern Clash*, 34–37, 69–75; "Need Man to Save Nation," *BDE*, June 9, 1916; "Hitchcock Explains Activity for Hughes," *NYT*, June 5, 1916; "Put Hughes Boom in Concrete Form," *NYT*, June 6, 1916.

13. WGH to CEH, June 10, 1916, CEH Manuscript Collection, LC; "Comments of this Morning's Newspapers on the Nomination," *NYT*, June 11, 1916; *CEHI*, 78. See also Jessup, *Elihu Root*, 335–352; Richard W. Leopold, *Elihu Root and the Conservative Tradition* (Little, Brown, 1954), 111–113; Clarence E. McCartney, *Men Who Missed It: Great Americans Who Missed the White House* (Dorrance, 1940), 114–116; Henry C. Beerits, "The Presidential Campaign of 1916," 1–9, CEH Manuscript Collection, LC; "Hughes Is Nominated

by G.O.P. Convention," *WT*, June 10, 1916; "Landslide for Hughes," *NYT*, June 11, 1916.

14. George E. Mowry, *Theodore Roosevelt and the Progressive Movement* (University of Wisconsin Press, 1946), 352, 357.

15. Mowry, *Theodore Roosevelt and Progressive Movement*, 340–360; "I Am Out of Politics," Says Roosevelt," *WH*, June 11, 1916; "Landslide for Hughes." See also Fred L. Israel, "Bainbridge Colby and the Progressive Party, 1914–1916," *New York History* 40 (January 1959): 33–46.

16. "Judicial Robes Gone, Hughes Is Revealed as Real Human Being," *WT*, June 11, 1916; Gould, *First Modern Clash*, xi–xii, 134–135. See also William C. Widenor, *Henry Cabot Lodge and the Search for an American Foreign Policy* (University of California Press, 1980), 244; "Hughes in Town: Opens Campaign for the Presidency," *BDE*, June, 12, 1916.

17. CEHMP, 331–332; "Telegram Accepting the Nomination of the Republican Convention," *AP*, 3–7; Arthur S. Link and William M. Leary Jr., "Election of 1916," in *History of American Presidential Elections, 1789–1968*, vol. 3, ed. Arthur M. Schlesinger Jr. (McGraw Hill, 1971), 2247–2252.

18. TR to William Austin Wadsworth, June 23,1916, in *The Letters of Theodore Roosevelt*, ed. Elting Morison et al. (Harvard University Press, 1951–1954), 1078. See also *CEHMP*, 332–334; Gould, *First Modern Clash*, 75–78; Arthur S. Link, *Wilson Campaigns for Progressivism and Peace, 1916–1917* (Princeton University Press), 1965, 6–7, 101; Beerits, "Presidential Campaign 1916," 11; Bruce Allen Murphy, *The Brandeis/Frankfurter Connection: The Secret Political Activities of Two Supreme Court Justices* (Oxford University Press, 1982), 260–261; "They're Off at the Hughes Headquarters," *NYT*, June 18, 1916.

19. Henry F. Pringle, *The Life and Times of William Howard Taft* (Archon Books, 1964), 895. See also R. W. Austin to W. H. Calder, June 14, 1916, CEH Manuscript Collection, LC; David Lawrence, "Man to Man," *The Independent*, July 24, 1916, "Persons in the Foreground," *Current Opinion*, August 1916; "Hughes Pilot Chosen," *WP*, June, 28, 1916; "The Republican Management," *WP*, September 14, 1916.

20. Gould, *First Modern Clash*, 99–100; Randall Le Boeuf to CEH, June 16, 1916; CEH to TR, June 26, 1916, CEH Manuscript Collection, LC.

21. Gould, *First Modern Clash*, 82, Mark Sullivan, *Our Times*, vol. 3 (Charles Scribner's Sons, 1933), 67; TR to CEH, August 11, 1916; CEH Manuscript Collection, LC.

22. *CEHMP*, 350–351; Throntveit, *Power Without Victory*, 9. See also John Milton Cooper Jr., *Woodrow Wilson, a Biography* (Random House, 2011), 338; Link, *Woodrow Wilson and Progressive Era*, 231; O'Toole, *Moralist*, 29–34, 209; Arthur S. Link, "Wilson: Idealism and Realism," in *Woodrow Wilson*, ed. Arthur S. Link (Hill & Wang, 1968), 163–177.

23. "Hughes Accepts, Attacks Record of his Opponent," *NYT*, August 1, 1916.

24. "Acceptance Speech by Charles Evans Hughes," New York, July 31, 1916, in Link and Leary, "Election of 1916," 2294. See also Michael Beschloss, *Presidents of War* (Crown, 2018), 303.

25. "Acceptance Speech by Charles Evans Hughes," 2294–2295, 2300.

26. "Acceptance Speech by Charles Evans Hughes," 2305–2307.

27. "Acceptance Speech by Charles Evans Hughes," 2295, 2307.

28. Gould, *First Modern Clash,* 81; William Allen White, *Woodrow Wilson* (Houghton Mifflin, 1924), 315–316. See also Cooper, *Warrior and Priest,* 305–308.

29. Gould, 61, 68; Cooper, 341–342. See also Link, *Wilson Campaigns,* 56–65; S. D. Lovell, *The Presidential Election of 1916* (Southern Illinois University Press, 1980), 1–9; Dominick C. Lizzi, *Governor Martin H. Glynn, Forgotten Hero* (Valatie Press, 2007), 67–71.

30. Cooper, *Woodrow Wilson,* 329–332. See also Link, *Woodrow Wilson and Progressive Era,* 224–230; David Sarasohn, *The Party of Reform: Democrats in the Progressive Era* (University Press of Mississippi, 1989), 198–201; Heather Cox Richardson, *To Make Men Free: A History of the Republican Party* (Basic Books, 2014), 173–175; Cooper, *Warrior and Priest,* 229–247, 248–264.

31. Link, *Wilson Campaigns,* 130; "Acceptance Speech by President Woodrow Wilson," 2311. See also Link, *Woodrow Wilson and Progressive Era,* 224–230, 240–241; O'Toole, *Moralist,* 55, 207–208; Lewis L. Gould, "Theodore Roosevelt, Woodrow Wilson, and the Emergence of the Modern Presidency: An Introductory Essay," *Presidential Studies Quarterly* 19 (Winter 1989): 48; Cooper, *Warrior and Priest,* 229–255

32. "Acceptance Speech by President Woodrow Wilson," 2312, 2315, 2317; Link, *Wilson Campaigns,* 41.

33. Throntveit, *Power Without Victory,* 9, 48.

34. Michael E. McGerr, *The Decline of Popular Politics, The American North, 1865–1928* (Oxford University Press, 1986), 162–168.

35. Pringle, *Life and Times,* 892; "It Will Pay to Think Before Voting for Wilson," *(Albuquerquo, New Mexico) Evening Herald,* November 6, 1916; Charles Seymour, ed., *The Intimate Papers of Colonel House,* vol. 2 (Houghton Mifflin, 1926), 364–365. See also Betty Glad, "Charles Evans Hughes and the Campaign of 1916," in *Lessons from Defeated Presidential Candidates,* ed. Kenneth W. Thompson (University Press of America, 1994), 1–21; Edward C. McKay to Major F. M. Crossett, November 10, 1916, CEH Manuscript Collection, LC; "What He Stands For," *NYS,* November 2, 1916; "When in the Course of Human Events," *(Norwich) Bulletin,* November 6, 1916.

36. *CEHMP,* 339, 352, 358; "Success Marks Hughes' Career in All Efforts," *Chicago Daily Tribune,* November 8, 1916. See also "Hughes a Regular Person, Laugh and Handclasp Show," *Los Angeles Times,* July 9, 1916; "Has Hughes Won the West?," *Literary Digest,* September 9, 1916; "Hughes Warming Up," *WP,* September 22, 1916.

37. *CEHMP,* 336–339; Gould, *First Modern Clash,* 76; "Obituary Notice for Mrs. Charles Evans Hughes," *NYT,* December 7, 1945.

38. Jacob Gould Schurman, "Why Progressives Want Hughes," *The Independent,* October 2, 1916; "Wilson a Failure, Says Elihu Root," *NYT,* October 4, 1916; "Labor Leaders Endorse Hughes," *NYS,* November 6, 1916; "City Acclaims Hughes: 65,000 March in Parade," *New York Tribune,* November 5, 1916;

"Horoscopes Predict Victory for Hughes" and "Hughes the Favorite with Odds of 10 to 8," *WH,* November 5, 1916.

39. Gould, *First Modern Clash,* 99–100, 118–119; *AN,* 18. See also "Man of Peace Shouts Hughes," *WH,* October 16, 1916; "Hughes for Peace, Not War, He Avers," *WP,* Oct.13, 1916; "Roosevelt Denounces Wilson's Hypocrisy," *New York Tribune,* October 29, 1916; "Will the Election of Hughes Plunge Us into War?" *Current Opinion,* November 1916.

40. Gould, *First Modern Clash,* 106–108; Adam Tooze, *The Deluge: The Great War, America and the Remaking of the Global Order, 1916–1921* (Penguin Books, 2014), 179, 193–195; "You Are Working," *New York Evening World,* November 4, 1916; *CEHMP,* 357. See also Link, *Wilson Campaigns,* 1–5; O'Toole, *Moralist,* 209–210, 231; Sarasohn, *Party of Reform,* 207–209.

41. "Hughes Aspires to Lead Patriots," *NYT,* October 29, 1916; "What He Stands For," *NYS,* November 2, 1916. See also *CEHMP,* 350–359; Gould, 78, 97–100; *CEHADS,* 56–58; Lovell, *Presidential Election,* 60–70; TR to CEH, August 28, 1916, 10; TR to James R. Garfield, September 28, 1916, in *Letters of Theodore Roosevelt,* 1108–1110, 1119; TR to CEH, August 11, 1916; Henry L. Stimson to CEH, August 1, 1916; CEH to Henry Pratt Judson, October 13, 1916, CEH Manuscript Collection, LC; Beerits, "Presidential Campaign 1916," 15–27, 39–42, CEH Manuscript Collection, LC; "Say Hughes Made a Deal with Hyphens," *New York Tribune,* October 23, 1916; "Hughes Denies All Alliances," *WH,* October 25, 1916.

42. Oswald Garrison Villard, *Fighting Years: The Memoirs of a Liberal Editor* (Harcourt, Brace, 1939), 187; CEH, "Speech before the New England Dry Goods Association," Boston, March 10, 1908, CEH Manuscript Collection, NYPL, box 1; CEH, "Address Delivered at Youngstown, Ohio, September 5, 1908," *AP,* 313–316; "True Americanism Will Elect Hughes," *Norwich Bulletin,* November 4, 1916.

43. Gould, *First Modern Clash,* 56, 101–103; Sarasohn, *Party of Reform,* 201. See also Hughes, "Address before the Republican Club of the City of New York," January 31, 1908, *AP,* 104; Beerits, "Presidential Campaign 1916," 28; Gould, *The William Howard Taft Presidency,* 9–10, 50–64; O'Toole, *Moralist,* 70–77.

44. Richard A. Epstein, *How Progressives Rewrote the Constitution* (Cato Institute, 2006), 83–87; *Campaign Bulletin* no. 7, 6–7, and *Campaign Bulletin* no. 8, 8, Women's Committee of the National Hughes Alliance, Hughes Campaign Service, *Collection of Campaign Bulletins* (Women's Committee of the National Hughes Alliance, 1916). See also *CEHADS,* 27; CEH, "Shall Force or Reason Rule?" *The Independent,* October 9, 1916.

45. CEH, "Shall Force or Reason Rule?"; Gould, *First Modern Clash,* 95.

46. Cooper, *Woodrow Wilson,* 346. See also Women's Committee, *Campaign Bulletin* no. 3, 5–8; *Campaign Bulletin* no. 6, 6–8; *Campaign Bulletin* no. 7, 2, 6–7; *Campaign Bulletin* no. 10, 10; "The Labor Question: Hughes or Wilson?," Election broadside, Hughes Cornell University League, CEH Manuscript Collection, LC; Sarasohn, *Party of Reform,* 203–207; "Hughes Defends Record on Labor," *New York Tribune,* September 30, 1916.

47. Cooper, *Warrior and Priest,* 256–257. See also Richard l. McCormick,

From Realignment to Reform: Political Change in New York State, 1893–1910 (Cornell University Press, 1979), 215–216.

48. Women's Committee, *Campaign Bulletin* no. 10, 10; Gould, *First Modern Clash,* 94–97, 102–103, 117. See also Lovell, *Presidential Election,* 79–88; Edward C. McKay to Major F. M. Crossett, November 10, 1916, CEH Manuscript Collection, LC; Beerits, "Presidential Campaign 1916," 31–33; Cooper, 256–260.

49. Anne Firor Scott and Andrew Mackay Scott, *One Half the People: The Fight for Woman Suffrage* (University of Illinois Press, 1982), 33–38; Christopher Cox, *Woodrow Wilson, The Light Withdrawn* (Simon and Schuster, 2024), 224–229.

50. Ann Marie Nicolosi, "'The Most Beautiful Suffragette': Inez Milholland and the Political Currency of Beauty," *Journal of the Gilded Age and Progressive Era* 6 (July 2007): 286–309.

51. J. Leonard Bates and Vanette Schwartz, "Golden Special Campaign Train: Republican Women Campaign for Charles Evans Hughes for President in 1916," *Montana: The Magazine of Western History* 37 (Summer 1987): 32.

52. Frances Kellor, "Women in the Campaign," *Yale Review,* 1917, 1–14. See also Gould, *First Modern Clash,* 108–110, 129–130; O'Toole, *Moralist,* 220–221; Jacqueline Van Vorster, *Carrie Chapman Catt, a Public Life* (Feminist Press, 1987), 162; Robert H. Fuller, "Memorandum for Governor Hughes," July 18, 1916, CEH Manuscript Collection, LC; Women's Committee, *Campaign Bulletin* no. 10, 6–7; *Campaign Bulletin* no. 11, 6–7, *Campaign Bulletin* no. 12, 10; Beerits, "Presidential Campaign 1916," 30; Alma Whitaker, "Hughes Campaign Pressed by Country's Brightest Women," *Los Angeles Times,* October 15, 1916; "Hughesettes Egged by Crowd in Chicago," *WH,* November 2, 1916; "Hughes to Aid Anthony Bill," *New York Tribune,* July 5, 1916; "Wilson Dodges on Federal Suffrage," *New York Tribune,* September 9, 1916.

53. *AN,* 111–113; *CEHMP,* 110–111, 288–289; Gould, 112–115; Women's Committee, *Campaign Bulletin* no. 7, 2; "The Labor Question: Hughes or Wilson?," CEH Manuscript Collection, LC.

54. Women's Committee, *Campaign Bulletin* no. 10, 5, and no. 12, 7. See also Link, *Woodrow Wilson and Progressive Era,* 63–66; O'Toole, *Moralist,* 79–80, 226–227; Sidney M. Milkis, *Theodore Roosevelt, the Progressive Party, and the Transformation of American Democracy* (University Press of Kansas, 2009), 273–276; David Levering Lewis, *W. E. B. Du Bois, Biography of a Race, 1868–1919* (Henry Holt, 1993), 522–523; Francis L. Broderick, "Du Bois and the Democratic Party, 1908–1916," *Negro History Bulletin* 21 (Nov. 1957): 44; Cox, *Woodrow Wilson,* 232, 247–248.

55. *CEHMP,* 335, 350–351; Medill McCormick to CEH, August 25, 1917; CEH to TR, August 27, 1916; George W. Perkins to CEH, September 6, 1916, CEH Manuscript Collection, LC; "Say Wilcox May Go," *WP,* September 3, 1916; "Wilcox to Stay as G.O.P. Campaign Head," *WH,* September 4, 1916.

56. *CEHADS,* 54–55; CEH to E. K. Davis, June 26, 1916, CEH Manuscript Collection, LC; Frederick M. Davenport, "Did Hughes Snub Johnson? An Inside Story: How and Why Charles Evans Hughes Lost California and the Presidency in 1916," *American Political Science Review* 43 (April 1949), 221–332; Frederick

M. Davenport, "The Case of Hiram Johnson: Not Guilty," *North American Review* 205 (Feb. 1917): 203–220.

57. George E. Mowry, *The California Progressives* (University of California Press, 1951), 261.

58. *CEHMP*, 340–344. See also Beerits, "Presidential Campaign 1916," 37–39; Israel, "Bainbridge Colby," 33–44; Davenport, "The Case of Hiram Johnson," 203–209; Alfred Holman, "The Case of Hiram Johnson: Guilty," *North American Review* 205 (Feb. 1917): 195–197; "Far too Momentous a Crisis to Play Politics," *BDE*, August 1, 1916; "Hughes Quiets Political Strife in California," *New York Tribune*, August 19, 1917.

59. *AN*, 182–185; *CEHMP*, 335–349; *CEHP*, 121; Gould, *First Modern Clash*, 82–86; Davenport, "Did Hughes Snub Johnson?," 221–332; Davenport, "Case of Hiram Johnson," 213–217; Holman, "Case of Hiram Johnson," 197–202; Spencer C. Olin Jr., "Hiram Johnson, the California Progressives, and the Hughes Campaign of 1916," *Pacific Historical Review* 31 (Nov. 1962): 403–412; Mowry, *California Progressives*, 246–277; CEH to Hiram Johnson, telegram, July 6, 1916, CEH Manuscript Collection, LC; "California in Doubt," *NYT*, November 8, 1916; "Snub to Johnson, California's Idol, Defeated Hughes?," *BDE*, November 10, 1916.

60. *CEHMP*, 360–336; Gould, *First Modern Clash*, 123–126.

61. Gould, 122–130; *CEHMP*, 362–364; *CEHADS*, 61–63; O'Toole, *Moralist*, 229–231; Lovell, *Presidential Election*, 171–180; White, *Woodrow Wilson*, 312–314; "Why Wilson Won" and "Women's Hand in the Election" in *Literary Digest*, November 18, 1916; "Progressives Cost Hughes Election," *NYT*, November 11, 1925.

62. Gould, 98, 121, 126, 130–135; Link, *Wilson Campaigns*, 124–153, 162–163; Sarasohn, *Party of Reform*, 211–238; Cooper, *Woodrow Wilson*, 356–361.

63. *AN*, 181, 200; CEH to HCL, November 22, 1916, CEH Manuscript Collection, LC. See also *CEHMP*, 363–364; Gould, 77, 126; CEH to John Lord O'Brien, December 4, 1916, CEH Manuscript Collection, LC; TR to Meyer Lissner, October 10, 1916, in *Letters of Theodore Roosevelt*, 1114–1115.

64. CEH to Joseph Buffington, July 24, 1916, CEH Manuscript Collection, LC.

65. Villard, *Fighting Years*, 317, 320–321; William Allen White, "Who Killed Cock Robin?," *Collier's Weekly*, December 16, 1916, 5–6, 26–27. See also White, *Woodrow Wilson*, 315–319.

66. Herbert Croly, "The Two Parties in 1916," *New Republic*, October 21, 1916, in Link and Leary, "Election of 1916," 2332–2340. See also *CEHADS*, 55; Link, *Wilson Campaigns*, 128–130; Israel, "Bainbridge Colby," 33–44; "Progressives Cost Hughes Election," *NYT*, November 11, 1916.

67. Link, *Wilson Campaigns*, 100–102; Pringle, *Life and Times*, 895; Glad, "Charles Evans Hughes and the Campaign of 1916," 10–13. See also TR to CEH, November 28, 1916, CEH Manuscript Collection, LC; Israel, "Bainbridge Colby," 33–44.

68. Gould, *First Modern Clash*, 128. See also *CEHADS*, 61; David Pietrusza, *TR's Last War: Theodore Roosevelt, the Great War, and a Journey of Triumph and Trag-*

edy (Globe Pequot, 2018), 123–143, 163–180; TR to Arthur Hamilton Lee, November 10, 1916; TR to William Allen White, January 1, 1917; TR to William Allen White, November 1, 1917, in *Letters of Theodore Roosevelt*, 1124, 1135–1138; New York Democrats to Mrs. Charles E. Hughes, November 10, 1916; New York Democrats to TR, November 10, 1916, CEH Manuscript Collection, LC.

69. CEH, "Memorial Address for Theodore Roosevelt at the Republican Club of New York," February 9, 1919, NYPL pamphlets; CEH to TR, June 26, 1916; TR to CEH, November 28, 1916, CEH Manuscript Collection, LC.

70. Norman Hapgood, "Is Hughes Going Downhill?," *The Independent*, August 21, 1916, 272; Cooper, *Warrior and Priest*, 256.

71. *AN*, 185; *CEHMP*, 364–366, 403. See also "Charles Evans Hughes, Presidential Contender," C-SPAN, October 11, 2011, https://www.c-span.org/video/?301272-1/charles-evans-hughes-presidential-contender.

72. *AN*, 186–187, 195. See also *CEHMP*, 367–368, 383; Henry C. Beerits, "Activities During the Years 1916–1921," CEH Manuscript Collection, LC; "Work Done by Legal Aid," *NYT*, January 27, 1919.

73. *CEHMP*, 369–370.

74. Matthew C. Waxman, "The Power to Wage War Successfully," *Columbia Law Review* 117 (April 2017): 614–628, 680–686.

75. *AN*, 189–190; *CEHMP*, 370–382; Beerits, "Activities 1916–1921," 1–6, CEH Manuscript Collection, LC; "Work Done by Legal Aid."

76. *AN*, 194; *CEHMP*, 386–391, 420; *CEHADS*, 65–66; *SC*, 93. See also Spencer Ervin, *Henry Ford vs. Truman H. Newberry* (Richard R. Smith, 1935).

77. "End War Policies Now, Says Hughes," *NYT*, December 1, 1918; CEH, "Our After-War Dangers: In Saving the World, Have We Lost Our Republic?" *The Forum*, 1919, 237–242.

78. Frank I. Cobb, "On the Eve of War," in *Woodrow Wilson, a Profile*, ed. Arthur S. Link (Hill & Wang, 1968), 127–129.

79. *CEHMP*, 391–394; Villard, *Fighting Years*, 467; Beerits, "Activities 1916–1921," 16; Zechariah Chafee Jr., *Freedom of Speech* (Harcourt, Brace & Howe, 1920), 14–15, 332–335. See also Henry M. Greenberg, "The Role of the New York State Bar in a Time of Crisis for the Rule of Law," YouTube, 2019, https://www.youtube.com/watch?v=gKweT8lIu3E.

80. Beerits, "Activities 1916–1921," 17.

81. *CP*, 87; *CEHADS*, 70. See also Charles H. Parkhurst, "Roosevelt, Hughes and Americanism," address delivered at the Madison Square Presbyterian Church, November 18, 1907, NYPL pamphlets; Gould, *First Modern Clash*, 118.

Chapter 6: Becoming Secretary of State, 1921–1925

1. CEH, "Remarks Made to Pressmen," March 11, 1922, *PP*, 245–248.

2. CEH, "Remarks," 248.

3. James MacGregor Burns, *Leadership* (Harper & Row, 1978), 4–5, 169–171.

4. *CEHS*, 11–12; William C. Widenor, *Henry Cabot Lodge and the Search for*

an American Foreign Policy (University of California Press, 1980), 154. See also *CEHMP*, 618; *CEHADS*, x, xxiv.

5. John Chalmers Vinson, "Charles Evans Hughes, 1921–1925," in *An Uncertain Tradition: American Secretaries of State in the Twentieth Century*, ed. Norman A. Graebner (McGraw-Hill, 1961), 148. See also *CEHI*, 321–327.

6. CEH, "The Pathway of Peace," September 4, 1923, *PP*, 8, 14–18; CEH, "Some Aspects of the Department of State," May 18, 1922, *PP*, 251–252; CEH, "Some Observations on the Conduct of Our Foreign Relations," *American Journal of International Law* 16 (1922): 366.

7. CEH, "Some Observations on Conduct," 365–367; Bertram D. Hulen, *Inside the Department of State* (McGraw Hill, 1939), 371; *AN*, 208.

8. CEH, "Some Observations on Conduct," 367–369; Hulen, Inside Department, 144–149. See also CEHI, 144–148.

9. "Rediscovering the First Miracle Drug," *NYT*, October 4, 2021; "Elizabeth Hughes Gossett," Wikipedia, accessed September 28, 2024, https://en.wikipedia.org/wiki/Elizabeth_Hughes_Gossett.

10. *CEHMP*, 401–403; *AN*, 196.

11. Andrew Sinclair, *The Available Man: The Life Behind the Masks of Warren Gamaliel Harding* (Quadrangle, 1965), 136–154; Robert K. Murray, *The Politics of Normalcy: Governmental Theory and Practice During the Harding-Coolidge Era* (W. W. Norton, 1973), 7–9; Eugene P. Trani and David L. Wilson, *The Presidency of Warren G. Harding*. (Regents Press of Kansas, 1977), 21–23; Lewis L. Gould, *Grand Old Party: A History of the Republicans* (Random House, 2003), 215–223.

12. Sinclair, *Available Man*, 181–197.

13. *CEHMP*, 405–409; Herbert Hoover, *The Memoirs of Herbert Hoover: The Cabinet and the Presidency, 1920–1933* (Macmillan, 1952), 36; Warren I. Cohen, *Empire Without Tears: American Foreign Relations, 1921–1933* (Temple University Press, 1987), 16. See also R. Murray, *Politics*, 22–34; Ryan S. Walters, *Jazz Age President: Defending Warren G. Harding* (Regenery, 2022), ch. 7; Philip C. Jessup, *Elihu Root*, vol. 2 (Dodd Mead 1938), 414–417.

14. Cohen, *Empire*, 15.

15. Robert K. Murray, *The Harding Era: Warren G. Harding and His Administration* (University of Minnesota Press, 1969), 131–133, 157–158, 327–328; Kenneth J. Grieb, *The Latin American Policy of Warren G. Harding* (Texas Christian University Press, 1977), 7–10.

16. *CEHMP*, 414–415, 610; CEH, "Remarks to New Consuls," July 20, 1921, *PP*, 241–244; Hugh R. Wilson, *Diplomat Between Wars* (Longmans, Green, 1941), 162.

17. *CEHMP*, 420–421; CEH, "Some Aspects of Department," *PP*, 253, 259.

18. Charles Cheney Hyde, "Charles Evans Hughes, Secretary of State," in *The American Secretaries of State and Their Diplomacy*, ed. Samuel Flagg Bemis (Cooper Square Publishers, 1963), 231–235.

19. CEH, "Aspects of Department," 260–265; *AN*, 204–206.

20. Richard W. Leopold, *Elihu Root and the Conservative Tradition* (Little, Brown, 1954), 47–69; Jonathan Zasloff, "Abolishing Coercion: The Jurispru-

dence of American Foreign Policy in the 1920s," *Yale Law Journal* 102 (May 1993): 1700–1704.

21. Zasloff, "Abolishing Coercion," 1690–1698; Jonathan Zazloff, "Law and the Shaping of American Foreign Policy; The Twenty Years' Crisis," *Southern California Law Review* 77 (2004): 586–588; Richard H. Steinberg and Jonathan M. Zasloff, "Power and International Law," *American Journal of International Law* 100 (Jan. 2006): 65–69; Juan Pablo Scarfi, "Pan American Legal Designs: The Rise and Fall of American International Law in the Western Hemisphere," in *Cooperation and Hegemony in US-Latin American Relations: Revisiting the Western Hemisphere Idea*, ed. Juan Pablo Scarfi and Andrew R. Tillman (Macmillan, 2016), 172; Benjamin Allen Coates, *Legalist Empire: International Law and American Foreign Relations in the Early Twentieth Century* (Oxford University Press, 2016), 61–81.

22. Hyde, "Charles Evans Hughes, Secretary," 233. See also Coates, *Legalist Empire*, 81–85; Scarfi, "Pan American," 196–198.

23. Zazloff, "Law," 584–588, 601–610, 677; Zasloff, "Abolishing Coercion," 1717.

24. Hugo Grotius, "The Rational Basis of International Law," in *A Treasury of Philosophy*, vol. 1, ed. Dagobert D. Runes (Grolier, 1955), 447–451; Hugo Grotius, *The Rights of War and Peace*, ed. David J. Hill (Anodos Books, 2019), 11–22. See also David H. Burton, *Taft, Wilson and World Order* (Fairleigh Dickinson Press, 2003), 21–22; Oona Hathaway and Scott J. Shapiro. *The Internationalists: How a Radical Plan to Outlaw War Remade the World* (Simon & Schuster, 2017), xix–xx, 10–12.

25. Steven Forde, "Hugo Grotius on Ethics and War," *American Political Science Review* 92 (Sept. 1998): 639–648; Grotius, "Rational Basis," 452–453; Grotius, *Rights of War*, 11–22.

26. CEH, "Pathway," *PP*, 3, 4, 6.

27. CEH, 5–13. See also Grotius, *Rights of War*, 155–162; Hathaway and Shapiro, *Internationalists*, 21–30.

28. CEH, "The Development of International Law," *Proceedings of the American Society of International Law at Its Annual Meeting* 19 (April 23–25, 1925): 1–3.

29. CEH, "Development of International Law," 3–4, 7–11; CEH, "Pathway," *PP*, 19. See also *SC*, 111–117; Richard D. Friedman, "Charles Evans Hughes as International Lawyer," *Proceedings of the Annual Meeting of the American Society of International Law* 90 (March 27–30, 1996): 145–146; Zasloff, "Abolishing Coercion," 1691–1700.

30. John Chalmers Vinson, *The Parchment Peace: The United States Senate and the Washington Conference, 1921–1922* (University of Georgia Press, 1955), 213–217. See also *CEHI*, 153–162, 321–327; Vinson, "Charles Evans Hughes," 128–148; William A. Williams, "The Legend of Isolationism in the 1920s," *Science & Society* 18 (Winter 1954): 1–20; William A. Williams, *The Tragedy of American Diplomacy* (W. W. Norton, 1972, 109–128; Zasloff, "Abolishing Coercion," 1691–1698, 1707–1711.

31. Hans J. Morgenthau, "The Primacy of the National Interest," *American Scholar* 18, no. 2 (Spring, 1949): 209; Hans J. Morgenthau, "The Mainsprings of American Foreign Policy: The National Interest vs. Moral Abstractions," *Amer-*

ican Political Science Review 44 (Dec. 1950): 849–850. See also *CEHI*, 158–160, 210–211, 321–327; Hans J. Morgenthau, "What Is the National Interest of the United States?," *Annals of the American Academy of Political and Social Science* 282 (July 1952): 1–4; Hans J. Morgenthau, "Diplomacy," *Yale Law Journal* 55 (Aug. 1946): 1067–1073.

32. George F. Kennan, *American Diplomacy, 1900–1950* (University of Chicago Press, 1964), 71–73, 80–85; Melvyn P. Leffler, "Political Isolationism, Economic Expansionism, or Diplomatic Realism: American Policy Toward Western Europe, 1921–1933," in *U.S. Foreign Policy and National Security, 1920–2015*, ed. Melvyn P. Leffler (Princeton University Press, 2017), 114. See also John Braeman, "Power and Diplomacy: The 1920s Reappraised," *Review of Politics* 44 (July 1982): 342–369; Burl Noggle, "The Twenties: A New Historiographical Frontier," *Journal of American History* 53 (Sept. 1966): 299–314.

33. William E. Leuchtenburg, *The Perils of Prosperity, 1914–32* (University of Chicago Press, 1958), 104–119; Selig Adler, *The Uncertain Giant, 1921–1941: American Foreign Policy Between the Wars* (Macmillan, 1965), viii; Joan Hoff Wilson, *American Business and Foreign Policy, 1920–1933* (University Press of Kentucky, 1971), 44; Niall Palmer, *The Twenties in America: Politics and History* (Edinburgh University Press, 2006), 71–72. See also Michael Kammen, "The Problem of American Exceptionalism: A Reconsideration," *American Quarterly* 45 (March 1993): 6–11, 31–32; Warren F. Kuehl and Lynn K. Dunn, *Keeping the Covenant: American Internationalists and the League of Nations, 1920–1939* (Kent State University Press, 1979), xvi–xvii; Hilde Eliassen Restad, "Old Paradigms in History Die Hard in Political Science: US Foreign Policy and American Exceptionalism," *American Political Thought* 1 (May 2012): 54–57.

34. CEH, "Observations on Conduct," 365, 373; CEH, "The Monroe Doctrine—a Review: Its Relation to American Foreign Policy in the Twentieth Century," November 30, 1923, *PP*, 142–143; Thomas H. Buckley, "Review of Charles Evans Hughes and the Illusions of Innocence: A Study in American Diplomacy by Betty Glad," *Journal of American History* 54 (June 1967): 187–188; CEH, "Pathway," *PP*, 4; CEH, "Aspects of Department," *PP*, 253. See also CEH to WGH, December 25,1916, CEH Manuscript Collection, LC.

35. *CEHMP*, 611; Karen Miller, "Charles Evans Hughes," in *Secretaries of State from John Jay to Colin Powell*, ed. Edward S. Mihakanin (Greenwood Press, 2004), 254–262; Buckley, "Review of Charles Evans Hughes," 187–188; Margot Louria, "The Boldness of Charles Evans Hughes," *National Interest* 72 (Summer 2003): 107–117.

36. *AN*, 209; Walter Lippmann, *United States Foreign Policy: Sheild of the Republic* (Little, Brown, 1943), 9–10.

37. John Milton Cooper Jr., *Breaking the Heart of the World: Woodrow Wilson and the Fight for the League of Nations* (Cambridge University Press, 2001), 1; "Acceptance Speech by Charles Evans Hughes," New York, July 31, 1916, in *History of American Presidential Elections, 1789–1968*, ed. Arthur M. Schlesinger Jr., vol. 3 (McGraw Hill, 1971), 2303–2204. See also *CEHMP*, 395–400; *CEHADS*, 71–94.

38. John Milton Cooper Jr., *Woodrow Wilson, a Biography*. (Vintage, 2011), 370–371. See also Patricia O'Toole, *The Moralist, Woodrow Wilson and the World*

He Made (Simon & Schuster, 2018), 239–242; John Milton Cooper Jr., *The Warrior and the Priest: Woodrow Wilson and Theodore Roosevelt* (Harvard University Press, 1983), 312–314.

39. *AN*, 188.

40. *CEHI*, 163–170; *CEHMP*, 395–400; Elizabeth, Cobbs Hoffman, *American Umpire* (Harvard University Press, 2013), 207–208; CEH to Senator Frederick Hale, July 24, 1919, CEH Manuscript Collection, LC; "Hughes Criticizes Article Ten Alone," *NYT*, August 5, 1919.

41. CEH, "Address to the Union League Club of New York City," March 26, 1919, CEH Manuscript Collection, LC; *AN*, 210–212. See also *CEHMP*, 395–400; *CEHADS*, 76; William G. Ross, "Constitutional Issues Involving the Controversy over American Membership in the League of Nations, 1918–1920," *American Journal of Legal History* 53 (Jan. 2013): 29–33.

42. Kuehl and Dunn, *Keeping Covenant*, 1–9. See also CEH, "Speech at the National Arbitration and Peace Congress," April 15, 1907, *AP*, 209–216; *CEHI*, 163–173; Stephen Wertheim, "The League that Wasn't: American Designs for a Legalist-Sanctionist League of Nations and the Intellectual Origins of International Organization, 1914–1920," *Diplomatic History* 35 (Nov. 2011): 810–817, 833–835; Coates, *Legalist Empire*, 154–162.

43. *AN*, 214; Hatsue Shinohara, "International Law and World War I," *Diplomatic History* 38 (Sept. 2014): 885–886.

44. Michael Beschloss, *Presidents of War* (Crown, 2018), 336. See also *CEHADS*, 70–80; Lewis L. Gould, *The Modern American Presidency* (University Press of Kansas, 2003), 42–54; Ross, "Constitutional Issues," 7–15, 65–71; H. W. Brands, *Woodrow Wilson* (Henry Holt, 2003), 103–107.

45. HCL to CEH, November 13, 1916, CEH Manuscript Collection, LC. See also Widenor, *Henry Cabot Lodge*, 221–246; John A. Garraty, *Henry Cabot Lodge, a Biography* (Alfred A. Knopf, 1953), 51–69, 294–300, 315–335; Brands, *Woodrow Wilson*, 107–111.

46. Widenor, *Henry Cabot Lodge*, 300–320.

47. Henry Cabot Lodge, "Opposing the League of Nations," in *Ideas in American Foreign Policy*, ed. Andrew Bacevich (Oxford University Press, 2018), 180–181; Ross, "Constitutional Issues," 34–35, 55–57.

48. O'Toole, *Moralist*, 440; Nancy Unger, *Fighting Bob La Follette, the Righteous Reformer* (University of North Carolina Press, 2000), 263–270; John Braeman, *Albert Beveridge, American Nationalist* (University of Chicago Press, 1971), 259–263; Richard Lowitt, *George W. Norris: The Persistence of a Progressive, 1913–1933* (University of Illinois Press, 1971), 107–123. See also William E. Borah, "Speech on the League of Nations, Nov. 19, 1919," in *Great Issues in American History from Reconstruction to the Present Day, 1864–1969*, ed. Richard Hofstadter (Vintage Books, 1969), 231–239: John Milton Cooper Jr., "William E. Borah, Political Thespian," *Pacific Northwest Quarterly* 56 (Oct. 1965): 150–151; Richard Coke Lower, "Hiram Johnson: The Making of an Irreconcilable," *Pacific Historical Review* 41 (Nov. 1972): 505–510; Howard De Witt, "Hiram Johnson and World War I: A Progressive in Transition," *Southern California Quarterly* 56 (Fall 1974): 295–305.

49. CEH to Senator Frederick Hale, July 24, 1919, CEH Manuscript Collection, LC; *AN*, 212; Cooper, *Woodrow Wilson*, 514. See also O'Toole, 412–415; Cooper, *Breaking Heart*, 131; Garraty, *Henry Cabot Lodge*, 336–356; John Morton Blum, *Woodrow Wilson and the Politics of Morality* (Little, Brown, 1956), 181–187; Michael P. Weatherson and Hal W. Bochin, *Hiram Johnson, Political Revivalist* (University Press of America, 1995), 83–90; Henry Cabot Lodge, *The Senate and the League of Nations* (Charles Scribner's Sons, 1925), 405–410; HCL, "Opposing the League of Nations," 181–185; Robert James Maddox, *William E. Borah and American Foreign Policy* (Louisiana State University Press, 1969), 50–64.

50. O'Toole, 415–423; Cooper, *Breaking Heart*, 185–187, 191. See also Blum, *Woodrow Wilson*, 180–199; Weatherson and Bochin, *Hiram Johnson*, 83–107; Beschloss, *Presidents*, 346–349; Arthur S. Link, *Woodrow Wilson: Revolution, War, and Peace* (AHM Publishing, 1979), 104–128; Brands, *Woodrow Wilson*, 116–130; Cooper, "William E. Borah," 145–153.

51. Cooper, *Breaking Heart*, 234; O'Toole, 436–447, 454–456. See also Garraty, *Henry Cabot Lodge*, 383–390; Maddox, *William E. Borah*, 67–72; Link, *Woodrow Wilson*, 104–128.

52. Garraty, *Henry Cabot Lodge*, 399–401; *CEHI*, 163–183. See also *AN*, 212–213; *CEHMP*, 431–434; Kuehl and Dunn, *Keeping the Covenant*, 11–17; Cooper, 390–386; "Hughes Praises Harding," *NYT*, August 26, 1920.

53. *AN*, 209–218; *CEHMP*, 436; CEH, "The Hughes-Holt Correspondence Clears the Air," *Advocate of Peace through Justice* 84 (Aug. 1922): 306–308; CEH to Hamilton Holt, July 19, 1922, CEH Manuscript Collection, LC. See also *CEHADS*, 83–86; Kuehl and Dunn, *Keeping Covenant*, 19–29; Thomas T. Thalken, "The Papers of Charles Evans Hughes," *Quarterly Journal of Current Acquisitions* (Nov. 1953): 5.

54. *AN*, 213–218; *CEHMP*, 433–438; Rollin Kirby, "I Sympathize with You, Madame, but I Cannot Associate with You," *The World*, December 4, 1923. See also *CEHI*, 173–179; *CEHADS*, 86–94; Kuehl and Dunn, *Keeping Covenant*, 128–135.

55. *AN*, 218–221; Walter LaFeber, *The American Age: United States Foreign Policy at Home and Abroad since 1750* (W. W. Norton, 1989), 312; Melvyn P. Leffler, "Political Isolationism," 101; Adam Tooze, *The Deluge: The Great War, America and the Remaking of the Global Order, 1916–1921* (Penguin Books, 2014), 516. See also *CEHI*, 159, 183–184; Edward, Rhodes, "Charles Evans Hughes Reconsidered, or Liberal Isolationism in the New Millennium," in *The Real and the Ideal: Essays on International Relations in Honor of Richard H. Ullman*, ed. Anthony Lake and David Ochmanek (Rowman & Littlefield, 2001), 161–176, 192–195.

56. Frank Ninkovich, *The Wilsonian Century: United States Foreign Policy Since 1900* (University of Chicago Press, 1999), 10–15, 48–49, 66–69; Correspondence from Edward Rhodes, January 5, 2023. See also Cooper, *Woodrow Wilson*, 416–424; Beschloss, *Presidents*, 308–316; Adler, *Uncertain Giant*, 43–46; Michael Patrick Culinane and Alex Goodall, *The Open Door Era: United States Foreign Policy in the Twentieth Century* (Edinburgh University Press, 2017), 75–80; Hyde, "Charles Evans Hughes, Secretary," 363–374.

57. *AN*, 221; Rhodes, "Charles Evans Hughes Reconsidered," 161–165. See

also Melvyn P. Leffler, "American Policy Making and European Stability, 1921–1933," *Pacific Historical Review* 46 (May 1977): 216–221; Zasloff, "Abolishing Coercion," 1691–1698.

58. Patrick O. Cohrs, "The First 'Real' Peace Settlements after the First World War: Britain, the United States and the Accords of London and Locarno, 1923–1925," *Contemporary European History* 12 (Feb. 2003): 9, 20.

59. *AN*, 225–230; CEH, "The Hughes-Holt Correspondence," 306–308; *CEHMP*, 440–442. See also Kurt Wimer and Sarah Wimer, "The Harding Administration, the League of Nations, and the Separate Peace Treaty," *Review of Politics* 29 (Jan. 1967): 13–24; Hyde, "Charles Evans Hughes, Secretary," 225–230.

60. Niall Palmer, *Twenties*, 79–80; CEH, "Pathway," *PP*, 19. See also *CEHMP*, 442–444.

61. CEH, "Some Aspects of Foreign Policy," *PP*, 55–58. See also Zasloff, "Abolishing Coercion," 1707–1711; Tooze, *Deluge*, 442–449; Leffler, "Political Isolationism," 80–85.

62. Leffler, 85–93.

63. Zasloff, "Law," 617–622; Jon Jacobson, "Is There a New International History of the 1920s?," *American Historical Review* 88 (June 1983): 621–623. See also Tooze, *Deluge*, 452–458; Hyde, "Charles Evans Hughes, Secretary," 374–393.

64. Emily S. Rosenberg, *Financial Missionaries to the World: The Politics and Culture of Dollar Diplomacy, 1900–1930* (Duke University Press, 2003), 100–101.

65. Lowitt, *George W. Norris*, 77–93, 529; *AN*, 257–261; CEH, "Some Aspects of Foreign Policy," 32–58; CEH, "A Better Understanding—Support of the Dawes Plan," *PP*, 102–109; *CEHMP*, 579–593; *CEHIADS*, 119–123; Murray, *Harding Era*, 360–367; LaFeber, *American Age*, 326–329; Cohen, *Empire*, 19–22; Hyde, "Charles Evans Hughes, Secretary," 374–393; Leffler, "American Policy," 209–216.

66. Rollin Kirby, "But, Monsieur, Where Does It Bend?" *The World*, October 4, 1927.

67. Allan Nevins, *The United States in a Chaotic World: A Chronicle of International Affairs, 1918–1933* (Yale University Press, 1950), 72–78; *CEHADS*, 125; *CEHI*, 220; Leffler, "Political Isolationism," 85–92; Sinclair, *Available Man*, 250–251; J. H. Wilson, *American Business*, 74–87; David A. Lake, *Power, Protection and Free Trade: International Sources of U.S. Commercial Strategy, 1887–1939* (Cornell University Press, 1988), 166–167, 173–178.

68. *CEHMP*, 570–571. See also William Appleman Williams, *The Tragedy of American Diplomacy* (W. W. Norton, 1972), 137; Sumner Welles, *Naboth's Vineyard: The Dominican Republic, 1844–1924* (Paul P. Appel Publishers, 1966), 930–931; Rhodes, "Charles Evans Hughes Reconsidered," 189–190; James Grafton Rogers, "Hughes as Secretary of State," *American Bar Association Journal* 27 (July 1941): 411–412.

69. Hyde, "Charles Evans Hughes, Secretary," 289–296.

70. CEH, "Recent Questions and Negotiations," *PP*, 96–98; *CEHMP*, 575–578; Lawrence Spinelli "Sailing into Dry Dock: The Harding Administration's

Shipping Policy and Prohibition," *Presidential Studies Quarterly* 19 (Fall 1989): 747–761; Charles Cheney Hyde, "Remarks of," in *Proceedings of the Bar and Officers of the Supreme Court of the United States, November 4, 1949. Proceedings before the Supreme Court of the United States May 8, 1950, in Memory of Charles Evans Hughes* (Washington, DC, 1950), 34–36.

Chapter 7: The Washington Naval Conference, 1921–1922

1. Thomas H. Buckley, *The United States and the Washington Conference, 1921–1922* (University of Tennessee Press, 1970), vii–viii.

2. Herbert Croly, "What the Conference Means," *New Republic: Roads to Peace: A Handbook to the Washington Conference* (Republic Publishing, 1921), 9–13; Mark Sullivan, *The Great Adventure in Washington: The Story of the Conference* (Doubleday, Page, 1922), viii, 116–117, 285; Frank. Ninkovich, *The Wilsonian Century: United States Foreign Policy Since 1900* (University of Chicago Press, 1999), 86–89; Walter Lippmann, *United States Foreign Policy: Shield of the Republic* (Little, Brown, 1943), ix–10, 54–58. See also Winston B. Thorson, "Pacific Northwest Opinion on the Washington Conference of 1921–1922," *Pacific Northwest Quarterly* 37 (April 1946): 111–112.

3. Herbert Croly, *The Promise of American Life* (Capricorn Books, 1964), 289; Selig Adler, *The Uncertain Giant, 1921–1941: American Foreign Policy Between the Wars* (Macmillan, 1965), 61.

4. John Chalmers Vinson, *The Parchment Peace: The United States Senate and the Washington Conference, 1921–1922* (University of Georgia Press, 1955), 43–68; Harold Sproat and Margaret Sproat, *Toward a New Order of Sea Power: American Naval Policy and the World Scene, 1918–1922* (Princeton University Press, 1940), 100–117; Robert Gordon Kaufman, *Arms Control During the Pre-Nuclear Era: The United States and Naval Limitation Between the Two World Wars* (Columbia University Press, 1990), 24; Elizabeth Cobbs Hoffman, *American Umpire* (Harvard University Press, 2013), 210–212; C. Leonard Hoag, *Preface to Preparedness: The Washington Disarmament Conference and Public Opinion* (American Council on Public Affairs, 1941), 89–125.

5. Allan Nevins, *The United States in a Chaotic World: A Chronicle of International Affairs, 1918–1933* (Yale University Press, 1950), 4–5; Vinson, *Parchment Peace*, 78–96; Rhodri Jeffrey-Jones, *Changing Differences: Women and the Shaping of American Foreign Policy, 1917–1994* (Rutgers University Press, 1995), 17–33; Adler, *Uncertain Giant*, 22–42, 62; Robert H. Van Meter Jr., "The Washington Conference of 1921–1922: A New Look," *Pacific Historical Review* 46 (Nov. 1977): 603–624; Kaufman, *Arms Control*, 23–31.

6. Adam Tooze, *The Deluge: The Great War, America and the Remaking of the Global Order, 1916–1921* (Penguin Books, 2014), 401. See also *AN*, 454–459; *CEHADS*, 98–100; Sproat and Sproat, *Toward New Order*, 47–56, 118–131.

7. *CEHADS*, 100–101. See also *AN*, 240–247; Sproat and Sproat, 131–144; Ernest Andrade Jr., "The United States Navy and the Washington Conference," *The Historian* 31 (May 1969): 345–363.

8. *CEHI*, 326; CEH, "Some Aspects of Our Foreign Policy," December 20, 1922, *PP*, 47. See also Philip C. Jessup, *Elihu Root*, vol. 2 (Dodd Mead, 1938), 445–466; *AN*, 247–248; *CEHMP*, 453–465; Buckley, *United States*, 35–47; Vinson, *Parchment Peace*, 115–129; Hoag, *Preface*, 126–141; Robert K. Murray, *The Harding Era: Warren G. Harding and His Administration* (University of Minnesota Press, 1969), 140–149.

9. Murray, *Harding Era*, 150–151. See also *CEHMP*, 461–468.

10. Buckley, *United States*, 70, 63–74; CEH, "Limitation of Naval Armament," November 12, 1921, *PP*, 20–27; *CEHMP*, 468–471; Jonathan Zasloff, "Law and the Shaping of American Foreign Policy: The Twenty Years' Crisis," *Southern California Law Review* 77 (2004): 588–591.

11. CEH, "Limitation," *PP*, 27–31; William E. Leuchtenburg, "Review of Charles Evans Hughes and American Democratic Statesmanship by Dexter Perkins," *Mississippi Valley Historical Review 83* (Dec. 1956): 512–513.

12. Tooze, *Deluge*, 11–12; Cobbs Hoffman, *American Umpire*, 215–216; CEH, "Limitation," 25; Buckley, *United States*, 74. See also *CEHI*, 269–273.

13. Buckley, 70.

14. Mark Sullivan, *Our Times, the United States, 1900–1925*, vol. 5 (Charles Scribner's Sons, 1933), 191–195; *CEHMP*, 472–473; *CEHADS*, 101–102. See also Vinson, *Parchment Peace*, 130–139; Robert K. Murray, *The Politics of Normalcy: Governmental Theory and Practice during the Harding-Coolidge Era* (W. W. Norton, 1973), 60–61; Raymond L. Buell, *Washington Conference* (D. Appleton, 1922), 137–152; Sproat and Sproat, *Toward New Order*, 145–156; William E. Leuchtenberg, *The Perils of Prosperity, 1914–32* (University of Chicago Press, 1958), 113–115; John Milton Cooper Jr., "The Shock of Recognition: The Impact of World War I on America," *Virginia Quarterly Review* 76 (Autumn 2000): 584.

15. *CEHMP*, 467, 481–485; Buckley, *United States*, 104–126; Sullivan, *Great Adventure*, 166–187; *CEHADS*, 105–106.

16. CEH, "Some Aspects of Foreign Policy," *PP*, 37, 39, 50; Sproat and Sproat, *Toward New Order*, 287–29. See also *CEHI*, 275–280; Buckley, *United States*, 125–126; Stanley Huddleston, "What France Wants," *New Republic: Roads to Peace: A Handbook to the Washington Conference* (Republic Publishing, 1921), 34–39.

17. Sullivan, *Our Times*, 191n4; Sproat and Sproat, 267–269. See also *CEHI*, 275–280; Emily O. Goldman, *Sunken Treaties: Naval Arms Control Between the Wars* (Penn State University Press, 1994), 153–156; Kaufman, *Arms Control*, 73–82; John Chalmers Vinson, "Charles Evans Hughes, 1921–1925," in *An Uncertain Tradition: American Secretaries of State in the Twentieth Century*, ed. Norman A. Graebner (McGraw Hill, 1961), 137–143; Frank H Simonds, *American Foreign Policy in the Post-War Years* (Johns Hopkins University Press, 1935), 49–76; Thorson, "Pacific Northwest Opinion," 120.

18. *AN*, 248; CEH, "Some Aspects of Foreign Policy," *PP*, 44. See also *CEHMP*, 510–511; George F. Kennan, *American Diplomacy, 1900–1950* (University of Chicago Press, 1964), 64–65; Andrade, "United States Navy," 345–363.

19. Niall Palmer, *The Twenties in America: Politics and History* (Edinburgh University Press, 2006). 77–78. See also Kaufman, *Arms Control*, 12–14.

20. Jessup, *Elihu Root,* 465; John Braeman, "Power and Diplomacy: The 1920s Reappraised," *Review of Politics* 44 (July 1982): 364–365. See also *CEHMP,* 474–490; Sproat and Sproat, *Toward New Order,* 85–99; Goldman, *Sunken Treaties,* 59–68; Walter LaFeber, *The Clash: A History of U.S.-Japan Relations* (W. W. Norton, 1997), 138–140; Sidney Pash, *The Currents of War: A New History of American-Japanese Relations, 1899–1941* (University Press of Kentucky, 2014), 57–61; John Edward Joseph Chusid, "The Concurrent Conferences: The Washington Naval Conference and the Far Eastern Affairs Conference of 1922" (MA thesis, Eastern Michigan University, 2008), 1–3, 19–23, 74–94. Zasloff, "Law," 629–635.

21. Kaufman, *Arms Control,* 32–41; Kennan, *American Diplomacy,* 35.

22. Hoag, *Preface,* 155–160; Buckley, *United States,* 180. See also Joan Hoff Wilson, *American Business and Foreign Policy, 1920–1933* (University Press of Kentucky, 1971), 45–48.

23. *CEHMP,* 499–500; Adler, *Uncertain Giant,* 65–67. See also Goldman, *Sunken Treaties,* 23–24; Chusid, "Concurrent Conferences," 6–7, 23–24, 67–74.

24. CEH, "The Development of International Law," *Proceedings of the American Society of International Law at Its Annual Meeting* 19 (1925): 5; Sproat and Sproat, *Toward New Order,* ix–xi, 3–15, 278–292; Arthur A Ekirch Jr., "Review of Charles Evans Hughes and the Illusions of Innocence: A Study in American Diplomacy by Betty Glad," *History of Education Quarterly* 8 (Spring 1968): 139–140. See also Pash, *Currents of War,* 53–54; Vinson, *Parchment Peace,* 149–169; Richard W. Leopold, *The Growth of American Foreign Policy: A History* (Alfred A. Knopf, 1962), 428–433; Jessup, *Elihu Root,* 445–466; Murray, *Harding Era,* 153–162; Chusid, "Concurrent Conferences," 74–94; Graham H. Stuart, *The Department of State: A History of its Organization, Procedure, and Personnel* (Macmillan, 1949), 264–267; Charles Cheney Hyde, "Charles Evans Hughes, Secretary of State," in *The American Secretaries of State and Their Diplomacy,* ed. Samuel Flagg Bemis (Cooper Square Publishers, 1963), 241–248.

25. Tooze, *Deluge,* 397–407. See also CEH, "Some Aspects of Foreign Policy," *PP,* 50–53; LaFeber, *Clash,* 141–143; Jonathan Zasloff, "Abolishing Coercion: The Jurisprudence of American Foreign Policy in the 1920s," *Yale Law Journal* 102 (May 1993): 1714–1717; Buckley, *United States,* 145–156, 185–187.

26. *CEHMP,* 501–506. See also CEH, "The Monroe Doctrine—a Review: Its Relation to American Foreign Policy in the Twentieth Century," November 30, 1923, *PP,* 147–153; *CEHADS,* 109; *CEHI,* 288–303; Nevins, *United States,* 104–112; Chusid, "Concurrent Conferences," 58–63; Buckley, *United States,* 157–171; Cobbs Hoffman, *American Umpire,* 195–196; Noel H. Pugach, "American Friendship for China and the Shantung Question at the Washington Conference," *Journal of American History* 64 (June 1977): 67–86.

27. Vinson, *Parchment Peace,* 213–217; CEH, "The Pathway of Peace," September 4, 1923, *PP,* 10; Thomas J. McCormick, *America's Half-Century: United States Foreign Policy in the Cold War and After* (Johns Hopkins University Press, 1995), 25–27. See also Buckley, *United States,* 185–187; Sadao Asada, "Japan's 'Special Interests' and the Washington Conference," *American Historical Review* 67 (Oct. 1961): 62–70.

28. CEH, "Some Aspects of Foreign Policy," *PP*, 50–53; *CEHADS*, 108–110; William Appleman Williams, "The Legend of Isolationism in the 1920s," *Science & Society* (Winter 1954): 19; William A. Williams, *The Tragedy of American Diplomacy* (W. W. Norton, 1972), 158–161; Buell, *Washington Conference*, 240–279, 280–300; J. H. Wilson, *American Business*, 41–45, 184–218; Leopold, *Growth*, 433–438; Chusid, "Concurrent Conferences," 4–6; Goldman, *Sunken Treaties*, 146–150; Emily Rosenberg, *Spreading the American Dream: American Economic and Cultural Expansion* (Hill & Wang, 1982), 158–160; A. Whitney Griswold, *The Far Eastern Policy of the United States* (Harcourt, Brace, 1938), 305–320; Warren I. Cohen, *Empire Without Tears: American Foreign Relations, 1921–1933* (Temple University Press, 1987), 24–25, 31–32, 38.

29. *CEHMP*, 506–510, 522; Arthur S. Link and William B. Catton, *American Epoch: A History of the United States Since 1900*, vol. 2 (Alfred A. Knopf, 1973), 82–87. See also CEH, "To the President," final report on the Washington Conference, CEH Manuscript Collection, LC; Murray, *Harding Era*, 162–163; Herbert Feis, *The Diplomacy of the Dollar, 1919–1932* (W. W. Norton, 1966), 15–16; "What Uncle Sam Has Done for World Peace," *BDE*, February 12, 1922; Hyde, "Charles Evans Hughes, Secretary," 248–252.

30. John Dewey, "Public Opinion in Japan," *New Republic: Roads to Peace: A Handbook to the Washington Conference* (Republic Publishing, 1921), 24–29; Bruce Bliven, "A Japanese Rebuttal," *New Republic: Roads to Peace: A Handbook to the Washington Conference* (Republic Publishing, 1921), 39–44.

31. Timothy P. Maga, "Prelude to War? The United States, Japan, and the Yap Crisis, 1918–1922," *Diplomatic History* 9 (Summer 1985): 225–231.

32. Mae M. Ngai, "The Architecture of Race in American Immigration Law: A Reexamination of the Immigration Act of 1924," *Journal of American History* 86 (June 1999): 81–88.

33. Mae M. Ngai, "Nationalism, Immigration Control, and the Ethnoracial Remapping of America in the 1920s," *OAH Magazine of History* 21 (July 2007): 11–15. See also Kristofer Allerfeldt, "And We Got Here First: Albert Johnson, National Origins and Self-Interest in the Immigration Debate of the 1920s," *Journal of Contemporary History* 45 (Jan. 2010): 7–13.

34. *CEHMP*, 512–515; *AN*, 249–252.

35. "Statement by Representative Albert Johnson," April 21, 1924, CEH Manuscript Collection, LC; Lon Kurashige, *Two Faces of Exclusion: The Untold History of Anti-Asian Racism in the United States* (University of North Carolina Press, 2016), 115–116.

36. *CEHMP*, 515–517; *CEHADS*, 115–119; LaFeber, *Clash*, 144–146; Leopold, *Growth*, 436–437; Kurashige, *Two Faces*, 118–123.

37. *AN*, xxiv, 249–252. See also "Memorandum of Interview with Mr. A. C. Bedford of the Standard Oil Company," July 6, 1923, CEH Manuscript Collection, LC; Hugh R. Wilson, *Diplomat Between Wars* (Longmans, Green, 194),184–189; A. Whitney Griswold, *The Far Eastern Policy of the United States.* (Harcourt, Brace, 1938), 370–379; Vinson, "Charles Evans Hughes," 142–143; Leopold, *Growth*, 436–437; Stuart, *Department*, 277; Hyde, "Charles Evans Hughes, Secretary," 318–326.

38. CEH, "Russia," March 21, 1923, *PP*, 62–63. See also *CEHMP*, 524–528; *CEHADS*, 125–128; Hyde, "Charles Evans Hughes, Secretary," 280–288, 318–326.

39. CEH, "Russia," 59–64; Douglas Little, "Anti-Bolshevism and American Foreign Policy, 1919–1939: The Diplomacy of Self Delusion," *American Quarterly* 35 (Autumn 1983): 227, 379–380. See also W. A. Williams, *Tragedy*, 142–143; Cohen, *Empire*, 83–88; Paul Dukes, *The USA in the Making of the USSR: The Washington Conference, 1921–1922, and Uninvited Russia* (Routledge Curzon, 2004), 1–13, 68–73.

40. *AN*, 261–263; CEH, "Liberty Under Law," *Advocate of Peace Through Justice* (March 1920): 89–91; *CEHI*, 312–314; Hyde, "Charles Evans Hughes, Secretary," 287–288.

41. Kennan, *American Diplomacy*, 82–84, 126. See also Murray, *Harding Era*, 348–354; Palmer, *Twenties*, 81–83.

42. CEH, "Possible Gains," *Advocate of Peace Through Justice* 89 (Aug. 1927): 483; CEH, "Some Aspects of Foreign Policy," *PP*, 38–40.

43. Vinson, *Parchment Peace*, 213–217; Vinson, "Charles Evans Hughes, 1921–1925," 129; *CEHADS*, 111–113; Charles Cheney Hyde, "The Election of Charles Evans Hughes to the World Court," *American Journal of International Law* (Oct. 1928): 638; CEH, "Some Aspects of Foreign Policy," 38, 40; *CEHI*, 279, 310–303.

44. CEH, "Possible Gains," 475–485; Leuchtenburg, *Perils*, 114–119.

45. CEH, "Development of International Law," *AP*, 3–4; 11; CEH, "Some Observations on Recent Events," *Proceedings of the American Society of International Law* 20 (1926): 4, 11; CEH, "Some Observations on the Conduct of our Foreign Relations," *American Journal of International Law* 16 (1922): 365.

46. CEH, "Some Observations on the Conduct of our Foreign Relations," 365; CEH, "Development of International Law," *AP*, 11; CEH, "Some Observations on Recent Events," 4. CEH, "Peace," *Proceedings of the American Society of International Law* 23 (1929): 1; Edward Rhodes, "Charles Evans Hughes Reconsidered, or Liberal Isolationism in the New Millennium," in *The Real and the Ideal: Essays on International Relations in Honor of Richard H. Ullman*, ed. Anthony Lake and David Ochmanek (Rowman & Littlefield, 2001), 157.

47. CEH, "Possible Gains," 484; CEH, "Development of International Law," *AP*, 14. See also *CEHMP*, 507–510; Quincy Wright, "The Washington Conference," *American Political Science Review* 16 (May 1922): 285–297.

48. *CEHMP*, 4; CEH, "Possible Gains," 477. See also Oona Hathaway and Scott J. Shapiro, *The Internationalists: How a Radical Plan to Outlaw War Remade the World* (Simon & Schuster, 2017), 113–115; Zasloff, "Abolishing Coercion," 626–629.

49. CEH, "Pathway of Peace," *PP*, 3, 6–7, 15–16; Hughes, "Possible Gains," 475–479. See also *CEHMP*, 645–646; Leopold, *Growth*, 458–462; Melvyn P. Leffler, "Political Isolationism, Economic Expansionism, or Diplomatic Realism: American Policy Toward Western Europe, 1921–1933," in *U.S. Foreign Policy and National Security, 1920–2015*, ed. Melvyn P. Leffler (Princeton University Press, 2017), 104–113.

50. Hathaway and Shapiro, *The Internationalists,* ix–xix; Correspondence from Edward Rhodes, January 5, 2023. See also Tooze, *Deluge,* 474

51. Tooze, 517–518.

Chapter 8: Empire or Umpire? 1921–1925

1. *CEHMP,* 551–552; Harold Sproat and Margaret Sproat, *Toward a New Order of Sea Power: American Naval Policy and the World Scene, 1918–1922* (Princeton University Press, 1940), 100–117; "Hughes by Fiery Speech Ends Intervention Crisis," *NYT,* February 19, 1928.

2. *CEHMP,* 552–558; *CEHADS,* 339–340; "Hughes Fiery Speech."

3. *CEHMP,* 551–561.

4. *CEHMP,* 559–560; Paul A. Freund, "Charles Evans Hughes as Chief Justice," *Harvard Law Review* 81 (Nov. 1967): 35.

5. *CEHMP,* 559–560; CEH, "United States and Nicaragua, Remarks made at the Plenary Session, Sixth International Conference of American States, Havana, Cuba," February 18, 1928, *Current Speech Digest* 2, April 1928, CEH Manuscript Collection, LC; "Hughes Pledges US to Non-Aggression in This Hemisphere," *NYT,* February 17, 1928; "Hughes Fiery Speech."

6. Elizabeth Cobbs Hoffman, *American Umpire* (Harvard University Press, 2013), 17, 169–178, 210–211; Thomas J. McCormick, *America's Half-Century: United States Foreign Policy in the Cold War and After* (Johns Hopkins University Press, 1995), 27–28.

7. *CEHMP,* 559–561, "Hughes Fiery Speech."

8. CEH, "Latin American Relations," January 20, 1925, *PP,* 164–165; Arnulf Becker Lorca, "Human Rights in International Law? The Forgotten Origins of Human Rights in Latin America," *University of Toronto Law Journal* 67 (Fall 2017): 475–481.

9. "Pan-American Pact Extolled by Hughes," *NYT,* March 24, 1929; *AN,* 274–279; Juan Pablo Scarfi, "Pan American Legal Designs: The Rise and Fall of American International Law in the Western Hemisphere," in *Cooperation and Hegemony in US-Latin American Relations: Revisiting the Western Hemisphere Idea,* ed. Juan Pablo Scarfi and Andrew R. Tillman (Macmillan, 2016), 174–175, 179–186. See also *CEHADS,* 134–136; "Intervention's Victory at Havana" and "The Havana Conference in Latin American Eyes," *Literary Digest,* March 3, 1928; Stuart Beach, "Mr. Hughes and Latin America at Havana," *Independent,* March 3, 1928; William Hard, "What Happened at Havana," *Review of Reviews,* February 13, 1928; David M. K. Sheinin, *Argentina and the United States: An Alliance Contained* (University of Georgia Press, 2006), 56–59; Lars Schoultz, *Beneath the United States: A History of U.S. Policy Toward Latin America* (Harvard University Press 1998), 282–289; Samuel Flagg Bemis, *The Latin American Policy of the United States: An Historical Interpretation* (Harcourt, Brace, 1943), 250–252; Lester D. Langley, *America and the Americas: The United States in the Western Hemisphere* (University of Georgia Press, 2010), 127; Joan Hoff Wilson, *American Business and Foreign Policy, 1920–1933* (University Press of Kentucky, 1971), 163–164; *CEHI,* 260–268.

10. CEH, "The Outlook for Pan Americanism: Some Observations on the Sixth International Conference of American States," *Proceedings of the American Society of International Law* 22 (1928): 2–4. Scarfi, "Pan American," 183

11. *CEHMP*, 530–531.

12. David Dent, T*he Legacy of the Monroe Doctrine* (Greenwood Press, 1999), 1–4; William A. Williams, *The Contours of American History* (Quadrangle, 1966), 215–218; Cobbs-Hoffman, *American Umpire*, 170. See also Dexter Perkins, *A History of the Monroe Doctrine* (Little, Brown, 1963), 149–191; Joseph Smith, *The United States and Latin America: A History of American Diplomacy, 1776–2000* (Routledge, 2005), 67–68; Langley, *America and Americas*, 104–105; David. Healy, *United States Expansionism: The Imperialist Urge in the 1890s* (University of Wisconsin Press, 1970), 34, 110–126.

13. Smith, *United States and Latin America*, 71–74. See also Perkins, *History*, 228–232; Richard W. Leopold, *The Growth of American Foreign Policy: A History* (Alfred A. Knopf, 1962), 255–258.

14. Edmund. Morris, *Theodore Rex* (Random House, 2001), 177–192, 205, 325–326; Gail Bederman, *Manliness and Civilization* (University of Chicago Press, 1995), 190. See also Perkins, *History*, 232–235.

15. Perkins, 241. See also Morris, *Theodore Rex*, 217–219; Adam Burns, *American Imperialism: The Territorial Expansion of the United States, 1783–2013* (Edinburgh University Press, 2017), 137. See also Emily S. Rosenberg, *Financial Missionaries to the World: The Politics and Culture of Dollar Diplomacy, 1900–1930* (Duke University Press, 2003), 41–52; Cyrus Veeser, *A World Safe for Capitalism: Dollar Diplomacy and America's Rise to Global Power* (Columbia University Press, 2002), 1–6, 127–142; Noel Maurer, *The Empire Trap: The Rise and Fall of U.S. Intervention to Protect American Property Overseas, 1893–2013* (Princeton University Press, 2013), 88.

16. Benjamin Allen Coates, *Legalist Empire: International Law and American Foreign Relations in the Early Twentieth Century* (Oxford University Press, 2016), 124–128; A. Burns, *American Imperialism*, 174; James Hudson, *Bankers and Empire: How Wall Street Colonized the Caribbean* (University of Chicago Press, 2017), 228–235; Frank Ninkovich, *The Wilsonian Century: United States Foreign Policy Since 1900* (University of Chicago Press, 1999), 25–33. See also Lewis L. Gould, *The William Howard Taft Presidency* (University Press of Kansas, 2009), 79–92.

17. Warren I. Cohen, *Empire Without Tears: American Foreign Relations, 1921–1933* (Temple University Press, 1987), 8–11. See also Perkins, *History*, 248–257; Herbert Feis, *The Diplomacy of the Dollar, 1919–1932* (W. W. Norton, 1966), 2–6.

18. Perkins, 258, 314–326; John E. Fagg, *Pan Americanism* (Robert E. Krieger Publishing, 1982), 33–37; Paul W. Drake, "From Good Men to Good Neighbors," in *Exporting Democracy: The United States and Latin America; Themes and Issues*, ed. Abraham F. Lowenthal. (Johns Hopkins University Press, 1991), 3–5, 12–22. See also John Milton Cooper Jr., *Woodrow Wilson, A Biography* (Random House, 2011), 237–248; W. A. Williams, *Contours*, 409–412; Patricia O'Toole, *The Moralist, Woodrow Wilson and the World He Made* (Simon & Schuster, 2018), 90–108; Langley, *America and Americas*, 110–119; Maurer, *Empire Trap*, 92–103, 117–125.

19. Schoultz, *Beneath United States*, 255–256; Cobbs Hoffman, *American Um-*

pire, 168. See also Perkins, *History*, 332–335; Kenneth Grieb, *The Latin American Policy of Warren G. Harding* (Texas Christian University Press, 1977), ix–13; Eugene P. Trani and David L. Wilson, *The Presidency of Warren G. Harding* (Regents Press of Kansas, 1977), 132–133.

20. CEH, *Our Relations to the Nations of the Western Hemisphere* (Princeton University Press, 1928), 112–119; Max Paul Friedman and Tom Long, "Soft Balancing in the Americas: Latin American Opposition to U.S. Intervention, 1898–1936," *International Security* 40 (Summer 2015): 131. See also Schoultz, *Beneath United States*, 282–289.

21. Clifford B. Casey, "The Creation and Development of the Pan American Union," *Hispanic American Historical Review* 13 (November 1933): 437–456; "Hall of Americas for Arms Meeting," *NYT*, August 27, 1921.

22. Friedman and Long, "Soft Balancing," 120–140.

23. CEH, "The Pathway of Peace," September 4, 1923, *PP*, 6–10. See also CEH, "Observations on the Monroe Doctrine," August 30, 1923, *PP*, 113–141; CEH, "The Monroe Doctrine, Its Relation to American Foreign Policy in the Twentieth Century," November 30, 1923, *PP*, 142–163; Sumner Welles, *Naboth's Vineyard: The Dominican Republic, 1844–1924* (Paul P. Appel Publishers, 1966), 922–925; Ninkovich, *Wilsonian Century*, 81–85; *CEHI*, 254–259.

24. Philip C. Jessup, *Elihu Root*, vol. 1 (Dodd Mead, 1938), 469. See also Richard W. Leopold, *Elihu Root and the Conservative Tradition.* (Little, Brown, 1954), 62–69; Juan Pablo Scarfi, "In the Name of the Americas: The Pan-American Redefinition of the Monroe Doctrine and the Emerging Language of American International Law in the Western Hemisphere, 1898–1933," *Diplomatic History* 40 (April 2016): 201–206.

25. Healy, *United States Expansionism*, 144–158; Jessup, *Elihu Root*, 418–424, 488–492; Graham H. Stuart, *The Department of State: A History of its Organization, Procedure, and Personnel* (Macmillan, 1949), 202–209; Charles L. Stansifer, "Application of the Tobar Doctrine to Central America," *Americas* 23 (Jan. 1967): 252–255; Coates, *Legalist Empire*, 107–111.

26. CEH, "Latin American Relations," *PP*, 169. See also *CEHMP*, 411–412; Grieb, *Latin American Policy*, 17–36; *CEHI*, 242–249, Maurer, *Empire Trap*, 10–11.

27. Maurer, 8, 149, 184–185. See also CEH, "Monroe Doctrine," *PP*, 162; Joseph S. Tulchin, *The Aftermath of War: World War I and United States Policy Toward Latin America* (New York University Press, 1971), 99–103; Robert K. Murray, *The Harding Era: Warren G. Harding and His Administration* (University of Minnesota Press, 1969), 339–341.

28. *CEHMP*, 530–532; See also Grieb, *Latin American Policy*, 41–56; Schoultz, "*In Their Own Best Interest*," 73–74; Stansifer, "Application of Tobar," 260–265; Charles Cheney Hyde, "Charles Evans Hughes, Secretary of State," in *The American Secretaries of State and Their Diplomacy*, ed. Samuel Flagg Bemis (Cooper Square Publishers, 1963), 266–270.

29. *CEHMP*, 551; Perkins, *History*, 329–332; Fagg, *Pan Americanism*, 38–40; Grieb, *Latin American Policy*, 177–188.

30. *CEHMP*, 540–541; Murray, *Harding Era*, 335–341; Hyde, "Charles Evans Hughes, Secretary," 261–265.

31. Thomas Bender, *A Nation Among Nations: America's Place in World History* (Hill & Wang, 2006), 228–233.

32. CEH, "Observations on Monroe Doctrine," *PP*, 120–121; CEH, "Monroe Doctrine," *PP*, 159. See also CEH, *Our Relations to the Nations of the Western Hemisphere* (Princeton University Press, 1928), 11–16; *CEHMP*, 535–537.

33. CEH, "Observations on Monroe Doctrine," *PP*, 122–124; 136–137; CEH, "Monroe Doctrine," *PP*, 158–159; Perkins, *History*, 332–335; William A. Williams, *The Tragedy of American Diplomacy* (W.W. Norton, 1972), 128–130, 136; J. Varela, "The Meaning of the Monroe Doctrine to the Republic of Uruguay," *Annals of the American Academy of Political and Social Science* 3 (Jan. 1924): 21–23. See also Scarfi, "In the Name," 207–209.

34. CEH, "Observations on Monroe Doctrine," *PP*, 122, 124, 127–128; Perkins, 332–335; J. H. Wilson, *American Business*, 160–164. See also CEH, "Latin American Relations," *PP*, 164–169; CEH, *Our Relations to Nations*, 16–20; Welles, *Naboth's Vineyard*, 838, 922–925; *CEHI*, 237–242; Hyde, "Charles Evans Hughes, Secretary," 336–349.

35. CEH, "Acceptance Speech by Charles Evans Hughes, July 11, 1916," in Arthur S. Link and William M. Leary Jr., "Election of 1916," in *History of American Presidential Elections, 1789–1968*, vol. 3, ed. Arthur M. Schlesinger Jr. (McGraw Hill, 1971), 2295–2299; O'Toole, *Moralist*, 91–98, 101–108, 110–111; Cooper, *Woodrow Wilson*, 237–245; Coates, *Legalist Empire*, 128–235; E. Bradford Burns, *Latin America: A Concise Interpretive History* (Prentice Hall, 1994), 195–200; Smith, *United States and Latin America*, 56–59; Grieb, *Latin American Policy*, 129–148; Benjamin C. Montoya, *Risking Immeasurable Harm: Immigration Restriction and U.S.-Mexican Diplomatic Relations, 1924–1932* (University of Nebraska Press. 2020), 19–24; Maurer, *Empire Trap*, 137–147.

36. Memorandum of Interview with Mr. Paul D. Cravath of New York City, May 26, 1923, CEH Manuscript Collection, LC; *CEHMP* 541–548; R. Murray, *Harding Era*, 328–331; *CEHADS*, 138–139; Schoultz, *Beneath United States*, 272–277; Grieb, *Latin American Policy*, 129–148; Niall Palmer, *The Twenties in America: Politics and History* (Edinburgh University Press, 2006), 85–88; Montoya, *Immeasurable Harm*, 19–26; Richard Lowitt, *George W. Norris: The Persistence of a Progressive, 1913–1933* (University of Illinois Press, 1971), 369–373; Jonathan Zasloff, "Law and the Shaping of American Foreign Policy: The Twenty Years' Crisis," *Southern California Law Review* 77 (2004): 635–639; *CEHI*, 249–253.

37. *CEHMP*, 532–535; Kenneth J. Grieb, "Warren G. Harding and the Dominican Republic U.S. Withdrawal, 1921–1923," *Journal of Inter-American Studies* 11 (July 1969): 425–440; Grieb, *Latin American Policy*, 61–78; Welles, *Naboth's Vineyard*, 840, 853–900, 926–929; Burns, *American Imperialism*, 144–146; Drake, "From Good Men," 25–26; Maurer, *Empire Trap*, 92–103, 164–166; Cohen, *Empire*, 72.

38. Grieb, *Latin American Policy*, 109–123; Lowitt, *George W. Norris*, 368; Drake, "From Good Men," 24–26.

39. Lowitt, 145–146. See also Hudson, *Bankers*, 81–83, 107–116; Grieb, 85–102; Maurer, *Empire Trap*, 117–125, 166–168.

40. Lowitt, 372.

41. Maurer, 104–116, 158–163; Virginia L. Greer, "State Department Policy in Regard to the Nicaraguan Election of 1924," *Hispanic American Historical Review* 34 (Nov. 1954): 445–467.

42. Tulchin, *Aftermath of War*, 79–80; Wilson, *American Business*, 102; Fred H. Harrington, "Review of Charles Evans Hughes. by Merlo J. Pusey," *Hispanic American Historical Review* 32 (Aug. 1952): 426–427.

43. Hudson, *Bankers*, 5–8.

44. Herbert Feis, *The Diplomacy of the Dollar, 1919–1932* (W. W. Norton, 1966), v; Williams, *Tragedy*, 129. See also CEH, "Observations on Monroe Doctrine," 135–136; William A. Williams, "The Legend of Isolationism in the 1920's," *Science & Society* 18 (Winter 1954): 1–20.

45. Tulchin, *Aftermath*, 110–114, 175. See also David Burner, *Herbert Hoover, A Public Life* (Alfred A. Knopf, 1979), 84; William E. Leuchtenberg, *Herbert Hoover* (Henry Holt, 2009), 51–70; Herbert Hoover, *The Memoirs of Herbert Hoover: The Cabinet and the Presidency, 1920–1933* (Macmillan, 1952), 40; Maurer, *Empire Trap*, 149–150; Feis, *Diplomacy*, 6–17, 26–31; Wilson, *American Business*, 101–122; Williams, *Tragedy*, 127–137.

46. Rosenberg, *Financial Missionaries*, 107, 111–121. See also Maurer, *Empire Trap*, 175–187; Williams, *Tragedy*, 130.

47. Rosenberg, *Financial Missionaries*, 109–110.

48. Hudson, *Bankers*, 14–17, 253–276.

49. Rosenberg, *Financial Missionaries*, 120–121.

50. CEH, "Observations on Monroe Doctrine," *PP*, 137; Hans Morgenthau, "The Mainsprings of American Foreign Policy: The National Interest vs. Moral Abstractions," *American Political Science Review* 44 (Dec. 1950): 839.

51. CEH, "Latin American Relations," *PP*, 166, 168. See also CEH, "Monroe Doctrine," *PP*, 128–134; *CEHMP*, 534–535; *CEHADS*, 130–133; Langley, *America and Americas*, 124–127; Smith, *Latin America*, 59–65; Drake "From Good Men," 26–72.

52. *CEHMP*, 548–550.

53. Private correspondence from Edward Rhodes to author, January 5, 2023.

54. Correspondence from Rhodes; *CEHADS*, 128; Scarfi, "Pan American," 173–175; Scarfi, "In the Name," 214–215.

55. Tulchin, *Aftermath of War*, v, 251–253. See also *AN*, 263–264; Bemis, *Latin American Policy*, 202; Leopold, *Growth*, 463–471; Cobbs Hoffman, *American Umpire*, 177, 210–211; Karen Miller, "Charles Evans Hughes," in *Secretaries of State from John Jay to Colin Powell*, ed. Edward S. Mihakanin (Greenwood Press, 2004), 254–262.

56. Denna Frank Fleming, *The United States and the World Court* (Russell & Russell, 1968), 43, 49–50; Wilson, *American Business*, 55–58; Hyde, "Charles Evans Hughes, Secretary," 394–401.

57. CEH, "The Permanent Court of International Justice," April 27, 1923, *PP*, 69; Fleming, *United States and World Court*, 15–18.

58. CEH, "The Development of International Law," *Proceedings of the American Society of International Law* 19 (1925): 4; *SC*, 115–117; Richard D. Friedman,

"Charles Evans Hughes as International Lawyer," *Proceedings of the Annual Meeting of the American Society of International Law* 90 (1996): 145–147; "Hughes Asks Nation to Join World Court," *NYT*, November 11, 1925.

59. Fleming, *United States and World Court*, 19–23; Cobbs Hoffman, *American Umpire*, 188; Leopold, *Elihu Root*, 54–57.

60. CEH, "Permanent Court," *PP*, 65–88; Appendix A, "The Permanent Court of International Justice, Message from the President of the United States," February 24, 1923, and Appendix B, "A Letter to the President of the United States Regarding the Permanent Court," March 1, 1923, *PP*, 311–329; CEHMP, 596–599; *CEHADS*, 89–92; *CEHI*, 175–176; Leopold, *Elihu Root*, 161–164.

61. *AN*, 222–225; *CEHI*, 185–195; Michael Dunne, *The United States and the World Court, 1920–1935* (St. Martin's, 1988), 73–80.

62. Palmer, *Twenties*, 90; Andrew Sinclair, *The Available Man: The Life Behind the Masks of Warren Gamaliel Harding* (Quadrangle, 1965), 276. See also Fleming, *United States and World Court*, 40–51; Eugene P. Trani and David L. Wilson, *The Presidency of Warren G. Harding* (Regents Press of Kansas, 1977), 146–149; Lowitt, *George W. Norris*, 367–368.

63. Palmer, 91–93; Sinclair, *Available Man*, 277. See also Murray, *Harding Era*, 368–373; Dunne, *United States and World Court*, 88–91.

64. Sinclair, vi–viii, 283–288; Robert K. Murray, *The Politics of Normalcy: Governmental Theory and Practice during the Harding-Coolidge Era* (W. W. Norton, 1973), 99–101; Trani and Wilson, *Presidency*, 172–178.

65. CEH, "Warren G. Harding: Memorial Address, Feb. 27, 1924," *PP*, 283, 294, 302–303.

66. CEH, "Permanent Court," *PP*, 65–88; Appendix A and Appendix B, *PP*, 311–329; *CEHMP*, 600–603.

67. Fleming, *United States and World Court*, 95–116, 117–137; Manley O. Hudson, "The United States Senate and the World Court," *American Journal of International Law* 29 (April 1935): 301–307.

68. *CEHMP*, 600, 640–647. See also CEH, "The Organization and Methods of the Permanent Court of International Justice," Address before the Association of the Bar of the City of New York, January 10, 1930, CEH Manuscript Collection, LC; "Mr. Hughes in the International Court," CEH Manuscript Collection, LC; CEH, "The World Court as Going Concern," *American Bar Association Journal* 16 (March 1930): 151–157; Perkins, *History*, 306–308; Leopold, *Growth*, 454–457; Trani and Wilson, *Presidency*, 113; "Hughes Is Elected World Court Judge by the League," *NYT*, September 9, 1928, "Hughes Says Nation Is Fully Protected in The World Court," *NYT*, January 17, 1930, "World Court Vital to Peace Program, Hughes Declares," *NYT*, April 26, 1931.

69. *CEHI*, 152.

70. "Hughes a Failure as Seen by Pat Harrison," *NYT*, February 4, 1923. See also *CEHMP*, 654.

71. CEH, "Monroe Doctrine," *PP*, 142, 148.

72. CEH, "Monroe Doctrine," *PP*, 142–154: CEH, "Observations on Monroe Doctrine," *PP*, 140–141.

73. Stuart, *Department of State,* 277; *CEHMP,* 610–614. See also *CEHI,* 150–151; "Changes Cause Surprise," *NYT,* January 11, 1925.

74. *AN,* 281–283; *CEHI,* 149–150.

75. *CEHMP,* 614–615; *CEHI,* 151.

76. *AN,* 281–283; *CEHI,* 149–150.

77. "Hughes Asks Nation to Join World Court as 1,000 Honor Him," *NYT,* November 11, 1925.

78. Hughes Asks Nation."

79. Zasloff, "Law," 676–677; *CEHI,* 313–314; Hyde, "Charles Evans Hughes, Secretary," 394–401; *CEHADS,* 139–140.

80. CEH, "Pathway of Peace," *PP,* 8; John Milton Cooper Jr., "The Shock of Recognition: The Impact of World War I on America," *Virginia Quarterly Review* 76 (Autumn 2000): 579–584; James Grafton Rogers, "Hughes as Secretary of State," *American Bar Association Journal* 27 (July 1941): 411–412.

81. *CEHMP,* 632–636, 656; *AN,* 148n29, 285; "Fare Case Re-Appeal Cost IRT $120,000," *NYT,* March 9, 1929.

82. *AN,* 285–287; *CEHMP,* 384, 605, 619–630, 638–647.

83. *CEHMP,* 623–624; Robert A. Slayton, *Empire Statesman: The Rise and Redemption of Al Smith* (Free Press, 2001), 160–163.

84. *AN,* 339–343; *CEHMP,* 620–625.

85. *CEHMP,* 628–630; Ronald Reagan, "Remarks in New York City on Receiving the Charles Evans Hughes Gold Medal of the National Conference of Christians and Jews," March 23, 1982, American Presidency Project, accessed October 5, 2024, https://www.presidency.ucsb.edu/documents/remarks-new-york-city-receiving-the-charles-evans-hughes-gold-medal-the-national.

86. *CEHMP,* 626–627, 635–636; *AN,* 287–288.

87. *CEHMP,* 619

Chapter 9: Becoming Chief Justice, 1930–1941

1. *SC,* 56; Albert P. Blaustein and Roy M. Mersky, "Rating Supreme Court Justices," *American Bar Association Journal* 58 (Nov. 1972): 1183–1184.

2. *CEHMP,* 649, 652; Alphaeus Thomas Mason, *The Supreme Court from Taft to Burger* (Louisiana State University Press, 1979), 67.

3. *CEHMP,* 652. See also *AN,* 290–294; *CEHCJ,* 4–9; William G. Ross, *The Chief Justiceship of Charles Evans Hughes, 1930–1941* (University of South Carolina Press, 2007), 10–11; Paul A. Freund, "Charles Evans Hughes as Chief Justice," *Harvard Law Review* 81 (Nov. 1967): 5–8; Michael E. Parrish, *The Hughes Court: Justices, Rulings, and Legacy* (ABC-CLIO, 2006),10; Drew Pearson and Robert S. Allen, *The Nine Old Men* (Doubleday, Doran, 1936), 74–75; Alpheus Thomas Mason, *Harlan Fiske Stone, Pillar of the Law* (Viking, 1956), 274–283.

4. *CEHMP,* 654; Stephen Budiansky, *Oliver Wendell Holmes: A Life in Law, War and Ideas* (W. W. Norton, 2019), 445. See also Brad Snyder, *Democratic Justice: Felix Frankfurter, the Supreme Court and the Making of the Liberal Establishment* (W. W.

Norton, 2022), 194–195; "President Names Hughes Chief Justice," *NYT*, February 4, 1930; "Action on Hughes Set for Next Week," *NYT*, February 5, 1930.

5. *CEHMP*, 654–663; Women's Committee of the National Hughes Alliance, Hughes Campaign Service, *Bulletin* no. 7, September 21, 1916, 1–2; Mason, *Supreme Court*, 13. See also "Fight to Bar Hughes from Bench Opened by Senator Norris," *NYT*, February 11, 1930; *CEHSC*, 78–79; Richard Lowitt, *George W. Norris: The Persistence of a Progressive, 1913–1933* (University of Illinois Press, 1971), 435–437; Parrish, *Hughes Court*, 10; "President Names Hughes Chief Justice," *NYT*, February 4, 11, 1930.

6. "Hughes Is Attacked by Borah and Glass," *NYT*, February 12, 1930.

7. "Hughes Attacked"; *CEHSC*, 80–88; "Hughes Is Confirmed by Senate, 52–26," *NYT*, February 14, 1930.

8. "Hughes Attacked"; "Hughes Confirmed."

9. Hughes Confirmed"; "Hughes Attacked"; Lowitt, *George W. Norris*, 436–437. See also *CEHMP*, 657–662.

10. "The Opposition to Mr. Hughes," *BDE*, February 12, 1930; "Hughes Confirmed"; Richard Coke Lower, *A Bloc of One: The Political Career of Hiram W. Johnson* (Stanford University Press, 1993), 248.

11. Elizabeth Hughes Gossett, "My Father the Chief Justice," *Supreme Court Historical Society Yearbook, 1976* (Supreme Court Historical Society, 1975). 12; "Hughes Attacked;" "Hughes Confirmed; J. N. Ding, "Life of Public Service," *NYHT*, February 1930; Ross, *Chief Justiceship*, 1, 12–16. See also *AN*, 295–297; *CEHSC*, 78–90.

12. Zechariah Chafee Jr., "Charles Evans Hughes, " *Proceedings of the American Philosophical Society* 93 (1949): 272; Joel Richard Paul, *Without Precedent: Chief Justice John Marshall and his Times* (Riverhead Books, 2018), 1–4; "Hughes Takes Oath as Chief Justice," *NYT*, February 25, 1930.

13. Peter G. Fish, "William Howard Taft and Charles Evans Hughes: Conservative Politicians as Chief Judicial Reformers," *Supreme Court Review* 1975 (1975): 140–144; Mason, *Supreme Court*, 64–73.

14. Ross, *Chief Justiceship*, 16–19.

15. *AN*, 300; Ross, 20–21.

16. Arthur M. Schlesinger Jr., *The Age of Roosevelt: The Politics of* Upheaval, *1935–1936* (Houghton Mifflin, 1966), 455–457, 460. See also *CEHMP*, 670; Ross, 21–24; Parrish, *Hughes Court*, 13–15.

17. *CEHMP*, 670–671; Ross, 22–23, 28; Parrish, 14; Melvin I. Urofsky, *Louis D. Brandeis, a Life* (Schocken Books, 2009), 479–480; Freund, "Charles Evans Hughes Chief Justice, " 8–9; Andrew L. Kaufman, *Cardozo* (Harvard University Press,1998), 479–480; Jeff Shesol, *Supreme Power: Franklin Roosevelt vs. The Supreme Court* (W. W. Norton, 2010), 34.

18. *AN*, 301; Benjamin N. Cardozo, *The Nature of the Judicial Process* (Yale University Press: 1921), 137, 168–173; Schlesinger, *Politics of Upheaval*, 461–462; Kaufman, *Cardozo*, 3, 144; See also Ross, *Chief Justiceship*, 25–27; *CEHMP*, 682.

19. Mason, *Harlan Fiske Stone*, 3–6, 304–306; Schlesinger, *Politics of Upheaval*, 462–464; *AN*, 298; *CEHMP*, 787–788; Parrish, *Hughes Court*, 12, 15–16.

20. *OWHDH*, 1146–1151, 1163–1164; Finley Peter Dunne, *Mr. Dooley's Opin-*

ions (R. H. Russell, 1901), 26; Robert G. McCloskey, *The American Supreme Court* (University of Chicago Press, 1994), 12–13; Alphaeus T. Mason, "Politics and the Supreme Court: President Roosevelt's Proposal," *University of Pennsylvania Law Review* 85 (May 1937): 666; Schlesinger, *Politics of Upheaval*, 451, 459. See also G. Edward White, "Constitutional Change and the New Deal: The Internalist/Externalist Debate," *American Historical Review* 110 (Oct. 2005): 1094–1096; William E. Leuchtenburg, *The Supreme Court Reborn: The Constitutional Revolution in the Age of Roosevelt* (Oxford University Press, 1995), 142–162, 213–236; Laura Kalman, "The Constitution, the Supreme Court, and the New Deal," *American Historical Review* 110 (Oct. 2005): 1052–1067; William E. Leuchtenburg "Comment on Laura Kalman's Article," *American Historical Review* 110 (Oct. 2005): 1081–1092; Laura Kalman, *FDR's Gambit: The Court Packing Fight and the Rise of Legal Liberalism* (Oxford University Press, 2022), 283–289; Mason, *Harlan Fiske Stone*, 293–304; Michael E. Parrish, "The Hughes Court, the Great Depression, and the Historians," *Historian* 40 (Feb. 1978): 286–293.

21. Alexander M. Bickel, *The Least Dangerous Branch: The Supreme Court at the Bar of Politics* (Bobbs-Merrill, 1975), 16–33; G. Edward White, *The Constitution and the New Deal* (Harvard University Press, 2000).11–32; White, "Constitutional Change," 1094–1096; Barry Cushman, *Rethinking the New Deal Court: The Structure of a Constitutional Revolution* (Oxford University Press,1998), 3–7, 33–43; Parrish "Hughes Court, Great Depression," 293–298; Kalman, *FDR's Gambit*, 289–291.

22. Kalman, "The Constitution," 1055, 1074; Stephen M. Feldman, "The Rule of Law or the Rule of Politics? Harmonizing the Internal and External Views of Supreme Court Decision Making," *Law & Social Inquiry* 30 (Winter 2005): 93, 108, 129.

23. *SC*, 2, 236; Parrish, *Hughes Court*, 178–179; Parrish, "Hughes Court, Great Depression," 307–308.

24. CEH, "President Hughes in Westminster Hall," *American Bar Association Journal* 27 (July 1941): 416–418.

25. CEH, "President Hughes," 418–419. See also *CEHMP*, 588–590.

26. Robert H. Jackson, *The Supreme Court in the American System of Government* (Harvard University Press, 1967), 55–56.

27. McCloskey, *Supreme Court*, 212–213.

28. *CEHMP*, 688–690; Ross, *Chief Justiceship*, 226; "Home," Supreme Court of the United States, accessed October 5, 2024, https://www.supremecourt.gov; "Home," Architect of the Capitol, accessed October 5, 2024, https;//www.aoc.gov.

29. Jean Edward Smith, *John Marshall, Definer of a Nation* (Henry Holt, 1996), 284–285.

30. *AN*, 161–163; Ross, *Chief Justiceship*, 227; *CEHMP*, 688–690; Shesol, *Supreme Power*, 34, 176–177. See also Urofsky, *Louis D. Brandeis*, 587; Kaufman, *Cardozo*, 477; Pearson and Allen, *Nine Old Men*, 1–15.

31. Edwin McElwain, "The Business of the Supreme Court as Conducted by Chief Justice Hughes," *Harvard Law Review* 63 (Nov. 1949): 6.

32. Felix Frankfurter, "The Administrative Side of Chief Justice Hughes,"

Harvard Law Review 63 (Nov. 1949): 4; See also *AN*, 313–318; *CEHMP*, 683–690; White, *Constitution and New Deal*, 213; Ross, *Chief Justiceship*, 225; Peter G. Fish "The Judicial Conference: Formative Years under Taft and Hughes," in Peter G. Fish, *The Politics of Federal Judicial Administration* (Princeton University Press, 1973), 51–52, 62–70, 86–90.

33. McElwain, "Business," 21–26. Harlan F. Stone, "The Chief Justice," *American Bar Association Journal* 27 (July 1941): 407–408.

34. *SC*, 45–46, 57–58; Frankfurter, "Administrative Side," 4.

35. *CEHMP*, 665–666, 670; Ross, *Chief Justiceship*, 222; Felix Frankfurter, "Chief Justices I Have Known," *Virginia Law Review* 39 (Nov. 1953): 898–899; Alphaeus T. Mason, "President by Chance, Chief Justice by Choice," *American Bar Association Journal* 55 (Jan. 1969): 38; Merle William Loper, "The Court of Chief Justice Hughes: Contributions to Civil Liberties," *Wayne Law Review* 12 (Spring 1966): 537.

36. Ross, 219; *CEHMP*, 663; Robert H. Jackson, "The Judicial Career of Chief Justice Hughes," *American Bar Association Journal* 27 (July 1941): 408, 411; Frankfurter, "Chief Justices," 901. See also Freund, "Charles Evans Hughes Chief Justice, "38.

37. Frankfurter, 901; McElwain, "Business," 16–17. See also Freund, 13–21; Ross, 222–224.

38. McElwain, 12, 17; Frankfurter, "Administrative Side," 4. See also Frankfurter, "Chief Justices," 902; Freund, "Charles Evans Hughes Chief Justice," 38.

39. *AN*, 302; *SC*, 60; Frankfurter, "Administrative Side," 4. See also *CEHMP*, 676; Parrish, *Hughes Court*, 93; Ross, *Chief Justiceship*, 28n118.

40. *SC*, 58–60; McElwain, "Business," 14; *CEHMP*, 682; Mason, *Harlan Fiske Stone*, 788–789; Ross, 219–222. See also Parrish, 91–93; Urofsky, *Louis D. Brandeis*, 675.

41. *SC*, 61; Harlan F. Stone, "The Chief Justice," *American Bar Association Journal* 27 (July 1941): 408; Frankfurter, "Administrative Side," 3. See also Mason, 316–317, 789–791; McElwain, –15.

42. *AN*, 302. See also *SC*, 67–68; *CEHMP*, 675–677; McElwain, 13–14, 19–20; Frankfurter, "Administrative Side," 3–4; Ross, *Chief Justiceship*, 232–233; White, *Constitution and New Deal*, 213; Kaufman, *Cardozo*, 481; *CEHSC*, 94.

43. *CEHMP*, 678–679; Ross, 228–230.

44. Stone, "Chief Justice," 408; Kenneth M. Holland, "FDR and Charles Evans Hughes, President Versus Chief Justice," in *Franklin D. Roosevelt and the Transformation of the Supreme Court*, ed. Stephen K. Shaw, William D. Pederson, and Frank J. Williams (M. E. Sharpe, 2004), 95–96.

45. Irving Brant, "How Liberal Is Justice Hughes?," *New Republic*, July 21, 1937, and July 28, 1937; *CEHCJ*, 144–145a, 165a–d; Freund, "Charles Evans Hughes Chief Justice, "41. See also Ross, *Chief Justiceship*, 230–231; Mason, *Harlan Fiske Stone*, 459–460 and note.

46. G. Edward White, *The American Judicial Tradition: Profiles of Leading American Judges* (Oxford University Press, 1976), 213–215; Schlesinger, *Politics of Upheaval*, 465.

Chapter 10: *Packing the Court,* 1933–1937

1. James MacGregor Burns, *Roosevelt: The Lion and the Fox* (Harcourt, Brace & World, 1956), 119.

2. William E. Leuchtenburg, *The Perils of Prosperity, 1914–1932* (University of Chicago Press, 1958), 251–259; Arthur M. Schlesinger Jr., *The Age of Roosevelt: The Crisis of the Old Order, 1919–1933* (Houghton Mifflin, 1967), 230–247.

3. Bernard Bellush, *Franklin D. Roosevelt as Governor of New York.* (Columbia University Press, 1955), xii, 76–102, 129–149, 282; Arthur M. Schlesinger Jr., *The Age of Roosevelt: The Coming of the New Deal* (Houghton Mifflin, 1958), 263–273; Schlesinger, *Crisis of Old Order,* 224–247, 386–393; Burns, *Roosevelt,* 105–117.

4. "Franklin D. Roosevelt, First Inaugural Address," in *Great Issues in American History from Reconstruction to the Present Day, 1864–1969,* ed., Richard Hofstadter (Vintage, 1969), 351–357.

5. William E. Leuchtenburg, *Franklin D. Roosevelt and the New Deal* (Harper & Row, 1963), 45; Burns, *Roosevelt,* 163–168; 234–241; Schlesinger, *Coming of New Deal,* 4–13.

6. "*Franklin D. Roosevelt,* First Inaugural," 356; Leuchtenburg, *Franklin D. Roosevelt,* 46–62; Schlesinger, *Coming of New Deal,* 20–23.

7. Alpheus Thomas Mason, *The Supreme Court from Taft to Burger* (Louisiana State Press, 1979), 70; Norman Williams, "The Commerce Clause and the Myth of Federalism," *UCLA Law Review* 54 (Aug. 2007): 1884.

8. Stephen Budiansky, *Oliver Wendell Holmes: A Life in Law, War and Ideas* (W. W. Norton, 2019), 362–363; "Hammer v. Dagenhart," in *Great Issues,* 312–315.

9. Budiansky, *Oliver Wendell Holmes,* 294–295, 412; Daniel J. Hulsebosch, "The New Deal Court: Emergence of a New Reason," *Columbia Law Review* 90 (Nov. 1990): 1977, 1980–1985; Robert G. McCloskey, *The American Supreme Court* (University of Chicago Press, 1960/1994), 95–108.

10. *CEHMP,* 712–713; *CEHSC,* 193–194, 227–228.

11. G. Edward White, *The Constitution and the New Deal* (Harvard University Press, 2000), 277–279; William G. Ross, *The Chief Justiceship of Charles Evans Hughes, 1930–1941* (University of South Carolina Press, 2007), 36–37; Melvin I. Urofsky, *Louis D. Brandeis, a Life* (Schocken Books, 2009), 678–680; Alpheus Thomas Mason, *Brandeis: A Free Man's Life* (Viking, 1956), 607–610.

12. Ross, *Chief Justiceship,* 48–49. See also Richard D. Freidman, "Switching Time and Other Thought Experiments: The Hughes Court and Constitutional Transformation," *University of Pennsylvania Law Review* 142 (June 1994): 1911–1912.

13. *CEHMP,* 699; Ross, 50–51; *CEHSC,* 171–179; White, *Constitution,* 211–213.

14. *CEHMP,* 699; White, 212–213.

15. *CEHMP,* 699; White, 213; Edward S. Corwin, *The Twilight of the Supreme Court: A History of Our Constitutional Theory* (Yale University Press, 1934), 1, 181–184. See also *CEHADS,* 159–161; William E. Leuchtenburg, *The Supreme Court Reborn, The Constitutional Revolution in the Age of Roosevelt* (Oxford University

Press, 1995), 115–119; Joel Richard Paul, *Without Precedent: Chief Justice John Marshall and his Times* (Riverhead Books, 2018), 380–383; Jeff Shesol, *Supreme Power: Franklin Roosevelt vs. The Supreme Court* (W. W. Norton, 2010), 65–70; F. D. G. Ribble, "The Constitutional Doctrines of Chief Justice Hughes," *Columbia Law Review* 41 (Nov. 1941): 1204–1205.

16. Friedman, "Switching Time," 1918; White, *Constitution*, 6, 213–215. See also Edward A. Purcell Jr., "The New Deal 'Constitutional Revolution' as an Historical Problem," *Virginia Quarterly Review* 78 (Spring 2002): 238–255.

17. Ross, *Chief Justiceship*, 51–52.

18. Robert F. Cushman, *Cases in Civil Liberties* (Prentice Hall, 1989), 23–26; Ross, 51–52, Barry Cushman, *Rethinking the New Deal Court: The Structure of a Constitutional Revolution* (Oxford University Press,1998), 78–83; *OWHDH*, 137–145, 268–269. See also *CEHSC*, 124–125, James F. Simon, *FDR and Chief Justice Hughes: The President, The Supreme Court and the Epic Battle over the New Deal* (Simon & Schuster, 2012), 247–249; Shesol, *Supreme Power*, 70–73; Friedman, "Switching Time," 1919–1922.

19. Frank Freidel, "The Sick Chicken Case," in *Quarrels That Have Shaped the Constitution*, ed. John A. Garraty (Harper & Row, 1964), 195–199, 206; Schlesinger, *Coming of New Deal*, 94–102.

20. *CEHSC*, 214–217; White, *Constitution*, 111.

21. CEH, "President Hughes in Westminster Hall," *American Bar Association Journal* 27 (July 1941): 418; *CEHSC*, 218. See also *CEHMP*, 733–735; Ross, *Chief Justiceship*, 60; Shesol, *Supreme Power*, 88–92; Simon, *FDR and Chief Justice*, 249–251.

22. Simon, 240.

23. Shesol, *Supreme Power*, 99; *CEHMP*, 736. See also Simon, 251–254; Friedman, "Switching Time," 1923.

24. Ross, *Chief Justiceship*, 61–64; *CEHSC*, 202, 204.

25. *CEHSC*, 202, 204; Ross, 63; Leuchtenburg, *Supreme Court*, 85–88; *CEHMP*, 735–738. See also Shesol, *Supreme Power*, 100–106; Simon, *FDR and Chief Justice*, 255–257; Alpheus Thomas Mason, *Harlan Fiske Stone: Pillar of the Law* (Viking, 1956), 388–392; Friedman, "Switching Time," 1923–1927; Sebastian Edwards, *American Default: The Untold Story of FDR, the Supreme Court and the Battle Over Gold* (Princeton University Press, 2018), 136–140; David Glick, "Conditional Strategic Retreat: The Court's Concession in the 1935 Gold Clause Cases," *Journal of Politics* 71 (July 2009): 802–812.

26. Ross, 65. See also Shesol, 116–118; Simon, 257–8; *CEHSC*, 229–230; "Justice Roberts Holds NRA's Future in His Hands," *BDE*, May 7, 1935.

27. Ross, 65–66.

28. Ross, 65–66; *CEHMP*, 738. See also Shesol, *Supreme Power*, 116–118; Simon, *FDR and Chief Justice*, 257–258; *CEHSC*, 229–233; Leuchtenburg, *Supreme Court*, 39–48; Friedman, "Switching Time," 1928–1930; *CEHCJ*, 217–218; "Roberts Holds NRA's Future," *BDE*, May 7, 1935.

29. Ross, 70.

30. Shesol, *Supreme Power*, 143–144. See also Ross, 70–71; Leuchtenburg, *Supreme Court*, 70–81.

31. Freidel, "Sick Chicken," 202. See also Simon, *FDR and Chief Justice*, 258–260.

32. Mason, *Harlan Fiske Stone*, 397; *CEHABH*, 7.

33. *CEHMP*, 739–741

34. Freidel, "Sick Chicken," 204; Shesol, *Supreme Power*, 135–136; See also Ross, *Chief Justiceship*, 67–69; *CEHADS*, 148–149; Cushman, *Rethinking*, 156–159; Freidman, "Switching Time," 1930–1932; Kenneth M. Holland, "FDR and Charles Evans Hughes, President Versus Chief Justice," in *Franklin D. Roosevelt and the Transformation of the Supreme Court*, ed. Stephen K. Shaw, William D. Pederson, and Frank J. Williams (M. E. Sharpe, 2004), 83–85.

35. Simon, *FDR and Chief Justice*, 259.

36. Simon, 264. See also Freidel, "Sick Chicken," 207–208; *CEHMP*, 739–742; Cushman, *Rethinking*, 156–159; Burns, *Roosevelt*, 222–223; Schlesinger, *Coming of New Deal*, 102, 152–176.

37. Freidel, 206; Shesol, *Supreme Power*, 140–146, 152–157; Ross, *Chief Justiceship*, 71–72; Leuchtenburg, *Supreme Court*, 82–98; "Washington Studies Plan for a Quick Amendment to the Federal Constitution," *NYT*, June 2, 1935.

38. Drew Pearson and Robert S. Allen, *The Nine Old Men* (Doubleday, Doran, 1936), 37, 40, 74, 96.

39. Simon, *FDR and Chief Justice*, 238, 279.

40. Ross, *Chief Justiceship*, 74–75.

41. Ross, 74–75; *AN*, 309–310. See also *CEHMP*, 743–745; Burns, *Roosevelt*, 231–233; Shesol, *Supreme Power*, 174–179, 184–190; Simon, *FDR and Chief Justice*, 275–282; Friedman, "Switching Time," 1953–1956.

42. Mason, *Harlan Fiske Stone*, 410; Ross, 74–77. See also Parrish, *Hughes Court*, 32–33, 184–185.

43. Shesol, *Supreme Power*, 210–211. See also *CEHSC*, 205–210; Leuchtenburg, *Supreme Court*, 103–104; Schlesinger, *Coming of New Deal*, 319–334; Parrish, *Hughes Court*, 32–33, 67, 69, 132–134; Urofsky, *Louis D. Brandeis*, 708–709.

44. Shesol, *Supreme Power*, 211–212. See also Ross, *Chief Justiceship*, 79–86.

45. *AN*, 342–343; Ross, 82–83; Holland, "FDR and Charles Evans Hughes," 91. See also *CEHSC*, 105–107.

46. Simon, *FDR and Chief Justice*, 288. See also White, *Constitution*, 70–71, 112; B. Cushman, *Rethinking*, 92–93.

47. Simon, *FDR and Chief Justice*, 288.

48. Simon, 290. See also *AN*, 310–311; *CEHMP*, 746; Ross, *Chief Justiceship*, 77–79; Shesol, *Supreme Power*, 213–214; Cushman, *Rethinking*, 161–162; *CEHSC*, 223; Parrish, *Hughes Court*, 34–35; Kaufman, *Cardozo*, 522–524; Friedman, "Switching Time," 1961; Samuel J. Konefsky, "Review of Charles Evans Hughes by Merlo J. Pusey," *Yale Law Journal* 61 (May 1952): 773–774.

49. *CEHSC*, 127.

50. *CEHMP*, 700–702. See also Friedman, "Switching Time," 1937.

51. Ross, *Chief Justiceship*, 91; *CEHABH*, 9; Mason, *Harlan Fiske Stone*, 425; *CEHMP*, 747. See also Simon, *FDR and Chief Justice*, 289–291; Shesol, *Supreme Power*, 219–225; B. Cushman, *Rethinking*, 92–104; *CEHSC*, 128–129.

52. Simon, 290–291; Leuchtenburg, *Supreme Court*, 105–106; Shesol, 222–

223. See also Ross, *Chief Justiceship*, 92–93; B. Cushman, 94–105; Parrish, *Hughes Court*, 35; Mason, *Harlan Fiske Stone*, 424–426.

53. Burns, *Roosevelt*, 271, 275. See also Shesol, 239–242; Simon, 291–298; *OWHDH*, 416–418.

54. Shesol, 282. See also Simon, 306–316; Ross, *Chief Justiceship*, 101–105; Burns, 291–297.

55. Shesol, 203–210: Ross, 104; Leuchtenburg, *Supreme Court*, 91–96; Burns, 295–297; Parrish, *Hughes Court*, 24, 233–235; James MacGregor Burns, *Packing the Court* (Penguin Books, 2009), 122.

56. *SC*, 74–77; "Publius, No. 79," Alexander Hamilton, James Madison, John Jay, *The Federalist Papers* (New American Library, 1961), 474–475.

57. Leuchtenburg, *Supreme Court*, 133–134; *CEHSC*, 250. See also Shesol, *Supreme Power*, 273, 291–298; Michael Nelson, "The President and the Court: Reinterpreting the Court-packing Episode of 1937," *Political Science Quarterly* 103 (Summer 1988): 276–280; Laura Kalman, "The Constitution, the Supreme Court, and the New Deal," *American Historical Review* 110 (Oct. 2005): 1052–1055, 1074–1079.

58. Burns, *Roosevelt*, 291–292.

59. Burns, 291–315; *CEHMP*, 753. See also Laura Kalman, *FDR's Gambit: The Court Packing Fight and the Rise of Legal Liberalism* (Oxford University Press, 2022), 268–271; Burns, *Packing Court*, 153–154; Leuchtenburg, *Supreme Court*, 160; Nelson, "President and Court," 276–287; Theresa Niedziela, "Franklin D. Roosevelt and the Supreme Court," *Presidential Studies Quarterly* (Fall 1976): 51–57; Jamie L. Carson and Benjamin Kleinerman, "A Switch in Time Saves Nine: Institutions, Strategic Actors, and FDR's Court-Packing Plan," *Public Choice* 113 (Dec. 2002): 301–319.

60. "President's Shocking Message," *BDE*, February 6, 1937. See also Shesol, *Supreme Power*, 298–306; Ross, *Chief Justiceship*, 105–111; Kalman, *FDR's Gambit*, 122.

61. "To Furnish the Supreme Court Practical Assistance" *WP*, February 6, 1937. See also Shesol, 324–331, 353–367; Simon, *FDR and Chief Justice*, 316–319; Robert H. Jackson, *The Supreme Court in the American System of Government* (Harvard University Press, 1967), 22–23; William G. Ross, "The Role of Religion in the Defeat of the 1937 Court Packing Plan," *Journal of Law and Religion* 23 (2007/2008): 629, 639–645, 648–662.

62. Burns, *Roosevelt*, 299–300. See also *CEHMP*, 754; Shesol, 315–331, 350–357; Ross, *Chief Justiceship*, 107–108; Simon, *FDR and Chief Justice*, 318–319; Kalman, *FDR's Gambit*, 125–129.

63. *CEHMP*, 755. See also Shesol, 384–401; Simon, 321–323; Burns, *Roosevelt*, 301–302; Ross, 114–118; B. Cushman, "Rethinking," 218–220; "Hughes, Brandeis Hit Court Plan," *BDE*, March 22, 1937.

64. *AN*, 303–307; Ross, 115–119; Burns, 301–303. See also Simon, 323–324; *CEHABH*, 10–12; Urofsky, *Brandeis*, 715–718; Mason, *Louis D. Brandeis*, 624–627; Kalman, *FDR's Gambit*, 160–166; Brad Snyder, *Democratic Justice: Felix Frankfurter, the Supreme Court and the Making of the Liberal Establishment* (W. W. Norton, 2022), 272–274; *CEHCJ*, 285–301.

65. *AN*, 307–308; B. Cushman, *Rethinking*, 36–37; Arthur M. Schlesinger Jr., *The Age of Roosevelt: The Politics of Upheaval, 1935–1936* (Houghton Mifflin, 1966), 395. See also Cushman, "Rethinking," 250–255; *CEHABH*, 9–10; G. Edward White, "Constitutional Change and the New Deal: The Internalist/Externalist Debate," *American Historical Review* 110 (Oct. 2005): 1101–1103.

66. Ross, *Chief Justiceship*, 97–98.

67. Simon, *FDR and Chief Justice*, 303; Edward A. Purcell Jr., "Understanding "Curtiss-Wright," *Law and History Review* 31 (Nov. 2013): 669–678.

68. *CEHSC*, 256–257. See also Ross, *Chief Justiceship*, 98–100; Simon, 303–305.

69. Ross, 120–121; Urofsky, *Louis D. Brandeis*, 719.

70. *AN*, 311–313; *CEHMP*, 751; Shesol, *Supreme Power*, 404–405, 414–415.

71. *CEHMP*, 757; Simon, *FDR and Chief Justice*, 300; Shesol, 405.

72. Shesol, 406.

73. Shesol, 406, 407; *CEHMP*, 703; Ross, *Chief Justiceship*, 119–120; Friedman, "Switching Time," 1936–1938. See also Hulsebosch, "New Deal Court," 2011–2014; Konefsky, "Review of Charles Evans Hughes," 771–774; Ribble, "Constitutional Doctrines," 1203–1207.

74. Shesol, *Supreme Power*, 407–409.

75. Shesol, 409–415; *CEHSC*, 133–135; Mason, *Harlan Fiske Stone*, 455–456; "Spring Practice," *Pittsburgh Post-Gazette*, April 1, 1937.

76. Shesol, 434, 407–415; Ross, *Chief Justiceship*, 119, 125–127; Leuchtenburg, *Supreme Court*, 142–144, 177, Friedman, "Switching Time," 1947–1953.

77. Ribble, "Constitutional Doctrines," 1203–1207; Richard A. Epstein, *How Progressives Rewrote the Constitution* (Cato Institute, 2006), 92–100. See also Friedman, 1937–1938; *CEHSC*, 130–135.

78. Shesol, *Supreme Power*, 421–428.

79. Ross, *Chief Justiceship*, 121–122; *CEHSC*, 261–262. See also Konefsky, "Review of Charles Evans Hughes," 771–774; Edward S. Corwin, "Review of Charles Evans Hughes by Merlo J. Pusey," *American Political Science Review* 46 (Dec. 1952): 1171–1173.

80. Shesol, *Supreme Power*, 430–431; *CEHMP*, 758–759.

81. Shesol, 430–431; *CEHMP*, 758–759.

82. *AN*, 311–313; Ross, *Chief Justiceship*, 122–123; *CEHSC*, 261–265; Cushman, *Rethinking*, 107–138; Friedman, "Switching Time," 1961–1967; *CEHCJ*, 313–333; Ribble, "Constitutional Doctrines," 1191–1192, 1199; Hulsebosch, "New Deal Court," 2008–2015.

83. Parrish, *Hughes Court*, 160; Ross, 147. See also *CEHSC*, 165–166; Schlesinger, *Coming of New Deal*, 397–406.

84. Shesol, *Supreme Power*, 432–433; Ross, 122–123.

85. Simon, *FDR and Chief Justice*, 329; Shesol, 433–437; Ross, 123–124.

86. Shesol, 435.

87. Shesol, 435–439, 506. See also Ross, *Chief Justiceship*, 131; Leuchtenburg, *Supreme Court*, 145–149.

88. Ross, 128; *AN*, 302–303; Simon, *FDR and Chief Justice*, 334; Cushman, "Rethinking," 214–215; "Several Justices Expected to Resign," *BDE*, February 6, 1937.

89. *CEHMP*, 760–761; Simon, 334–338; Shesol, *Supreme Power*, 444–453.

90. Ross, *Chief Justiceship*, 128–129; Parrish, *Hughes Court*, 37, 66. See also Kaufman, *Cardozo*, 527–529; Cushman, *Rethinking*, 22–23.

91. Ross, 129. Parrish, 37.

92. Shesol, *Supreme Power*, 453–454; Irving Brant, "How Liberal Is Justice Hughes?" *New Republic*, July 21, 1937.

93. Shesol, 468–469.

94. Shesol, 470; Kalman, *FDR's Gambit*, 198, 215–221, 262. See also Simon, *FDR and Chief Justice*, 339; Ross, *Chief Justiceship*, 131–132. Leuchtenburg, *Supreme Court*, 146–148.

95. Simon, 340.

96. Shesol, *Supreme Power*, 481, 483–484; Schlesinger, *Coming of New Deal*, 568

97. Shesol, 486–489.

98. Simon, *FDR and Chief Justice*, 341. See also Leuchtenburg, *Supreme Court*, 151–153.

99. Shesol, *Supreme Power*, 518, Kalman, *FDR's Gambit*, 279–303. See also Leuchtenburg, *Supreme Court*, 155–156; Nelson, "President and Court," 286–293.

100. Kalman, 291–292; William E. Leuchtenburg, "Comment on Laura Kalman's Article," *American Historical Review* 110 (Oct. 2005): 1081–1092; Shesol, 501–502; 519; Ross, *Chief Justiceship*, 133–136; White, *Constitution*, 13; Cushman, *Rethinking*, 3–4; Konefsky, "Review of Charles Evans Hughes," 771–774; James MacGregor Burns, *Packing the Court* (Penguin Books, 2009), 148–150.

101. *CEHSC*, 279; William E. Leuchtenburg, "Charles Evans Hughes: The Center Holds," *North Carolina Law Review* 83 (2005): 1200–1203.

102. James A. Henretta, "Charles Evans Hughes and the Strange Death of Liberal America," *Law and History Review* 24 (Spring 2006): 117; Holland, "FDR and Charles Evans Hughes," 107.

103. Ross, *Chief Justiceship*, 230.

104. *CEHMP*, 771–772; Konefsky, "Review of Charles Evans Hughes," 774; Cushman, "Rethinking," 243–249; Cushman, *Rethinking*, 3–5; Kalman, *FDR's Gambit*, 261.

105. Cushman, *Rethinking*, 3–5, 40–43, 224–225.

106. Cushman, 42; Cushman, "Rethinking," 260; Kalman, *FDR's Gambit*, 260, 292–295, 300–303.

107. Cushman, "Rethinking," 201–208, 256–261; *AN*, 307–313; Friedman, "Switching Time," 1892–1903; Henretta, "Charles Evans Hughes and Strange Death," 115–118, 149–150; White, *Constitution*, 302–312; White, "Constitutional Change," 1101–1112; Konefsky, "Review of Charles Evans Hughes," 766–772; Parrish, *Hughes Court*, 39; Ross, *Chief Justiceship*, 136.

108. Ross, 117; *CEHCJ*, 353–354, 358–359; *AN*, 307.

109. Ross, 242. See also Parrish, *Hughes Court*, 177–179.

110. Leuchtenburg, *Supreme Court*, 161–162. See also Holland, "FDR and Charles Evans Hughes," 102–108; Simon, *FDR and Chief Justice*, 341–342.

Chapter 11: Reorienting the Court, 1937–1941

1. Michael E. Parrish, *The Hughes Court: Justices, Rulings, and Legacy* (ABC-CLIO, 2006), 177–179.

2. Jeff Shesol, *Supreme Power: Franklin Roosevelt vs. The Supreme Court* (W. W. Norton, 2010), 514. See also *CEHMP*, 773–774; William G. Ross, *The Chief Justiceship of Charles Evans Hughes, 1930–1941* (University of South Carolina Press, 2007), 138; Parrish, *The Hughes Court*, 114–116; Noah Feldman, *Scorpions: The Battles and Triumphs of FDR's Great Supreme Court Justices* (Hatchette, 2010), 53–59, 133–143; Tony Freyer, *Hugo L. Black and the Dilemma of American Liberalism* (Scott, Foresman, 1990), 16–71.

3. Parrish, *Hughes Court*, 116–118; Ross, *Chief Justiceship*, 138.

4. Feldman, *Scorpions*, 161, 28–31, 157–163. See also Ross, *Chief Justiceship*, 139–140; Parrish, *Hughes Court*, 118–120; Brad Snyder, *Democratic Justice: Felix Frankfurter, the Supreme Court and the Making of the Liberal Establishment* (W. W. Norton, 2022), 309, 313–331.

5. Feldman, 60–67, 170–174; Ross, 140; Parrish, 120–122; Melvin I. Urofsky, *Louis D. Brandeis, a Life* (Schocken Books, 2009), 750–751.

6. Ross, 138–139. See also Parrish, 122–124; Feldman, *Scorpions*, 182–184.

7. Ross, 141–156, 171.

8. Ross, 147, 154–55; *CEHSC*, 271–272.

9. Ross, 147–148, 152, 163; *CEHSC*, 267, 271–272.

10. *CEHSC*, 199–200, 269–270. Ross, 80, 161–162.

11. *CEHSC*, 267, 279; *CEHCJ*, 363–366; Robert H., Jackson, "The Judicial Career of Chief Justice Hughes," *American Bar Association Journal* 27 (July 1941): 408–409. See also F. D. G. Ribble, "The Constitutional Doctrines of Chief Justice Hughes," *Columbia Law Review* 41 (Nov. 1941): 1200–1203.

12. *SC*, 50–51, 55.

13. *SC*, 170, 228; *CEHMP*, 729. See also Ross, *Chief Justiceship*, 172, 202–203; *CEHSC*,158; Merle William Loper, "The Court of Chief Justice Hughes: Contributions to Civil Liberties," *Wayne Law Review* 12 (Spring 1966): 536–537; Joseph Percival Pollard, "Hughes the Humanitarian," *North American Review* 229 (April 1930): 444–448.

14. *SC*, 225–228.

15. *SC*, 187–188, 192; CEH, "Address before the New York State Bar Association, Jan. 14, 1916: Some Aspects of the Development of American Law," *AP*, 349–352.

16. *AN*, 339–343; *SC*, 193–199. See also CEH, "Address before NYS Bar," *AP*, 349–351.

17. *CEHSC*, 140.

18. *CEHSC*, 140; *CEHMP*, 718; Ross, *Chief Justiceship*, 172–175; *OWHDH*, 686–689.

19. *CEHSC*, 139. See also Richard D. Freidman, "Switching Time and Other Thought Experiments: The Hughes Court and Constitutional Transformation," *University of Pennsylvania Law Review* 142 (June 1994): 1907.

20. Ross, *Chief Justiceship*, 175–177.

21. *CEHMP*, 720–721; *CEHSC*, 147. See also Friedman, "Switching Time," 1907–1908; *OWHDH*, 693–702.

22. *CEHSC*,141–142; Stephen Budiansky, *Oliver Wendel Holmes: A Life in Law, War and Ideas* (W. W. Norton, 2019), 441.

23. Ross, *Chief Justiceship*, 186; *CEHSC*, 143; *OWHDH*, 729–746.

24. Ross, 183–184.

25. Ross, 183–184. See also Alpheus Thomas Mason, *Harlan Fiske Stone, Pillar of the Law* (Viking Press, 1956), 513–516; Barry Cushman, "Carolene Products and Constitutional Structure," *Supreme Court Review* 2012 (January 2013): 326–330; Snyder, *Democratic Justice*, 351.

26. *CEHMP*, 721.

27. *CEHMP*, 721–722. See also *CEHSC*, 150–152; *OWHDH*, 702–706.

28. *CEHMP*, 721–722; Ross, *Chief Justiceship*, 181–182; *CEHSC*, 150–152; Parrish, *Hughes Court*, 44, 61, 100, 164–165; Joseph Proskauer in *Proceedings of the Bar and Officers of the Supreme Court of the United States, November 4, 1949. Proceedings before the Supreme Court of the United States, May 8, 1950, in Memory of Charles Evans Hughes* (Washington, DC, 1950), 26.

29. Ross, 188. See also Loper, "Court," 584–586.

30. *CEHCJ*, 41–43; Snyder, *Democratic Justice*, 353–356; Ross, 188.

31. Loper, "Court," 584–588, 591–593; Snyder, *Democratic Justice*, 350–356; Parrish, *Hughes Court*, 47–48, 120, 169; Ross, 188–189; *CEHCJ*, 41–44.

32. Snyder, *Democratic Justice*, 355–359; Parrish, 169; Ross, 188–189; *CEHCJ*, 42–44.

33. Snyder, 356–362, 422–429; CEH, "Roger Williams," in *PP*, 271–272; *CEHMP*, 728–729; Mason, *Harlan Fiske Stone*, 525–535; James A. Henretta, "Charles Evans Hughes and the Strange Death of Liberal America," *Law and History Review* 24 (Spring 2006): 152–153.

34. Robert F. Cushman, *Cases in Civil Liberties* (Prentice Hall, 1989), 203–204; Donald L Drakeman, "Everson v. Board of Education and the Quest for the Historical Establishment Clause," *American Journal of Legal History* 49 (April 2007): 127.

35. *CEHSC*, 155. See also Loper, "Court," 586–588.

36. *SC*, 175–176.

37. Dan Carter, *Scottsboro: A Tragedy of the American South* (Louisiana University Press, 2007), 3–25, 26–50, 232.

38. Hugh T. Murray Jr., "Changing America and the Changing Image of Scottsboro," *Phylon* 38 (1977): 177; Langston Hughes, *The Collected Poems of Langston Hughes*, ed. Arnold Rampersad (Alfred A. Knopf, 1996), 168.

39. Hugh T. Murray Jr., "The NAACP Versus the Communist Party: The Scottsboro Rape Cases, 1931–1932," *Phylon* 28 (1967): 277–278, 284; Carter, *Scottsboro*, 3–50; Michael J. Klarman, "The Racial Origins of Modern Criminal Procedure," *Michigan Law Review* 99 (Oct. 2000): 48–50.

40. Ross, *Chief Justiceship*, 178. See also *CEHMP*, 724; Carter, *Scottsboro*, 160–163.

41. Ross, 177–181; *CEHSC*, 158; Parrish, *Hughes Court*, 80, 84, 146, 172, 183; Carter, 160–164; Loper, "Court," 542–152; R. Cushman, *Cases*, 37–44.

42. Ross, 209. See also *CEHMP*, 723–724; Carter, 155–173.

43. Klarman, "Racial Origins," 62–64; Ross, 210.

44. Ross, 210; Carter, *Scottsboro*, 326, 411–414, 425–427. See also Loper, "Court," 560–561.

45. Ross, 196, 208. See also Loper, 542–557.

46. *CEHMP*, 724–726. See also Ross, 196–197.

47. *CEHSC*, 97; Klarman, "Racial Origins," 93. See also Loper, "Court," 544–545.

48. Ross, *Chief Justiceship*, 197–199. See also Freyer, *Hugo L. Black*, 82–83.

49. Ross, 215–216. See also Richard. Kluger, *Simple Justice: The History of Brown v. Board of Education and Black America's Struggle for Equality* (Alfred A. Knopf, 1987), 202–204, 212–221.

50. *CEHMP*, 726; *CEHSC*, 163–164; Ross, 215–216.

51. Kluger, *Simple Justice*, 213; Ross, 217; Parrish, *Hughes Court*, 171.

52. *CEHSC*, 164–165. See also *CEHMP*, 726–727; Ross, 8, 216; Loper, "Court," 570–572.

53. Ross, 208, 212–215; *CEHMP*, 621–622; *SC*, 183–184; *CEHSC*, 161–162; Parrish, *Hughes Court*, 43, 170–171.

54. *CEHMP*, 622.

55. *OWHDH*, 702–706, 1142–1143; Loper, "Court," 588.

56. Shesol, *Supreme Power*, 432; *CEHMP*, 370, 770–771.

57. B. Cushman, "Carolene Products," 320–322.

58. B. Cushman, 330–334, 353–361.

59. B. Cushman, 330–341.

60. B. Cushman, 353–363.

61. B. Cushman, 363–367. See also Ross, *Chief Justiceship*, 141–142.

62. B. Cushman, 368–371; Parrish, *Hughes Court*, 216–217.

63. *CEHCJ*, 383–388; B. Cushman, 371–374. See also Ross, *Chief Justiceship*, 150; Mason, *Harlan Fiske Stone*, 551–552.

64. B. Cushman, 374; Mason, 552.

65. *CEHSC*, 266.

66. *SC*, 192. See also *CEHMP*, 770–771; B. Cushman, "Carolene Products," 373–377; Mason, *Harlan Fiske Stone*, 553–556.

67. *SC*, 193, 197; Proskauer, *Proceedings*, 28. See also Ross, *Chief Justiceship*, 179–180; Klaus H. Heberle, "From Gitlow to Near: Judicial 'Amendment' by Absent-Minded Incrementalism," *Journal of Politics* 34 (May 1972): 458–460, 473–483.

68. Henretta, "Charles Evans Hughes and Strange Death," 115–116, 161–178.

69. Ross, *Chief Justiceship*, 119.

70. Nathan Miller in *Proceedings*, 17–20.

71. Joel Richard Paul, *Without Precedent: Chief Justice John Marshall and his Times* (Riverhead Books, 2018), 3–4; Jean Edward Smith, *John Marshall, Definer of a Nation* (Henry Holt, 1996), 19.

72. Paul A. Freund, "Charles Evans Hughes as Chief Justice," *Harvard Law Review* 81 (Nov. 1967): 43.

73. Freund, "Charles Evans Hughes as Chief Justice," 43; *CEHSC*, 280–281; Paul, *Without Precedent*, 239–240; Drew Pearson and Robert S. Allen, *The Nine Old Men* (Doubleday, Doran, 1936), 90. See also William S. Murray, "Review of Charles Evans Hughes and the Supreme Court by Samuel Hendel," *University of Pennsylvania Law Review* 99 (May 1951): 1045–1047.

74. *CEHMP*, 692–693. See also Henretta, "Charles Evans Hughes and Strange Death," 161–178; CEH, "Madison," *American Bar Association Journal* 18 (Jan. 1932): 854–859.

75. CEH, "Address before NYS Bar," *AP*, 355; *SC*, 45–46. See also Ribble, "Constitutional Doctrines," 1210.

Conclusion, 1941–1948

1. *CEHMP*, 782, 802.

2. CEH, "Unity to Keep Our Democratic Form," *World Affairs* 102 (June 1939): 86–87.

3. *CEHMP*, 782–786; *CEHI*, 111.

4. *CEHMP*, 786.

5. *SC*, 75–77; *CEHCJ*, 391–392. See also *CEHMP*, 787.

6. *CEHMP*, 787–788; "That's the Question," *Buffalo Courier-Express*, June 7, 1941.

7. *CEHMP*, 792.

8. *CEHMP*, 793–796.

9. *CEHMP*, 796, 801.

10. *CEHMP*, 796–798.

11. Elizabeth Hughes Gossett, "My Father the Chief Justice," *Supreme Court Historical Society Yearbook, 1976* (Washington, DC: Supreme Court Historical Society, 1975), 14; *CEHMP*, 789–801.

12. *CEHMP*, 802–804.

13. "Final Tribute Paid to Charles E. Hughes," *NYT*, September 1, 1948. See also *CEHMP*, 805; "Chief Justice Charles Evans Hughes Had Long and Notable Career in Service of His Country," *NYT*, August 28, 1948.

14. "Hughes Left $100,000 to Higher Learning, $140,000 in Gifts and Residue to Family," *NYT*, September 15, 1948; Earl Warren, "Hughes and the Court," commemorative pamphlet, address delivered on April 11, 1962, at Colgate University, Hamilton, New York; Ronald Reagan, "Remarks in New York City on Receiving the Charles Evans Hughes Gold Medal of the National Conference of Christians and Jews," March 23, 1982, Ronald Reagan Presidential Foundation and Library, https://www.reaganfoundation.org/ronald-reagan/reagan-quotes-speeches/remarks-in-new-york-city-on-receiving-the-charles-evans-hughes-gold-medal-of-the-national-conference-of-christians-and-jews-1/; Personal communication with Sandra H. Waddell, president, Charles Evans Hughes Memorial Foundation, January 19, 2022, and September 30, 2022.

15. "Charles Evans Hughes," *NYT*, August 28, 1948; American Bar Asso-

ciation, "Charles Evans Hughes, 1862–1948: America's Great Diplomat-Jurist Dies," *American Bar Association Journal* 34 (Oct. 1948): 902–903; Learned Hand, "Charles Evans Hughes," in *The Spirit of Liberty*, ed. Irving Dilliard (Knopf, 1952), 221–222.

16. *CEHMP*, 788–790; Paul A. Freund, "Charles Evans Hughes as Chief Justice," *Harvard Law Review* 81 (Nov. 1967): 43; "Chief Justice Charles Evans Hughes Had Long and Notable Career in Service of His Country," *NYT*.

17. Edwin McElwain, "The Business of the Supreme Court as Conducted by Chief Justice Hughes," *Harvard Law Review* (Nov. 1949): 9–10; "Letter from the Justices of the Supreme Court to Mr. Chief Justice Hughes upon his Retirement from the Court" *Proceedings of the Bar and Officers of the Supreme Court of the United States, November 4, 1949. Proceedings before the Supreme Court of the United States, May 8, 1950, in Memory of Charles Evans Hughes* (Washington, DC, 1950), 71–72; William G. Ross, *The Chief Justiceship of Charles Evans Hughes, 1930–1940* (University of South Carolina Press, 2007), 136.

18. Proskauer in *Proceedings*, 28.

19. "Arthur T. Vanderbilt, Chief Justice of the New Jersey Supreme Court," in *Proceedings*, 64–65.

20. "Columbia to Honor Justice Hughes," *NYT*, April 11, 1962; "Warren, at Hughes Centennial, Hails His Predecessor's Record," *NYT*, April 12, 1962; Warren, "Hughes and the Court," 1–6.

Case Index

General Index

www.ingramcontent.com/pod-product-compliance
Lightning Source LLC
Chambersburg PA
CBHW030017291025
34684CB00011B/131/J
* 9 7 8 0 7 0 0 6 3 8 8 6 4 *